GW01403006

Studies in Diversity Linguistics

Editor: Martin Haspelmath

In this series:

1. Handschuh, Corinna. A typology of marked-S languages.

2. Rießler, Michael. Adjective attribution.

3. Klamer, Marian (ed.). The Alor-Pantar languages: History and typology.

4. Berghäll, Liisa. A grammar of Mauwake (Papua New Guinea).

5. Wilbur, Joshua. A grammar of Pite Saami.

6. Dahl, Östen. Grammaticalization in the North: Noun phrase morphosyntax in Scandinavian vernaculars.

7. Schackow, Diana. A grammar of Yakkha.

8. Liljegren, Henrik. A grammar of Palula.

9. Shimelman, Aviva. A grammar of Yauyos Quechua.

10. Rudin, Catherine & Bryan James Gordon (eds.). Advances in the study of Siouan languages and linguistics.

11. Kluge, Angela. A grammar of Papuan Malay.

12. Kieviet, Paulus. A grammar of Rapa Nui.

13. Michaud, Alexis. Tone in Yongning Na: Lexical tones and morphotonology.

14. Enfield, N. J. (ed.). Dependencies in language: On the causal ontology of linguistic systems.

15. Gutman, Ariel. Attributive constructions in North-Eastern Neo-Aramaic.

16. Bisang, Walter & Andrej Malchukov (eds.). Unity and diversity in grammaticalization scenarios.

17. Stenzel, Kristine & Bruna Franchetto (eds.). On this and other worlds: Voices from Amazonia.

18. Paggio, Patrizia and Albert Gatt (eds.). The languages of Malta.

19. Seržant, Ilja A. & Alena Witzlack-Makarevich (eds.). Diachrony of differential argument marking.

20. Hölzl, Andreas. A typology of questions in Northeast Asia and beyond: An ecological perspective.

21. Riesberg, Sonja, Asako Shiohara & Atsuko Utsumi (eds.). Perspectives on information structure in Austronesian languages.

22. Döhler, Christian. A grammar of Komnzo.

23. Yakpo, Kofi. A Grammar of Pichi.

24. Guérin Valérie (ed.). Bridging constructions.

25. Aguilar-Guevara, Ana, Julia Pozas Loyo & Violeta Vázquez-Rojas Maldonado *eds.). Definiteness across languages.

26. Di Garbo, Francesca, Bruno Olsson & Bernhard Wälchli (eds.). Grammatical gender and linguistic complexity: Volume I: General issues and specific studies.

27. Di Garbo, Francesca, Bruno Olsson & Bernhard Wälchli (eds.). Grammatical gender and linguistic complexity: Volume II: World-wide comparative studies.

ISSN: 2363-5568

Grammatical gender and linguistic complexity

Volume II: World-wide comparative studies

Edited by

Francesca Di Garbo

Bruno Olsson

Bernhard Wälchli

language
science
press

Di Garbo, Francesca, Bruno Olsson & Bernhard Wälchli (eds.). 2019.
Grammatical gender and linguistic complexity: *Volume II: World-wide
comparative studies* (Studies in Diversity Linguistics 27). Berlin: Language
Science Press.

This title can be downloaded at:
http://langsci-press.org/catalog/book/237
© 2019, the authors
Published under the Creative Commons Attribution 4.0 Licence (CC BY 4.0):
http://creativecommons.org/licenses/by/4.0/
Indexed in EBSCO
ISBN: 978-3-96110-180-1 (Digital)
        978-3-96110-181-8 (Hardcover)

ISSN: 2363-5568
DOI:10.5281/zenodo.3446230
Source code available from www.github.com/langsci/237
Collaborative reading: paperhive.org/documents/remote?type=langsci&id=237

Cover and concept of design: Ulrike Harbort
Typesetting: Bruno Olsson, Sebastian Nordhoff
Proofreading: Alena Witzlack, Carmen Jany, Gracious Temsen, Jeroen van de
Weijer, Laura Arnold, Martin Haspelmath, Tom Bossuyt
Fonts: Linux Libertine, Libertinus Math, Arimo, DejaVu Sans Mono, SIL Doulos,
Sarabun Light, SIL Annapurna, ITF Hind Madurai
Typesetting software: X꯭ΗᴽΤᴇX

Language Science Press
Unter den Linden 6
10099 Berlin, Germany
langsci-press.org

Storage and cataloguing done by FU Berlin

Freie Universität Berlin

Contents

1 Introduction
Francesca Di Garbo, Bruno Olsson & Bernhard Wälchli   1

2 The evolving complexity of gender agreement systems
Francesca Di Garbo & Matti Miestamo   15

3 The feminine anaphoric gender gram, incipient gender marking,
maturity, and extracting anaphoric gender markers from parallel texts
Bernhard Wälchli   61

4 On the distribution and complexity of gender and numeral classifiers
Kaius Sinnemäki   133

5 The dynamics of gender complexity
Bernhard Wälchli & Francesca Di Garbo   201

Index   365

Chapter 1

Introduction

Francesca Di Garbo
Stockholm University

Bruno Olsson
Australian National University

Bernhard Wälchli
Stockholm University

This chapter introduces the two volumes *Grammatical gender and linguistic complexity I: General issues and specific studies* and *Grammatical gender and linguistic complexity II: World-wide comparative studies*.

Grammatical gender is notorious for its complexity. Corbett (1991: 1) characterizes gender as "the most puzzling of the grammatical categories". One reason is that the traditional definitional properties of gender – noun classes and agreement – are very intricate phenomena that can affect all major areas of language structure. Gender is an interface phenomenon par excellence and tends to form elaborate systems, which is why the question of how systems emerge in language development and change is highly relevant for understanding and modeling the evolution of gender systems. In addition, some of the recent literature on linguistic complexity claims that gender is 'historical junk' without any obvious function (Trudgill 2011: 156) and is likely to be lost in situations of increased non-native language acquisition (McWhorter 2001; 2007; Trudgill 1999). Not only are its synchronic functions a matter of debate, but gender also tends to be diachronically opaque due to its high genealogical stability and entrenchment (Nichols 1992: 142; Nichols 2003), making gender a core example of a mature phenomenon (Dahl 2004). However, despite the well-established connection between gender and linguistic complexity, and recent attempts to develop complexity metrics for gender systems (Audring 2014; 2017; Di Garbo 2016) and metrics for addressing

Francesca Di Garbo, Bruno Olsson & Bernhard Wälchli. 2019. Introduction. In Francesca Di Garbo, Bruno Olsson & Bernhard Wälchli (eds.), *Grammatical gender and linguistic complexity: Volume I: General issues and specific studies*, 1–12. Berlin: Language Science Press. DOI:10.5281/zenodo.3462754 the relationship between gender and classifiers (Passer 2016), there is so far no collection of articles particularly devoted to the relationship between grammatical gender and linguistic complexity.

The two companion volumes introduced here are an attempt to fill this gap. They address the topics of gender and linguistic complexity from a range of different perspectives and within a broadly functional–typological approach to the understanding of the dynamics of language. Specific questions addressed are the following:

- **Measurability of gender complexity**:
  What are the dimensions of gender complexity, and what kind of metrics do we need to study the complexity of gender cross-linguistically? Are there complexity trade-offs between gender and other kinds of nominal classification systems? Does gender complexity diminish or increase under the pressure of external factors related to the social ecology of speech communities?

- **Gender complexity and stability**:
  How does gender complexity evolve and change over time? To what extent do the gender systems of closely related languages differ in terms of their complexity and in which cases do these differences challenge the idea of gender as a stable feature? How complex are incipient gender systems?

- **Typologically rare gender systems and complexity**:
  How do instances of typologically rare gender systems relate to complexity? What tools of analysis are needed to disentangle and describe these complexities?

Discussion around these topics was initiated during a two-day workshop on "Grammatical gender and linguistic complexity" that took place at the Department of Linguistics at Stockholm University, Sweden, November 20–21, 2015. Most chapters included in the two volumes are based on papers first presented and discussed during this workshop. However, some additional authors came on board after the workshop and all contributions went through considerable modifications on their way to being included in the collection of articles. The result consists of 14 chapters (including this introduction) in two volumes, which address the questions listed above, while investigating the many facets of grammatical gender through the prism of linguistic complexity.

The chapters discuss what counts as complex or simple in gender systems, and whether the distribution of gender systems across the world's languages relates to the language ecology and social history of speech communities. The contributions demonstrate how the complexity of gender systems can be studied synchronically, both in individual languages and across large cross-linguistic samples, as well as diachronically, by exploring how gender systems change over time.

Organization of the two volumes

The first volume, *Grammatical gender and linguistic complexity I: General issues and specific studies* (henceforth referred to as Volume I), consists of three chapters on the theoretical foundations of gender complexity, and six chapters on languages and language families of Africa, New Guinea and South Asia. The second volume, *Grammatical gender and linguistic complexity II: World-wide comparative studies* (henceforth referred to as Volume II), consists of three chapters providing diachronic and typological case studies, and a final chapter discussing old and new theoretical and empirical challenges in the study of the dynamics of gender complexity. The rest of this section is a roadmap providing summaries of the following thirteen chapters.

Volume I: General issues and specific studies

Part I, General issues, in Volume I, starts with **Jenny Audring**'s contribution. Building on previous work in Canonical Typology, Audring proposes that a maximally canonical gender system is one in which formal clarity and featural orthogonality reign, unperturbed by morphological cumulation and cross-category interactions. Canonical gender is also populated by well-behaved targets exhibiting unambiguous agreement, in accordance with the (transparently assigned) gender of their controllers. Alongside this hypothetical clustering of canonical properties, Audring, building on earlier literature, establishes three main dimensions according to which the complexity of a gender system can be gauged: economy (a system with fewer distinctions is less complex than one with many distinctions), transparency (a one-to-one mapping between meaning and form is less complex than a one-to-many mapping) and independence (a system in which all features are independent of each other is less complex than one where they interact). Starting from the postulate that the maximally canonical gender system should also be minimally complex, Audring examines how the canonicity parameters fare against the complexity measures, and finds that the criteria from canonicity and complexity largely converge, with economy being the glaring exception: a canonical gender system is an uneconomical one. The discussion then turns to the notion of difficulty, here understood as the speed with which children acquire the gender system of their first language. With the premise that a gender system of maximal canonicity and minimal complexity should also be the least difficult to acquire, Audring compares the criteria for canonicity and complexity with factors that are known to facilitate the acquisition of a gender system. The result of this comparison is general convergence between the three dimensions, again except for economy. An otherwise canonical and simple gender system will be easier to acquire if it also features ample redundancy.

Exploring the relationship between language structures and sociohistorical and environmental factors is one of the most debated issues in recent quantitative typological research. In his contribution, **Östen Dahl** asks whether there is a negative correlation between the complexity of grammatical gender and community size in line with the general claim that languages with large populations feature simpler morphology than smaller languages. Gender systems presuppose non-trivial patterns of grammaticalization and complex types of encoding in inflectional morphology. In addition, contact-induced erosion and loss of grammatical gender are well documented in the literature. Yet, Dahl shows that it is very hard to find any clear-cut statistically significant correlation between gender features as documented in the *World atlas of language structures* (*WALS*) and language size. Similarly, gender features do not clearly correlate with any of the inflectional categories represented in *WALS*, with the exception of systems of semantic and formal gender assignment, which tend to be found in languages with highly grammaticalized nominal number marking. Dahl argues that in order to better understand the impact that language-external factors may have on the complexity of gender systems, areal and genealogical skewing in the distribution of types of gender systems and the demographic profile of the languages need to be taken into account. Furthermore, he suggests that more elaborate classifications of gender systems than those currently available in typological databases are needed in order to identify those aspects of gender marking that are most likely to adapt to the pressure of language-external factors, as well as a shift in perspective from synchronic to diachronic typologies.

Johanna Nichols uses canonicity as a starting point for her discussion of the relative complexity of gender agreement. As in Audring's contribution, exponence of gender is non-canonical inasmuch as it departs from the structuralist ideal of biunique form–function correspondence. Nichols proposes the reasonable hypothesis that gender systems are in fact not complex in themselves. Rather, their complexity is a side-effect of gender arising primarily in languages that have already cultivated considerable complexity elsewhere in their grammars. But empirical testing of this hypothesis suggests that it must be rejected, because Nichols shows – surprisingly perhaps – that languages with grammatical gender do not display a higher degree of overall morphological complexity than languages without gender. The question is then which diachronic processes cause gender systems to accumulate complexity over time, even when the rest of the morphological system manages to avoid increased complexification. Nichols identifies one clue to this puzzle by comparing gender to participant indexation, and, more specifically, to cases in which such systems display hierarchical patterning (as when a verb form indexes the participant that ranks highest on a hierarchy such as 1, 2 > 3). In Nichols' view, this is an example of a "self-correcting mechanism" that can act as a cap on complexification within indexation systems. Gender systems, on the other hand, do not have recourse to such mechanisms, because markers of gender agreement lack the referential function that participant indexes, such as pronouns, have.

Part II of Volume I focuses on languages of Africa. Gender systems in Niger-Congo languages are among the most studied instances of grammatical gender cross-linguistically. Yet to a large extent this body of research is based on a tradition of analysis which is strongly Bantu-centered and not easily applicable to other language families within and outside Africa. The chapter by **Tom Güldemann** and **Ines Fiedler** seeks to overcome this limitation by proposing a novel toolkit for the analysis of Niger-Congo gender systems. The kit rests upon four notions: agreement class, nominal form class, gender and deriflection, and aims to be universally applicable to the description of any language-specific gender system as well as for the purpose of cross-linguistic comparison. While the notions of nominal form class and agreement class have to do with the concrete morphosyntactic contexts in which nominal and non-nominal gender marking occur, gender and deriflection are more concerned with the abstract, lexical dimension of grammatical gender. By using these analytical tools, Güldemann and Fiedler dismiss the notion of noun class which has been largely used in Niger-Congo studies and which rests on the problematic assumption that there is a systematic one-to-one mapping between nominal form classes and agreement classes. The authors demonstrate the descriptive adequacy of the proposed approach by focusing on data from three genealogically and/or geographically coherent Niger-Congo groups in West Africa: Akan, Guang and Ghana-Togo-Mountain. They show how the new method reveals some important generalizations about Niger-Congo gender systems. For instance, agreement class inventories are always simpler (or at least not more complex) than nominal form class inventories, both in terms of number of distinctions and types of structures. Diachronically, this means that the systems of nominal form classes can be more conservative than those of agreement classes.

The contribution by **Don Killian** discusses the gender system of Uduk, a Koman language of the Ethiopian-(South) Sudanese borderland, with special emphasis on some unusual properties of the agreement and assignment principles operating in the language. Gender agreement in Uduk is primarily realized in a set of clitics that attach to the verb, and which mark the case role and gender of a core argument that immediately follows the verb. The fact that these postverbal clitics only appear when immediately followed by the corresponding argument points to the fundamental role of adjacency in this gender system, a point also illustrated by conjunctions and complementizers, which agree in gender with the following nominal. According to Killian, gender assignment is largely arbitrary, even for the highest segments of the animacy hierarchy, where one could expect to find assignment based on salient features of the referent (such as sex). Furthermore, the irrelevance of the referent for gender assignment extends to pronouns and demonstratives, which invariably trigger agreement according to Class I. Apart from a few formal rules (targeting derived nouns), there seem to be no clear-cut semantic patterns that could bring order to this unwieldy assignment system. Killian proposes that the Uduk gender is non-canonical but relatively simple – features that would easily make this gender system slip under the typologist's radar.

In the first of three contributions focusing on languages of New Guinea (Part III of Volume I), **Matthew Dryer** presents an overview of gender in Walman, a Torricelli language. Gender agreement in Walman is shown in third person agreement on verbs, where the sets of subject and object affixes distinguish feminine and masculine agreement. Agreement is also found, albeit less systematically, on a subset of nominal modifiers, including some adjectives and demonstratives. Gender assignment is sex-based for humans and large animals, arbitrary for lower animals, whereas almost all inanimates are feminine, with spill-over into the masculine for some natural phenomena (which, like animates, are capable of autonomous force). Dryer presents two analytical puzzles for the description of Walman gender. The first concerns the large group of pluralia tantum nouns, which trigger invariant plural agreement instead of the standard masculine or feminine (singular) agreement. This group of nouns is about twice as large as that of masculine nouns, so if the number of members is taken as decisive for the status of a category, then the pluralia tantum category in Walman is clearly on a par with the two uncontroversial genders. The second puzzle concerns diminutive agreement. The Walman diminutive is not marked on the noun itself (unlike some more familiar derivational diminutives), rather it is realized by dedicated diminutive affixes that replace the usual feminine and masculine gender agreement markers. This makes the diminutive look like an additional gender value, but Dryer points to the lack of inherently diminutive nouns and the fact that the diminutive sometimes co-occurs with masculine/feminine agreement as good reasons for questioning its status as a gender value. Like other contributions to this book, Dryer's discussion is a good illustration of how interactions between gender and other categories of grammar conspire to make gender systems (as well as the task of analyzing them) more complex.

Bruno Olsson shows that the complexity of gender can be addressed from a diachronic point of view by advanced methods of internal reconstruction in the case of a family in which all languages except one are so far poorly documented. The language investigated is Coastal Marind, an Anim language of the Trans-Fly area of South New Guinea. Coastal Marind gender is covert except in a few nouns displaying stem-internal vowel alternation (*anem* 'man [I sg]', *anum* 'woman [II sg]', *anim* 'people [I/II pl]'). Olsson endorses earlier comparative research arguing that vowel alternation within Anim words derives from umlaut triggered by postposed articles inflecting for gender (as they still exist in the perhaps distantly related and areally not too remote Ok languages). By means of statistical analysis, he identifies traces of umlaut for two classes even in non-alternating nouns. The lack of any statistical effect in a third class is explained by class shift of nouns for animals. In Coastal Marind, gender and number are intricately intertwined in an unexpected way. The joint plural of the two animate classes behaves almost identically to gender IV, one of the two inanimate classes (which do not distinguish number). Olsson speculates that gender IV might have originated from pluralia tantum, but since there is no longer a semantic link (no inanimate plural), it is not possible to view gender IV as plural synchronically, despite systematic syncretism with the animate plural throughout a large number of different formal exponents, including stem suppletion. The case of Coastal Marind thus demonstrates that a gender system can become more complex through very specific kinds of interaction with phonology on the one hand and with number on the other.

In the traditional literature on gender, not all continents are equally well represented. New Guinea is a major area that has been notoriously underrepresented so far. **Erik Svärd** investigates gender in New Guinea in an areally restricted variety sample of twenty languages and compares it to gender in Africa and beyond. Unlike Africa, where gender is amply represented in the large language families, the two large families in New Guinea, Austronesian and Trans-New Guinea, mostly lack gender, unlike many small language families and isolates in which gender is attested. As a consequence, gender in New Guinea is diverse and more akin to the global profile of gender in comparison with Africa. Despite the diversity of gender in New Guinea, Svärd is able to identify characteristic properties of gender in New Guinea. Most languages with gender have a masculine–feminine opposition (where either member can be unmarked), and several gender targets, typically including verbs. Unlike Africa and the Old World in general, formal assignment and overt marking of gender on nouns is rare in New Guinea and, in the few languages having formal assignment, it is usually limited to a subset of the gender classes. However, gender assignment in New Guinea is not typically simple, since many languages have what Svärd calls "opaque assignment", which does not mean lack of assignment patterns, but rather that exceptions abound. The relevance of size and shape, the existence of multiple noun class systems, and lack of gender in pronouns are further properties characteristic of many languages of New Guinea with gender. Svärd's comparison of New Guinea and Africa concludes the part on languages in Africa and New Guinea.

In Part IV of Volume I, **Henrik Liljegren** investigates the properties of gender systems and their complexity in 25 of 28 Hindu Kush Indo-Aryan languages. The languages under study are those for which there is enough data in published sources and/or the author's field data, and are examined against the background of other languages spoken in the area, namely other Indo-Aryan, Nuristani, Iranian, Tibeto-Burman, Turkic and Burushaski. The result is a cross-linguistic survey, which is an intra-genealogical, areal and micro-typological study in one. Despite the close genealogical relationship between the Hindu Kush Indo-Aryan languages, their gender systems are remarkably diverse, ranging from languages with the inherited masculine–feminine distinction pervasively marked on many agreement targets in the southwest (for instance, in Kashmiri) to the Chitral languages Kalasha and Khowar in the northwest, which instead have an innovated copula-based animacy distinction. These two languages also reflect the earliest northward migration of Indo-Aryans in the region. In some languages in the southeast, the sex-based and animacy-based oppositions are combined in concurrent gender systems, as is the case in the Pashai languages and Shumashti, which yield the highest complexity scores among Hindu Kush Indo-Aryan languages. Liljegren shows that the distribution of various kinds of gender systems has both genealogical and areal implications, with different Iranian contact languages in the southeast and southwest yielding a variety of contact effects. Liljegren traces in detail how the entrenchment of gender in this language grouping gradually declines from the southeast to the northwest. Generally in Hindu Kush Indo-

Aryan, gender is stable only to the extent that related languages with inherited gender are neighbors. But there are also language-internal factors. The functional load of gender is higher in languages with ergative rather than accusative verbal alignment.

Volume II: World-wide comparative studies

After having introduced all chapters of Volume I, we now turn to Volume II. To date, the study of gender complexity has largely focused on synchrony. **Francesca Di Garbo** and **Matti Miestamo** demonstrate that diachrony is indispensable for a deeper understanding of the relationship between gender and complexity. They investigate four types of diachronic changes affecting gender systems – reduction, loss, expansion and emergence – in fifteen sets of closely related languages (36 languages in total) from various families and continents. In exploring how the detected types of changes relate to complexity, they find that reduction of gender agreement does not necessarily entail reduction of complexity. Rather complexity can increase both in reducing and emerging gender systems. Across the languages of the sample, there are strong regularities in how different kinds of changes are mapped onto the Agreement Hierarchy. The two opposite poles of the hierarchy, attributive modifiers and personal pronouns, can often be identified as the places of origin for both the decline and rise of gender. Di Garbo and Miestamo argue that two opposite forces, syntactic cohesion and semantic agreement, are at work at the two different poles of the implicational hierarchy. In a similar vein, the two different processes involved in reduction – morphophonological erosion and redistribution of agreement – display different directions of change along the Agreement Hierarchy. Di Garbo and Miestamo consider various cases of language-internal rise of gender and contact-induced gender emergence, and detect striking similarities. The cases under consideration suggest that gender in the process of emergence is non-pervasive and constrained. While gender can disseminate by means of borrowing of lexical items, emergent gender systems in borrowing languages differ in structure from gender systems in donor languages.

Traditional definitions of grammatical gender rely on the notions of noun class, agreement and system. **Bernhard Wälchli** demonstrates that dispensing with these notions and pursuing a radically functional approach to the study of grammatical gender is possible and worthwhile. The chapter is a typological investigation of feminine anaphoric gender grams (as in English *she/her*) in a world-wide convenience sample of 816 languages, based on a corpus of parallel texts (the New Testament). The functional equivalence between the forms extracted from the corpus is ensured by the fact that they cover a single search space across all languages considered. Through this methodology, which is applied to the domain of grammatical gender for the first time, the study finds instances of simple patterns of gender marking in a large number of languages for which no such constructions had been documented before. Three types of simple gender are extracted from the corpus and analyzed in the paper: non-compositional complex noun phrases, reduced nominal anaphors and general nouns. These instances of simple gender are interpreted as incipient types of gender systems from a grammaticalization perspective. Conversely, cumulation with case in the encoding of grammatical relations is taken as a characteristic feature of complex and mature (i.e. highly grammaticalized) feminine anaphoric gender grams. After discussing the differences between simple and mature gender, the chapter concludes by proposing a functional network for the grammatical gender domain in which the gram approach is reconciled with more traditional approaches based on the notions of noun classes, agreement and system.

While languages can have both gender and classifier systems, the co-occurrence of the two is rare. This suggests that these two different types of nominal classification systems may actually be in complementary distribution with one another. **Kaius Sinnemäki** validates this claim statistically by investigating the distribution of gender and numeral classifier systems in a stratified sample of 360 languages. Complexity is operationalized as the overt coding of a given pattern in a given language and thus, in this case, as the presence of gender and/or numeral classifiers. The study's main hypothesis is that there is an inverse relationship between presence of gender and presence of numeral classifiers. The hypothesis is tested using generalized mixed effect models, which also control for the impact of genealogical and areal relationships between languages on the distribution of the variables of interest. The results reveal a statistically significant inverse relationship between presence of gender and presence of numeral classifier systems and that in addition the two types of nominal classification systems have a roughly complementary areal distribution. Languages spoken within the Circum-Pacific region are more likely to have numeral classifiers than languages spoken outside this area, whereas the opposite distribution applies to gender. This inverse relationship also exists independently of language family and area and thus confirms the study's main hypothesis. According to Sinnemäki, these results, which should be interpreted as a probabilistic rather than an absolute universal, suggest that there is a functionally motivated complexity trade-off between gender and numeral classifiers, whereby languages tend to avoid developing and maintaining more than one system at a time within the functional domain of nominal classification.

The concluding chapter, by **Bernhard Wälchli** and **Francesca Di Garbo**, presents a wide-ranging enquiry into the diachrony and complexity of gender systems, with an emphasis on gender systems as dynamic entities evolving over time. The authors re-examine a variety of phenomena that will be familiar to students of gender, such as gender and the animacy hierarchy, assignment rules, gender agreement, and cumulative expression with other inflectional categories. But casting the net wider, the chapter also examines various issues that have received less attention in the literature, and which arguably are crucial for understanding the origin, development and synchronic characteristics of gender systems. These include the introduction of inanimate nouns into sex-based gender classes, opaque assignment and the development from semantic to phonological assignment, nouns – and clauses – as targets of gender agreement, and relationships between controller and target that go beyond co-reference and syntactic dependency. Among the 12 sections of the chapter (all of which can be read independently), we also find an exploratory survey of accumulation of nominal marking in the NP (including markers that fall outside the realm of noun classification, such as *one* in the NP *the red one*), and a proposal for a definition of agreement that is intended to capture the fundamental asymmetry between controller and target (as the sites where gender originates and is realized respectively). These and other sections of the chapter question the solidity of some commonly made distinctions, such as that between agreement features and conditions on agreement, or the binary splits between e.g. semantic and formal assignment systems, or the assumption that the category of gender can always be distinguished from that of number. These emerge in a new guise once the dynamic perspective favored by the authors is adopted.

Acknowledgments

The two volumes are the result of a collaborative endeavor in which not only the editors and authors of the chapters were involved. We would like to thank in particular Yvonne Agbetsoamedo, Jenny Audring, Lea Brown, Greville Corbett, Östen Dahl, Michael Daniel, Deborah Edwards-Fumey, Sebastian Fedden, Jeff Good, Pernilla Hallonsten Halling, Martin Haspelmath, Robert Hepburn-Gray, Dan Ke, Marcin Kilarski, Matti Miestamo, Manuel Otero, Robert Östling, Frank Seifart, Ruth Singer, Krzysztof Stroński, Anna Maria Thornton and 9 anonymous reviewers, whose comments have contributed to considerable improvement of all chapters. We would also like to thank the editorial board of the series Studies in Diversity Linguistics for having supported the book project from its very beginning. In particular, the words of encouragement of the series' editor, Martin

Haspelmath, have been very important from the outset to the final stages of the volumes' production. We would also like to thank the Language Science Press team, and in particular Sebastian Nordhoff and Felix Kopecky, for their eagerness in supporting us in all matters of producing open access books. As mentioned earlier, the book project started with the workshop "Grammatical gender and linguistic complexity" which was held in Stockholm, November 20th–21st, 2015. We thank the Department of Linguistics at Stockholm University for hosting the workshop, as well as the workshop participants and the audience for contributing to a very inspiring and stimulating discussion venue. The workshop was ultimately made possible thanks to the vice-chancellor of Stockholm University, Astrid Söderbergh Widding, who, back in 2015, initiated a funding program for collaborative linguistics research between Stockholm University and the University of Helsinki. This funding scheme has since then sparked numerous collaborative projects between the two universities, under the coordination of its scientific committee, directed by Camilla Bardel. The Stockholm-Helsinki cooperation program has through the years led to a large number of joint publications of which the present two volumes are just one example.

References

Audring, Jenny. 2014. Gender as a complex feature. *Language Sciences* 43. 5–17.

Audring, Jenny. 2017. Calibrating complexity: How complex is a gender system? *Language Sciences* 60. 53–68.

Corbett, Greville G. 1991. *Gender*. Cambridge: Cambridge University Press.

Dahl, Östen. 2004. *The growth and maintenance of linguistic complexity*. Amsterdam: John Benjamins.

Di Garbo, Francesca. 2016. Exploring grammatical complexity crosslinguistically: The case of gender. *Linguistic Discovery* 14(1). 46–85.

McWhorter, John. 2001. The world's simplest grammars are creole grammars. *Linguistic Typology* 5(2-3). 125–166.

McWhorter, John. 2007. *Language interrupted: Signs of non-native acquisition in standard language grammars*. New York: Oxford University Press.

Nichols, Johanna. 1992. *Linguistic diversity in space and time*. Chicago: University of Chicago Press.

Nichols, Johanna. 2003. Diversity and stability in language. In Brian D. Joseph & Richard D. Janda (eds.), *The handbook of historical linguistics*, 283–310. Oxford: Blackwell.

Passer, Matthias Benjamin. 2016. *The typology and diachrony of nominal classifi-cation.* Utrecht: University of Amsterdam. (Doctoral dissertation).

Trudgill, Peter. 1999. Language contact and the function of linguistic gender. *Poznań Studies in Contemporary Linguistics* 35. 133–152.

Trudgill, Peter. 2011. *Sociolinguistic typology: Social determinants of linguistic com-plexity.* New York: Oxford University Press.

Chapter 2

The evolving complexity of gender agreement systems

Francesca Di Garbo
Stockholm University

Matti Miestamo
University of Helsinki

This paper proposes to integrate the diachronic dimension to the typological study of gender complexity, and focuses on the morphosyntactic encoding of gender distinctions via agreement patterns. After investigating the processes of language change that foster the reduction, loss, expansion and emergence of gender agreement in a sample of fifteen sets of closely related languages (N= 36 languages), we discuss how gender agreement systems in decline and on the rise pattern in terms of complexity. We show that declining and emerging gender agreement systems may exhibit increase or decrease in complexity and discuss how this relates to the fact that they represent transitional stages between absence of gender and full-fledged gender systems. In our analysis, we make use of typological implicational hierarchies in the domain of agreement as a tool to account for diachronic variation and for the patterns of simplification/complexification in the agreement systems of the sampled languages.

Keywords: agreement hierarchy, agreement redistribution, gender emergence, gender expansion, gender loss, gender reduction, morphophonological erosion, complexification, simplification.

1 Introduction and key notions

Within the last decade, pioneering research on the complexity of grammatical gender has contributed to identify a number of dimensions along which gender systems may vary in complexity (see Audring 2014; 2017; Di Garbo 2016 for

Francesca Di Garbo & Matti Miestamo. 2019. The evolving complexity of gender agreement systems. In Francesca Di Garbo, Bruno Olsson & Bernhard Wälchli (eds.), *Grammatical gender and linguistic complexity: Volume II: World-wide comparative studies*, 15–60. Berlin: Language Science Press. DOI:10.5281/zenodo.3462778 gender-specific complexity measures[1]), and to apply these dimensions of complexity variation to research on the typology of gender systems within specific language families and areas of the world (Di Garbo 2016). The approach followed in these studies has been predominantly synchronic. In this paper, we argue that integrating the diachronic dimension to the typological study of gender complexity is essential to understand how gender systems vary in complexity (i.e., along which dimensions of the proposed metrics) and how this variation is distributed crosslinguistically.

We investigate the evolution of complexity in the domain of grammatical gender by using a diachronic approach to the study of linguistic diversity in line with Greenberg (1978a). Greenberg addressed possible pathways of change between different types of structures and languages and argued that there would likely be a diachronic connection between all language types in a typology in the sense that change from any given type to any other type would be possible. This diachronic route would not always be direct, but rather mediated by other types, and the relative stability of the different types would differ, with some types qualifying as *stable, persistent*, and others as *unstable, transitional*. In this paper, we describe the patterns of language change whereby complexification and simplification in gender systems take place, explore possible functional explanations to the unfolding of these changes, and show how these explanations are ultimately grounded in well-known implicational tendencies in the typology of gender systems. In addition, by operationalizing gender complexity as a dynamic, evolving variable, we explore the relationship between the complexity and stability of gender systems.[2] The questions we attempt to answer are:

- Which complexities are most stable in the domain of grammatical gender?

- Which other aspects of gender complexity are more likely to change?

- To what extent can we identify complexification or simplification in the processes of emergence and expansion of gender on the one hand, and reduction and loss of gender on the other?

---

[1] Inaddition, see Passer (2016) for a discussion of gender complexity in comparison with other nominal classification strategies; and Leufkens (2015) for a discussion of grammatical gender in the context of a general model of complexity and transparency in grammar.

[2] On the stability of gender systems see the pioneering large-scale typological investigation by Nichols (1992) as well as the more recent overview by Nichols (2003). For a study of the diachrony and stability of grammatical gender in the Indo-European family, see Matasović (2004).

Following Miestamo (2006; 2008) we define complexity in absolute, theory-oriented, objective terms, paying attention to the number of elements in a system and connections between these. In an information-theoretic perspective, complexity can ultimately be reduced to description length: of two entities, for instance two grammatical systems, the less complex one is the one whose shortest possible description is shorter. In other words, the simpler entity can be compressed into a smaller space without losing information. This approach also aligns with complexity theories outside linguistics and thereby allows linguistic complexity to be viewed in a cross-disciplinary perspective as well. The notions of cost and difficulty of processing and learning are related to complexity, and some authors, such as Kusters (2003), take a relative, user-oriented, subjective approach, equating complexity with cost and difficulty. In a user-oriented approach, those aspects of language that increase processing load and learning difficulty are defined as complex. Dahl (2004) and Miestamo (2006; 2008) discuss some obvious problems with the cost- and difficulty-based approach and point out that it is important to keep the notions of complexity and difficulty apart. However, to what extent and in what ways complexity and difficulty are correlated is a highly interesting question. We believe that keeping these notions apart is a prerequisite for adequately addressing this issue.

Miestamo (2006; 2008) proposes two principles by which grammatical complexity can be measured:

- The Principle of Fewer Distinctions, which, paying attention to grammatical meaning, defines as less complex a grammatical system in which, other things being equal, fewer semantic/pragmatic distinctions are made grammatically.

- The Principle of One-Meaning–One-Form, which, paying attention to the relationship between meaning and form, defines as less complex those systems and structures in which, other things being equal, each meaning is expressed by one form and each form corresponds to only one meaning.

Violations of these two principles increase complexity.

To take some examples, by the Principle of Fewer Distinctions, a gender system with two grammaticalized gender distinctions is less complex in this respect than a gender system with, say, five grammaticalized distinctions. By the Principle of One-Meaning–One-Form, we can identify a higher degree of complexity in a gender system system in which: (a) the formal expression of one or more genders is combined with other categories in one morpheme (fusion, multiple exponence);

(b) one or more gender distinctions are expressed with multiple/discontinuous morphemes (fission); (c) the markers of one or more gender distinctions show two or more variants (allomorphy); and/or (d) the markers of some gender distinctions are identical in some grammatical contexts (syncretism).

While the Principle of One-Meaning–One-Form can handle the relation between meaning and form relatively exhaustively (relevant subcriteria need of course to be defined and refined), the Principle of Fewer Distinctions only covers parts of complexity on the level of meaning. Things get more complicated when we look at the interaction between different functional domains (e.g., gender and number). Dahl (2004) discusses the notion of choice structure, i.e. the dependency of available choices on choices made earlier (cf. also the notion of dependency hierarchies by Aikhenvald & Dixon 1998). To take an example from the domain of grammatical gender, in many languages gender distinctions are available only in the singular, but are neutralized in the plural. This is, for instance, the case in Russian (Indo-European, Slavic). In order to account for interactions between functional domains and their effect on the complexity of individual domains, Di Garbo (2014; 2016) proposes the Principle of Independence.

- The Principle of Independence defines as less complex those systems and structures which, other things being equal, are *independent* of other systems and structures.

Under the Principle of Independence, a gender system whose formal realization is dependent on number distinctions is more complex than a gender system which is not constrained by number distinctions.

The three principles, the Principle of One-Meaning–One-Form, the Principle of Fewer Distinctions, and the Principle of Independence, are all operationalized in the gender complexity metric proposed by Di Garbo (2014; 2016), as well as in the discussion of gender complexity and canonicality by Audring (2019 [in Volume I]).[3] In this paper, we will be especially concerned with the way in which morphosyntactic and semantic properties of reducing and emerging gender systems may be accounted for as violations of one of these principles.

The paper is organized as follows. §2 presents some of the parameters along which gender systems may vary, and the sampling method followed in the study. In §3, attention is given to the factors that explain synchronic variation in the domain of gender agreement and to the extent to which these can be mapped on

---

[3] Audring (2019 [in Volume I]) uses a different terminology for the Principle of One-Meaning–One-Form and the Principle of Fewer Distinctions. In her own terminology, these are the Principle of Transparency and the Principle of Economy, respectively.

diachronic change, too. Reducing gender agreement systems are presented in §4 whereas §5 focuses on emerging gender agreement systems, and §6 on expanding gender agreement systems. In §7, we discuss how changes in the domain of gender agreement affect the complexity of gender systems. Concluding remarks are given in §8.

2 The evolution of gender complexity

In this paper, we explore synchronic distributions of types of gender systems among closely related languages, and, based on these synchronic distributions, we try to infer how gender systems change through time becoming more or less complex. We draw our observations from a sample of fifteen language sets. Each set consists of two to three genealogically related languages. In addition, the sample includes one isolate within the Austronesian family, Chamorro, and one mixed language, Michif. The total number of languages is 36. The map in Figure 1 illustrates the geographic distribution and genealogical affiliations of the sampled languages. A list of the sampled languages can be found in Appendix 8.

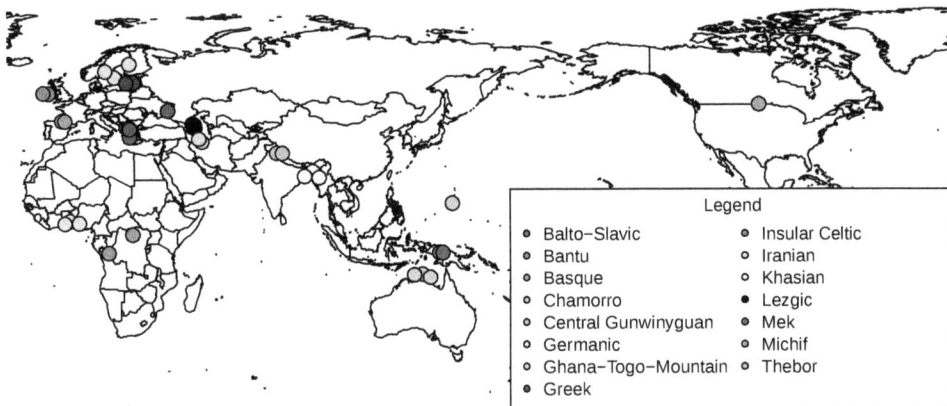

Legend	
Balto–Slavic	Insular Celtic
Bantu	Iranian
Basque	Khasian
Chamorro	Lezgic
Central Gunwinyguan	Mek
Germanic	Michif
Ghana–Togo–Mountain	Thebor
Greek	

Figure 1: The language sample

The data set studied stems from a larger project on the sociohistorical correlates of the evolution of gender complexity led by Francesca Di Garbo (for details, see Di Garbo forthcoming). The diachronic processes examined in the study are somewhat biased towards instances of contact-induced change, even though language-internal developments are also discussed. While the pace and nature of these developments may thus be specific to the type of contact situation in which they unfold, we believe that the data set under study offers insights of rather general relevance with respect to the diachrony of gender marking systems. Data were collected based on a questionnaire (Di Garbo 2015), as well as on consultation of reference grammars and language experts.

Typological research on grammatical gender systems has mostly focused on three broad domains of analysis:

- Number of genders

- Number and/or type of gender assignment rules

- Formal marking through agreement patterns.

We argue that these domains of synchronic variation can also be used to investigate how gender systems change through time. However, we suggest that any change in the number of gender values or the number and nature of gender assignment rules must ultimately hinge on variation and change in the domain of agreement patterns, that is, in the morphosyntactic encoding of gender distinctions. For instance, a gender value is lost when the corresponding gender agreement patterns fall out of use. Similarly, changes in the nature and distribution of gender assignment rules are reflected by the gender agreement patterns that the nouns affected by these changes trigger in discourse. For instance, we know that a former masculine noun is re-analyzed as neuter if patterns of neuter agreement are selected when the noun is used. Thus, we argue that studying synchronic and diachronic variation in patterns of gender agreement enables us to make generalizations about variation and ongoing change in the number of genders and/or the nature of the gender assignment rules that languages have. This suggestion aligns with recent observations in the literature on gender complexity where complexity in the domain of gender agreement has been shown to interact with complexity at the level of gender values and assignment rules (Audring 2017; Di Garbo 2016).[4]

We explore simplification and complexification of gender systems by focusing on reducing, emerging and expanding patterns of gender agreement. The sample languages are thus selected so as to represent instances of (1) reduction, (2) loss, (3) emergence, and (4) expansion of gender agreement. These are then compared with instances of retention or lack of gender agreement as attested in closely related languages. Naturally, loss, reduction and expansion presuppose the pre-existence of a gender system within the relevant language sets, whereas emergence of gender presupposes absence of gender within the relevant language sets.

---

[4]For instance, Di Garbo (2016) shows that manipulable gender assignment tends to presuppose rather pervasive gender agreement systems in the languages of her sample.

The data in Table 1 and the map in Figure 2 illustrate how the patterns of change in focus are distributed within the languages of the sample.[5]

Table 1: Patterns of change attested in the languages of the sample

Family by macroarea	Language	Pattern of change
Eurasia		
Khasian	Khasi	Expansion
	Lyngngam	Retention
	Pnar	Expansion
Basque	Standard Basque	Lack
	Lekeitio Basque	Emergence
Balto-Slavic	Latvian	Retention
	Tamian Latvian	Loss
Greek	Modern Greek	Retention
	Pontic Greek	Reduction
	Rumeic Greek	Reduction
	Cappadocian Greek	Loss
Insular Celtic	Irish	Reduction
	Irish (Ros Much)	Retention
North Germanic	Elfdalian	Retention
	Karleby Swedish	Reduction
	Standard Swedish	Reduction
Northwestern Iranian	Eshtehardi	Expansion
	Kafteji	Expansion
	Kelasi	Loss
Lezgic	Archi	Retention
	Aghul	Loss
	Udi	Loss
Thebor	Shumcho	Emergence
	Jangshung	Emergence
Papunesia		
Chamorro	Chamorro	Emergence
Mek	Nalca	Emergence
	Eipo	Emergence

[5]For language classification we follow the Glottolog (Hammarström et al. 2018).

Family by macroarea	Language	Pattern of change
Africa		
Bantu	Kinshasa Lingala	Reduction
	Makanza Lingala	Expansion
Ghana-Togo-Mountain	Selee	Retention
	Igo	Reduction (near loss)
	Ikposo	Loss
Australia		
Gunwinggu	Kunwinjku	Retention
	Kundjeyhmi	Reduction
	Kune	Loss
North America		
Mixed Language	Michif	Expansion

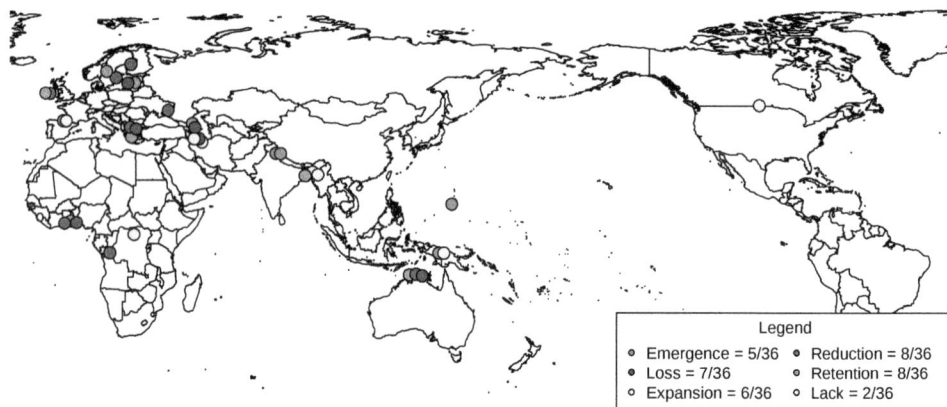

Figure 2: Distribution of patterns of change

It can be hypothesized that gender agreement systems in decline represent instances of reducing complexity, while gender agreement systems on the rise or under expansion represent instances of increasing complexity. A further possible hypothesis is that gender agreement systems on the rise or in decline are less complex than the more pervasive systems that they are moving towards or away from. We will come back to these hypotheses in §7 and evaluate them against our data.

3 The evolution of gender complexity in the domain of agreement

Starting with the pioneering work by Corbett (1979; 1991), a great deal of research has focused on unraveling constraints on the distribution of gender distinctions on different types of agreement targets. This research has shown that certain agreement targets (e.g., personal pronouns) are more likely than others (e.g., attributive modifiers) to index semantic rather than grammatical properties of nouns. In the terminology proposed by Corbett (1979; 1991), this is known as an opposition between *semantic* and *syntactic* agreement patterns. Preferences towards semantic or syntactic agreement per type of agreement target are captured in the form of an implicational hierarchy, which is known as the Agreement Hierarchy. The Agreement Hierarchy – illustrated in (1) – was first proposed by Corbett (1979) and is further discussed in Corbett (1991; 2000; 2006). It expresses the likelihood of semantic agreement to occur with different types of agreement targets as well as the degree of syntactic cohesion between agreement targets and their controllers.

(1)   The Agreement Hierarchy (adapted from Corbett 2010)

- SEMANTIC AGREEMENT
  attributive > predicate > relative pronoun > personal pronoun
- SYNTACTIC COHESION
  attributive < predicate < relative pronoun < personal pronoun

The directions of the arrows – ">" or "<" – stand for different directionalities in the two main chains of implications entailed by the hierarchy. The first row indicates that semantic agreement on any of the targets to the left implies the presence of semantic agreement on the targets to the right, with attributive modifiers being the least likely candidate for semantic agreement. The second row indicates that syntactic cohesion between nouns and any of the targets to the right of the hierarchy implies at least the same level of syntactic cohesion with any of the targets to the left, with personal pronouns being the agreement targets with the loosest syntactic integration to nouns. These hierarchical effects are connected with the fact that pronouns tend to be linearly more distant from their antecedents (low syntactic cohesion) as compared, for instance, with definite articles (high syntactic cohesion), which tend to occur linearly closer to the controller nouns.[6] Pronouns are therefore more prone to index semantic proper-

---

[6]Different types of agreement targets may occur within the noun phrase (articles, quantifiers, numerals etc.) and further hierarchical effects between such targets cannot be excluded. This, however, falls outside the scope of the present investigation.

ties of the discourse referent rather than lexico-grammatical properties of nouns, such as grammatical gender. Mismatches between the agreement patterns associated with different types of targets are especially likely to occur when the controller nouns are *hybrid nouns*. In the case of gender, these are nouns whose inherent gender assignment is in conflict with their semantics. A classic example is the German noun for 'girl', *Mädchen*, which is grammatically neuter, but denotes a human entity. Let us consider the types of gender agreement mismatches attested in German with the noun *Mädchen*.

(2) German (Indo-European, Germanic; Corbett 1991: 228)
   Schau dir   dieses Mädchen an, wie gut   sie/es Tennis spielt.
   look you this.N girl   at, how good she/it tennis plays

   'Look at this girl, see how well she plays tennis.'

The example shows that while gender agreement within the noun phrase (i.e., on the demonstrative) can only conform to the lexical gender of the noun (*dieses*, N), speakers can choose between feminine and neuter agreement for personal pronouns. Feminine agreement indexes the fact that the discourse referent is female (as in *sie*, F); neuter agreement indexes the fact that the noun for 'girl' is grammatically neuter (as in *es*, N).[7] Conflicts between "semantic" and "syntactic" agreement can also be understood in terms of mismatches between *referential* and *lexical* gender, as these terms are used by Dahl (2000) (see also the study of the evolution of gender marking in medieval English by Siemund & Dolberg 2011).

There are at least two ways in which the Agreement Hierarchy can be used to describe synchronic variation in gender complexity, one pertaining to the types and number of attested agreement domains, and one pertaining to the type and number of preferred agreement patterns per domain. Concerning type and number of attested agreement domains, a language that exhibits gender agreement in all the agreement domains represented along the hierarchy is, in this respect, more complex than a language that, other things being equal, has agreement in fewer domains. This is, for instance, the way in which the amount of gender agreement or gender indexation is treated in the metric proposed by Di Garbo (2016).[8] Concerning type and number of preferred agreement patterns, a lan-

---

[7]Corbett (1991: 228) further mentions that the older the age of the young woman that is being talked about, the more likely it is for speakers to use feminine agreement.

[8]For some observations on possible implicational tendencies constraining which agreement domains are more likely to be targets of gender marking in a sample of 20 languages from New Guinea see Svärd (2019 [in Volume I]).

guage in which gender agreement is only syntactic with all agreement targets is, in this respect, less complex than a language that, other things being equal, exhibits variation between syntactic and semantic agreement at any point along the hierarchy. For a broader discussion about the use of typological implicational hierarchies as cross-linguistic measures of complexity, see Miestamo (2009).

In this paper, we explore the extent to which not only synchronic, but also diachronic variation in the domain of gender agreement can be mapped onto the Agreement Hierarchy (for an overview of the role of the Agreement Hierarchy in the diachrony of nominal classification see also Seifart 2010). With respect to types and number of agreement domains, we find that, in the languages of our sample, both the rise and the decline of gender agreement tend to start off from the agreement domains at the two opposite ends of the Agreement Hierarchy, i.e., either from attributive modifiers or from personal pronouns and/or other type of anaphoric constructions, such as light nouns with anaphoric functions (for the latter, see also Wälchli 2019 [this volume]). With respect to types and number of preferred agreement patterns per domain we find that, in the languages of the sample, at least the decline and loss of gender agreement tend to be directional, and that the attested lines of directionality are reminiscent of the two opposite pulling forces described by the Agreement Hierarchy: syntactic cohesion between controllers and targets, and spread of semantic agreement. However, we make no claims about the universality of these tendencies, and we do not exclude that, in languages other than those sampled for this study, diachronic change in the morphosyntax of gender agreement occurs on other types of agreement targets first. Finally, while we argue that the hierarchy is a useful tool to *describe* tendencies in how gender marking systems change, we make no claims about it having a *predictive/explanatory* value concerning the spreading of such changes. On the contrary, we argue that explanations should be sought in the realm of those functional pressures that are reflected in the hierarchy.

In §4, we focus on reducing gender agreement systems; emerging gender agreement systems are discussed in §5 whereas the expansion of gender agreement patterns is treated in §6.

4 Reducing gender agreement systems

4.1 Attested processes of change

In our data, the reduction and, in some cases, the loss of gender agreement result from two distinct diachronic processes: (1) *morphophonological erosion* and (2) *redistribution* of agreement patterns.

By morphophonological erosion we refer to the wholesale patterns of change that lead to the loss of inflection. Sound changes (e.g., changes in stress patterns resulting in the loss of word-initial or word-final segments) can cause loss of segmental morphology, which ultimately determines the neutralization of previously overtly coded grammatical distinctions and the overall restructuring of inflectional paradigms. This process is also known in the literature under the label *deflection*. Within the domain of nominal morphology, morphophonological erosion often affects gender marking along with the marking of other nominal inflectional features, such as number and case, which are frequently cumulatively encoded with gender. It has been suggested (see Priestly 1983 for Indo-European; Audring 2009 for Germanic languages) that, when morphophonological erosion affects the encoding of gender distinctions, the word classes that are likely to lose gender marking first are the nouns themselves (in case of overt gender systems), followed by the agreement targets that are more adjacent to nouns, i.e., adnominal modifiers, such as definiteness markers, demonstratives, adjectives and numerals, with definiteness markers generally being yet more stable than, say, numerals or adjectives. Personal pronouns (both dependent and independent) are more likely to retain the encoding of gender distinctions as a means to signal semantic properties of the discourse referents. In other words, under morphophonological erosion, gender agreement is more likely to be retained on those agreement targets where it is most functional to reference tracking and reference identification, i.e. demonstrative and/or personal pronouns. These may then tend to inflect based on semantically transparent principles of gender assignment (animacy and/or biological gender). In English, for instance, the encoding of gender distinctions underwent massive erosion as part of a general weakening of inflectional morphology. As a result of this deflection process, gender marking was lost on all of the agreement targets (as well as on nouns) except for the personal pronouns, which nowadays signal the biological gender of discourse referents, and for the relative pronouns which make a distinction of the human/non-human type (Curzan 2003).

By *redistribution of agreement*, we refer to the process whereby one of the several agreement patterns available in a language (for instance, the neuter) starts being used with nouns that would normally trigger agreement in other genders (for instances, with nouns that are semantically inanimate, but grammatically masculine or feminine). If the redistribution of one agreement pattern comes to affect all agreement domains, and to effectively replace all the other competing agreement patterns independently of semantic or morphological properties of the controller nouns, then gender distinctions become neutralized. In many of the cases attested in our sample, the redistribution of agreement patterns appears to be at least initially semantically motivated: semantic oppositions generally pertaining to the domain of animacy start affecting the criteria according to which certain nouns trigger gender agreement on at least some targets. In general, the higher the number of nouns involved in the restructuring of the assignment criteria, the higher the chance that the overall gender assignment rules of a language may change. Similarly, the higher the number of agreement targets that align with the new assignment criteria, the more reasons to speak of an increase or decrease in the number of gender distinctions. For instance, when the semantic agreement patterns that are being redistributed are based on animacy, their generalization to all agreement targets may eventually lead to a bipartite, animate vs. inanimate, type of gender system, where gender assignment is semantically predictable. This is for instance the case of the Bantu language Kinshasa Lingala, in which all productive agreement targets index the animacy of the noun, whereas the nouns themselves retain prefixal remnants of the old, no longer productive system of gender distinctions (Maho 1999: 130–132; Meeuwis 2013: 28–29). In other cases, the most frequent (default) pattern of gender agreement is the one that takes over. This is for instance the case of Tamian Latvian (Indo-European, Balto-Slavic), where the masculine agreement pattern has replaced nearly all instances of feminine agreement leading to loss of grammatical gender. The redistribution of agreement patterns is ultimately a process of analogical levelling: the gender agreement system of a language is restructured on the basis of the more semantically motivated and/or more frequent agreement pattern, which gradually spreads at the expenses of others.

Table 2 illustrates the distribution of patterns of reduction and loss of gender agreement within the languages of the sample, and specifies whether these are due to morphophonological erosion, redistribution of agreement, a combination of both, or whether the exact pattern of change cannot be inferred based on the data at our disposal. For each of the relevant languages, the table also specifies if directionality applies, and if the distribution of a given pattern of change is at any rate semantically motivated. Given the limited size of our sample, the analysis proposed here is merely qualitative and we draw no generalization based on the relative frequencies of the observed patterns of change. Examples for each of the possible scenarios are discussed in §4.2, 4.3 and 4.4.

Table 2: Morphophonological erosion and redistribution of agreement in the languages of the sample where gender agreement reduction and loss are attested

	Languages	Directionality	Semantics
Morphophonological erosion	Standard Swedish	YES	NO
	Kelasi	Not clear	NO
Redistribution	Cappadocian Greek	YES	YES
	Pontic Greek	YES	YES
	Rumeic Greek	YES	YES
	Irish	YES	YES
	Kune	Not clear	No data
Both	Igo	YES	Not clear
	Karleby Swedish	Not clear	Partially
	Kinshasa Lingala	YES	YES
	Tamian Latvian	Partially	Partially
Not clear	Aghul	–	–
	Kundjeyhmi	–	–
	Lezgian	–	–
	Udi	–	–

Table 3: Personal Pronouns in Standard Swedish

	M	F	PL
Nominative	*han* 'he'	*hon* 'she'	*de* 'they'
Genitive	*hans* 'his'	*hennes* 'her'	*deras* 'their'
Accusative	*honom* 'him'	*henne* 'her'	*dem* 'them'

4.2 Reduction and loss by morphophonological erosion

In Standard Swedish, the opposition between masculine and feminine gender is retained in the inflectional paradigm of the independent third person pronouns (see Table 3), but has been lost elsewhere.[9]

The Masculine and Feminine singular forms of the third person pronouns are used to signal the biological gender of human and other animate referents.[10]

---

[9]In written language, a masculine suffix *-e* may still sometimes be used on adjectives to mark masculine agreement.

[10]During the last decade, a biological gender-neutral form, *hen* has been introduced. Its frequency of use has rapidly increased, both in written and spoken Swedish discourse.

With non-animate entities, the demonstrative pronouns *den*, Common Gender, and *det*, Neuter Gender, are used instead, and the choice between the two is based on the lexical gender of nouns. In sum, in the pronominal domain, Standard Swedish has a four-way gender distinction: Masculine, Feminine, Common, Neuter, with a split between animate and inanimate referents governing the distribution of these gender values. Within the domain of adnominal modification, Swedish distinguishes between a Common and a Neuter Gender only: *en person* 'a person' (Common Gender), and *ett hus* 'a house' (Neuter Gender). Historically, the Common Gender is the result of a merger between the Feminine and Masculine genders. Many nonstandard varieties of Swedish, as well as many other Scandinavian varieties, retain a tripartite gender system. Tripartite gender systems were found all over Scandinavia before the standard varieties with a bipartite gender system, such as Danish and Swedish, started spreading.[11] One of the Swedish dialects which still retains a fully productive tripartite gender system is Elfdalian, spoken in the Swedish region of Northern Dalarna by approximately two thousand people.[12] In Elfdalian, the opposition between Masculine, Feminine and Neuter gender runs productively through the whole agreement system. A tripartite gender system of the type retained by Elfdalian is also attested in Old Swedish texts.[13] The Masculine-Feminine merger in the domain of adnominal modification appears to be due to a combination of various morphophonological processes, such as the erosion and loss of the masculine *-er* ending in the inflectional paradigm of strong adjectives, the loss of the masculine suffix *-r* before the definite suffix in the nominative form of the noun, and the loss of final consonant length in the inflectional paradigm of the definite suffixes (Duke 2010: 652–654). Finally, pervasive reduction in gender agreement domains is attested in Karleby Swedish, the variety of Swedish spoken in the town of Karleby, located in the Finnish region of Ostrobothnia.[14] Gender agreement reduction in Karleby Swedish is best described as an instance of both morphophonological erosion and agreement redistribution. It is therefore discussed in §4.4.

---

[11]Before the spread of the standard languages, bipartite gender systems were only attested in Denmark, southern Sweden, the Mälaren valley in Sweden, and pockets of Norway where varieties heavily influenced by Danish were spoken (Östen Dahl, personal communication).

[12]Data from Åkerberg (2012), as well as from Östen Dahl (personal communication).

[13]The use of the Masculine and Feminine pronouns with inanimate antecedents continued in the written language until the nineteenth century, even though this distinction was lost in all other domains of nominal inflection and no longer maintained in spoken use (Östen Dahl, personal communication).

[14]It is worth mentioning that, contrary to Karleby Swedish, some other Ostrobothnian varieties of Swedish display quite conservative gender systems (for more details see Huldén 1972: 40–50.) However, it is perhaps unsurprising, that the near loss of gender distinctions is attested in the northernmost corner of the Swedish speaking area of Finland.

Loss of gender in Kelasi, a Northwestern Iranian language of the Tatic sub-branch, is also the result of a process of morphophonological erosion. Stilo (to appear) proposes a historical-comparative analysis of gender loss in Kelasi whereby the decline of gender marking is explained as originating from the domain of noun inflection. In Kafteji, a closely related language spoken at a distance of twelve kilometers from Kelasi, gender distinctions are still retained. However, in Kafteji, overt marking of gender on nouns is dropped when nouns are used in a generic sense or as citation forms, and gender is never marked on agreement targets when these occur in isolation. Based on this comparative evidence, Stilo (to appear: 27) hypothesizes that, at some point in the history of Kelasi, gender marking became increasingly optional and "went through gradual stages of erosion by becoming more and more rarely used in speech", to be finally dropped in all domains of encoding. Even though the individual stages of this process of erosion are not known, nouns – "the crucial locus of gender in the grammar" of Kelasi (Stilo to appear: 27) – are viewed as the word class from which the decline of gender marking originated. This is why we classify Kelasi as an instance of gender loss by morphophonological erosion.

The reduction and loss of gender inflections as a result of a more general erosion of nominal morphology are widely attested across different genera of the Indo-European language family. See Audring (2009: chapter 9) for an overview of patterns of gender reduction and loss across Germanic languages; Priestly (1983) for a broader overview of the Indo-European language family, and, in particular, of pronominal relics of the neuter gender in Romance (e.g., Italian, French) and Baltic (e.g., Lithuanian) languages.

4.3 Reduction and loss by redistribution of agreement

Gender reduction and loss as a result of the redistribution of agreement patterns are widely attested in our sample. In this section, we discuss a selection of the attested cases.

The Asia Minor Greek dialects are a group of Greek varieties that are or, prior to the 1923 population exchange between Greece and Turkey, used to be spoken in Turkey. Karatsareas (2014) identifies five main dialects within the Asia Minor Greek cluster: Cappadocian, Pharasiot, Pontic, Silliot, and Rumeic. While the first four varieties were spoken in different areas of modern Turkey, Rumeic is the variety spoken by the Greek inhabitants of Mariupol, Ukraine, and can be considered as the historical descendant of the Pontic spoken by Greek settlers in Crimea.

Due to their long-lasting history of isolation from mainland varieties of Greek, and, partially, to a history of prolonged contact and bilingualism with Turkish, the Asia Minor Greek dialects exhibit a wealth of grammatical innovations among which a significant reorganization of the gender agreement and gender assignment patterns. This is attested in all Asia Minor Greek varieties but Silliot, which rather retains a conservative system similar to the one attested in Standard Greek and in other Modern Greek varieties outside the Asia Minor area (Karatsareas 2014: 83). Examples (3), (4), (5), and (6) illustrate the innovations attested in the domain of gender agreement and gender assignment in four out of the five groups of Asia Minor Greek dialects. We present data from the dialects that display renewed gender systems and compare them with equivalent structures in Standard Greek, where these innovations are not attested.[15]

In Pontic, example (3), the inanimate feminine noun for 'door' triggers neuter agreement with agreement targets non-immediately adjacent to nouns. In the corresponding Standard Greek sentence, agreement is feminine with all targets.

(3)   a.   Argyroúpolis Pontic (Indo-European, Greek; Karatsareas 2014: 79)

      i   *pórta*   (...) *móno ímoson óran*   *estéknen*

      DEF.F.SG door.F.SG (...) only half.N.SG hour.F.SG stay.PST.3SG

      anixtón

      open.N.SG

      'The door would stay open for only half an hour.'

    b.   Standard Greek (Indo-European, Greek; Karatsareas 2014: 80)

      i   *pórta*   *móno misí*   *óra*   *émene*   *anixtí*

      DEF.F.SG door.F.SG only half.F.SG hour.F stay.PST.3SG open.F.SG

      'The door stayed open for only half an hour.'

In Pontic, the criteria of gender assignment are reorganized based on the animacy of the noun: semantically inanimate, but grammatically masculine and feminine nouns are to a large extent treated as neuter. This semantic reorganization is reflected at the level of agreement: semantic (neuter) agreement with inanimate masculine and feminine nouns is attested on all agreement targets but prenominal definite articles, which instead agree with the grammatical gender of the nouns (i.e. they take masculine or feminine inflection).

In Rumeic, example (4), the pattern of semantic agreement observed in Pontic is generalized to all targets: the inanimate noun for 'winter' (which is masculine in Standard Greek) triggers neuter agreement with all agreement targets.

---

[15]Notice that the Standard Greek examples reported by Karatsareas (2014) can be either full or partial translations of the corresponding example in one of the Asian Minor Greek dialects.

(4) a. Rumeic (Indo-European, Greek; Karatsareas 2014: 79)

      tu   ko   mas   to   ʃumós   en   xlísku

      DEF.N.SG POSS.N.SG 1PL.GEN DEF.N.SG winter.N.SG be.PRS.3SG tepid.N.SG

      'Our winter is tepid.'

   b. Standard Greek (Indo-European, Greek; Karatsareas 2014: 80)

      o   ðikós   mas   o   çimónas

      DEF.M.SG POSS.M.SG 1PL.GEN DEF.M.SG winter.M.SG

      'our winter'

In Rumeic, the gender system has been restructured based on semantic grounds: male entities are assigned to the Masculine Gender, female entities to the Feminine and inanimate entities to the Neuter.

A different path is taken by Pharasiot and Cappadocian, where the redistribution of the neuter gender agreement pattern leads to a more pervasive erosion of the gender system. In Pharasiot, as illustrated in example (5), the animate noun for 'woman' (feminine in Standard Greek) triggers neuter agreement with all targets but the definite article adjacent to the noun.

(5) a. Pharasiot (Indo-European, Greek; Karatsareas 2014: 79)

      férinke   adʒíno   i   néka   xortáre

      bring.PST.3.SG DEM.DIST.N.SG DEF.F.SG woman.F.SG herb.PL

      'that woman used to bring herbs.'

   b. Standard Greek (Indo-European, Greek; Karatsareas 2014: 80)

      ecíni   i   jinéka

      DEM.DIST.F.SG DEF.F.SG woman.F.SG

      'that woman'

In Pharasiot, the neuter agreement has been generalized to all nominal types (animate and inanimate) and the semantic opposition between animate and inanimate entities has been neutralized. Only the agreement targets that are most adjacent to nouns retain agreement with the original grammatical gender of the noun (in this case with the Feminine).

Finally, in Cappadocian, example (6), the neuter agreement pattern is generalized to all nouns, irrespective of animacy and type of target (the noun for 'wall' is masculine in Standard Greek).

(6) a. Axó Cappadocian (Indo-European, Greek; Karatsareas 2014: 79)

      t   *spitçú*   *ta*   *ndix(u)s xtizména*

      DEF.SG.GEN house.SG.GEN DEF.PL wall.PL built.PL

      'The walls of the house (are) built.'

  b. Standard Greek (Indo-European, Greek; Karatsareas 2014: 80)

      i   *tíçi*   *ine*   *xtixméni*

      DEF.M.PL wall.M.PL be.PRS.3PL built.M.PL

      'the walls are built'.

In Cappadocian, pervasive redistribution of the neuter agreement pattern has led to complete gender loss, whereby agreement patterns only index number distinctions, in this case that the noun is plural.[16]

Using internal reconstruction, historical data, and data from contemporary varieties of Pontic spoken in Greece, Karatsareas (2014) shows that two main orders of facts account for the rise and spread of semantic agreement in Pontic. On the one hand, the triggers of semantic agreement are nouns at the bottom of the Individuation Hierarchy (Sasse 1993), that is, inanimate mass and abstract nouns that are grammatically assigned to the masculine or feminine genders. These are typical instances of hybrid nouns, i.e., nouns whose denotational semantics is in conflict with their grammatical gender assignment (these nouns denote inanimate entities, but are grammatically masculine or feminine). On the other hand, according to Karatsareas' reconstruction, the spreading of semantic agreement starts from the personal (and demonstrative) pronouns. In Pontic, the sole agreement targets that are left untouched by these redistribution patterns are those that are most adjacent to nouns, i.e., prenominal definite articles. Rumeic is the only Asia Minor Greek dialect where semantic agreement has become generalized to all nouns and targets leading to a gender system which is still tripartite (Masculine, Feminine, Neuter), but in which assignment rules and agreement patterns are entirely semantic. Conversely, in Pharasiot and Cappadocian, the generalization of the neuter agreement pattern to human nouns has paved the way for a more pervasive erosion of gender marking.[17] This process of erosion has turned into complete loss in (varieties of) Cappadocian only. The loss of gender in Cappadocian Greek is seen by Karatsareas (2014: 99) as reasonably connected

---

[16]Feminine and masculine agreement survive in the singular form of definite articles preceding nouns only in the Delmesó, Potámia, and Sílata varieties of Cappadocian (Karatsareas 2014: 97).

[17]A similar development is attested in some more recent varieties of Pontic, where at least human nouns denoting female referents systematically trigger neuter agreement (Karatsareas 2014: 96–97).

with the fact that, among all Asia Minor Greek varieties, this is the one with the longest and tightest history of contact and bilingualism with Turkish. A summary of the patterns of agreement redistribution attested in Pontic, Rumeic, and Cappadocian Greek is given in Figure 3.

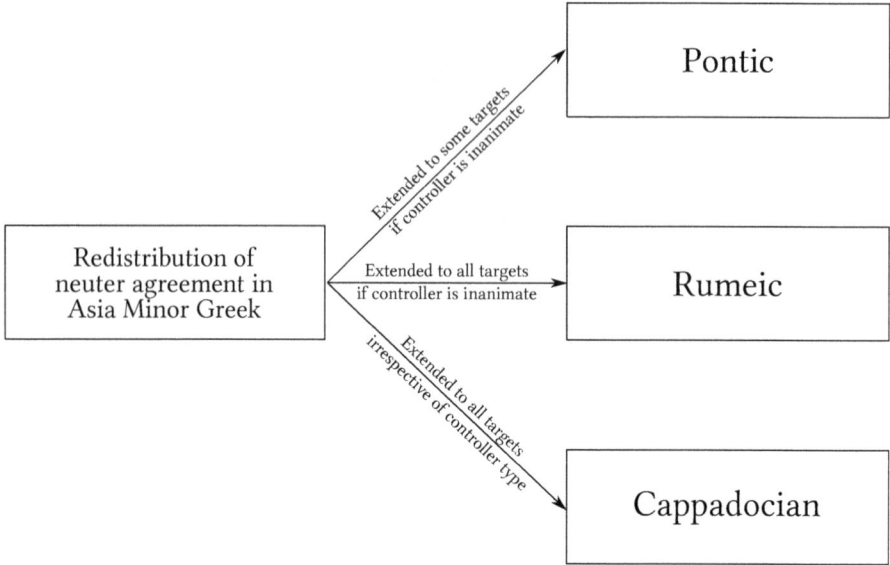

Figure 3: Neuter Agreement in the Asia Minor Greek dialects

Semantically motivated redistribution of gender agreement patterns also occurs in contemporary varieties of urban Irish as documented by Frenda (2011). In these non-standard varieties of Irish (which Frenda classifies as "non-native"), masculine agreement is increasingly used as the default agreement pattern for grammatically feminine nouns denoting inanimate entities. The redistribution is very pervasive in the domain of personal pronouns where the gender assignment system appears to be largely based on an opposition between "female referent" (marked by the Feminine Pronoun) and "everything else" (marked by the Masculine Pronoun). In the domain of adnominal modification, controller nouns that are grammatically feminine but semantically inanimate still trigger feminine agreement (this is attested in 88% of the examined cases; see Frenda 2011: 17, Figure 1).

In sum, the data from our sample suggest that patterns of agreement redistribution tend to be constrained by the syntactic cohesion between controller nouns and agreement targets. Those agreement targets that are most adjacent to nouns are the ones that are affected last by the spreading of innovations.

4.4 Combined and unclear cases

In some cases, both morphophonological erosion and agreement redistribution are attested in one and the same language, albeit not necessarily as the result of co-occurrent patterns of change. One such case is Igo, a Ghana-Togo-Mountain language of the Kwa subfamily of the Atlantic-Congo family, spoken by approximately 6.000 people (Gblem-Poidi 2007). In general, the Ghana-Togo-Mountain languages represent an ideal test case for an intragenealogical study of the diachrony of gender systems and their evolving complexity (for a historical-comparative overview, see also the contribution by Güldemann & Fiedler 2019 [in Volume I]). Some languages within the family, such as Selee (Agbetsoamedo 2014) and Siwi (Dingemanse 2009), display very productive gender systems characterized by a high number of (non-sex-based) gender distinctions, pervasive agreement and overt marking of gender on nouns. Some other languages (e.g., Animere) present heavily eroded and completely semanticized systems of gender assignment and gender agreement, whereby gender assignment and agreement are animacy-based, and traditional noun class marking on nouns is retained merely as a means of marking singular/plural distinctions. Finally, a few other languages, such as Ikposo (Soubrier 2013), have lost gender completely and retain relics of the extinct gender marking system only on nouns. Igo provides us with an example of a system in transition from animacy-based gender distinctions (of the Animere type) to complete loss of gender (of the Ikposo type). Gblem-Poidi (2007) argues that the original gender system of Igo consisted of eleven non-sex-based genders whose distribution paralleled the eleven pairings of singular and plural nominal prefixes still in use in the language. Nowadays, however, in formal registers of Igo,[18] only an animate/inanimate type of distinction is marked on the agreement targets. It can thus be assumed that this animacy-based gender system is already an eroded system, and that this process of erosion may have occurred through the spreading of semantic, animacy-based agreement. Albeit preferred in formal registers and still in use among the older generations, the animacy-based gender system of Igo is described by Gblem-Poidi (2007) as under threat, highly eroded in the speech of middle-aged speakers, and practically unused by the younger speakers. The ongoing loss of gender distinctions in Igo is the result of the erosion of segmental gender morphology. Gender agreement morphemes are omitted in actual discourse while their tonal patterns are retained in the form of floating tones that encroach upon the immediately fol-

---

[18]Those in use in the literacy program and in the New Testament Translation (Honorine Gblem-Poidi, personal communication).

lowing tonal segments. Interestingly, in spoken use, the former animate gender agreement markers (*ù-* and *bù-*) are resumed and reanalyzed as nominal number markers, whereby *ù-* marks the singular with both animate and inanimate nouns, and *bù-* the plural, but only with animate nouns. Example (7) shows overt plural marking with animate nouns and zero marking with inanimate.

(7) Igo (Niger-Congo, Kwa, Ghana-Togo-Mountain; Gblem-Poidi 2007: 59)

a. *bégù   lɔ́   bù ɖā   wūlū*
    children DEF PL PROG.SBJ dry.out

    'The children are losing weight.'

b. *ātī   lɔ́   ɖàā   wūlū*
    trees DEF PROG.SBJ dry.out

    'The trees are dying out.'

Based on the data at our disposal, it is not possible to determine whether the loss of segmental gender marking affects all agreement targets at once or is gradually spreading from one agreement domain to the other.

Another instance of pervasive reduction of gender agreement morphology which seemingly results from a combination of morphophonological erosion and agreement redistribution is Karleby Swedish. In this variety of Swedish, gender distinctions have been lost on all agreement targets except for the definite articles (immediately adjacent to nouns) and the demonstrative and personal pronouns. These retain a tripartite distinction between Masculine, Feminine and Neuter gender. The masculine and feminine forms are however used only when the controller noun denotes human beings; in all other cases only one form (the Neuter) is used both in the domain of definite and indefinite articles and with demonstrative and anaphoric pronouns (Huldén 1972; Hultman 1894). It is reasonable to think that this superimposed animacy-based distinction (whereby only nouns denoting humans trigger a masculine/feminine distinction) might have spread from the domain of anaphoric pronouns (where, for instance, it is also found in Standard Swedish) to the definite articles.

In the Tamian dialects of Latvian, loss of gender marking is also the result of a complex interplay between morphophonological erosion and agreement redistribution. According to the recent comparative study by Wälchli (2017), the loss of short vowels in final syllables caused the neutralization of the opposition between masculine and feminine gender in the accusative plural of nominal paradigms. The neutralization pattern later extended to the demonstratives. This paved the way to several processes of redistribution that led to the gradual generalization of masculine agreement to other types of targets (for instance, past participles and predicative adjectives), but never to all instances of gender agreement. As underscored by Wälchli (2017), and contrary to what suggested in previous literature (Rudzīte 1980), the unfolding of these developments varies substantially across different Tamian varieties and cannot be subsumed under one unitary model of change.

For three of the sampled languages, Kundjeyhmi (Central Gunwinyguan), Udi (Lezgic), and Aghul (Lezgic), the patterns of change behind the reduction and loss of gender agreement patterns cannot be fully inferred based on the data at our disposal.

4.5 Reducing gender agreement systems: summary

In our data, the reduction and loss of gender agreement can be described as the result of two distinct processes: morphophonological erosion and redistribution of agreement. We also found evidence for some directional effects in the way in which these developments spread. The morphophonological erosion of gender inflections tends to spread from nouns to those agreement targets that are syntactically more adjacent to nouns (i.e., adnominal modifiers). Conversely, the redistribution of agreement patterns affects anaphoric pronouns (i.e., the agreement targets that are least adjacent to nouns) first. In our sample, these directional effects are attested across different language families and different types of gender systems, which makes it reasonable to hypothesize that they may respond to more general, possibly universal, tendencies in language change. Furthermore, we believe that these directional effects are due to two distinct types of functional constraints: the syntactic cohesion between agreement targets and their controllers, on the one hand, and the sensitivity of agreement targets to semantic properties of discourse referents, on the other hand. The higher the syntactic cohesion (e.g. with definite and indefinite articles), the lower the sensitivity to referential properties, and vice versa (personal pronouns have looser syntactic cohesion with nouns and are therefore more sensitive to semantics). We suggest that the Agreement Hierarchy, a generalization over observed tendencies in the distribution of syntactic and semantic agreement, makes it possible to detect and describe the connection between these two opposite tendencies. This is because, as also outlined in §3, the two ends of the scale, attributive modifiers and personal pronouns, represent instances of highest and lowest degree of syntactic cohesion, and lowest and highest likelihood of semantic agreement, respectively. In §7 we discuss how these different diachronic developments pattern with the evolution of gender complexity.

5 Emerging gender agreement systems

The literature on the rise of grammatical gender is vast, and cannot be reported here in detail. Broadly speaking, two opposite scenarios have been proposed in order to account for the origin of grammatical gender systems. According to the first scenario, the development of classificatory strategies precedes the rise of gender agreement patterns. Gender systems originate from classifiers and classificatory nouns that grammaticalize as agreement markers and, eventually, as gender markers on nouns (Greenberg 1978b; Corbett 1991). According to the second scenario, the development of agreement precedes the development of classificatory distinctions. Nichols (1992: 139–142) argues that the development of classificatory distinctions encroaches on preexisting (person and/or number) agreement patterns whose distribution may be based on covert, in the sense of not morphosyntactically realized, animacy distinctions or on other highly cognitively salient types of distinctions. Against this background, the debate on the origins of grammatical gender systems has focused on a diverse variety of gendered language families, such as Indo-European (Matasović 2004; Luraghi 2011), Atlantic-Congo (Greenberg 1978b; Williamson 1994), Eastern Nilotic (Heine & Vossen 1983), or on individual languages such as the Boran language Miraña (Seifart 2005) or the Southern Daly language Ngan'gityemerri (Reid 1997).

In this section we focus on the hitherto understudied semantic and morphosyntactic properties of young, non-mature (in the sense of Dahl 2004) gender systems. Two main types of young gender agreement systems are brought to attention in this work: (1) emerging gender systems that result from the grammaticalization of light nouns, such as the noun for "woman", as generalized anaphoric devices (see Wälchli 2019 [this volume]) and (2) emerging gender systems that result from the rise of marginal agreement patterns in the domain of adnominal modification, which we discuss in this section. In line with the tendencies also observed for the decline and loss of gender agreement, the two types of emerging gender agreement systems discussed in this volume appear to flag the agreement domains at the two opposite ends of the Agreement Hierarchy (the attributive domain and the anaphoric domain). Neither of these systems, however, originates from classifiers or pre-existing agreement patterns.[19]

While it is impossible to predict whether these emergent patterns of gender agreement will develop into more grammaticalized types of systems, we believe

---

[19]The emergence of gender agreement from the grammaticalizion of classificatory light nouns is studied, for instance, by Grinevald & Seifart (2004) and Seifart (2005), with a special focus on Amazonian languages.

that they offer a unique insight into the rise of complexity in the domain of gender marking as well as into its stability and transmissibility. In the languages of our sample, the emergence of gender agreement in the domain of adnominal modification can result either from language-internal developments or from language contact. These two cases are discussed separately in the remainder of this section.

5.1 Language-internal development of gender: Nalca

Nalca is a Mek language of the Nuclear Trans-New Guinea family spoken in the Highlands of Tanah Papua. The gender system of Nalca is described by Wälchli (2018), both from a synchronic and diachronic perspective. Nalca has a sex-based gender system, with five gender distinctions and semantic and formal (phonological) assignment; gender distinctions are not overtly coded on nouns and the sole targets of gender agreement are a set of function words, which, beside marking gender, also work as case and deictic marking hosts. The gender markers of Nalca and their respective labels are given in Table 4.

Table 4: Gender in Nalca

Gender	Marker
Masculine (some human males)	*be-*
Feminine (some human females)	*ge-*
Neuter/nouns with Consonant + Vowel phonotactic structure (CV), 'the thing(s) that...'	*ne-*
Default Noun	*e-*
Default Phrase (locative, adverbs)	*a-*

Gender agreement in Nalca is noun phrase internal and strongly tied to linear adjacency between controller nouns and agreement targets. When the adjacency condition is not fulfilled, or when the controller noun is not preceded by attributive adjectives (which favor the expression of gender), inherent gender distinctions are neutralized and the agreement pattern triggered on the case/deictic host is that of the Default Phrase gender *a-*, which is typically used with non-prototypical controllers. This illustrated in (8).

(8) Nalca (Mek; Wälchli 2018: 71)

    me: *a-ra*   *gelelinga*   *sovb-vka*
    child(cv) DP-TOP unnoticed enclose.in.netbag-CVB
    bo-ba-lam-e:k.   *Nauba me:*   *ne:-ra* *al-biyvk.* *Me:k*
    carry-go-HAB/IPVF-PST.3PL. big   child(cv) CV-TOP 3SG-alone. small
    me: *ne:-ra* *sovb-vka*   *bo-ba-lam-e:k*
    child.cv CV-TOP enclose.in.netbag-CVB carry-go-HAB/IPVF-PST.3PL

    'They carried the boy away secretly in a netbag. A big boy went by himself. A small boy they carried in a netbag.'

The Nalca noun for 'child' *me:* is Neuter (it has a CV type of phonotactic structure). However neuter agreement is marked only when the noun is accompanied by the attributive modifiers for 'big' and 'small'. When it occurs on its own, as in the first of the three sentences exemplified in (8), the Default Phrase gender agreement *a-* is selected.

Wälchli (2018) describes gender in Nalca as a recent innovation within Mek languages. The gender markers of Nalca have cognates in all related Mek languages, but in none of these languages are these markers part of a system of classificatory distinctions in paradigmatic opposition with each other. In Nalca, an emergent system of nominal classification has resulted from a complex array of multiple, independent patterns of language change. The onset of this evolutionary process is the reinterpretation of a uniqueness/saliency marker targeting the top end of the Animacy Hierarchy (*bi-*) as an agreement marker in opposition with *a-*, probably marking non-uniqueness and low animacy (Wälchli 2018). This type of system is attested in the neighboring languages Eipo and Una, where a high degree of animacy is flagged by the marker *bi-*.

5.2 Contact-induced gender emergence

Contact-induced gender emergence presupposes borrowing of agreement patterns, a phenomenon which is argued to take place only in the context of prolonged contact between two or more speech communities, presupposing child bi-/multilingualism (Thomason & Kaufman 1992; Thomason 2001; Trudgill 2011). The three languages discussed in this section – Chamorro (Austronesian), Lekeitio Basque (Basque), Shumcho (Sino-Tibetan) – fit this scenario in that: (1) they show instances of borrowed gender agreement, (2) they are spoken in a situation of intense and prolonged contact with the languages from which the agreement patterns are borrowed.

We begin our overview of contact-induced gender systems with Chamorro, an independent branch within the Austronesian family, spoken in the Northern Mariana Islands. If borrowed patterns of gender agreement are excluded, in Chamorro, nominal classification is restricted to a small set of classifiers, which are almost exclusively used in possessive constructions. Definite articles vary depending on the information structure status of the nominal they modify (they are sensitive to focus), and there is no gender marking on personal pronouns nor noun-phrase internal agreement, apart from optional multiple plural marking (Stolz 2012: 111). Contact between Chamorro and Spanish starts on an occasional basis during the 16th century, it reaches its apex during the Spanish colonization (between the 17th to end of the 19th century), before it starts declining with the advent of the US occupation, and terminates after World War I. The emergent gender system of Chamorro is described in detail by Stolz (2012). Sex-based gender distinctions manifested through agreement on adnominal modifiers emerged in the language as a result of borrowing of nouns and property words from Spanish. The gender system of Spanish is based on a masculine vs. feminine type of opposition with a combination of semantic, morphological and opaque assignment rules. In Chamorro, the Spanish gender assignment rules are reanalyzed into a predictable system of semantic assignment. Agreement with human female controllers is marked by *-a* (Spanish feminine agreement) while human male controllers, as well as any other type of controller nouns, trigger *-o/-u* agreement (Spanish masculine agreement). This is illustrated in example (9).

(9)   Chamorro Feminine (a) and Non-Feminine (b) Gender (Austronesian; Stolz 2012: 123)

   a. *Ma-nobena-na-ye   i   mi-milagros-a   na   Bithen.*
      PASS-novena-RED-REF DEF RED-miraculous-F LINK Virgin

      'A novena is being conducted for the abundantly miraculous Virgin.'

   b. *Desde antitites   na   tiempo esta   gof bunit-u na   siuda i   ya*
      since RED:before LINK time   already very nice-NF LINK town DEF TN
      Hagåtña.
      Hagåtña

      'A very long time ago, Hagåtña was a very pretty town already.'

In (9b) the Spanish-borrowed noun for town, *siuda*, triggers non-feminine agreement. However its correspondent in Spanish, *ciudad*, is grammatically feminine. Gender assignment in Chamorro is thus predictable based on semantic properties of the controller nouns, and does not fully comply with the assignment rules of the donor language. The Chamorro corpus used by Stolz (2012) reveals 300 pairs of words that are sensitive to the distinction between Feminine and Non-Feminine gender. These can be both property words and nouns. Semantically, they cover a wide range of meanings from physical properties to character traits, from names of professions to kinships, ethnonyms, and young animals with sexual dimorphism (Stolz 2012: 117). Of these gender-sensitive lexical items, the property word *bunitu/a* 'pretty, nice, handsome' is the most frequent token for the encoding of sex-differentiation and agreement. With respect to the productivity of gender marking on nouns, Stolz (2012) finds that Spanish derivational rules for the encoding of gender distinctions on nouns may in some cases extend to Chamorro and English nominal stems as in *dander/a* 'male/female musician' from the Chamorro verb stem *dandan* 'to play music', and in *apostero/a* 'male/female upholsterer' from the English noun *upholsterer*. With respect to the productivity of gender marking outside nouns, adjectival adnominal modifiers borrowed from Spanish may index Feminine Gender when modifying a Chamorro noun denoting a female entity. However, the only set of words that are morphosyntactically suited to mark agreement are adnominal modifiers of Spanish origin. Finally, not all Spanish loanwords are sensitive to gender distinctions and there is a considerable amount of intra-speaker and regional variation as to which words are part of the system of gender distinctions and which are excluded; the range of this variation is still to be studied. In sum, Chamorro displays a semi-productive sex-based type of gender system, where gender assignment is semantically predictable and the only targets of gender agreement are a subset of property words borrowed from Spanish. While the system originated through prolonged and intense contact with Spanish, the evolution of gender agreement in Chamorro grammar and usage continues beyond the disappearance of Spanish as a local contact language, and follows patterns of development that do not completely overlap with those of the donor language.

Lekeitio Basque is another example of a language without gender in which marginal patterns of nominal gender marking and gender agreement have intruded through the borrowing of a (small) set of nouns and property words from Spanish, and are used to index semantic properties of discourse referents. Lekeitio Basque is a variety of western Basque spoken in Lekeitio, a town located in the province of Bisqay, within the Spanish Basque Country. According to Hualde et al. (1994: 1–2), Basque is the preferred language of interaction among Lekeitians, even though Lekeitio is a largely bilingual town, with the majority of speakers having an active command of both Basque (standard and local variety) and Spanish. In addition, the authors report that, even though Standard Basque is the official language of instruction, the local variety is generally preferred to the standard language in everyday communication outside the class environment as well as in formal registers of communication (e.g., communication from the mayor and other local authorities, at church). In Lekeitio Basque, -a is used to express reference to female entities, whereas -o is used for males. Similarly to the Chamorro case, the borrowed gender suffixes appear both on borrowed nouns, where they qualify as a word formation strategy for the overt coding of natural gender distinctions, and on borrowed modifiers, where they qualify as an instance of gender agreement. Examples of borrowed nouns and modifiers with overt gender distinctions are: *enano/a* 'dwarf'; *álto/a* 'tall'; *alúmno/a* 'student'; *tónto/a* 'stupid, silly', *txúlo/a* 'arrogant' (Hualde et al. 1994: 108–109). Interestingly, gender marking on nouns and adjectives is also extended to Basque lexemes: *gixájo/a* 'poor man/poor woman'; *sorristo/a* 'lousy'; *txotxólo/a* 'stupid, short witted' (Hualde et al. 1994: 109). Finally, when gender-sensitive adjectives are used as a base to derive verbs, gender markers are retained. In such cases, gender is marked through a suffix occurring between the root and the derivational suffix, leading to a pattern of affixation which is unknown to Spanish morphology. This pattern is shown in example (10).[20]

(10)   Deadjectival verbs indexing natural gender in Lekeitio Basque (Hualde et al. 1994: 109)
       morenotu = 'to become tanned (a male)' < *moréno* 'dark (male)'
       morenatu = 'to become tanned (a female)' < *moréna* 'dark (female)'
       majotu = 'to become handsome (a male)' < *májo* 'handsome (male)'
       majatu = 'to become handsome (a female)' < *mája* 'handsome (male)'

Contact-induced emergence of gender agreement is also attested in the Thebor (Bodic, Sino-Tibetan) language Shumcho, spoken in the Kinnaur district of Himchal Pradesh in the Indian Himalaya, a highly multilingual area at the crossroads between Bodic and Indo-Aryan languages, where Hindi is the language of administration and mass media. In general, natural gender distinctions in Shumcho are encoded lexically; there is no morphological gender marking on nouns and no gender agreement on adjectives and verbs. However, there exist a number of nouns and adjectives for which gender distinctions can be marked suffixally (-a = masculine; -e = feminine), e.g. *šara/e* 'beautiful', 'young person';

---

[20] An alternative analysis of the patterns illustrated in (10) is, of course, that the gender-differentiating adjectives are stored as independent lexical items.

laṭa/e 'deaf, dumb', 'deaf/dumb one'.[21] In the majority of cases, these words are of clear Indo-Aryan origin, other cases are less clear. Whenever gender-sensitive adjectives modify nouns denoting humans, gender must be marked, independently of whether the head noun is of Bodic or Indo-Aryan origin (Christian Huber, personal communication). With non-human animates and inanimate nouns gender-sensitive adjectives are invariably feminine. In naturally occurring discourse, however, speakers may sometimes choose to index the biological gender of animals, especially if they feel emotionally attached to them (Christian Huber personal communication; Huber 2011: 76). Some instances of masculine/feminine gender distinctions of the type attested in Shumcho are also found in Jangshung, the other Thebor language included in our sample, as well as in almost all West Himalayish languages; their origin is often connected with loanwords from neighboring Indo-Aryan languages (Christian Huber, personal communication). The distribution and spread of these marginal gender marking systems in the languages of the area are, however, still poorly investigated.

In sum, the three instances of borrowed gender agreement patterns attested in our sample and discussed in this section share a number of characteristics both at the morphosyntactic and semantic level:

1. They result from borrowing of nouns and adjectives, which leads to the emergence of instances of nominal gender marking and of gender agreement patterns, respectively.

2. They are noun-phrase internal.

3. They have purely semantic assignment rules: whatever the gender assignment rules of the donor language, the borrowed agreement patterns are used to signal semantic properties of nouns, and, typically, natural gender distinctions.

Finally, the productivity of these borrowed gender agreement patterns varies a great deal in native speakers' usage and from language to language.

5.3 Emerging gender systems: summary

The number of languages examined in this section is too small to formulate any valid generalization on crosslinguistic properties of young gender systems with

---

[21]Gendered adjectives can also be used as nouns, in the absence of an overt nominal head (Christian Huber, personal communication).

gender agreement restricted to the domain of adnominal modification. Yet, a couple of remarks can be made on what appear to be recurrent properties of such systems.

Firstly, all four languages examined exhibit non-pervasive gender agreement, which is restricted to one type of target only (case marking hosts in the case of Nalca, borrowed adnominal modifiers in the case of Chamorro, Leiketio Baque, and Shumcho). In all four languages, then, the syntactic cohesion between controllers and targets is maximal, and, in the case of Nalca, also tied to a rather rigid principle of linear adjacency.

Secondly, in all four languages, gender marking is *conditional* rather than *absolute* in the sense that it is constrained by (1) syntactic properties of noun phrases, whereby gender agreement occurs only if the target and the controller noun are adjacent to each other, as in Nalca, or (2) lexical restrictions, whereby only borrowed adjectival modifiers can agree in gender, as in Chamorro, Lekeitio Basque, and Shumcho.

Crosslinguistic similarities between the examined systems are even more striking in the case of contact-induced gender systems. As mentioned before, in the languages examined in this section, emergent gender agreement patterns result from lexical borrowing. Gender marking patterns are transferred along with borrowed nominal and adjectival stems, and the assignment principles that underpin their use in the donor languages are reanalyzed. The resulting assignment systems in the recipient languages are purely semantic in that they especially target the encoding of natural gender distinctions with human (or highly animate) referents. This is suggestive of a possible hierarchical tendency whereby semantic gender assignment rules are preferred to mixed types (semantic and formal) of assignment rules, even if the donor language has both semantic and formal rules. Finally, in the cases examined here, the recipient languages are not genealogically related (apart from Shumcho and Jangshung); they belong to language families that are typically genderless and that, prior to contact, display agreement in other grammatical domains (such as number or person).

It remains to be seen whether the similarities between the three contact-induced emerging gender systems are due to the fact that the donor languages themselves (Spanish, Indo-Aryan languages) have rather homologous, and in fact, genealogically related, gender systems, or whether these similarities speak of more general tendencies with respect to the kind of gender agreement systems that can emerge as a result of language contact (e.g. only semantic, only noun-phrase internal etc.). Only a larger crosslinguistic survey could tackle this question. However, what the instances of contact-induced gender emergence examined here suggest is that borrowing should be counted as a possible source scenario for the rise of gender systems crosslinguistically.

In §7, we will address how the emergent gender systems surveyed here pattern in terms of complexity.

6 Expanding gender agreement systems

In our sample, the expansion of gender agreement systems is attested under three different scenarios: (1) through the extension of gender marking to new agreement domains via grammaticalization processes (as in the Northwestern Iranian languages Kafteji and Eshtehardi, and in the Khasian languages Pnar and Khasi); (2) as a consequence of contact between languages with different types of gender systems (Michif); and (3) as a result of language planning and standardization (Makanza Lingala). The three scenarios are briefly surveyed in the following.

While the erosion and loss of gender distinctions is not uncommon within Northwestern Iranian varieties (as we observed with the Kelasi case discussed in Section 4.2), in some languages of this group new patterns of gender agreement have grammaticalized in the domain of verbal morphology. In Kafteji, for instance, all tense forms of the intransitive past verb stems inflect for gender in all three singular persons. In Eshtehardi, gender inflection in the domain of verbal morphology is somewhat less pronounced. While intransitive past verbs and copula verbs inflect for gender in the third person singular, only copula verbs inflect for gender even in the first and second person singular. According to Stilo (to appear), the construction through which gender agreement expanded to these domains of verbal inflection is: "PARTICIPLE$^{M/F}$ + COPULA". This construction consisting of participial forms inflecting for gender, followed by copula verb forms, later grammaticalized into a new type of synthetic perfect retaining the gender inflection of the original participial form. The marking of gender distinctions on these recently grammaticalized verb forms is thus directly connected with the source constructions from which these forms originate. The extent to which gender distinctions are marked on verbs across the three person values varies across languages (Stilo to appear: 29).

When compared with each other, the Khasian (Austroasiatic) languages Lyngngam, Pnar and Khasi display a continuum of increasing gender agreement domains. Lyngngam has a pronominal gender system, with gender distinctions marked on personal pronouns and deictic pronominal bases. In Pnar and Khasi, pronominal and deictic markers are used as pre-nominal gender clitics, which mark gender within the noun phrase. In Khasi, the encoding of gender distinctions has also extended to the verbal domain. According to Anne Daladier (personal communication) the pervasiveness of gender agreement and the degree of predictability of assignment rules in these three languages are inversely correlated: the higher the number of agreement targets, the less semantically transparent the gender assignment rules. The distribution of gender agreement systems across the three Khasian languages included in the sample is illustrated in Figure 4. These observations should be tested on a wider set of languages within the family.

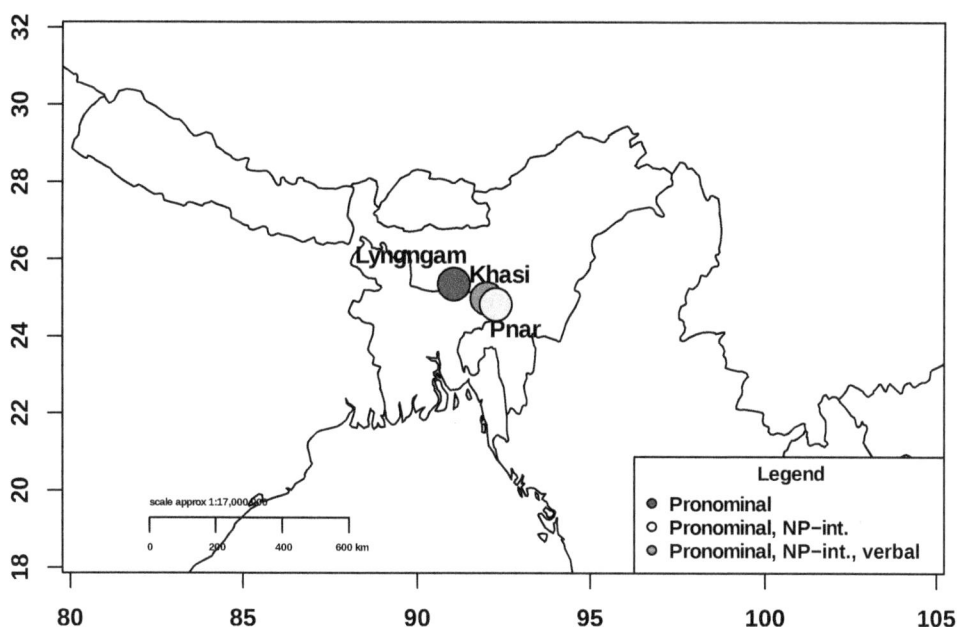

Figure 4: Expansion of gender agreement within Khasian

Michif (scenario 2) is a nearly extinct mixed language originated through intense contact and multilingual practices between female Cree speakers and male French speaking fur trade workers (thoroughly described by Bakker 1997). As a result of these intriguing dynamics of language contact and transmission, the lexicon and morphosyntax of Michif are split into two: nominal lexicon and morphosyntax are French-based while verbal lexicon and morphosyntax are Cree-based. Accordingly, Michif has two co-existing gender systems, with two different systems of gender assignment – sex-based and animacy-based – that manifest themselves through a sharp division between gender agreement within the noun phrase and gender agreement on verbs (with the exception of demonstratives, which comply to the verb-phrase agreement pattern). The noun-phrase gender system is taken from French, while the verb-phrase gender system is based on Cree. This unique split system of gender agreement is illustrated in (11) where the controller noun for 'mare' triggers feminine agreement within the noun phrase and animate agreement on the verb.

(11) Michif (Mixed Language, Canada and US; Bakker 1997: 87)

la	žyma:	ki:-aja:w-e:w	æ	pči	pulæ
DEF.AN.F.SG	mare	PST-have-TA.3→3[I]	INDEF.AN.M.SG	little	foal

'The mare had a foal.'

The last instance of expanding gender agreement systems in our sample is Makanza Lingala (scenario 3). In this variety of Lingala, non-sex-based, arbitrary gender distinctions (and corresponding gender agreement patterns) were reintroduced during the standardization process that the language underwent between 1901 and 1902 under the influence of the Scheutist missionaries, who wanted to create an official language that looked more like a 'proper Bantu language'. Kinshasa Lingala, which is nowadays the most widely spoken variety of Lingala and which did not undergo the standardization process attested in Makanza Lingala, exhibits a heavily reduced gender system where gender distinctions and gender agreement patterns are exclusively animacy-based. This reduced gender system is the result of the pidginization and creolization processes that are at the very origins of the history of Lingala, which is the historical descendent of the Bangala pidgin, developed at the Bangala state post on the northwestern banks of the Congo River (for more details on the history of different varieties of Lingala and their gender systems see Bokamba 1977; Di Garbo 2016; Meeuwis 2013).

To summarize, our data suggest that the patterns of change through which languages may acquire more domains of gender inflection tend to be rather heterogeneous and language-specific. However, the limited number of cases examined here does not allow us to formulate any far reaching generalization on the dynamics of gender agreement expansion. While this calls for further investigation, patterns of gender agreement expansion will not be discussed further in the remainder of the paper.

7 How simple/complex are gender agreement systems on the rise and/or in decline?

In §2, we brought up two hypotheses about the complexity of gender systems. Firstly, in viewing the complexity of gender as an evolving variable, instances of gender systems in decline could be considered as reducing complexity and instances of gender systems on the rise/under expansion as emerging/increasing complexity. Secondly, both reducing and rising gender systems could be expected to show less complexity than their full-fledged counterparts. The data presented in this paper do not, however, support these hypotheses. In this section, we show that many of the processes of reduction and emergence of gender agreement attested in our data contribute to increase the complexity of gender systems as matched against the proposed measures of gender complexity.

Starting with reducing gender agreement, we suggest that especially in those cases in which patterns of reduction only affect sub-parts of the agreement system, whether as a result of morphophonological erosion or of redistribution of agreement, this cannot be described as a straightforward simplification process. In Standard Swedish, for instance, the merger between the Masculine and Feminine genders in the domain of noun-phrase internal agreement gave rise to: (1) a sex-based, referential system of gender assignment, which is active only in the domain of pronominal agreement and for nouns that denote entities at the top end of the animacy hierarchy (humans and, occasionally, higher animals); (2) a non-sex-based, semantic and formal type of gender assignment system, which is active through agreement in the domain of adnominal modification. When mapped onto the model of gender complexity proposed by Audring (2017), this split in the type of classificatory distinctions that agreement targets are sensitive to qualifies as an increase in gender complexity, as illustrated in (12). (The symbol "<" here, as well as in (13), (14) and (15), reads as "less complex than".)

(12)   Split agreement system and gender complexity (adapted from Audring 2017)

   Matching values (between targets) < Mismatching values (between targets)

This effect can be analyzed as a violation of the Principle of Independence in that the type and number of gender distinctions available in a language vary depending on the type of agreement targets that inflect for gender. Mismatching gender values across different types of targets need to be separately specified in the description of a gender system, which leads to an increase in description length and thus in complexity.

Similarly, we saw that the redistribution of agreement is usually triggered by the reanalysis of the gender assignment of hybrid nouns. In the Asia Minor Greek dialects, for instance, the critical items are nouns that are grammatically masculine or feminine, but semantically denote inanimate entities. In some Asia Minor Greek varieties (such as Pontic), the ongoing reanalysis of the gender assignment rules associated with these nouns is reflected through mismatching agreement patterns whereby targets adjacent to nouns retain syntactic agreement and non-adjacent targets agree semantically. In Audring's model of gender complexity, hybrid nouns qualify as a "complexifying phenomenon in a gender system" because they engender mismatches in the agreement patterns that they control. This is schematized in (13) and (14).

(13) Hybrid nouns and gender complexity (Audring 2017)

Consistent controller < Hybrid controller

(14) Semantic agreement and gender complexity (Audring 2017)

Targets do not have a choice in value < Targets have a choice in value

When, due to mismatches between grammatical gender and semantic properties of hybrid nouns, agreement targets have a choice in value, these choices need to be specified in the description of a gender system. This increases the description length of the system, and thus its complexity.

Conversely, when the reduction, loss or semantic reanalysis of gender agreement patterns are more pervasive, this usually results in an uncontroversial simplification of the gender agreement system. Under morphophonological erosion, this is for instance the case of English, where sex-based gender distinctions are only preserved on third personal and possessive pronouns and index purely semantic distinctions.[22] Under agreement redistribution, this is the case of Rumeic Greek, where the gender system has become completely semanticized. Nouns denoting male entities are masculine, nouns denoting female entities are feminine, and nouns denoting inanimate entities are neuter.

Moving on to the emergence of gender agreement, the young gender systems examined in this paper also exhibit some features of high complexity when measured against the dimensions proposed by Audring (2017). We observe that, under contact-induced gender emergence, only a subset of lexical items within a given word class (nouns and/or adjectives) is sensitive to gender distinctions. For instance, in Chamorro, only property words borrowed from Spanish can inflect for gender, and there is a great deal of intraspeaker variation as for how productively gender agreement is used. Similarly, in Nalca, where the emergent gender system is the result of a language internal development, gender marking is also not fully productive, and it can be switched off whenever certain syntactic conditions within the noun phrase are not met. Low productivity and optionality

---

[22]On the use of the pronouns 'he' and 'she' with inanimate referents in varieties of American and Australian English see Pawley (2004).

in gender marking count as complexifying factors according to Audring (2017): they introduce variability in the gender agreement system of a language as a result of lexical and/or grammatical idiosyncrasies that are, in fact, independent of gender.

(15)   Low productivity and gender complexity (Audring 2017)

   Gender marking is obligatory < Gender marking is optional

   Gender marking is fully productive < Only a subset of lexical items per agreement target mark gender

   When gender is not fully obligatory or fully productive, specifying explicitly under which circumstances gender marking occurs adds to the system's description length, which means higher complexity. Conversely, the emergent gender systems examined in this paper are rather simple with respect to domains of gender agreement, given that they all display one agreement target, which in all cases examined is confined to the domain of adnominal modification.

   Reducing and emerging gender systems represent transitional stages between the *absence of gender* and *full-fledged gender systems*, two rather stable stages in the history of individual languages and language families. These transitional stages are to a large extent associated with phenomena that, we think, increase gender complexity as a side-effect of ongoing language change. In the case of gender reduction, we observed, for instance, a pervasive occurrence of mismatching agreements, which is due to the fact that innovations (a) do not immediately reach all available agreement targets, but rather spread gradually across agreement domains; and (b) do not immediately affect all controller nouns, but rather those with ambiguous semantics (that is, hybrid nouns) first. Under gender emergence, gender agreement tends to be non-obligatory and thus non-frequent. Therefore the main factors underlying increased complexity in reducing and emerging gender systems are partial distributions and optionality, which are ultimately connected to ongoing variation and change.[23] While we hope to have shown that some crosslinguistically recurrent patterns can be associated with these systems in transition, we think that their relative stability is harder to generalize over and depends on the interplay between internal and external dynamics of change, the understanding of which falls outside the scope of this paper.

---

[23]This has also been pointed out to us by Jenny Audring.

8 Concluding remarks and prospects for future research

We consider the main contribution of this paper to be bringing diachrony in focus in the typological study of gender complexity. We hope to have shown that investigating closely related languages enables us to formulate empirically grounded diachronic inferences about the decline, rise and expansion of gender agreement, as well as about how these dynamics of change affect the complexity of gender systems. In particular, we found that both gender agreement patterns in decline and gender agreement patterns on the rise feature properties of increased complexity when assessed against existing gender complexity metrics. We suggested that emerging and declining patterns of gender agreement represent transitional stages between two poles: genderless languages and full-fledged gender agreement systems. These poles often appear as less complex than the transitional stages, as represented in our sample. Whether this can be generalized over all cases of emerging and declining gender systems is a hypothesis that should be tested on a larger data set and, possibly, with the support of quantitative methodologies.

We think that one additional contribution of this paper is to have shown that implicational hierarchies can be used as schemas for investigating complexity variation across languages in a meaningful way, not only at the synchronic level (as previously suggested by Miestamo 2009), but also diachronically. In this respect, we found that, in the languages of our sample, the agreement domains at the two opposite ends of the Agreement Hierarchy, attributive modifiers and personal pronouns, often function as the place from which processes leading to both the rise and the decline of gender agreement begin. Furthermore, our data suggest that at least the reduction and loss of gender agreement tend to be directional in nature, and that the type of directionality at stake is predicted by whether loss and reduction are due to morphophonological erosion or redistribution of agreement patterns.

We hope that these results may spark further research on the relationship between the complexity of gender systems and other well-known implicational universals in the domain of gender marking, such as the series of implicational universals on the availability of gender distinctions in the plural as opposed to the singular (e.g., Universal 37), or in pronouns as opposed to nouns (e.g., Universal 43), formulated by Greenberg (1963). We believe that this line of research is particularly promising to shed new light on synchronic and diachronic interactions between gender and other grammatical domains, and their effect on the complexity of gender systems.

Finally, one important question that is left out from this paper is whether there are any external factors that contribute to explain why and under which conditions gender agreement systems complexify or simplify. Even though many of the instances of change discussed in this paper clearly involved language contact as a causal factor, the question of the relationship between the evolution of gender agreement systems and language ecology was not addressed systematically here. Thus the answer to this question must be left to further studies. Our impression so far is that gender agreement patterns – whose evolutionary dynamics we have tried to unravel in this paper – might be a better match for the study of the sociolinguistic correlates of gender complexity than, say, sheer number of genders and/or type of assignment systems. Patterns of gender agreement directly hinge on inflectional morphology, which has so far been one of the main foci of research in testing the effects of social structures and language ecologies on the rise and transmissibility of linguistic complexity.

Acknowledgments

We thank two anonymous reviewers, as well as Jenny Audring, Johanna Nichols, and Bernhard Wälchli for providing constructive comments on previous versions of the paper. For financial support, Francesca Di Garbo is thankful to the Wenner-Gren Foundations.

Special abbreviations

The following abbreviations are not found in the Leipzig Glossing Rules:

3→3	3rd person animate obviative	LINK	linker
AN	animate	HAB	habitual
CV	consonant + vowel phonotactic structure	NF	non-feminine
		RED	reduplication
DP	default phrase gender	TA	transitive animate verb
INAN	inanimate	TN	toponym
INDEF	indefinite		

References

Agbetsoamedo, Yvonne. 2014. Noun classes in Sɛlɛɛ. *Journal of West African Languages* 41(1). 95–124.

Aikhenvald, Alexandra Y. & Robert M. W. Dixon. 1998. Dependencies between grammatical systems. *Language* 74(1). 56–80.

Åkerberg, Bengt. 2012. *Älvdalsk grammatik*. Älvdalen: Ulum Dalska.

Audring, Jenny. 2009. *Reinventing pronoun gender*. Vrije Universiteit, Amsterdam. (Doctoral dissertation).

Audring, Jenny. 2014. Gender as a complex feature. *Language Sciences* 43. 5–17.

Audring, Jenny. 2017. Calibrating complexity: How complex is a gender system? *Language Sciences* 60. 53–68.

Audring, Jenny. 2019. Canonical, complex, complicated? In Francesca Di Garbo, Bruno Olsson & Bernhard Wälchli (eds.), *Grammatical gender and linguistic complexity: Volume I: General issues and specific studies*, 15–52. Berlin: Language Science Press. DOI:10.5281/zenodo.3462756

Bakker, Peter. 1997. *A language of our own: The genesis of Michif, the mixed Cree-French language of the Canadian Métis*. Oxford: Oxford University Press.

Balode, Laimute & Axel Holvoet. 2001. The Latvian language and its dialects. In Östen Dahl & Maria Koptjevskaja-Tamm (eds.), *The Circum-Baltic languages: Typology and contact*. Vol. 1: *The Latvian language and its dialects: Past and present*, 3–40. Amsterdam: John Benjamins.

Bokamba, Eyamba. 1977. The impact of multilingualism on language structures: The case of Central Africa. *Anthropological Linguistics* 19(5). 181–202.

Corbett, Greville G. 1979. The agreement hierarchy. *Journal of Linguistics* 15(2). 203–224.

Corbett, Greville G. 1991. *Gender*. Cambridge: Cambridge University Press.

Corbett, Greville G. 2000. *Number*. Cambridge: Cambridge University Press.

Corbett, Greville G. 2006. *Agreement*. Cambridge: Cambridge University Press.

Corbett, Greville G. 2010. Implicational hierarchies. In Jae Jung Song (ed.), *The Oxford handbook of linguistic typology*, 190–205. Oxford: Oxford University Press.

Curzan, Anne. 2003. *Gender shifts in the history of English*. Cambridge: Cambridge University Press.

Dahl, Östen. 2000. Animacy and the notion of semantic gender. In Barbara Unterbeck (ed.), *Gender in grammar and cognition*. Vol. 1: *Animacy and the notion of semantic gender: Approaches to gender*, 99–115. Berlin: Mouton de Gruyter.

Dahl, Östen. 2004. *The growth and maintenance of linguistic complexity*. Amsterdam: John Benjamins.

de Boeck, Egide. 1904. *Grammaire et vocabulaire du lingala, ou langue du Haut-Congo*. Brussels: Polleunis-Ceuterick.

Di Garbo, Francesca. 2014. *Gender and its interaction with number and evaluative morphology: An intra- and intergenealogical typological survey of Africa.* Stockholm University. (Doctoral dissertation).

Di Garbo, Francesca. 2015. Questionnaire: Grammatical gender and language ecologies.

Di Garbo, Francesca. 2016. Exploring grammatical complexity crosslinguistically: The case of gender. *Linguistic Discovery* 14(1). 46–85.

Di Garbo, Francesca. forthcoming. The complexity of grammatical gender and language ecology. In Peter Arkadiev & Francesco Gardani (eds.), *The complexities of morphology.* Oxford: Oxford University Press.

Dingemanse, Mark. 2009. *Noun classification in Siwu.* Paper presented at the Conference on African Languages and Linguistics. Leiden 2009.

Duke, Janet. 2010. Gender reduction and loss in Germanic: The Scandinavian, Dutch, and Afrikaans cases studies. In Antje Dammel, Sebastian Kürschner & Damaris Nübling (eds.), *Kontrastive germanistische Linguistik,* 643–672. Hildesheim: Olms.

Evans, Nicholas. 2003. *Bininj Gun-Wok: A pan-dialectal grammar of Mayali, Kunwinjku and Kune.* Canberra: Pacific Linguistics.

Frenda, Alessio. 2011. Gender in Irish between continuity and change. *Folia Linguistica* 45(2). 283–316.

Gblem-Poidi, Massanvi Honorine. 2007. Nominal classes and concord in Igo (Ahlon). In Mary Esther Kropp Dakubu, George Akanlig-Pare, Kweku E. Osam & Kofi K. Saah (eds.), *Proceedings of the annual colloquium of the Legon-Trondheim Linguistics Project 10–20 January 2005,* vol. 4, 52–60. Legon: Linguistics Department, University of Ghana.

Greenberg, Joseph H. 1963. Some universals of grammar with particular reference to the order of meaningful elements. In Joseph H. Greenberg (ed.), *Universals of language,* 73–113. Cambridge: MIT Press.

Greenberg, Joseph H. 1978a. Diachrony, synchrony and language universals. In Joseph H. Greenberg (ed.), *Universals of human language.* Vol. 1: *Diachrony, synchrony and language universals: Method and theory,* 61–92. Stanford: Stanford University Press.

Greenberg, Joseph H. 1978b. How does a language acquire gender markers? In Joseph H. Greenberg, Charles Ferguson & Edith Moravcsik (eds.), *Universals of human language.* Vol. 3: *How does a language acquire gender markers?: Word structure,* 47–82. Stanford: Stanford University Press.

Grinevald, Colette & Frank Seifart. 2004. Noun classes in African and Amazonian languages: Towards a comparison. *Linguistic Typology* 8(2). 243–285.

Güldemann, Tom & Ines Fiedler. 2019. Niger-Congo "noun classes" conflate gender with deriflection. In Francesca Di Garbo, Bruno Olsson & Bernhard Wälchli (eds.), *Grammatical gender and linguistic complexity: Volume I: General issues and specific studies*, 95–145. Berlin: Language Science Press. DOI:10.5281/zenodo.3462762

Hammarström, Harald, Robert Forkel & Martin Haspelmath (eds.). 2018. *Glottolog 3.2*. Jena: Max Planck Institute for the Science of Human History. http://glottolog.org/.

Heine, Bernd & Rainer Vossen. 1983. On the origin of gender in Eastern Nilotic. In Rainer Vossen & Marianne Bechhaus-Gerst (eds.), *Nilotic studies: Proceedings of the international symposium on languages and history of the Nilotic peoples, Cologne, January 4-6, 1982*, 245–268. Cologne: Reimer.

Hualde, José Ignacio, Gorka Elordieta & Arantzazu Elordeta. 1994. *The Basque dialect of Lekeitio*. Bilbo: Universidad del País Vasco/Euskal Herriko Univertsitatea.

Hualde, José Ignacio & Jon Ortiz de Urbina. 2003. *A grammar of Basque*. Berlin: Mouton de Gruyter.

Huber, Christian. 2011. Some notes on gender and number marking in Shumcho. In Gerda Lechleitner & Christian Liebl (eds.), *Jahrbuch des Phonogrammarchivs*, vol. 2, 52–90. Göttingen: Cuvillier.

Huldén, Lars. 1972. Genussystemet i Karleby och Nedervetil. *Folkmålsstudier* 22. 47–82.

Hultman, Oskar Fredrik. 1894. *De östsvenska dialekterna*. Helsinki: Svenska landsmålsföreningen.

Karatsareas, Petros. 2009. The loss of grammatical gender in Cappadocian Greek. *Transactions of the Philological Society* 107. 196–230.

Karatsareas, Petros. 2014. On the diachrony of gender in Asia Minor Greek: The development of semantic agreement in Pontic. *Language Sciences* 43. 77–101.

Koptjevskaja-Tamm, Maria & Bernhard Wälchli. 2001. The Circum-Baltic languages: An areal-typological approach. In Östen Dahl & Maria Koptjevskaja-Tamm (eds.), *Circum-Baltic languages: Typology and contact*, vol. 2, 615–750. Amsterdam: John Benjamins.

Kusters, Wouter. 2003. *Linguistic complexity: The influence of social change on verbal inflections*. University of Leiden. (Doctoral dissertation). Utrecht: LOT.

Leufkens, Sterre. 2015. *Transparency in language: A typological study*. Amesterdam: University of Amsterdam. (Doctoral dissertation).

Luraghi, Silvia. 2011. The origin of the Proto-Indo-European gender system: Typological considerations. *Folia Linguistica* 45(2). 435–464.

Maho, Jouni. 1999. *A comparative study of Bantu noun classes* (Orientalia et Africana Gothoburgensia 13). Göteborg: Acta universitatis gothoburgensis.

Matasović, Ranko. 2004. *Gender in Indo-European.* Heidelberg: Winter.

Meeuwis, Michael. 2013. Lingala. In Susanne Michaelis, Philippe Maurer, Martin Haspelmath & Magnus Huber (eds.), *The survey of pidgin and creole languages.* Vol. 3: *Lingala: Contact languages based on languages from Africa, Asia, Australia and the Americas,* 25–33. Oxford: Oxford University Press.

Miestamo, Matti. 2006. On the feasibility of complexity metrics. In Krista Kerge & Maria-Maren Sepper (eds.), *Finest Linguistics. Proceedings of the Annual Finnish and Estonian Conference of Linguistics, Tallinn, May 6–7, 2004,* 11–26. Tallinn: TLÜ.

Miestamo, Matti. 2008. Grammatical complexity in a cross-linguistic perspective. In Matti Miestamo, Kaius Sinnemäki & Fred Karlsson (eds.), *Language complexity: Typology, contact, change,* 23–41. Amsterdam: John Benjamins.

Miestamo, Matti. 2009. Implicational hierarchies and grammatical complexity. In Geoffrey Sampson, David Gil & Peter Trudgill (eds.), *Language complexity as an evolving variable,* 80–97. Oxford: Oxford University Press.

Nichols, Johanna. 1992. *Linguistic diversity in space and time.* Chicago: University of Chicago Press.

Nichols, Johanna. 2003. Diversity and stability in language. In Brian D. Joseph & Richard D. Janda (eds.), *The handbook of historical linguistics,* 283–310. Oxford: Blackwell.

Passer, Matthias Benjamin. 2016. *The typology and diachrony of nominal classification.* Utrecht: University of Amsterdam. (Doctoral dissertation).

Pawley, Andrew. 2004. Using *he* and *she* for inanimate referents in English: Questions of grammar and world view. In Nick J. Enfield (ed.), *Ethnosyntax, explorations in grammar and culture,* 110–137. Oxford: Oxford University Press.

Priestly, Tom M. S. 1983. On 'drift' in Indo-European gender systems. *The Journal of Indo-European Studies* 11(3-4). 339–363.

Reid, Nicholas. 1997. Class and classifier in Ngan'gityemerri. In Mark Harvey & Nicholas Reid (eds.), *Nominal classification in Aboriginal Australia,* 165–225. Amsterdam: John Benjamins.

Rudzīte, Marta. 1980. Läripärast liivi morfoloogias. In *Congressus quintus internationalis fenno-ugristarum. Turku, 20-27. VIII 1980,* vol. Pars VI, 231–236.

Sasse, Hans-Jürgen. 1993. Syntactic categories and subcategories. In Joachim Jakobs, Arnim von Stechow, Wolfgang Sternefeld & Theo Vennemann (eds.), *Syntax: Ein internationales Handbuch zeitgenössicher Forschung / An international handbook of contemporary research,* 646–686. Berlin: Walter de Gruter.

Seifart, Frank. 2005. *The structure and use of shape-based noun classes in Miraña.* Nijmegen: Radboud Universiteit Nijmegen. (Doctoral dissertation).

Seifart, Frank. 2010. Nominal classification. *Language and Linguistics Compass* 4(8). 719–736.

Siemund, Peter & Florian Dolberg. 2011. From lexical to referential gender: An analysis of gender change in medieval English based on two historical documents. *Folia Linguistica* 45(2). 489–534. DOI 10.1515/flin.2011.018.

Soubrier, Aude. 2013. *Description de l'ikposso uwi.* Lyon: Université Lumière Lyon 2. (Doctoral dissertation).

Stilo, Donald. to appear. Loss vs. expansion of gender in Tatic languages: Kafteji (Kabatei) and Kelasi.

Stolz, Thomas. 2012. Survival in a niche. On gender-copy in Chamorro (and sundry languages). In Martine Vanhove, Thomas Stolz, Aina Urdze & Hitomi Otsuka (eds.), *Morphologies in contact*, 93–140. Munich: Akademie-Verlag.

Svärd, Erik. 2019. Gender in New Guinea. In Francesca Di Garbo, Bruno Olsson & Bernhard Wälchli (eds.), *Grammatical gender and linguistic complexity: Volume I: General issues and specific studies*, 225–276. Berlin: Language Science Press. DOI:10.5281/zenodo.3462770

Thomason, Sarah G. 2001. *Language contact: An introduction.* Washington D.C.: Georgetown University Press.

Thomason, Sarah G. 2015. When is the diffusion of inflectional morphology not dispreferred? In Francesco Gardani, Peter Arkadiev & Nino Amiridze (eds.), *Borrowed morphology*, 27–46. Berlin: Mouton de Gruyter.

Thomason, Sarah G. & Terrence S. Kaufman. 1992. *Language contact, creolization and genetic linguistics.* Berkeley & Los Angeles: University of California Press.

Trudgill, Peter. 2011. *Sociolinguistic typology: Social determinants of linguistic complexity.* New York: Oxford University Press.

Wälchli, Bernhard. 2017. The incomplete story of feminine gender loss in Northwestern Latvian dialects. *Baltic Linguistics* 8. 143–214.

Wälchli, Bernhard. 2018. The rise of gender in Nalca (Mek, Tanah Papua): The drift towards the canonical gender attractor. In Sebastian Fedden, Jenny Audring & Greville G. Corbett (eds.), *Non-canonical gender systems*, 68–99. Oxford: Oxford University Press.

Wälchli, Bernhard. 2019. The feminine anaphoric gender gram, incipient gender marking, maturity, and extracting anaphoric gender markers from parallel texts. In Francesca Di Garbo, Bruno Olsson & Bernhard Wälchli (eds.), *Grammatical gender and linguistic complexity: Volume II: World-wide comparative studies*, 61–131. Berlin: Language Science Press. DOI:10.5281/zenodo.3462780

Williamson, Kay. 1994. Niger-Congo overview. In John Bendor-Samuel (ed.), *The Niger-Congo languages*, 3–45. Lanham, New York, London: University Press of America.

Yarshater, Ehsan. 1969. *A grammar of Southern Tati dialects*. The Hague - Paris: Mouton.

Appendix

The sampled genealogical units are listed by macroarea and higher levels of classification are mentioned, if applicable. (Q) indicates that, for any particular language, data have been collected through full questionnaire responses; (p.c.) stands for personal communication (i.e., data collected through consultation of language experts but no full questionnaire response).

Family by macroarea Language		Glottocode	Source
AFRICA			
Bantu (Atlantic-Congo)			
	Kinshasa Lingala	ling1263	Bokamba (1977); Meeuwis (2013)
	Makanza Lingala	ling1269	de Boeck (1904); Bokamba (1977); Meeuwis (2013)
Ghana-Togo-Mountain (Atlantic-Congo)			
	Selee	sele1249	Agbetsoamedo (2014)
	Igo	igoo1238	Gblem-Poidi (2007; p.c.)
	Ikposo	ikpo1238	Soubrier (2013); Ines Fiedler (p.c.)
AUSTRALIA			
Gunwinggu (Central Gunwinyguan, Gunwinyguan)			
	Kunwinjku	gunw1252	Evans (2003)
	Kundjeyhmi	gunw1252	Evans (2003)
	Kune	gunw1252	Evans (2003)
EURASIA			
Khasian (Austroasiatic)			
	Khasi	khas1269	Anne Daladier (p.c.)
	Lyngngam	lyng1241	Anne Daladier (p.c.)
	Pnar	pnar1238	Anne Daladier (p.c.)
Basque			
	Standard Basque	basq1248	Hualde & Ortiz de Urbina (2003)
	Lekeitio Basque	bisc1236	Hualde et al. (1994)
Balto-Slavic (Indo-European)			
	Latvian	latv1249	Balode & Holvoet (2001), Anna Kalnača (p.c.)
	Tamian Latvian	latv1249	Balode & Holvoet (2001); Thomason (2015); Koptjevskaja-Tamm & Wälchli (2001)
Greek (Indo-European)			
	Modern Greek	mode1248	Karatsareas (2009; 2014)
	Pontic Greek	pont1253	Karatsareas (2009; 2014) (Q)
	Rumeic Greek	mari1411	Karatsareas (2009; 2014)
	Cappadocian Greek	capp1239	Karatsareas (2009; 2014)

Continued

Family by macroarea	Language	Glottocode	Source
EURASIA			
Insular Celtic (Indo-European)			
	Irish	iris1253	Frenda (2011)
	Irish (Ros Much)	conn1243	Frenda (2011)
North Germanic (Indo-European)			
	Elfdalian	dic (ISO)	Åkerberg (2012); Östen Dahl (Q)
	Karleby Swedish	oste1241	Hultman (1894); Huldén (1972)
	Standard Swedish	swed1254	Duke (2010); Mikael Parkvall (Q)
Northwestern Iranian (Indo-European)			
	Eshtehardi	esht1238	Stilo (to appear); Yarshater (1969)
	Kafteji	kaba1276	Stilo (to appear; p.c.)
	Kelasi	kaba1276	Stilo (to appear; p.c.)
Lezgic (Nakh-Daghestanian)			
	Archi	arch1244	Michael Daniel, Nina Dobrushina (Q)
	Aghul	aghu1253	Nina Dobrushina (Q)
	Udi	udii1243	Nichols (2003);Wolfgang Schulze (Q)
Thebor (Bodic, Tibeto-Burman)			
	Shumcho	shum1243	Huber (2011; p.c.)
	Jangshung	jang1254	Huber (2011; p.c.)
NORTH AMERICA			
Mixed Language			
	Michif	mich1243	Bakker (1997)
PAPUNESIA			
Chamorro (Austronesian)			
	Chamorro	cham1312	Stolz (2012)
Mek (Nuclear-Trans-New-Guinea)			
	Nalca	nalc1240	Wälchli (2018)
	Eipo	eipo1242	Wälchli (2018)

Chapter 3

The feminine anaphoric gender gram, incipient gender marking, maturity, and extracting anaphoric gender markers from parallel texts

Bernhard Wälchli

Stockholm University

The aim of this paper is to carry out a typological study of feminine anaphoric gender grams (such as English *she/her*) in a large world-wide convenience sample of 816 languages based on a strictly procedural definition. The investigation pursues a radically functional approach where the functional equivalence of the forms under study is assured by exploring an identical search space in parallel texts (translations of the New Testament) in all languages of the sample. This is the first large scale typological study of grammatical gender based on parallel texts, and a large part of the paper is devoted to methodological aspects. The study shows that gender has a functional core like any other grammatical category, and that it can at least partly be studied without resort to the notions of noun class, agreement and system. The results show that a large number of languages possess simple forms of gender, often representing incipient gender from a grammaticalization perspective. The paper discusses how simple gender differs from more mature and genealogically more stable forms of anaphoric gender. Finally the feminine anaphoric gram type is considered in its wider context, reconciling it to the traditional global approach focusing on the notions of system, noun class and agreement.

Keywords: feminine gender, anaphora, anaphoric pronouns, grams, grammaticalization, grammatical relations, functional domains, constructional islands, cue validity, maturity, parallel texts.

Bernhard Wälchli. 2019. The feminine anaphoric gender gram, incipient gender marking, maturity, and extracting anaphoric gender markers from parallel texts. In Francesca Di Garbo, Bruno Olsson & Bernhard Wälchli (eds.), *Grammatical gender and linguistic complexity: Volume II: World-wide comparative studies*, 61–131. Berlin: Language Science Press. DOI:10.5281/zenodo.3462780

Bernhard Wälchli

1 Introduction

The traditional definition of gender ("Genders are classes of nouns reflected in the behavior of associated words"; Hockett 1958: 231) rests on the notions of noun class and agreement. With the exception of classifiers, for which noun classes are crucial as well, these notions do not figure in the definitions of other grammatical categories. This makes gender stand out among grammatical categories as very specific by definition. In this paper it is argued that it is also possible to address gender as any other grammatical category by defining it as "grammatical category expressing meaning X", where X can be feminine, masculine, animate and inanimate, given that the most widespread meanings in gender are animacy and sex (Dahl 2000: 101; Corbett 1991: 68; Luraghi 2011), at least as far as anaphoric gender is concerned.[1] In order to make clear that this paper mainly deals with gender marking in anaphoric contexts, I will use the term "anaphoric gender". The question of how grammatical gender is defined is highly relevant for assessing the complexity of grammatical gender.

Noun classes and agreement are complex phenomena. Acccpting the traditional definition of gender as the only option would mean to take for granted that grammatical gender is complex by definition. In order to assess the complexity of grammatical gender empirically it is indispensable to explore the possibility of simpler alternative definitions. Linguists nowadays often understand "gender" and "noun class" as full synonyms. This may be appropriate for the study of gender within noun phrases, but does not do justice to the use of gender in the anaphoric domain, which is the topic of this paper.

The major aim of this paper is to show that gender has a functionally motivated semantic core that can be considered in abstraction from the notions of noun class and agreement. This is done by formulating a procedural definition of feminine anaphoric gender which is so explicit that it can be implemented in a computer program in order to extract certain feminine gender markers from parallel texts (here translations of the New Testament). Feminine is chosen for practical reasons. It is the easiest to address in this particular corpus (see §2.2).

---

[1] One of the first things I was ever taught in linguistics is that gender and sex are absolutely not the same thing and, since my department found me highly suitable for teaching numerous courses in discourse studies, sociolinguistics, and pragmatics and intercultural communication, I am quite familiar with gender studies and the notion of performative gender. However, the approach pursued in this paper focuses exclusively on the semantic core of feminine and masculine grammatical genders and here the gross simplification that sex is the core meaning of masculine and feminine gender grams has proven to be very useful in practice.

The underlying idea is that grammatical categories can be captured in terms of GRAMS. A gram is a grammatical item in a particular language with specific form and specific meaning and/or function (Bybee & Dahl 1989; Dahl & Wälchli 2016). Grams can be considered in abstraction from the language-specific systems they are part of. For instance, perfect and progressive can be investigated in abstraction from tense and aspect systems. For gender grams this means that the units of research are feminine, masculine, animate and inanimate, rather than gender systems. Virtually all gender systems are sensitive to the meanings sex and/or animacy (whereby different segments of the animacy hierarchy can be affected). It is true that gender in many languages also comprises other meanings, such as size and shape, and these other meanings are very important for the study of gender as systems. With the gram approach, however, it is possible to address the semantic core areas and to study them cross-linguistically, without having to consider the entire gender systems. A strength of the gram approach is its selectivity. Only salient semantic core uses are considered and compared cross-linguistically. A gram necessarily has a semantic core, but not all of its uses need be semantically motivated. The gram approach focuses on the semantic core of grammatical categories and investigates to what extent grams across different languages share their semantic core, put differently, cluster to cross-linguistic gram types. In order to find out whether a language has a gram reflecting a cross-linguistic gram type, it is sufficient to consider the prototypical uses of a gram type.

Focusing on the semantic core means focusing on those uses of a grammatical category where it is most transparent semantically. We know, among other things, from Corbett's (1991, chap. 8) study of the Agreement Hierarchy that gender use tends to be most transparently semantic in third person anaphoric pronouns. According to Audring (2009), all pronominal gender systems (where gender is restricted to pronouns) are semantically organized, which further supports the view that gender is most semantic in anaphoric use.

A feminine gender gram – in its prototypical use – is a grammatical element picking up reference to a female human, such as the English third person singular pronominal forms *she* and *her* exemplified in (1). (1) is one of 74 parallel corpus passages that are used as a search space for feminine anaphoric gender grams in this paper.

(1) English (Indo-European; Matth. 15:26–27): gender marking on free pronouns
But he answered: "..." But **she** *said: "..."*

What I have said so far may suggest that this is a paper about gender in personal pronouns such as English *she* (see, e.g., Audring 2009), but the search space is much broader. In many languages the functional equivalent to *she* and *her* in English is an affix on verbs and/or adpositions as in (2) from Garifuna.

(2)   Garifuna (Arawakan; Matth. 15:26–27): gender marking on bound
      pronouns and prepositions
      Ába l-aríñagun Jesúsu t-un: "..." *Ába t-aríñagun:* "..."
      and 3SG.M-say Jesus 3SG.F-to   and 3SG.F-say
      'But he answered: "..." But she said: "..." '

Third person pronouns and affixes for third person have in common that they are REDUCED REFERENTIAL DEVICES in terms of Kibrik (2011; ch. 3), who calls them FREE and BOUND PRONOUNS. In (1) from English the gender marking is located in free pronouns, but in (2) from Garifuna and (3) from Ama it is in bound pronouns (pronominal affixes). While Garifuna has bound pronouns indexing subject, Ama has bound pronouns indexing absolutive (S, P and R[ecipient]). Hausa in (4) marks pronominal gender mainly on aspect words, a kind of auxiliary that is preposed to the verb, but also has optional free pronouns.

(3)   Ama (Arai/Left May; Matth. 15:26–27): gender marking on bound
      pronouns (S, P only)
      [...] no-na-ni   imo na i-so-ki,   *Isiso mo. Ulai*
         that-FOC-here talk FOC say-O.3SG.F-REM.PST Jesus TOP but
      no-na-ni   nukonu   mo na imo-ki,   "..."
      that-FOC-here woman.SPEC TOP FOC say[O3SG.M]-REM.PST
      'But he answered ("to her"): "..." But she said ("to him"): "..." '

(4)   Hausa (Afro-Asiatic; Matth. 15:26–27): gender marking on aspect words
      Ya   amsa ya   *ce:* "..." *Sai ta*   *ce:* "..."
      3SG.M answer PST.3SG.M say   then PST.3SG.F say
      'But he answered: "..." But she said: "..." '

However, even if we consider affixes on verbs to be bound pronouns following Kibrik, the search space is not restricted to pronouns. Many languages have anaphoric forms intermediate between nouns and pronouns, for which I will use the name "GRAMMATICAL ANAPHOR" in want of a better term. Third person pronouns are, of course, also grammatical and anaphors, but since pronoun and third person pronoun are established terms, there is little risk of confusion. A grammatical anaphor is illustrated in (5) from Kiribati. Kiribati has a personal pronoun not distinguishing gender (*e* 3SG), but there is also the "person demonstrative" (Trussel 1979: 176) *neierei* 'that woman', which is a noun phrase and displays the word order of a full noun phrase (VOS), but is different from the full demonstrative noun phrase *te aine arei* [ART woman DEM.DIST] 'that woman' and does not contain the noun *aine* 'woman'. Kiribati *neierei* (70 times in the N.T.) mostly translates to 'she' and can also pick up reference to *teinaine* 'girl' and *tina-* 'mother' whereas *te aine arei* (13 times) [ART woman DEM.DIST] translates to 'the woman'.

(5) Kiribati (Austronesian, Micronesian; Matth. 15:27): grammatical anaphor

    *Ao e   taku **neierei***   ...

    and 3SG say **that[DIST].woman**

    'But she said: "..." '

Grammatical anaphors, such as Kiribati *neierei* 'that[DIST].woman', are less grammaticalized than pronominal gender markers such as English *she*. Grammatical anaphors tend to be INCIPIENT GENDER MARKERS, nouns on their way to be grammaticalized to pronominal indexes.

One possibility of interpretation is to argue that pronominal gender is more MATURE than non-pronominal gender in anaphors. Mature phenomena imply some sort of non-trivial historical development (Dahl 2004: 2; Trudgill 2011). Pronouns often differ from nouns in being suppletive according to grammatical relation. English *she* (subject) and *her* (object, indirect object, possessor) illustrate this point. Nouns are not entirely precluded from suppletion according to grammatical relation, but such suppletion in nouns is rare. Free and bound pronouns, however, usually display some sort of suppletion and/or neutralization according to grammatical relation. In Ama (3), gender is distinguished in S, P and R, but not in A. Suppletion or neutralization in pronouns can be viewed as a feature of complexity and a feature of maturity.

Another possible interpretation is that gender cumulating with case (grammatical relation), as it often occurs in free and bound pronouns, is a different kind of phenomenon. Wälchli (2019 [this volume]) argue following Nichols (1992: 142) that agreement (and notably agreement in case and number) often triggers noun classification rather than vice versa. Put differently, at least in some instances, gender originates from case, and gender then tends to exhibit particular cumulation patterns with case from its very origin. While, following the second interpretation, cumulation and/or neutralization in certain grammatical relations might be incipient within gender, it is still mature in the sense of grammaticalization, as the development of gender then draws on preexistent grammatical categories (case, number and person).

In this paper I will extract feminine gender grams from translations of the New Testament (N.T.). Translations of the N.T. are parallel texts, and parallel texts allow us to define a semantic core in a very simple manner as a set of aligned passages. The N.T. comes segmented in chunks slightly larger than sentences (so-called verses), which is why no sentence alignment has to be made. The N.T. is translated into many languages and many translations are available electronically. Working with unannotated translations from many languages has the advantage that larger samples than usual can be used and that the dependence on individual grammar writers' reporting or not reporting relevant characteristics is reduced. The most important advantage, however, is that working with automatic extraction forces us to formulate a fully explicit PROCEDURAL DEFINITION of the wanted category, which is then applied in exactly the same way to all languages considered. In particular, the heuristic potential of automatic extraction is invaluable. The automatic device is naive and does not have any preconceived opinions about what kinds of markers should be included or not. In this particular study, this has helped me find various non-mature gender grams which have been overlooked in the gender literature so far, such as Kiribati (5).

The procedural definition of the feminine gender gram will be discussed in more detail in §2. It has essentially two components: (a) finding markers associated with a semantic core in a FUNCTIONAL DOMAIN (Givón 1981) and (b) filtering out markers which are also associated with other semantic cores (notably masculine gender and female light nouns such as 'woman', 'girl' and 'mother'). Despite differences concerning parts of speech (pronouns, verbs, auxiliaries) and grammatical relations (A, S, R, P) exhibiting or not exhibiting feminine gender, all languages exemplified in (1–5) mark feminine gender in the same context in the parallel text corpus. The markers all occur in the same functional domain. Nothing in the procedural definition is in any way related to the notions of noun class and agreement. This means that if the endeavor is successful, it is possible to define feminine anaphoric gender grams in abstraction from the notions of noun class and agreement.

What does all this mean for the understanding of gender? Corbett's Agreement Hierarchy is evidence that there is a semantic pole (anaphors) and a syntactic pole (NP-internal agreement) in gender. Traditional research focusing on noun classes and syntactic agreement considers the syntactic pole to be basic. This culminates in the Canonical Approach to gender, which focuses on gender values of nouns and considers redundant gender marking and local agreement domains to be canonical (Corbett & Fedden 2016). In this paper I argue that a shift of perspective is possible where semantic and referential gender in anaphora is the primary concern of grammatical gender, whereas syntactic, lexical and redundant gender is secondary.

The following sections are structured as follows. §2 motivates and formulates the procedural definition of the feminine anaphoric gender gram and §3 discusses its practical implication in the parallel text corpus and reports the results. §4 elaborates on the distinction between mature and non-mature grams and how it is related to grammatical relations. §5 focuses entirely on those non-mature gender grams that are non-pronominal and arguably incipient anaphoric gender markers. Finally, §6 discusses how the functional approach developed in this paper can be connected to the traditional system perspective on gender and §7 concludes this paper.

2 A procedural definition of the feminine anaphoric gender gram

2.1 Overview

This paper focuses on a domain where gender is most obviously used semantically and which is easiest to address by automatic extraction in the N.T. corpus. In §2.2 I am going to discuss why feminine is easiest to address. I will then discuss why feminine anaphoric can be viewed as a functional domain which can be defined as a set of passages in the parallel text corpus (§2.3). The next step is to discuss what makes markers of feminine gender differ from other markers closely associated with the feminine anaphoric functional domain (§2.4). This will allow us to formulate a procedural definition of the feminine gender gram which is sufficiently elaborate for the purposes of this paper. Finally, based on the notions of cue validity and constructional islands, §2.5 discusses why anaphoric gender grams in most languages are accessible without previous familiarity with the entire language system.

2.2 Why feminine, why singular and why anaphora?

We know from Corbett's Agreement Hierarchy that the semantically most transparent use of gender is found in third person anaphoric pronouns. However, this does not mean that grammatical gender has the function of reference tracking in discourse.[2] Within anaphoric use, the descriptive content of gender is most active in contrastive use in implicit or explicit focus (Bosch 1988: 227; Seifart 2018:

---

[2] According to Kibrik, gender is used as a deconflicter in reference tracking in an "opportunistic way" Kibrik (2011: 359). Languages rely on referential aids to various extent and some languages without gender such as Navajo (Na-Dene) are more strongly inclined to use reduced referential devices than some languages with gender such as Archi (Nakh-Daghestanian) (Kibrik 2011: 336).

25), and contrastive use ('but she') is represented in the clauses selected for the extraction from the corpus as in (1). Since gender is often neutralized in the plural (even though this is no strict universal, see Plank & Schellinger 1997), the search space is restricted to singular. The most widespread meanings in gender grams are animacy and sex. Sex is easier to identify than animacy, since animacy comes in many different forms in grammatical markers, not only as gender feature, but also as condition on gender (Corbett 2006, chap. 6) and is, among other things, also involved in the choice of case or adposition in differential object marking (Croft 2003: 166). This leaves us with masculine (singular) and feminine (singular) as possible choices. In the N.T. corpus, feminine is the much easier choice. Reference to male beings is strongly overrepresented in this text, which makes it difficult to distinguish between third person masculine and third person in general in automatic extraction. A further complication in this particular text is that the distinction between male and deity is fuzzy, which, in many languages, calls for specific solutions where this distinction is relevant in grammar. Thus, feminine singular in the anaphoric domain is clearly the easiest option to choose.

2.3 Feminine anaphoric as a functional domain

Defining feminine anaphoric gender as a functional domain in parallel texts means identifying a set of passages where this function is expressed recurrently across all translations of the text. Such a passage is Matthew 15:27, which has been illustrated from various languages in Section 1 and which is for convenience repeated here in English in (6).

(6) English (Indo-European; Matth. 15:27)
     *But **she** said: "..."*

Saying that (6) reflects the feminine anaphoric functional domain abstracts from the fact that this passage is related to another passage earlier in the text given in (7). In (7), the referent of the anaphor in (6) is introduced in the form of an indefinite noun phrase.

(7) English (Indo-European; Matth. 15:27)
     *And behold, **a Canaanitish woman** came out from those borders...*

Another way to put it is that anaphors tend to be coreferent with full noun phrases introduced earlier in the text, which is not strange given that anaphora "is the phenomenon whereby one linguistic element, lacking clear independent reference, can pick up reference through connection with another linguistic element" (Levinson 1987: 379). However, this does not mean that all anaphora have explicit antecedents with which they are exactly coreferent, as illustrated in (8).

(8)   Anaphors without explicit antecedent (Hintikka & Kulas 1985: 98):
      *A couple was sitting on a bench. **He** stood up and **she** followed **his** example.*

Not only pronouns, but even full NPs can be used in anaphoric function, and third person pronouns and full NPs have very similar properties in anaphoric function as shown, in (9). Pronominal anaphors and definite NPs can both be used to make attributions of gender and neither of them requires a syntactically explicit antecedent, but they are both definite expressions.

(9)   Pronouns and full NPs in anaphoric function (Hintikka & Kulas 1985: 98):
      a.   *The teacher addressed the children. **He/The man** was stern.*
      b.   *A couple was sitting on a bench. **He/The man** stood up and **she/the woman** followed **his/the man's** example*

However, when assembling a set of passages expressing feminine anaphoric in a parallel text corpus, it is possible to abstract from the fact that most anaphors have NP antecedents and that a lexical item in the NP can determine the gender value in a way that goes against the core meaning of gender.

2.4 Filtering out markers of feminine gender grams from the feminine anaphoric functional domain

All languages have some anaphoric expressions in the feminine anaphoric domain, but not all expressions are grammatical expressions and not all grammatical expressions are feminine. The anaphoric expressions in the feminine anaphoric domain can be nouns, such as 'woman' or 'girl', or they can be pronouns not distinguishing gender. This is both illustrated in (10) from Turkish with the noun *kadın* 'woman' and the general third person pronoun *o* 'he/she'.

(10)   Turkish (Matth. 15:24–27)
       İsa, «...» diy-e   cevap ver-di.   Kadın ise   yaklaş-ıp,   «...»
       Jesus   say-CVB answer give-PST3 woman however approach-CVB
       diyerek [...]. İsa o-na,   «...» de-di.   Kadın, «...» de-di.   «...»
       say-CVB   Jesus 3SG-DAT   say-PST3 woman   say-PST3
       'But **he** [=Jesus] answered and said, "..." But **she** [=the woman] came [...] saying, "...". And **he** [=Jesus] answered (to **her**) and said, "...". So **she** [=the woman] said, "..." '

It is thus not all expressions in the functional domain of picking up reference to female humans that instantiate feminine gender. If we extract the forms which are associated with the feminine anaphoric domain, which can easily be done by means of collocation measures (see §3), the recall will be too large. Put differently, many nouns, such as Turkish *kadın* '(a/the) woman', and general anaphoric pronouns, such as Turkish *o* 'he/she', will be extracted as well. One way to account for this is to define the search domain very narrowly by excluding such contexts where many languages use nouns instead of pronouns. But cross-linguistic and stylistic differences in the use of nouns, pronouns and zero anaphors are so large that a restrictive search domain is not sufficient.

The solution which is chosen here is to filter out expressions such as Turkish *o* 'he/she' and *kadın* '(a/the) woman'. By subtracting forms associated with anaphoric masculine and anaphoric in general, we can make sure that none of the extracted forms is third person masculine or third person general. Expressions for 'woman' have their own functional domain, which only marginally overlaps with the feminine anaphoric. Notably they also contain non-anaphoric uses, such as (7), where languages such as English have an indefinite article. Lexical nouns are not restricted to anaphoric uses, but can occur both in definite and indefinite uses. By subtracting all forms associated with the functional domain '(a/the) woman' from the set of forms associated with the feminine anaphoric we can make sure that none of the extracted forms means '(a/the) woman'. The same procedure can be applied to a few other critical lexical domains, such as 'girl' and 'mother'. Nouns are an open word class. Hence, the number of potential female lexical domains is potentially infinite. However, there is no need to care about rare lexical domains. It is sufficient to address the most frequent ones: 'woman', 'girl', 'mother', and 'daughter'. This is sufficient for the particular parallel corpus used. If in another parallel corpus another female lexical domain would be particularly frequent, it would have to be included in the filter as well. Filters must be adjusted to particular parallel corpora. However, their content can be described in general terms in the procedural definition: "frequent female lexical domains".

Filtering out all forms that might be associated with a lexical domain, we can also make sure that the remaining set of forms consists exclusively of grammatical markers. This does not restrict the set to pronouns. Grammatical anaphors, such as *neierei* in Kiribati (5), will still be included.

What has been said above, results in the procedural definition for feminine anaphoric gender grams given in (11):

(11) Procedural definition of feminine anaphoric gender markers:

    a. Extract all markers picking up reference to female humans

    b. unless they can also be used to pick up reference to male humans, and

    c. unless they express frequent female lexical domains (such as 'woman', 'mother', 'girl', and 'daughter')

The concrete implementation of this definition is discussed in §3.

2.5 Constructional islands and cue validity

The approach implemented in this paper rests on the assumption that markers expressing a grammatical or lexical meaning X can be viewed as constructional islands with high cue validity. I take these terms from the literature on first language acquisition (Tomasello 2003: 113). In general terms, constructional islands can be defined as utterance-meaning pairings, where one part of the utterance, the marker, is constant, such as in the set: *more milk,* *more grapes,* *more juice.* The marker has high cue validity, if it is sufficiently distinct from all other markers in the language and if it can be immediately recognized without any previous analysis of the morphology of a language, simply as a continuous sequence of sounds (a word form or a continuous segmental morph without allomorphs).

The notions of constructional island and cue validity can be directly applied to parallel text corpora, where a constant meaning can be defined as a set of passages in which a meaning is instantiated. In written corpora we have to take continuous sequences of characters instead of phonemes. All word forms and all continuous substrings of words are candidates for markers that are directly accessible without any previous analysis of the language system. Constructional islands with high cue validity can be detected in the corpus without any knowlegde about the structure of a language and without any resort to parts of speech, grammatical or lexical categories, paradigms or systems.

My assumption is that if a language has a feminine anaphoric gender gram, there will usually be at least one marker with high cue validity. Not all markers will have high cue validity, so the extraction will not be complete. But the approach will be sufficient in most cases for finding out whether or not the language has a feminine anaphoric gender gram. For this purpose, it is sufficient to find one marker if there is more than one.

Put succinctly, if there is no gram, no marker is detected, if there is a gram, at least one of its markers is extracted.

There may be languages where the cue validity of anaphoric gender grams is low, where gender is highly integrated in grammatical systems. These may be cases where the marker is short (just a single phoneme within words of a particular word class) and often neutralized or where the marker is zero (as opposed to a non-zero masculine marker). However, my assumption is that in the vast majority of languages, feminine gender grams have high cue validity and can be viewed as constructional islands, at least to some extent.

3 Extracting feminine gender grams from parallel texts

3.1 Sample, data, and procedure

The sample consists of 816 languages (listed in Appendix A and B) and is not stratified. It simply contains the languages for which I happened to have an electronic version of the New Testament available when I started this work, and, as in other work based on Bible translations, some areas, in particular North America and Australia, are strongly underrepresented. The texts arc not annotated. Some texts which are not in Roman script have been Latinized, but differences in writing systems have very little impact on the extraction procedure. Where the writing system is relevant, this is discussed below. For a few languages, more than one translation has been used (a total of 858 texts). The differences within languages are not reported, since in most cases the results were largely constant within a language,[3] but this does not change the fact that the translations represent particular varieties (doculects), and in a few cases there may be intra-language variety that has not been detected. In one case, Uduk, feminine anaphors have been deliberately created by missionaries (see §5.1), but language planning is an issue only for few languages of the sample, which is why it is not excessively discussed in this paper.

While the theoretical notion of procedural definition of a category type (11) is very general, there are several practical details in the extraction process that can be adjusted and must be adjusted (see below). As is usually the case in typological investigations, there is no gold standard. It is not known what the result is going to be before the investigation has been carried out. Hence, the automatic extraction must be complemented by an evaluation by means of grammars and other reference material. However, since grammatical gender is known to be genealogically stable in many language families, it was very useful to have a large

---

[3]There are some minor differences as in German where the form *ihr* [3SG.F.DAT] is not extracted in some texts.

number of languages from a few large families in the sample. I expected feminine anaphoric gender to be lacking in most languages of the following families: Austronesian (134 lgs.), Niger-Congo (127 lgs.), Trans-New Guinea (90 lgs.; except Ok-branch known to have gender), Quechuan (25 lgs.), Sino-Tibetan (24 lgs.), Uto-Aztecan (18 lgs.), Turkic and Uralic (17 lgs.), and to be present in most languages in the following families: Indo-European (50 lgs.; except for some Indo-Iranian languages and Armenian known to lack gender), Arawakan (17 lgs.) and Tucanoan (13 lgs.). This means that for roughly two thirds of the sample there was an expected result and the details of the extraction mechanism (set of verses included in the search space, filters, how to compare a filter with the search space, see below) could be adapted in a process of trial and error until the outcome largely matched the expected result. In practice, the most difficult thing was to avoid extraction of forms in languages without anaphoric gender grams, so it is very important that the sample contains a large number of such languages (Appendix B). This means that only about a third of the languages of the sample had to be checked manually with grammars and other reference material. Hence, due to its genealogical stability, gender is an exceptionally favorable domain for a typological investigation based on parallel texts with many languages.

In the course of investigation it then turned out that in several dozens of languages the results yielded other forms than just the expected third person free and bound pronouns even after the necessary practical adjustments in the algorithm. At closer introspection, it became clear that many of these languages had incipient anaphoric gender; put differently, anaphoric gender that is so simple that it has not figured prominently in the literature on gender so far, which traditionally focuses on complex cases of gender. This made it necessary to devote a large part of this paper to languages with incipient gender (§5) and these languages also turned out to be typical exceptions to the expected genealogical stability of gender. The rest of the unexpected forms could be accounted for as various types of systematic errors due to the naive mechanic nature of the extraction algorithm (§3.3).

3.2 Extract all markers picking up reference to female humans

The starting point for the extraction of feminine gender from the N.T. parallel corpus is the procedural definition in (11).

First, the algorithm extracts markers picking up reference to female humans, based on collocation with a set of contexts where feminine anaphoric gender occurs.

In parallel texts, meaning can be equated with a set of contextually embedded situations where the markers encoding that meaning (which are language-particular form classes) are expected to occur (Wälchli & Cysouw 2012: 672). In order to identify the situations across translations into different languages, the texts must be aligned with each other on a level coming close to sentences (sentence alignment). The N.T. is aligned in verses and verses are often somewhat larger than sentences, but verse alignment comes close to sentence alignment. Extraction is much easier if the texts are also word-aligned, but here I use only verse alignment which is a crude approach.

For the sake of simplicity it is assumed that a marker is either a word form or a morph (a continuous part of a word form; in concrete terms, any continuous sequence of characters in a word form). This makes it possible to explicitly define the set of potential markers as all word forms and all continuous sequences of characters within word forms.

The easiest way to design a search domain is to take one or several SEED GRAMS (Dahl & Wälchli 2016), forms from particular languages where it is known that they more or less accurately instantiate a gram. Such forms are the third person singular feminine personal pronoun forms in English (*she/her*) or in Scandinavian languages (Swedish *hon/henne/hennes*). The English forms *she* and *her* occur together in 292 verses in the N.T. (American Standard translation). An extraction of potential markers is nothing else than a list of the word forms and character sequences (approximating morphs) that collocate best with the search space above a certain threshold with an appropriate collocation measure. If these 292 verses are used as a search space, an extraction of collocating forms will contain many of the wanted markers, but it will also contain many forms that should not be extracted (boldface in Table 1).

A good extraction must meet two conflicting criteria. There should be as many correct extracted forms as possible (high recall), but there should also be as few wrongly extracted forms as possible (high accuracy). Since the majority of languages in the sample lack feminine gender grams, high accuracy is not as trivial as it might seem at first glance.

There are three ways to improve accuracy: (i) We can use a higher threshold, but this is no good solution, since it has devastating effects on the recall. (ii) We can filter out wrongly extracted forms, since they can be grouped according to certain meanings which we can search for as well, such as 'woman' or general third person singular. (iii) We can reduce the search domain, so that the conflicting meanings are removed from it.

After many attempts I have decided to use a combination of (ii) and (iii). Probably it would be possible to work with the 292 verse search space and filtering, but I have not managed to design the filters such that the extraction is optimal.

Table 1: Word forms and morphs best collocating with English *she+her*.
Here and elsewhere the notation >x< will be used for morphs and # is
used for word boundaries.

Language	Forms	Gloss of forms in boldface
Turkish	**kadın**	'woman'
Swedish	hon, henne, hennes, **kvinna**	'woman'
English	her, she, **woman**	'woman'
Koine Greek	αυτης, αυτη, >σα#<, **γυνη, η**	'woman', DEF.NOM.SG.F
Estonian	**naine, ta, tema**	'woman', 3SG, 3SG.EMPH
Tok Pisin	**meri, en, maria**	'woman', 3SG, 'Mary'
Indonesian	**perempuan, >nya#<**	'woman', POSS.3SG

In the best attempt, there are wrongly extracted forms in 33 more languages and
10 languages are lost in comparison to the extraction reported here. The larger
the search space, the more sophisticated the filters have to be. In larger search
spaces there are simply more meanings represented and there is more that can
go wrong.

In the extraction reported in this paper I have used a subset of 74 clauses as
search space. The clauses have been selected manually, but more important than
which clauses are selected is the simple fact that the set has about that size. If
smaller sets are chosen it is increasingly more difficult to extract short bound
morphemes, such a Garifuna >#t-< in (2). Explicit marking of word boundaries
by a character makes peripheral morphs more salient and easier to extract.

The following criteria have been used to select the 74 clauses.

(i) Include verses where feminine anaphoric gender is instantiated several
times, for instance, as in (12):

(12) Two of 76 verses of the trigger domain (given in the English
Lexham translation)
42015009 (=Luke 15:9) And when **she** has found it, **she** calls
together **her** friends and neighbors, saying, 'Rejoice with me,
because I have found the drachma that I had lost!'
44016015 (=Acts 16:15) And after **she** was baptized, and **her**
household, she urged us, saying, "If you consider me to be a
believer in the Lord, come to my house and stay." And **she**
prevailed upon us.

(ii) exclude long verses (where many other meanings are expressed);

(iii) exclude clauses containing words for 'woman' in most texts;

(iv) exclude most verses where feminine anaphoric gender is contrastive ('but she'), because many texts have nouns for 'woman' there;

(v) exclude verses with 'Mary', so this proper name need not be filtered, and

(vi) exclude (as far as possible) clauses with masculine anaphoric contexts (in fact, this cannot be strictly implemented, because masculine anaphoric contexts are omnipresent in the text).

This results in a set of 74 verses[4] two of which have been illustrated in (12). Choosing the verse (or sentence/clause) as unit of alignment has an important consequences for the extraction of gender. It is not easily possible to distinguish between different grammatical relations, since the same verse often contains the feminine gender gram in various functions. This is notably true of reflexive possessors (as in *she calls together **her** friends*) where even the clause is too large as a unit of alignment. Thus, the extraction applied here is not helpful in deciding which grammatical relation a marker encodes; only that it is some sort of feminine gender marker. The classification of markers according to grammatical relations in Appendix A has therefore been made manually with the help of reference grammars.

Furthermore, it needs to be pointed out that the N.T. is a text where feminine anaphoric gender is strongly underrepresented. Together with the considerable number of verses that have been excluded, this results in a quite small search domain, less than 1% of the text. However, there are enough examples in the text for a mostly correct automatic extraction of frequent feminine gender grams, even if this sometimes means that only some, not all, markers of a feminine anaphoric gender gram are extracted. Extraction works quite well, despite the fact that the algorithm used here is crude. This testifies to the high cue validity of feminine

---

[4] 40001019 (i.e., 40 1:19 or Matth. 1:19; Matthew is the 40th book in the Bible), 40002018, 40008015, 40009025, 40012042, 40014008, 40014011, 40015023, 40015027, 40026012, 41005042, 41006024, 41006025, 41006028, 41007030, 41010004, 41014005, 41014006, 41014008, 42001029, 42001035, 42001036, 42001057, 42001058, 42001061, 42002006, 42002007, 42002036, 42002037, 42002038, 42007013, 42007035, 42007038, 42007047, 42008054, 42008055, 42008056, 42010040, 42010041, 42011031, 42013012, 42015009, 42018005, 42020031, 43004013, 43004016, 43004026, 43008005, 43011023, 43011033, 43011040, 43012007, 43019027, 43020014, 43020017, 44005008, 44005009, 44005010, 44009037, 44009040, 44012014, 44016015, 44016019, 44019027, 45007003, 45009012, 45016002, 46007028, 54005010, 58011031, 59002025, 66002021, 66002022, 66021011.

gender markers. Put differently, in most languages identifying feminine gender grams is not particularly complex and does not presuppose any knowledge about gender systems.

The algorithm goes through all candidates and checks which of them matches best with the trigger domain according to a collocation measure (here T-score as defined by Fung & Church 1994 is used) above a certain threshold. The threshold is determined empirically so that no or few incorrect forms appear. In order to demonstrate that this can be done in slightly different ways, two different thresholds have been applied: t = 3.4 and t = 3.19. The higher threshold prevents the first entirely wrong form to be extracted (Buglere *chku* [arrive:PFV] 'arrived'). However, with the higher threshold we also lose three languages with a feminine gender gram: Kabyle, Angami Naga and Owa (Owa is actually a borderline case, see 5.4), but there are also a large number of arguable errors among the 44 forms that are not extracted with the higher threshold. Since many errors are very interesting from a methodological point of view, I have chosen not to use only the higher threshold, which would probably have been the most reasonable thing to do for an optimal extraction. Forms only extracted with the lower threshold are given in curly braces in Table 2 and in Appendix A.

Table 2: Selected languages where feminine anaphoric gender markers have been extracted

Language	Extraction	T-value of first form
Akateko (knj)	[ix]1	7.682
Ama (amm)	[isoki]1	4.113
Carapana (cbc)	[cõ]1 [>upo#<]2 [>ñupõ#<]3 [>mo#<]4	7.738
English (eng) [amstd]	[her]1 [she]2	7.2
Garifuna (cab)	[>#t<]1	6.008
Hausa (hau)	[ta]1 [>ta#<]2	5.309
Kaingang (kgp)	[fi]1	7.636
Latvian (lav)	[viņai]1 {[>usi<]2 }	4.152
Owa (stn)	{[kani]1 }	{3.191}
Zapotec, Miahuatlan (zam)	{[xa']1 }	{3.310}

Although Indo-European languages have been the starting point for determining the distribution, it is rather languages from other families that have the best extraction values (the top three are Carapana *cõ*, Kaingang *fi* and Akateko *ix*; see Table 2).

3.3 Filtering out conflicting meanings

While the procedure described in §3.2 yields the correct result for most languages with anaphoric gender, the recall is too large in languages where anaphoric gender is lacking. The kind of forms wrongly extracted fall mainly into two semantic groups:

(i) Indexes for third person singular not distinguishing gender. Forms expressing third person singular in general without making a gender distinction also collocate with feminine gender.

(ii) Words for 'woman', 'girl/daughter', and 'mother'. This is surprising at first glance since most texts in Indo-European languages of Europe do not contain instances of 'woman' in the smaller search domain of 74 verses and too few for 'girl/daughter' and 'mother' to be extracted. These "errors" reflect the fact that many translations into languages without feminine anaphoric gender use words for 'woman' in contexts where languages with feminine gender use forms such as *she* and *her*, as in (10) from Turkish. For determining whether a language has feminine anaphoric gender, the procedure must be refined so that such forms are not extracted.

If forms collocating with the feminine third singular also include some forms for third person singular general and some forms for 'woman' and other general feminine nouns, extraction must take this into account by excluding forms which have a better correlation with third person singular masculine and with 'woman', 'girl' and 'mother'.[5] The best way of doing this would be to define sets of verses for all conflicting meanings as carefully as for feminine anaphoric gender. Here, a cruder approach is used where these conflicting domains are simply represented by some characteristic instances in particular languages (Table 3).

(i) *The masculine filter*: For excluding general third person use, a form is not extracted if it correlates better with at least one of the following sets: (a) English *he*, (b) English *him*, (c) all uses of anaphoric masculine singular in English together (*he, him* and *his*), and (d) all uses of *said to him*. These

---

[5]To identify better correlations is not trivial since T-score values with larger search domains are generally higher than with small domains. Since there happen to be roughly two kinds of sizes of domains (smaller than 164 and larger than 742, see Table 3), it is for practical reasons possible to apply a very crude solution by dividing all values of the larger domains by two before comparison. If this correction is not applied, a considerable number of feminine gender markers, for instance those in Kuot and Paumari, are filtered out.

Table 3: Filters in the extraction of feminine gender grams

Masculine filter (relates to (11b))	English *he* [2347 verses], English *him* [1836 verses], English *he/him/his* [3570 verses], English *said to him* [164 verses]
'Woman' filter (11c)	English *woman* [54 verses], Xaasongaxango *muso* 'woman' [39 verses] Yau (yuw) *owi* 'woman, grandmother' [1953 verses]
'Mother' filter (11c)	English *mother* [76 verses]
'Girl' filter (11c)	Nalca *gelma* 'girl, daughter' [40 verses], Upper Pokomo *mwanamuke* 'girl' [41 verses]
'Child' filter	Tok Pisin *pikinini* [743 verses]

four distributions all serve the same purpose, but conflicting forms can have different extensions, so all four of them are needed. Together they constitute the masculine filter.

(ii) *The 'woman', 'mother' and 'girl' filters*: For the exclusion of lexical feminine meanings, a form is not extracted if it correlates better with at least one of the following sets: (a) the English singular form *woman*, Xaasongaxango *muso* 'woman', and Yau *owi*, which is an instance of a very extensive use of a word for 'woman' occurring also in the co-compound *owi amna* [woman man] 'people' (Sarvasy 2014: 104), (c) English *mother*, (d) Nalca *gelma* 'girl, daughter', (e) Upper Pokomo *mwanamuke* 'girl'. This is to make sure that the basic meaning of an extracted form is not 'woman', 'mother' or 'girl' and only incidentally also occurs in the anaphoric domain. Several forms are needed since the semantic extension of words can vary (in some languages 'daughter' and 'girl' is expressed by the same word, in others by different words).

After this is done, a smaller problem area remains which is presented here directly with the remedy resolving it:

(iii) *The 'child' filter*: In a few languages a word for 'child' is extracted. This is because children, child bearing, giving birth to children happens to collocate with the search domain in the N.T. This is solved by removing all forms that collocate better with Tok Pisin *pikinini* 'child' than with the search domain. This is a practical complication that is so specific that I have not included it in the more abstract procedural definition in (11).

To paraphrase the whole procedure in a simple way: a feminine singular anaphoric gender marker is any form that collocates with the feminine singular anaphoric gender domain unless it rather means third person singular in general, 'woman', 'mother', 'girl, daughter', or 'child'. Put differently, forms collocating with the feminine anaphoric singular gender must pass the masculine, 'woman', 'girl', 'mother' and 'child' filters before it is likely that they really represent the feminine anaphoric gender gram.

If the larger search space of English *she+her* is used, further filters have to be added, notably 'wife', 'husband' and 'Mary' filters. There are also complex adjustments required for comparing T-score values with search spaces of different magnitudes.

3.4 Unexpected extracted forms and whether they are errors

Since there is no gold standard, extracted forms were checked with grammars and dictionaries. Checking revealed that after markers with conflicting meanings have been removed by filtering, there remain some unexpected extracted forms which could be considered errors. However, almost all "errors" are highly interesting in that they are somehow associated with the meaning of the feminine anaphoric gram. They fall into five types:

(a) anaphoric (demonstrative or definite) forms of a word for 'woman',

(b) demonstrative pronouns,

(c) person name markers (determiners or titles), mostly female person name markers,

(d) gender markers within noun phrases, and

(e) the masculine gender form by female speakers.

Finally, four occasional forms for 'woman', third person singular personal pronouns, and an entirely occasional verb form meaning 'arrived' escaped filtering with the lower threshold.

(a) *Anaphoric (demonstrative or definite) forms of a word for 'woman':* In South Tairora the form *nraakyeva* [*nraakye-va* 'woman-DEM'] is extracted, because the naive algorithm cannot recognize that it contains *nraakye* 'woman' and should therefore be removed by the 'woman' filter. In South Tairora demonstrative NPs are formed by a free demonstrative, *mwi, mwa*, or *mwatai* in the N.T. text, followed by a noun with an obligatory *-va* suffix (Vincent 2010: 584). The form *nraakyeva* has the correct distribution since it only occurs in the feminine anaphoric domain; it is not a general form for 'woman' and passes therefore the 'woman' filter. This error thus derives from the fact that the algorithm applied here does not have the capacity to segment word forms into morphemes. Extracted forms with the same kind of error include Sabaot *(:)cheebyoosyaanaa* 'this woman', Endo *cheepyoosoonoonëë*, Ayautla Mazatec *chjunbiu*, Safeyoka (Wojokeso) *a'musi*, Umbu-Ungu *ambomo*, and Rawa *barega* (see Appendix A IV). Several similar forms are slightly below the lower threshold for extraction, such as Low Tarahumara (*muki-ka* 'woman-EMPH') and Auhelawa (*waihi-una-ne* woman-DEM/DEF'). Also Ama *nukonu* [woman.SPEC] (see (3)) sorts here, with an irregular form of the specifier (suffix *-ta* in other nouns; Årsjö 1999: 92); however, this form is not extracted.

Generally, a demonstrative or definite form of 'woman' tends to be extracted whenever the demonstrative or definite marker is synthetic. This kind of error is particularly instructive because it shows us how anaphoric gender markers may emerge. Expressions for 'that woman' may qualify as anaphoric gender markers to the extent that the noun and demonstrative have become opaque. This is exactly what has happened in languages with non-compositional complex NPs such as Japanese (see §5.2). The errors made by the computer derive from the fact that more forms are opaque for the computer than for humans.

(b) *Demonstrative pronouns:* Since complex expressions of 'that/the woman' are common feminine anaphoric expressions, it is not entirely unexpected that demonstratives and articles are occasionally wrongly extracted. This happens in several Trans-New Guinea languages such as Mountain Koiali *ke-u* [that-SUBJECT] (Garland & Garland 1975: 428; in the N.T. in *keate keu* 'woman that', *ma keu* 'girl that'), Folopa *kale* 'the' (Anderson 1989: 85; in *kale so[-né]* 'the woman[-ERG]'), Fore *kana-* 'this mentioned one, the aforementioned' (Scott 1989: 45), and Awa *mi* 'that' (Lowing & Lowing 1975) (Appendix A VI). I have not tried to add a demonstrative filter because demonstratives are too different in their distribution from each other and there is no point in adding filters that remove just one or two problematic cases.

(c) *(Female) person name markers*: It is not uncommon for anaphoric gender markers to also be used together with person names. In a few languages the form is slightly different, thus Kiribati uses *Nei* as a female person name marker and *neierei* as anaphoric gender form. In North Halmaheran languages of the sample female names contain a form *ngo*, which combines with the general determiner *o*. A few languages in the sample have female person name markers but lack anaphoric gender. If the language at the same time happens to use many person names in the anaphoric domain, the person name marker can be wrongly extracted (Appendix A III). This is the case for Iraya *bayi* (probably a shortening of *babayi* 'woman'), Uab Meto *bi*, Satere-Mawe *mana*, and Huave *müm*.

(d) *Gender markers within noun phrases are special cases of (b) and (c)*: demonstratives or extended person name markers that happen to bear NP-internal gender. In a sense these are not errors, since the forms mark feminine gender, but they mark feminine gender only NP-internally with common nouns and person names. This holds for Abau (*sokwe* [DIST.DEM.F.OBJ]; Lock 2011: 87), where there are also correctly extracted anaphoric forms, and for Kadiweu, Mocoví, and Nalca.

The Guaicuruan languages Kadiweu and Mocoví have so-called local classifiers (standing, sitting, lying, coming, going, absent; Sándalo 1997: 62) in attributive demonstratives, which combine with masculine and feminine gender markers. In both languages only the form with the 'going' classifier is extracted: Kadiweu *nag-a-jo* CLOSE-F-going and Mocoví *a-so'-maxare* F-GOING-PRO (Appendix A VI).

Nalca (Mek, Trans-New Guinean) has developed a gender system from person name markers (Wälchli 2018), and the female person marker *ge-* grammaticalized from *gel* 'woman' has extended also to some female kinship terms and the word for 'woman'. The extracted form is the topic form *ge-ra* [F-TOP], which occurs in the search domain 15 times with female person names, 12 times with *gel* 'woman' and twice with two different words for mother (Appendix A III). In the whole N.T. this form is only used once anaphorically, but not within the search domain.

It is not unexpected that some NP-internal non-feminine anaphoric gender forms, as in Abau, Kadiweu, Mocoví, and Nalca, are extracted by the
algorithm, because, as far as anaphoric NPs occur in the search domain,
they have the right distribution and are not filtered since they are both
dedicated to feminine and non-lexical.

Some languages have derivational noun suffixes in female nouns, such as
Parecis *-halo*, Esperanto, and Iraqw *o'o* (Mous 1992: 63). The Iraqw form is
not extracted, the Esperanto form is eliminated by the 'woman' filter and
the Parecis form is eliminated by the 'girl' filter.

(e) *Masculine gender for female speakers and second person feminine*: Kayabi
(Tupian) distinguishes both speaker and referent gender (see §4). The verses
of the search domain happen to contain a considerable number of quotations from female speakers which are basically useless for the extraction
of the feminine gender gram. While the quotations do not do any harm for
most languages, for Kayabi they cause with the lower threshold the error
that *kĩã* 'M 3SG (female speaker)' is wrongly extracted. Also due to direct
speech in the search domain is the extraction of Mwaghavul *yi*, a form for
second person feminine reference, even this only with the lower threshold.

Finally, the most problematic wrongly extracted forms are four forms that escaped filtering. But three of them are extracted only with the lower threshold
t=3.19. One form for 'woman' Ama *iní* 'woman' escaped filtering (Appendix A
V). General third person pronouns in two Zapotecan languages were wrongly extracted (Appendix A VII). In Chichicapan Zapotec *bi* is opposed to third person
respect *ba* (Benton 1975) and escapes the masculine filter, probably because Jesus
is referred to with the respect form. For Chichicapan Zapotec *bi* even using the
higher threshold does not help; the T-value is high (t=5.24). Miahuatlan Zapotec
xa' is another general anaphoric marker for third person (both masculine and
feminine) that happens to have escaped filtering with masculine domains. These
cases show that filtering is not always reliable, especially if forms for 'woman'
and general third person singular deviate from their expected distribution in the
text. Finally, as mentioned in §3.2, Buglere *chku* 'arrived' is the first fully unsys-
tematic kind of error at t=3.39.

3.5 Languages where the automatic extraction fails to detect gender

Languages that have gender but where it is not extracted can be ordered into the
following groups:

(a) There is agreement gender or there are noun classifiers reminiscent of agreement gender within the NP, but no or virtually no anaphoric gender: Limbu (van Driem 1987: 21), Baruya, Biangai, and Mopan Maya (Contini-Morava & Danziger 2018) (for Nalca, Kadiweu and Mocoví, see §3.4 above).

(b) Gender is distinguished in pronouns, but only in the second or in the second and first persons: Basque, Paez (Jung 2008: 136, first and second person, but not third person) and Iraqw. However, in Mwaghavul some second person singular form *yi* has been wrongly extracted, since second person with female referent often occur in direct speech in the search domain (see §3.4 (e)).

(c) There is feminine anaphoric gender, but it only covers the domain of girls or young women, the adult women domain is covered by a general human respect gender: Coatzospan Mixtec and Texmelucan Zapotec. These are removed by the 'girl' filter. The 'girl' filter is also responsible for eliminating the reduced nominal anaphor *tɑhn* in Teutila Cuicatec. In Tlalcoyalco Popoloca the anaphoric forms generally correspond to specific feminine lexemes and are therefore filtered out (see §5.3) by the 'woman' and 'girl' filters. A more problematic case is Southern Puebla Mixtec, where the gender marker has many allomorphs (*-nè, -ne, -né, -ñá, -ña* F), and the only one that is detected happens to be removed by the 'woman' filter.

(d) Gender marking is restricted to a limited part of the S and P domain and the markers do not have high cue validity: Chechen, Hindi, Gujarati, and Eastern Panjabi. These are languages with feminine genders, but the anaphoric function in those languages is marginal or non-existing. In Avar only gender on free pronouns is detected.

(e) The marker is partly zero as opposed to a non-zero masculine marker: This holds for the Arawakan languages Ashéninka Pajonal, Asháninka, Caquinte, Pichis Ashéninka and Nomatsiguenga. The algorithm as implemented here is simply not smart enough for recognizing zero as the marker of the feminine gender gram. The recognition of zero morphemes requests some understanding of systems or at least oppositions.

(f) Gender is too inconsistently marked to be extracted: In Iraqw (Cushitic, Afro-Asiatic; Mous 1992), masculine and feminine are not distinguished in third person free pronouns, and in affixes in verbs and auxiliaries, the markers are manifold both for the expression of subject and object (e.g., *ó'* 'she said' vs. *óo'* 'he said'). It is not possible to detect feminine marking as constructional island without previous analysis of the paradigms. The algorithm fails to detect feminine anaphoric gender in Iraqw.

(g) The dominant marker is orthographically identical with another form: Teutila Cuicatec.

The types (a) and (b) are no real errors since the algorithm only extracts feminine anaphoric gender in third person. The cases in (c) are too weakly grammaticalized or do not have general feminine gender grams, and can therefore not really be counted as errors. The cases in (d) are errors, but these are all languages where anaphoric gender has a very weak functional load. In Chechen only a small proportion of verbs have a feminine prefix *j-*[6] in S and P. In Hindi and some other Indo-Aryan languages, some verbs in some tenses have a feminine singular suffix *-ī*, not restricted to third person. The errors in (e) are due to the unsophisticated design of the algorithm that cannot recognize zero marking as a marker. All errors of the types (d), (e), and (f) concern languages where there are only bound gender markers consisting maximally of two phonemes; in most instances there is even only a single character. These are most difficult to identify.

Finally the failure in (g) is probably an artifact of the orthography not distinguishing tone, but I do not have any description of Teutila Cuicatec available to check whether te occurring 3573 times in the N.T., only a small part of which is the feminine gender marker, is a case of homonymy or undifferentiated orthography. But Cuicatec languages also have a general respect gender that makes extraction more difficult.

Using a larger search domain would be helpful for a few languages. With a search space of 293 verses mainly based on English *she/her* markers are extracted even for Ashéninka Pajonal >#ok, >#op<, Asháninka >#o<, Caquinte >#o<, and more markers in other languages, such as Avar, >й<, Tachelhit >#t<, Tamasheq >#tě<, >#tă<, Maltese >et<, Machiguenga >#os< are extracted. (Note also that Kabyle >#te< is only extracted with the lower threshold.) However, using a larger search domain comes at the cost of more wrong forms not filtered and nine languages with non-mature feminine gender markers and Yagua not extracted. I have not managed to extract any forms in Hindi, Gujarati, Eastern Panjabi, Chechen, and Iraqw, however the extraction is designed.

Explaining away exceptions is always problematic. However, the discussion shows that there are good reasons why the algorithm misses gender in a few languages.

---

[6] The Cyrillic alphabet not representing /j/ with a single letter is an additional difficulty, but the extraction does not succeed even when the text is transliterated.

3.6 Cases where the automatic extraction fails to extract particular forms

It is quite astonishing that in most languages anaphoric gender markers can be identified without previous analysis of any other grammatical categories or lexemes. This means that in most languages at least some anaphoric gender markers tend to have very high cue validity and are constructional islands (item-based constructions with a constant element; Tomasello 2003; see §2.5) which can be considered in abstraction from most other aspects of grammar as a form-meaning relationship in the text. The only exception the extraction algorithm has to make is that it must consider the feminine anaphoric singular domain in opposition to the anaphoric masculine singular domain and to the lexical domain 'woman', however, without having acquired the grammar of how feminine and masculine gender interact with other categories. This entails that the algorithm fails to recognize cases of "diagonal" syncretism involving cumulation (Table 4). Diagonal syncretism is similar to neutralization in that a form is used for more than one category. However, the opposition is not neutralized since there is another cumulating category that keeps the values distinct. An example is the Latvian third person feminine nominative singular pronoun *viņa* 'she', which has the same form as the masculine genitive singular form. The algorithm used here excludes it, because this form is also used in the masculine singular anaphoric gender domain. The algorithm fails to recognize that there is cumulation with an entirely different category: case. Another case in point is Afrikaans *sy* 'she' which is also used for possessive masculine 'his'; only *haar* 'feminine oblique' is extracted. "Diagonal" syncretism only occurs in mature gender markers.

Table 4: Cases of "diagonal" syncretism

Latvian			Afrikaans		
	F	M		F	M
NOM.SG	*viņa*	*viņš*	3SG	*sy*	*hy*
GEN.SG	*viņas*	*viņa*	POSS.3SG	*haar*	*sy*

Interestingly, there is no language in the sample where a feminine gender gram is missed due to "diagonal" syncretism. All languages of the sample with "diagonal" syncretism also have another feminine anaphoric gender marker with higher cue validity.

Some forms are not extracted due to other cases of homonymy where the other homonymous form is much more frequent. French *la* '3SG.F.ACC' is not extracted, because this form is primarily used as a definite article outside the anaphoric gender domain.

Affixes, especially short affixes, are more difficult to extract than free forms. This holds especially of affixes restricted to object, absolutive, and/or recipient marking. In some cases the form for 'said to her' is extracted instead of the feminine recipient affix. This holds for some languages of New Guinea and for some languages of South America: Ama *i-so-ki* [say-O3SG.F-REM.PST], Mian *baa-b-o-n-e-a* [say.PFV-BEN:PFV-IO.3SG.F.PFV-SS.SEQ-S.3SG.M-MED] (Fedden 2007), Bine *jo-ji-ge* [ABS.3SG.F-say-ERG.3SG] (as opposed to *je-ji-ge* [ABS.3SG.M-say-ERG.3SG] 'said to him'). In Kamasau the only form extracted is *w-uso* [3SG.F-go] 'she went' (Sanders & Sanders 1994: 21). This is partly an artifact of the size of the search space. With larger search spaces, short bound morphs are more easily detected.

Due to the statistical nature of the algorithm, rare forms cannot be extracted since it cannot be known whether rare forms only accidentally occur in the search domain. This means in practice that forms occurring in less than eleven verses (or 15% of the search domain) cannot be extracted. This affects, for instance, contrastive subject forms, such as Welsh *hithau*, possessive forms with gender agreement, such as German *ihr-e/en/es/er* [3SG.F-AGR], demonstratives used for referents of relatively low activation (Kibrik 2011: 327), such as Latvian *t-ā* [DEM.DIST-NOM.SG.F] and Latin *hæc*, and the Latin relative pronoun *quæ* [REL.NOM.F.SG] in non-relative use marking text coherence. Since there can be many feminine anaphoric gender markers, especially when markers are mature, there is a considerable amount of forms missed in languages with mature gender.

Gender markers for special groups of female beings, such as young women or female deities, as they frequently occur in Mesoamerican languages, are not extracted by the algorithm. Forms for young women are mostly filtered by the lexical 'girl' filter. Other groups, such as female deities, are not represented with sufficiently high frequency in the text.

3.7 Conclusions

As can be seen in more detail in Appendix A and B, there are 629 languages in the sample lacking a feminine anaphoric gender gram and 187 languages where such a gram is attested. Furthermore, it can be seen in Appendix A that the automatic extraction fails to detect feminine gender in 18 languages (3 Indo-Aryan, 1 Nakh-Daghestanian, 1 Cushitic, 5 Tucanoan, 1 Mayan, and 7 Otomanguean). Wherever extraction fails, there is a good reason for it (anaphoric function for animate nouns highly restricted, very short bound or different bound affixes on verbs, zero exponence, or low degree of grammaticalization of the gram).

With one exception the wrongly extracted forms are all closely related semantically to feminine anaphoric gender and include feminine person name markers (5 lgs.), forms of a noun for 'woman' with a demonstratrive or definite affix (9 lgs.), other forms of 'woman' (1 lg.), demonstratives and definite articles (5 lgs., 2 of them distinguishing gender within the NP), and general third person pronouns (2 lgs). With the higher threshold, a feminine anaphoric gender gram is missed in 21 languages and a marker is wrongly extracted in 15 languages (all with some semantic resemblance to feminine anaphoric gender).

We can therefore conclude that almost all errors are systematic errors. Some are due to the crude nature of the algorithm that cannot segment word forms into morphemes. Some are due to the fact that some other grammatical phenomena are very closely related to anaphoric gender. Some failures are due to the fact that anaphoric gender has low cue validity in some languages. Rare forms are not detected. Throughout this section we have also seen that errors are sometimes even more valuable than correct results as they reveal where gender is particularly complex in certain ways. The procedure is highly useful as a heuristic device to check whether there are feminine anaphoric singular gender markers in a language.

4 Cumulation with grammatical relations and maturity of anaphoric gender

Once feminine anaphoric gender grams have been extracted for the languages of the sample, we can arrange the forms as they are distributed over various grammatical relations. This has been done by means of manual analysis and Table 5 illustrates the results for a few languages of the sample where there is some suppletion and/or neutralization for some grammatical relations. The languages listed in Table 5 represent different patterns of suppletion and/or neutralization and are discussed in more detail later in this section. The grammatical relations listed are A (transitive subject), S (intransitive subject), P (monotransitive object), R (recipient, indirect object), Poss1 (non-reflexive possessor or alienable possessor) and Poss2 (reflexive possessor or inalienable possessor; i.e., any less independent kind of possessor). Bound forms are indicated as affixes to the verb (-)V(-) or noun (-)N(-). See Appendix A for the whole sample. The examples in Table 5 are discussed in more detail below.

Table 5: Feminine gender grams (third person singular) in selected languages

	A	S	P	R	Poss1	Poss2
English	she	she	her	her	her	her
Belize Kriol	shee	shee	–	–	–	–
German	sie	sie	ihr	ihr	ihr-AGR	ihr-AGR
Welsh	hi	hi	hi	wrthi	ei+ASPIR	ei+ASPIR
Latin	illa, quæ, hæc	illa, quæ, hæc	eam, illam	–	–	–
Latvian	viņa, (V-usi)	viņa, viņa, (V-usi)	–	viņai	viņas	–
Northern Kurdish	wê	–	–	wê	wê	–
Hindi	–	V-ī	– (V-ī)	–	–	–
Ama	–	V-mo-	V-mo-	V-mo-	–	–
Au	hire / w-V	hire / w-V	V-p	V-we	AGR-ire	AGR-ire

As argued in §1, feminine anaphoric gender grams as those listed in Table 5 are mature. The markers have the function of noun phrases, but suppletion and neutralization is not characteristic of nouns. While mature anaphoric gender markers are often shorter phonologically than non-mature markers, a more reliable token of maturity is higher complexity in the sense of formal variability. The incipient anaphoric gender markers discussed in §5 are typically invariant across grammatical relations and not systematically absent from any grammatical relations (except sometimes reflexive possessor). This makes them differ from most pronominal anaphoric gender markers which exhibit cumulation and/or neutralization. English *she* (subject) and *her* (object, indirect object, and possessor) illustrate this point. Nouns are not entirely precluded from suppletion according to grammatical relation, but such suppletion in nouns is rare. Vafaeian (2013) shows that suppletion in nouns is common according to number, possession, and vocative case. In her sample of 63 languages there is only one language, Archi (Nakh-Daghestanian) with suppletion according to grammatical relation (absolutive/ergative in two nouns). Pronouns, however, and especially if bound pronouns are included, usually display some sort of suppletion and/or neutralization according to grammatical relation. In Turkish third person, for instance, the free pronoun has the stem *o* and the possessive suffix is *-i/ı/u/ü*. Pronouns can lack suppletion or neutralization according to grammatical relation, such as Mandarin Chinese *ta¹* 's/he', but in pronouns this is the less frequent option cross-linguistically.

Anaphoric gender grams exhibiting suppletion or neutralization must have undergone some kind of grammaticalization process. They presuppose earlier stages with simpler gender grams which are more similar to nouns or have developed from markers of other grammatical categories (such as case or number). How anaphoric gender grams can develop from nouns and noun phrases will be discussed in §5 based on the languages of the sample lacking suppletion and neutralization according to grammatical roles. Suppletion and/or neutralization are not necessary properties of gender grams with a long prehistory, but since most grams extracted here with long prehistories of gender exhibit these properties, I will refer to grams lacking suppletion and neutralization as "non-mature". Figure 1 shows the distribution of mature and non-mature feminine anaphoric gender grams in the languages of the sample.

Let us now discuss the languages listed in Table 5 one-by-one:

While English has a feminine marker for all relations – *she* for subject and *her* for all other ones – Belize Kriol English (at least the N.T. version) distinguishes feminine *shee* only for S and A (subject); object *ahn* and the possessor *ih* do not distinguish gender. Even though there is only one form, there is different behavior across grammatical relations since the single feminine form does not occur as non-subject, where gender is neutralized in Belize Kriol English.

Agreement of possessors with head nouns is indicated by AGR in Table 5 and illustrated in (13) for German and (14) for Au. These examples show that gender indexation (boldface) and NP-internal gender agreement (arrow) can be expressed on the same word form.

(13)   German (Indo-European; Mk. 3:31 ; Matth. 14:8)

    a. **sein**-*e*   *Mutter*
        POSS.3SG.**M**-NOM.SG.F← Mutter(F)[NOM]
        '**his** mother'

    b. *von* **ihr**-*er*   *Mutter*
        from POSS.3SG.**F**-DAT.SG.F← mother(F)[DAT]
        'by **her** mother'

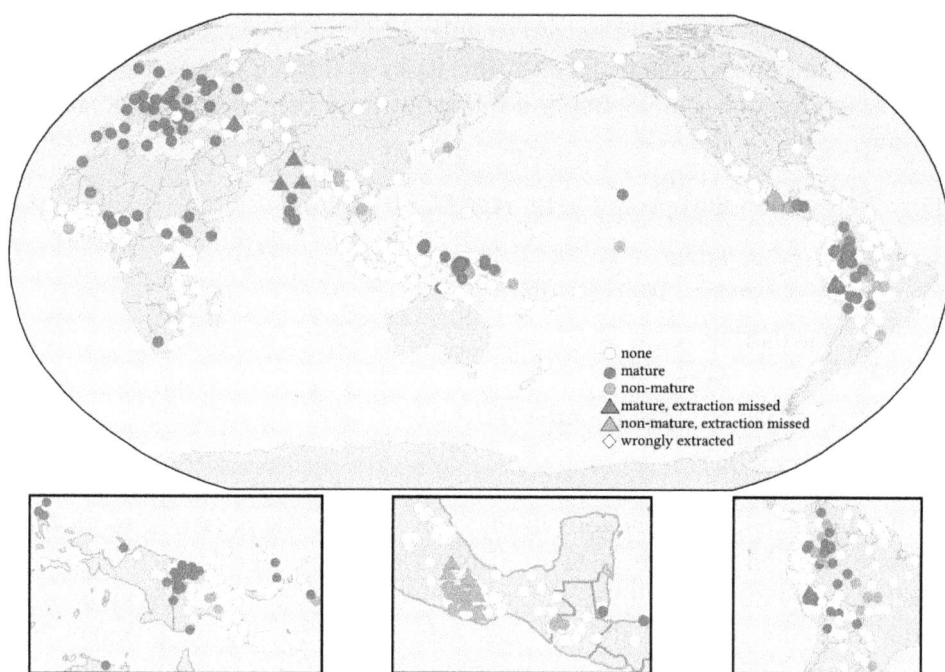

Map designed with the WALS Interactive Reference Tool by Hans-Jörg Bibiko.

Figure 1: Languages of the sample with mature and non-mature feminine gender grams

(14) Au (Torricelli; Mk. 3:31, Mk. 9:21, Matth. 14:11)

    a. *miye   p-irak*
       mother(F) →SG.F-POSS.3SG.M
       '**his** mother'

    b. *haai   k-irak*
       father(M) →SG.M-POSS.3SG.M
       '**his** father'

    c. *miye   p-ire*
       mother(F) →SG.F-POSS.3SG.F
       '**her** mother'

Welsh (15) represents a special case in that anaphoric gender in possessive pronouns is marked only as a sandhi phenomenon spread to the following head noun. The third person singular masculine form *ei* causes soft mutation (among other things *m->f-*); the third person singular feminine form *ei*, however, causes aspirate mutation (no change for *m-*). This looks as if there was agreement into the wrong direction, but is simply a rather intricate case of anaphoric gender marking.

(15)   Welsh (Indo-European; Matth. 14:8, Matth. 12:46)

   a. **ei**   *fam*
      POSS.3SG POSS.3SG.M:mother(F)

      'his mother'

   b. **ei**   *mam*
      POSS.3SG POSS.3SG.F:mother(F)

      'her mother'

Latin lacks gender distinctions in the dative and in the possessor (both non-reflexive *eius* and reflexive *su*-AGR). Latvian lacks a gender distinction for the direct object (*viņu* ACC.SG.M/F) and for reflexive possessors (*sav*-AGR RPOSS.M/F). In the subject, gender in Latvian is indexed not only by the free pronoun, but sometimes also in participles (-*usi* PTCP.PST.ACT.NOM.SG.F). Northern Kurdish distinguishes gender in the oblique (*wî* M, *wê* F), which covers A (ergative), R and non-reflexive possessor, but not in the absolutive (*ew* M/F) S and P relations. Hindi lacks gender in free pronouns, and in the perfective past, which I take here as the most representative form since it is used in narrative function, gender is marked on the verb (-*ī* F) only in intransitive verbs and in some transitive verbs for the object. Ama (see also (3)) marks gender on the verb, but only for the absolutive, which, however, also covers the primary object (P and R): *ko-so-ki* [see-O.3SG.F-REM.PST] 's/he saw her' vs. *ki-Ø-ki* [see-O.3SG.M-REM.PST] 's/he saw him', *i-so-ki* [say-O.3SG.F-REM.PST] 's/he said to her' vs. *i-mo-ki* [say-O.3SG.M[7]-REM.PST] (Årsjö 1999).[8]

In all languages listed in Table 5, anaphoric gender is well entrenched, which can be seen from the fact that its marker interacts in some way with grammatical relations, either by means of cumulation or neutralization. This situation is characteristic of mature gender grams where anaphoric gender has a long history. This is opposed to incipient gender marking where the gender gram is less

---

[7]The masculine form is zero except for a few relics with -*mo*- as in the verb 'say'.

[8]Some predicates are especially salient in terms of frequency in the corpus with animate participants, these are notably 'go/come/arrive' for S, 'see' for P, and 'say' for R. However, the indexes listed in Table 5 are not always equivalent in translation; for instance, not in all languages 'see' is transitive.

complex and usually only has a single form irrespective of grammatical relation and where the use of the gram tends to be optional.

All examples in Table 5 have in common that anaphoric gender marking is pronominal (whether free or bound) and has variable formal expression across grammatical relations as opposed to the invariant anaphoric gender markers of nominal origin or supposedly nominal origin discussed in §5. However, not all invariant anaphoric gender markers can be proven to have nominal origin. There are, for instance, two Tupian languages in the sample with invariant markers. Kayabi *ẽẽ* F (male speaker) M, *kyna* F (female speaker), M *'ga* (male speaker), and *kĩã* M (female speaker), distinguishing both speaker and referent gender. These markers also follow person names and animate nouns in anaphoric use. Tenharim has *hẽa* F and *'ga* M (singular and plural), which also occur as suffixes on referring person names and animate nouns. Like in other Tupian languages the pronominal prefixes on nouns and verbs do not distinguish gender in Kayabi (Dobson 2005: 27) and Tenharim (Betts 1981: 17). The lack of gender markers in most Tupian languages might suggest that anaphoric gender in Kayabi and Tenharim are innovations.

However, invariant marking does not always testify to recent origin of gender. Malayalam (Dravidian) has the constant pronominal stem *aval(-)* 3SG.F and no bound pronouns. But Old Malayalam still had subject indexes on the verb (*-ā̆ḷ* 3SG.F) (Andronov 1996: 120). Anaphoric gender marking was thus not invariant in Old Malayalam. While all Indo-European languages and all Creole languages with anaphoric gender in the sample have variant anaphoric gender marking, the artificial language Esperanto has invariant marking with the constant markers *sxi(-)* F and *li(-)* M.

Anaphoric gender can occasionally have quite unexpected sources. In Yagua, women who have borne children are referred to by dual forms (Payne 1985: 42) – 3DU *naada-* (often realized as *naan-*), *naadá*, 2DU *sáána-*, *saadá*. Men, however, are referred to with singular bound pronouns: 3SG *sa-* [I], *-níí* [II], 2SG *jiy-* [I], *jíy* [II].[9] In the N.T. dual forms are used as a default for adult women for whom it is not specified in the text whether they have given birth to children. Even if this is lack of gender from the point of view of the system – and Payne (1985: 42) says explicitly that Yagua lacks gender – this is an anaphoric gender marking opposition from the point of view of language use. Anaphoric gender in Yagua hijacks another highly grammaticalized category, number. This is why the markers are mature even if they are presumably young as gender markers. Yagua is thus an example of a very specific origin of an anaphoric gender opposition which has a

---

[9] Set II forms are used for direct objects and some intransitive subjects.

mature marker from the very beginning. However, since the origin of gender is often associated with case or number (Wälchli & Di Garbo 2019 [this volume]), the example of Yagua is perhaps less parochial than it seems at first glance.

To summarize: Even though there are a few exceptions, cumulation and/or neutralization testify to mature anaphoric gender marking whereas lack of cumulation and/or neutralization typically goes hand in hand with incipient gender marking. Since cumulation and neutralization can be considered to reflect an increase in complexity, this is evidence that complexity in anaphoric gender increases over time.

5 Grammatical anaphors and incipient anaphoric gender markers

5.1 Introduction

Third person pronouns (*he/she*) and full NPs have very similar properties in anaphoric function. Notably, there is very little semantic difference between a gender marked anaphoric pronouns (*he/she*) and a full definite NPs containing a light noun (a noun with a very general meaning, such as 'man', 'woman', 'thing'). This contrasts with their very different form – pronoun vs. noun – which assigns them entirely different roles in the typology of referential devices. As mentioned above, Kibrik (2011) makes a distinction between full referential devices (common nouns with or without modifiers, and person names) and reduced referential devices (pronouns and zero forms) and claims that it is universal: "The only truly universal opposition is that between full and reduced referential devices" (Kibrik 2011: 42). Grammatical anaphors are intermediate referential devices in the sense that they are neither lexical nouns nor third person pronouns. However, the distinction is still clear-cut in the sense that grammatical anaphors are grammatical in the same way as personal pronouns and hence to be included when discussing gender grams. Kibrik (2011: 123–136) discusses several of the grammatical anaphors considered here, such as Jacaltec classifiers and Japanese *kare* 'he' and *kanojo* 'she', under the heading "functional analogues" of personal pronouns.

Describing grammatical anaphors is essentially a synchronic aim. However, since grammaticalization tends to be unidirectional (Haspelmath 1999) and intermediate forms do not seem to evolve from more grammaticalized pronominal anaphoric gender markers, there is automatically also a diachronic dimension. Put differently, forms intermediate between nouns and indexes also tend to be INCIPIENT GENDER MARKERS. Intermediate forms (grammatical anaphors) keep from their lexical origin the property of distinguishing the basically lexical meanings 'woman' and 'man', but they are decategorialized from the lexical category of nouns. However, since the diachrony of grammatical anaphors often remains opaque, this is in some cases only a hypothesis. It is important to point out that incipient gender markers do not necessarily further grammaticalize to mature gender markers. It is very well possible that incipient gender markers can be lost or remain incipient. As discussed in §4, mature gender markers can develop from other grammatical categories, such as number, case or person, and need not necessarily develop from incipient anaphoric gender markers.

Grammatical anaphors have both pronominal and nominal properties. Three different subtypes are discussed in this section as illustrated in Table 6.

Table 6: Three subtypes of grammatical anaphors

Subtype	Example	Subsection
Non-compositional complex NP	Japanese *kano(-)jo* *'that(-)woman'	§5.2
Reduced nominal anaphor	Chalcatongo Mixtec *-ña* (*ñã'ã* 'woman')	§5.3
General noun	Northern Khmer *niang* 'girl; she'	§5.4

Non-compositional complex NPs differ from the other types in that they are diachronically complex (more than one morpheme). Reduced nominal anaphors differ from the other two simplex types in that they diachronically reflect reduced nouns. General nouns have the form of a non-reduced noun, but they are so extended in use that they are semantically difficult to distinguish from pronouns. What makes them pronoun-like is not their form or word class, but the fact that their use is broader than in their lexical nominal use. Put differently, general nouns have specific meaning when used as nouns and more general meaning when used as grammatical anaphors.

Two further issues need to be specified. The first one is that not all instances of incipient anaphoric gender markers reflect genuine grammaticalization developments since linguistic gender categories can be subject to deliberate language planning. As there are sometimes attempts to eliminate anaphoric gender by language planning (for instance, in Swedish, a gender neutral form *hen* has been suggested to replace *han* 'he' and *hon* 'she' and is now partly gaining ground especially in generic use; see Milles 2011: 27), there have been attempts to implement gender distinctions in pronouns where there a none. A case in point is Uduk where the N.T. uses the noun *(a)yim* [CLASS2] 'female friend' for 'she' even though this noun does not have any anaphoric use in spoken Uduk (Don Killian, p.c.). Thus, Bible translation Uduk has a special pronominal noun whereas there are no indications of a grammaticalization of an anaphoric gender gram in spoken Uduk (for more information on gender in Uduk, see Killian 2019 [in Volume I]).

The second one is that the presence of a masculine grammatical anaphor does not entail the presence of a feminine form.[10] As other Mek languages, Yale (13) has a masculine, but no feminine grammatical anaphor. Yale does not distinguish gender in third person pronouns (*el* 3SG), but has a special form *bone* glossed 'this.man' by Heeschen (1992), which does not contain the noun *nimi* 'man', but rather looks like a demonstrative pronoun as it cumulates the expression of spatial deixis with its nominal meaning (*ane* 'this here', *ani* 'that up there', *anu* 'that down there', *bini* 'that man up there', *bunu* 'that man down there'; Heeschen 1992: 15). All three devices, demonstrative NP, grammatical anaphor and personal pronoun, occur in example (16) and are summarized in Table 7.

(16) Yale (Mek, Trans-New Guinea phylum; Heeschen 1992: 29)
Nimi ane dinge, **bone** dinge dane, **el-di** kwaneng
man   this property, this.man property DEM:PL 3SG-GEN sweet.potato
wa-m-la=ba,   na do-do   de-n.
be-PRF-PRS.3SG=CONNECT 1SG take-CVB eat[PFV].PRS.1SG
'I have taken and eaten (earlier today) this man's sweet potatoes.'

While the etymology of *bone* 'this.man' is opaque, there is a second grammatical anaphor in Yale which obviously derives from a full NP: *mene* 'this.child' (*mini* 'that child up there', *munu* 'that child down there' < *me ane/ani/anu*).

This section does not discuss all languages in the sample where gender has emerged recently. Due to genealogical considerations, in some languages feminine gender must have emerged recently (all related languages lack feminine; this holds, e.g., for Northern Wè within Niger-Congo; Paradis 1983), but it is not possible to trace a non-pronominal origin of gender markers.

It should be also stressed that automatic extraction of anaphoric gender (§3) has been the dominant heuristic in identifying the relevant set of languages. Many languages discussed here are not traditionally considered gender languages

---

[10]I do not know of any case of the contrary, a feminine grammatical anaphor without a corresponding masculine form.

Table 7: Yale third person pronouns, grammatical anaphors and demonstrative NPs

3SG	Grammatical anaphors	N DEM
	bone 'this.man'	*nimi ane/ene* 'this man'
el 'she/he'	—	*kel ane/ene* 'this woman'
	mene 'this.child'	*me ane/ene* 'this child'

and when I obtained forms in the automatic extraction I first thought that there must be some mistake in the algorithm.[11]

Some of the forms to be discussed in this section figure prominently in the literature on classifiers, especially NOUN CLASSIFIERS. This is no surprise since anaphoric use is a well-recognized function of noun classifiers in some languages. According to Aikhenvald (2000: 87) "noun classifiers are typically used with anaphoric function". Aikhenvald discusses especially Mayan languages of the Kanjobalan branch (Jacaltec and Akateko) and some Australian languages (notably Yidiny). It is thus not unexpected that some noun classifier languages are found to exhibit anaphoric gender which does not presuppose agreement as definitional property.

The literature on noun classifiers has in common with the literature on gender that it considers anaphoric use to be secondary. Noun classifiers as grammatical markers co-occurring with nouns in the same NP are not the topic of this paper, and in the same way as anaphoric gender can be considered without making reference to the notion of agreement, it can also be considered without making reference to the notion of noun classifiers.

5.2 Non-compositional complex NPs

Non-compositional complex NPs have similar uses as expressions for 'that man/ woman', and sometimes they are entirely opaque, as the example from Kiribati illustrated in §1. However, non-compositional complex NPs are not usually condensed forms of 'that woman/man'; rather they contain other nouns that have been generalized to general meanings of feminine or masculine, such as 'mother' or 'elder sister' or 'body' or they contain obsolete or irregular forms of demonstrative pronouns.

---

[11]Since many languages also have third person singular forms not distinguishing gender they are not usually captured in Siewierska's (2005) typology (except Japanese where the third person singular pronoun is zero anaphor).

English has no anaphoric non-compositional NPs, but a related phenomenon is indefinite pronouns originating from NPs, such as *somebody*. *Somebody* contains the noun *body*, but does not have the meaning that the noun *body* has. For a typology of indefinite pronouns, see Haspelmath (1997). In the languages of the sample, non-compositional complex NPs are attested in Kiribati (Austronesian), Japanese (isolate), Kannada (Dravidian), Zome (Sino-Tibetan), Golin and Chuave (Chimbu, Trans-New Guinea phylum). Anaphoric gender markers in some South American languages with noun classifiers, notably Nambikuara and in Guahiban and Witotoan languages, are highly reminiscent of non-compositional complex NPs and can perhaps be interpreted as more advanced stages of grammaticalization. Table 8 summarizes the forms of the languages discussed in this section.

Table 8: Languages with non-compositional complex NPs for female reference

	Index (3sg general)	Grammatical anaphor	NP 'that woman'	'woman'
Japanese	zero anaphor	*kanojo*	*sono onna*	*onna*
Kannada	*avaḷu* (F), V-*aḷu* (F)	*āke* (honorif.)	*ā strīyu*	*strīyu*
Zome	*amah*	*tuanu*	*tua numei*	*numei*
Kiribati	*ngaia, e*	*neierei*	*te aiine aarei*	*aiine*
Golin	V-*m*, V-*ngw*	*abalini*	*abal i*	*abal*
Chuave	V-*m*, V-*ngu*	*oparomi*	*opai,*	*opai*
S. Nambikuara	*te²na²*, zero, V-*la¹*	*ta¹ka³lx(ai²n)a²*	*txu¹h(a³ka³lx)ai²na²*	*txu¹ha²*
Cuiba	–	*barapowa*	*barapo petsiriwa, yabuyo*	*yabuyo, petsiriwa*
Guayabero	–	-*ow, hapow*	*ampow pawis*	*pawis*
Huitoto Murui	*ie*	*naiñaiño*	*naie riño*	*riño*
Huitoto Minica	*ie*	*afengo*	*afe ringo*	*ringo*
Bora	(*i-*)	*diílle, -lle*	*áalle*	*walle*

Japanese *kanojo* 'she' means originally 'that woman', but it is not a reduced form of *sono onna* [that woman] 'that woman'. *Kano* is originally the attributive form of a distal demonstrative (free form *kare*) that has come out of use except in a few fixed archaic expressions such as *kare kore* 'that and this'. *Jo* is the Sino-Japanese expression for 'woman' (Ishiyama 2008: 141). *Kanojo* and its masculine counterpart *kare* 'he' (originally 'that') were established in the Meiji period (1868–1912) in the literary movement *genbun-itchi* (unification of written and spoken language) where translations from European languages played an important role (Ishiyama 2008: 139). There is some element of deliberate manipulation in this grammaticalization process and there is no reduction or erosion contributing to the grammaticalization of *kanojo* 'she'. The reason why *kanojo* cannot be analyzed as a compositional NP anymore is that the demonstrative *kano* has disappeared. Although *kanojo* usually is translated with 'she' it could also still be translated as 'that woman'. In the N.T. *kanojo* competes in the anaphoric domain with *onna* 'woman' and *sono onna* 'that woman' (*suruto onna ha itsut-ta* [and woman TOP say-PST] 'So she said'; Matth. 15:27). *Kanojo* and *kare* cannot be compared to *she* and *he* in terms of text frequency (Ishiyama 2008: 36). Japanese prefers zero anaphor as reduced referential device (Kibrik 2011: 44). *Kanojo* also has some rather nominal uses: *kanojo wa?* [she TOP] 'Do you have a girlfriend?' (Ishiyama 2008: 232). It can also be used as a term for address (Ishiyama 2008: 232) which further shows that it is not a canonical third person pronoun.

Kannada (Dravidian) has so called honorific pronouns *āke* 'that woman, she', *īke* 'this woman', which have developed from the demonstratives *ā* 'that', *ī* 'this' and *akka* 'elder sister'. The second component in *ātanu* 'that man, he', *ītanu* 'this man' (honorific) is of Sanskrit origin: *dēha-* 'person, body'. Similar forms are found in Telugu (Andronov 2003: 171). Kannada and Telugu are the only languages I am aware of which have both gender-distinguishing third person pronouns (Kannada *avaḷu* 'she', *avanu* 'he') and grammatical anaphors.

Zome (Sino-Tibetan) *nu* and *pa* mean 'mother' and 'father' when possessed (*ka/na/a nu* [1SG/2SG/3SG mother]), but with the demonstratives *tua* 'that' and *hih* 'this' they are non-compositional complex NPs: *tuanu* 'that woman, she', *hih nu* 'this woman, she'. The corresponding nouns are *numei* 'woman' and *mi* 'man'. Rather than just pronouns and NPs there are three sets of forms in Zome: *ama(h)* 'he/she', *tuanu* 'she, that woman', and *tua numei* 'that woman'. It might be argued that *tuanu* 'that woman, she' is not sufficiently opaque to qualify as a non-compositional complex NP and is not much different from cases such as South Tairora *nraakyeva* [*nraakye-va* 'woman-DEM'] that have been removed as errors (see §3.4(a)). Indeed, no form is extracted for Zome if the form is spaced *tua nu*, where *nu* 'mother' is removed by the 'mother' filter. However, Zome is different from South Tairora in that the demonstrative is written without space only in few forms where it is semantically non-compositional, it is not generally an affix. Looking more closely for non-univerbated collocations of 'that mother' in the search domain in other Sino-Tibetan languages did not yield any further cases like Zome *hih nu* 'this woman, she', which suggests that Zome is different from other Sino-Tibetan languages in the sample.

In the variety of Golin (Trans New Guinea, Chimbu; documented by Bunn 1974: 55) which is the same as in the N.T., the pronouns for third person plural *abalíni* 'she' < *abál inín* [woman REFL] and *yalíni* 'he' < *yál inín* [man REFL],[12] are not reflexive although they seem to contain reflexive markers. The variety documented by Evans et al. (2005) does not seem to have the same forms, but even this variety uses almost consistently NPs containing *abal* 'woman' or *gi* 'girl' and *yal* 'man' wherever the English translation has 'she' or 'he' as in (17) while in few cases where the reference is repeated within the same sentence there is only a bound affix for third person which does not distinguish gender.

(17) Golin (Lee 2005: 35)
      abal   i   takal no-m
      woman TOP what eat-3
      'What did she eat?'

In the closely related language Chuave *opai* 'woman' and *yai* 'man' are opposed to *opa-rom-i* 'woman-?-DIST and *ya-rom-i/day* 'man-?-DIST/PROX' (Thurman 1987) where the element *-rom-*, misleadingly glossed 'this' by Thurman, only occurs in these two non-compositional anaphoric forms.

In Southern Nambikuara *txu¹ha²* 'woman' is opposed to *ta¹ka³lxai²na²* 'the woman, she' (*in³txa²* 'man' vs. *jah¹lai²na²* 'the man, he'). Lowe (1999: 283) lists *ta¹ka³lxai²na²* and *jah¹lai²na²* as third singular feminine free pronouns although they contain the demonstrative nominal ending *-ai²na²* and the base can take many other nominal endings including demonstrative emphatic *-ai²li²* and indefinite *-su²* (*ta¹ka³lxu²su²* once in the N.T. for 'a woman').[13] Kroeker (2001: 71) gives instead the forms with definite suffix (*-a²*) as third person forms (*ta¹ka³lxa²* and *jah¹la²*). There is also a third person form *te²na²* not distinguishing gender, which is used mostly in generic contexts where gender is not specified. Nambikuara has a large set of noun classifiers including *-a³ka³lx(i³)* feminine and *-(j)ah¹lo²* masculine which are always followed by nominal endings. These classifiers are placed at the end of NPs following adjectives and relative clauses. Thus, example (18) is one noun phrase. I interpret *Ta¹ka³lx(ai²n)a²* and *jah¹l(ai²n)a²* as non-compositional complex NPs.

(18) Southern Nambikuara (Rev. 17:18)
      txu¹ha² ta¹ka³lx-a²   ī²-in¹-ta³ka³lx-ai²na²
      woman woman[ANA]-DEF see-2SG-F-DEM
      'the woman whom thou sawest'

---

[12]The N.T. also has a few occurrences of *ibalini* (*ibal* 'people').

The documentation of Golin by Evans et al. (2005) has *yal (i) inin* 'he' [man (TOP) REFL] only twice and in both cases *inin* can be interpreted reflexively.

[13]Note, however, that even the free forms for first and second person have the demonstrative and emphatic noun suffixes *txai²na²/txai²li²* 'I', *wxãi²na²/wxãi²li²* 'you', but they do not take the definite and the indefinite endings.

In Guahiban and Witotoan languages feminine anaphoric and masculine forms consist of demonstratives with classifier suffixes which can perhaps be considered opaque grammaticalized forms of non-compositional complex NPs.

Guahiban languages use demonstratives with classifier suffixes as special anaphoric forms. Guayabero differs from Cuiba and Guahibo in that the forms have become bound indexes on verbs, which suggests a higher degree of grammaticalization. Cuiba (Guahiban) has the demonstratives *ba(ra)po-wa, po-wa* [this-F, that-F] and *ba(ra)po-n, po-n* [this-M, that-M]. Machal (2000: 237) lists the proximal <*bajapowa/bajaponü*> as personal pronouns, Merchán (2000: 589) the distal *powa/pon*; neither source mentions the forms *barapowa/barapon*. In the N.T. mainly the forms *ba(ra)powa/ba(ra)pon* are used anaphorically – both longer and shorter forms very much in similar contexts – often also preposed to person names in anaphoric use. *Powa/pon* are mostly used NP-internally as a relative clause introducer. The suffixes *-wa* F and *-n* M make part of a larger set of classifier suffixes. Merchán (2000: 589) lists eight other inanimate suffixes, which do not seem to occur with demonstrative stems, however. Attributive demonstratives usually lack classifier markers. For the closely related language Guahibo, de Kondo (1985, 1: 15) gives *pówa̱* F and *pónẹ̈* M as personal pronouns (which are, however, used only in relative function in the N.T. and rare) and the forms with proximal circumfix *ma̱-je* and distal prefix *baja-* as demonstratives (de Kondo 1985: 2: 49). In the N.T. *barapova* is the dominant feminine anaphoric form; *mapovaje* is mainly used for 'this woman', a combination of demonstrative and *petiriva* woman (*bajarapova petiriva*) is attested only once; for definite uses of 'woman' the demonstrative with the feminine classifier suffix is preferred in proximal or distal form. Guayabero, a third Guahiban language, is different in that F *-(p)ow* and M *-(p)on* are used as bound indexes on verbs if there is no NP subject (they are two of at least nine third person markers, including various diminutive and neuter forms, Keels 1985: 79, 86) and have become the major anaphor in the subject relation rather than the demonstratives *japow* and *japon*. According to Keels (1985: 79), subject and object indices can be combined on the same verb, but in the N.T. the object is usually expressed by the full pronoun *japow/japon*. The tendency to reduce subject markers more often than object markers can be seen as a first trait of maturity in Guayabero anaphoric indexes.

The special anaphoric form in Huitoto Minica (Witotoan) *afengo* 'she, that woman' (masculine *afemɨe*) consists of the demonstrative *afe* 'that' and the feminine noun classifier *-ngo* (masculine *-mie*) and is opposed to the noun *ringo* 'woman' (*ɨima* 'man') (Minor et al. 1982). The demonstrative can also combine with the noun: *afe ringo* 'that woman', *bie ringo* 'this woman'. The numeral for 'one' can combine both with the noun *daa ringo* 'a woman' and the classifier *daa-ngo* 'a woman' (rare). There is also a third person singular pronoun *ie* not distinguishing gender which is predominantly used in possessive function. Huitoto Murui is structurally very similar, except that the feminine classifier has various forms (*-ño*, *-ñaiño*) and is freer in combining with different pronominal stems (*nai-ñaiño* DEM.DIST-F, *bai-ñaiño* DEM.VIS-F, *bi-ñaiño* DEM.PROX-F, *i-ñaiño* 3SG-F). However *i-ñaiño* 3SG-F is rare and never used as a pronominal form (it is rather a free form of the classifier suffix). The most dominant anaphoric form is the distal *naiñaiño* 'she; that/the woman'. It is a matter of debate how closely related Bora and Huitoto are, but as far as the domain discussed here is concerned, the structural parallels are very strong. The major difference is that the Bora classifiers are not restricted to nouns and nominalizations but have extended to indexation on verbs, which is why Bora *-lle* 'F' and Muinane *-go* 'F' are much more frequent than Huitoto Minica *-ngo*. A special property of the Bora text is that the noun for 'woman', *walle*, is very rare in the N.T.; it is used almost exclusively in generic contexts. Almost the whole range of the nominal domain is covered by the classifier suffix *-lle*. With numerals, the classifier is used: *tsáápille* 'one/a woman'. The possessive prefix for third person *i-* does not distinguish gender.

Non-compositional complex NPs tend not to be genealogically pervasive. They pop up occasionally in most different language families, except in Guahiban and Witotoan where we also encounter the most mature exemplars. It can be assumed that non-compositional complex NPs originate from transparent complex NPs when one of their parts becomes opaque or as they acquire a non-compositional meaning. However, the nominal origin is a hypothesis as far as Kiribati and the South American languages are concerned, where the etymology of the forms cannot be traced.

5.3 Reduced nominal anaphors

While the non-compositional complex NPs discussed in §5.2 are found in a wide range of language families, the reduced nominal anaphors in the sample all come from Mesoamerica and almost exclusively from one family, Otomanguean. Table 9 lists examples from six Otomanguean examples, where reduced nominal anaphors occur in subject and reflexive possessor roles.

Reduced nominal anaphors in Otomanguean are both more grammaticalized and less grammaticalized than non-compositional complex NPs discussed in §5.2. They are rather highly grammaticalized in that they quickly increase in token frequency as they extend to all grammatical relations including reflexive possessors. However, they tend to remain more restricted in use semantically. There can be

Table 9: V-subject and N-reflexive possessor in 'and she (=the girl) brought it to her mother' (Matth. 14:11) in selected Otomanguean languages with anaphoric gender

Tlalcoyalco Popoloca	*co*	*jehe*	*xan*	*joanjo* **xan**		*ngain janné*	**xan**
	and	3	child	gave **child[ANA]**		give mother	**child[ANA]**
San Miguel Mixtec	*te*	*máá-i,*	*ni*	*janchɑka-i*	*nuu nǎɑ-i*		
	and	self-YOUNG	COMPL	gave-YOUNG	to mother-YOUNG		
Tepeuxila Cuicatec	*ní*	*tá^n'ā*	*mii^n*	*ní ca'a*		*tá* *chɛɛcu* *tá*	
	and	**woman.F**	there/DEF	? COMPL:give:3		F mother F	
San Martín Itunyoso Triqui	*ni*	*naga'ui'*	*ún'*	*ra'a nni*	*ún'*		
	and	gave	F	to mother	F		
Chiquihuitlan Mazatec	*ca-sua*	**na**	*naa*	*rë*	**na**		
	COMPL-give	F	mother	POSS	F		
Amatlan Zapotec	*nu*	*lee*	**me**	*m-zaaya*	*lo xnaa*	**me**	
	and	FOC	F	COMPL-give	to mother	F	

separate forms for young humans, as in San Miguel Mixtec, and often there are separate forms for human respect and for deities.

In some languages the nominal origin of the reduced forms can clearly be traced. This is most obvious in Tlalcoyalco Popoloca (Stark 2011). Although Tlalcoyalco Popoloca has a third person pronoun *je'e* not distinguishing gender there is a large number of short forms of nouns with anaphoric use (termed "short pronouns" in Stark 2011: 3). The most common include *xii* 'man[SG]' (anaphoric *xa*) and *nchrii* 'woman[SG]' (anaphoric *nchra*). Example (19) illustrates a plain noun *janna'a* 'mother' and its corresponding anaphoric form *jan*:

(19) Tlalcoyalco Popoloca (Stark 2011: 4)
  *Naa **janna'a** jian anseen **jan*** *ixin* *rinao **jan*** *kain*
  one mother fine heart mother[ANA] because loves mother[ANA] all
  xe'en **jan.**
  children mother[ANA]
  'A mother has a good heart because she loves all her children.'

Some condensed anaphoric NPs are reminiscent of noun classifiers ("pronouns that echo a prefix"; Stark 2011: 4) and some uses are compatible with a noun class with agreement interpretation as when animals take the pronoun *ba*. However, anaphoric noun formation is productive and applies even to Spanish loanwords (*guitaarra*, anaphoric *guitarra*).

Tlalcoyalco Popoloca *nchra* 'woman[ANA]' is so specific in its meaning that it can hardly be considered a grammaticalized feminine gram. It has the distribution of a word for 'woman', and other female nouns have other anaphoric forms.

All Mixtec languages have clitic anaphoric gender markers usually following their head (following a verb for subject and object, following a relational noun for oblique and following a noun for possessor) which mostly have the phonological structure CV (see Macri 1983 for a survey of several Mixtec languages) and are much more strongly grammaticalized than Popoloca anaphoric nouns. Unlike first and second person, there are no full free forms for third person clitics, or rather the corresponding full free forms are nouns. Chalcatongo Mixtec (Macaulay 1996: 139) has the following six sets (in parentheses the nouns corresponding to the reduced nominal anaphors): masculine *-ðe* (*čàà* 'man'), feminine *-ña* (*ñá'ã* 'woman'), polite, older *-to* (*to'ò* 'older person'), supernatural *-ža* (*í'a*, *íža* 'god'), *-tɨ* animal, and *-ži* (no related noun, *žii* is 'male'). The clitics are usually not tenacious (i.c., they are dropped if there is an explicit NP), unless the NP preposed to the verb is a topic (Macaulay 1996: 140). A way to supplete the missing full forms needed for contrastive purposes is to add the clitic to the emphatic form *máá* 'self' (Macaulay 1996: 106, see also Table 4 above). The meaning of Mixtec genders is much more general than those of Tlalcoyalco Popoloca genders. But 'girl, young women' is often covered by the child gender in many Mixtec languages (see Table 9 for an example from San Miguel Mixtec). In Coatzospan Mixtec, feminine gender is of limited use since there is a general adult respect human gender *ña* that does not distinguish men and women. "[T]he use of a specifically masculine or feminine noun or pronoun to refer to an adult is usually considered disrespectful" (Small 1990: 406).

Reduced nominal anaphors or forms reminiscent of reduced nominal anaphors can also be found in Cuicatec (Bradley 1991), in Chiquihuitlan Mazatec (Capen 1996; but not in three other Mazatec languages included in the sample), and in Triqui (see Table 9).

Most Zapotec languages have some forms that are intermediate between nouns and third person pronouns. Feminine is not always a salient category though, because many Zapotec languages have a special respectful form used for both genders, especially for women by men speaking. In Texmelucan Zapotec respect is used for deity, respect human in women's speech and respect feminine in men's speech (Speck 1972: 290). Texmelucan Zapotec has masculine (*yu*, *-y*), feminine (*fiñ*, *ñi*, *-ñ*), respect (*mi*, *-m*), animal (*ma*, *bañ*) and neuter (*ñi*, *-ñ*), which occur both in fuller and more reduced forms. As shown in (20), masculine and feminine can be modified by adjectives, numerals, and demonstratives, which makes them look rather like nouns, but they can even be reduced subject indexes on verbs.

(20) Texmelucan Zapotec (Speck 1972: 32)

Benu sac **fiñ** *feñ* *nu* *gusht ni* **yu** *feñ* *ze´ lugaar ze´ nu*
if not.be **3F** young COMP please PP **3M** young that place that COMP

cyiiñ **yu, yu** *ze´ neñ* **yu** *nu* *zu* *tub* **ñi** *ca* *zi´l na tub*
POT:live **3M 3M** that hear **3M** COMP POT:stand one **3F** where only be one

ranch nu *zet, ze´ a´* **yu´** *lo* *nap* **yu-ñ**, *orze´ uz* **yu**
ranch COMP far but NEG PROG.be.in face good **3M-3F** then father **3M**

gzuu *nez* **yu** *i´ñ* **yu** **yu** *feñ* *ze´ nu* *cha-y* *cha*
POT:CAUS:stand trail **3M** child **3M 3M** young that COMP POT:go-**3M** POT:go

gwii-y **fiñ** *mñaa ze´* *ben a gyet* *lagy* **yu-ñ**.
POT:see-**3M 3F** woman that if Q POT:descend liver **3M-3F**

'If there are no young women who appeal to the young man at the place where he lives, but if he hears that there is one at some ranch or another that is far away, but if he doesn't know her well, his father will send his child, the young man, to go see if he likes her or not.'

For Mixtepec Zapotec, Hunn et al. (n.d.: 11) list fourteen categories of third person pronouns, twelve of which refer to persons and only one of which is a reduced form (C-*á*, V-*w* inanimate). Their use depends on the speaker as is quite common across Zapotec: e.g., *nîip, nîib* is used by men for a young man and by women for a man of their age or younger. Several categories refer to men and women of lesser respect. *Zhó* <zho> 'person of minor respect, group of people' is used, for instance, in the N.T. for the Samaritan (Lk. 10:33). Shifting use depending on speaker attitude is not easily understandable in terms of noun classes, but well in-line with the idea of anaphoric gender.

Gender is more strongly grammaticalized in Southern Rincón Zapotec, where the familiar forms lack a gender opposition and respectful forms distinguish masculine and feminine gender (Earl & de Earl 2006: 363). While the feminine consistently has the form *-nu* (free form *lë-nu*), the masculine form varies (free form *lë-'*): *blé'i-***në***'=nu* [COMP.saw-3SG.M.RESP=3SG.F.RESP] 'he saw her', *blé'i-nu=***në***'* [COMPL.see-3SG.F.RESP=3SG.M.RESP] 'she sees him', *cati' blé'i-***në***' **lë***'* [when COMPL. see-3SG.M.RESP 3SG.M.RESP] 'when he saw him', *rë-'-nu* [CONT.say-3SG.M.RESP-3SG.F.RESP] 'he said to her'. The allomorphs cannot be clearly ascribed to different grammatical relations, however: *-(ë)'*, *-në'*, and *-lë'* all occur in direct object function. Aside from familiar (*-bi'*), feminine respect, and masculine respect, there are also forms for animal (*-ba*) and neuter in the third person singular.

The only non-Otomanguean language to be discussed in this section is Todos Santos Mam (Mayan). Mam has a set of twelve human classifiers which are reduced forms of nouns, non-compositional forms, or pronominal nouns (common noun *txiin* 'young woman' CL *txin*; *xu7j* 'woman' CL *xu7j* 'woman', CL *xuj* 'old woman (respectfully)'; *yaab'aj* 'grandmother' CL *xhyaa7* 'old woman'; England 1983: 158). While their use in Northern and Central Mam is mostly restricted to one occurrence per clause, Todos Santos Mam has extended them even to reflexive possessors as in (21).

(21)   Todos Santos Mam (40014011)
     *[...] bix e xi'   t-k'o-'n-tl-**txin***   *t-e*
        and ? go/DIR ERG.3-SG-give-DIR-again-CL.girl POSS.3SG-to
     *t-txu-**txin**.*
     POSS.3SG-mother-CL.girl
     'and she (=the girl) brought it to her mother'

Note that both the ergative subject (A) and the reflexive possessor are indexed twice in (21), by the suffixed anaphoric gender marker and by the general third person singular prefix *t-*.

5.4 General nouns

General nouns have the form of a non-reduced noun, such as 'woman', 'girl' or 'wife', but because of their extension in use they are difficult to distinguish from pronouns. In the sample general nouns occur in four Mayan languages: Jacaltec, Akateko, Ixil Nebaj and Chuj, in Northern Khmer, and perhaps in the Austronesian language Owa.

It may seem strange at first glance that general nouns can be extracted by the algorithm since they have the same form as lexical nouns whose domains of use are applied as filters in the algorithm. The reason they can be extracted is that their use as general nouns is so pervasive that it is quite different from what the use of a lexical noun would be if everything is taken together.

The same Jacaltec form *ix* 'woman' is used all the way from the nominal low activation domain up to the top pronominal domain. *Naj* 'he (non-respected, non-kin)' is a reduced nominal anaphor (*winaj* 'man'). *Ix* 'woman; she (non-respected, non-kin)' and *naj* 'he' belong to the set of noun classifiers and are notably used with thematically salient NPs in referential anaphoric function (Craig 1986: 267; Aikhenvald 2000: 323). There are no free third person pronominal forms except classifiers. Example (22) illustrates the non-respect feminine classifier *ix* 'woman' in non-reflexive possessor and subject function and the non-respect masculine classifier *naj* 'man' as a noun classifier in the anaphoric NP with a person name:

(22) Jacaltec (Matth. 14:8)

Y-al-ni	is-mi'	ix	t-et	tato
ERG.3-say-DETRANS	POSS.3-mother	CL.woman/F	3-to	COMPL
ch-is-k'an	ix	is-wi'	naj	Juan.
INCOMPL-ERG.3-ask	CL.woman/F	POSS.3-head	CL.man/M	John

'Her mother said that she should ask for John's head.'

However, it is not the entire top activation domain that is covered by the general nouns. Reflexive possessors lack general nouns. Grinevald Craig (1977: 159), who describes the phenomenon in detail, calls this "noun classifier deletion under identity of reference". Diachronically classifiers are not deleted from reflexive possessor function; rather they have never been expanded to that domain. Note that reflexive possessor even includes co-reference with object as shown in (23) ("no constraint on the controller NP", Grinevald Craig 1977: 152).

(23) Jacaltec (Lk. 7:15)

y-a-ni-co	Comam	naj	t-et	is-mi'.
ERG.3-give-DETRANS-DIR	CL.male.deity	CL.man/M	3-to	POSS.3-mother

'and he gave himⱼ to hisⱼ mother'

The wider extension of possessive prefixes even to obligatory use with prepositions (*t-et* 3SG-to) testifies to their higher degree of maturity. Not all noun classifiers in Jacaltec (Day 1973: 125) are general or reduced nouns.

For Akateko, which is closely related to Jacaltec, see Zavala (1992). In Nebaj Ixil, which is only distantly related to Jacaltec and Akateko within Mayan, the nominal and general uses of *ixoj(e)* 'woman' and *naj* 'man' differ in that the former have a preposed determiner *u*. Thus, from the point of view of the whole NP the general forms could also be considered to be reduced forms. Chuj *'ix* 'woman' also arguably sorts here, although it is not as easily extracted as the forms in the other three Mayan languages.

In Northern Khmer (Austroasiatic) the noun used prominently in the high activation domain is เนียง *niang* 'girl' rather than ซแร็ย *srej* 'woman'. เนียง *niang* 'girl' also occurs as a term of address and it has probably become a special pronominal form by extension from deictic second person use to anaphoric third person use. Special pronominal nouns are a feature of Southeast Asia. Vietnamese has a general human special pronominal noun *người* for adult human beings, which is also used as a noun classifier, but Vietnamese lacks a general feminine anaphoric noun.

Owa (Austronesian) *kani* 'she, the woman, that woman; wife', which is just above the lower threshold for extraction, is difficult to classify. One possibility is to interpret it as a general noun with the specific meaning 'wife', but it is not clear to me whether the nominal meaning 'wife', restricted to use with following possessor, is the original one. Mellow's (2013: 273) dictionary analyzes *kani* as "pronoun", but the form is not listed in the grammar's pronoun section, where just the general third person singular form *ngaia* is given (Mellow 2013: 7). As elaborated below, there is some evidence that *kani* might contain the female person name article *ka-*, but personal pronouns can also have articles, although most pronouns are in the i-class. Owa distinguishes five different genders in noun-phrase-initial articles listed here in their cumulative forms with coordination/comitative *mi*, where there are most clearly marked and distinguished: male person names *m-o*, female person names *mi-ka*, some nouns beginning in e- (mostly kinship terms, phonologically assigned) *m-e*, location nouns, some pronouns and the word *kare* 'child' *m(-)i*, and default *mi-na* (see also Mellow 2013: 26). The male and female person name classes are extended to some common nouns, especially kinship terms, but not 'father' and 'mother', which are e-class, and to the pronoun 'who' (mostly in the male form *mo o-tai* 'and who?'). The male counterpart of *kani* 'she, the woman, that woman; wife' usually co-occurs with the male person name article *o* as *o wani* 'he, the man, that man, husband', which suggests that *kani* is a condensation of **ka-wani* (compare also *o goana* 'brother' vs. *ka goana* 'sister', *na goana* 'friend(s), sibling(s)'), especially also because all traditional Owa names have the female person article fused as a prefix *ka-* (Mellow 2013: 20). In the N.T. *kani* is i-class in some instances (object *ki kani*; *mi kani* could also be interpreted as lack of article following *mi* 'and'), perhaps in phonological analogy to *kare* 'child' or in functional analogy to pronouns. In the automatic extraction *kani* is only extracted because there is no 'wife' filter. Whatever the origin of *kani*, it is a grammatical anaphor, but it remains unclear whether of the subtype general noun or the subtype non-compositional NP, which suggests that these two subtypes are not neatly different.

There are no examples with 'mother' as a general noun, but Zome, discussed in §5.2 comes close to it.

5.5 Conclusions

The three subtypes of grammatical anaphors discussed above reflect different parameters of grammaticalization that tend to behave differently in different non-mature anaphoric gender grams as summarized in Table 10. The definitional properties, marked with asterisks in Table 10, relate to different parameters. Hence, the types are not strictly opposed to each other, so that some forms, such as Zome *tuanu* (§5.2) and Owa *kani* (§5.4) can have properties characteristic of various subtypes. In reduced nominal anaphors (§5.3) the grammaticalization of form (reduction) is most advanced, which goes together with a high text frequency, whereas generalization can be almost absent as in Tlalcoyalco Popoloca. In general nouns (§5.4), generalization is the relevant factor of grammaticalization whereas formal reduction is absent. Non-compositional complex NPs (§5.2) can have low text frequency, as Japanese *kanojo*, unlike reduced nominal anaphors. The degree of decategorialization from nouns varies greatly. In most cases, grammatical anaphors retain at least some properties of nouns.

Table 10: Different properties of the subtypes of grammatical anaphors

Subtype	Complex	Opaque	Reduced	Frequent	General
Non-compositional complex NP	+*	+	−/+	−	+
Reduced nominal anaphor	−	+	+*	+	−
General noun	−	−	−	+/−	+*

The grammaticalization of grammatical anaphors is gradual for general nouns, while there is a more categorial border for reduced nominal anaphors and for non-compositional complex NPs (for the latter to the extent they are opaque). General nouns are not distinct in form from lexical nouns and generalization must have gone a long way before the markers escape filtering by the lexical noun their form instantiates.

6 Reconciling the gram approach with the system perspective

In the previous sections I have shown that it makes perfect sense to consider feminine anaphoric singular markers as a gram type (dedicated markers with a particular grammatical meaning, prototypically instantiated in a particular functional domain), and a typology of feminine singular anaphoric gender grams in a sample of 816 languages has been presented, which abstracts away from viewing gender as a system phenomenon resting on the notions of noun class and agreement. However, it is undeniable that gender values form systems and that – even if not always canonical noun classes and canonical agreement – at least some kind of noun-class-like and agreement-like phenomena are crucial for the understanding of gender. The question thus arises as to what the gram approach can contribute to a better understanding of gender systems and of noun-class-like and of agreement-like phenomena in gender.

All gram types are alike in that they are markers instantiating a grammatical meaning X. However, beyond this common ground, different gram types may have different properties, and this is how they may become engaged in complex grammatical structures of particular kinds.

Feminine singular anaphoric gender grams are special in that they almost always are engaged in an opposition to another gram type, masculine singular anaphoric gender grams. This is no strict universal though. In §5.1 we have seen that Yale and some other Mek languages only have masculine anaphoric grams without parallel feminine anaphoric grams. However, Yale and other Mek languages are quite exotic in this respect. Oppositions are nothing strange for gram types. Most tense and aspect grams have some kind of oppositions. Perfect grams, for instance, are opposed to narrative (Dahl & Wälchli 2016: 327), but this does not make every perfect gram to be opposed to a narrative gram. Within the realm of aspect it is certainly perfective and imperfective that are most inclined to engage in a pair of oppositions and, not unexpectedly, perfective and imperfective grams are usually the core of aspect systems.

In the extraction of feminine anaphoric gender grams, I have made practical use of the opposition to anaphoric masculine by using the anaphoric masculine as a filter. I have not been able to design an implementable procedural definition of feminine gender grams that can dispense with filters. Filters are kinds of oppositions and oppositions are the building blocks of systems. Here it is important to point out that the filters that have been used are semantic domains rather than language specific structural elements. Put differently, semantics predestines the feminine anaphoric gender gram type for structural oppositions. However, feminine anaphoric gender grams are not only engaged in one kind of opposition, they are generally and necessarily engaged in two kinds of oppositions: (i) to masculine and (ii) to nominal lexical domains for the designation of female referents, the most important ones being 'woman', 'girl', 'mother', and 'daughter', and these are also indispensable as filters in the procedural definition.

What makes feminine anaphoric and masculine grams grammatical from a semantic point of view is their virtual restriction to anaphoric use. Nouns, even nouns that are typically used to designate individual items, such as *mother, sun,* and *god,* can be used non-anaphorically: *a mother, a sun, a god.* Unlike lexical nouns, anaphoric grams are not only dedicated to anaphoric use, they also tend to be more general than lexical nouns. They are almost always in a hyperonymic relation to lexical nouns (see also Seifart 2018). This can also hold when an anaphoric gram is not syntactically a pronoun as in Kiribati where *neierei* 'this woman' picks up reference to a range of female nouns. The least general feminine anaphoric grams we have encountered in Otomanguean languages (§5.3), most markedly in the extreme case of Tlalcoyalco Popoloca, where "short pronouns" are an open set.

As soon as anaphoric grams are "hyperonymic", they are noun-class-like, since they collocate with a set of hyponymic nouns. The Tlalcoyalco Popoloca "short pronoun" for animals is already reminiscent of a noun class, whereas the "short pronouns" for 'woman', 'mother', and 'girl' mainly correspond to particular lexical domains (this is why Tlalcoyalco Popoloca is filtered out in the automatic extraction). Here it is important to emphasize the difference between "noun class" and "noun-class-like". English, *she/her,* for instance, is noun-class-like. In practice, *she* and *her* tend to pick up reference to such nouns as *woman, wife, girl,* and *mother* etc., but that does not make feminine gender strictly lexical in English.

At the same time, the anaphoric character of "picking up reference" makes anaphoric grams agreement-like, which does not mean that anaphoric gender is agreement. It is important to emphasize the difference between "agreement" and "agreement-like". The agreement-like character of anaphoric grams derives from their semantic properties, it is not a syntactic process. However, due to the similarity of agreement and agreement-like anaphors, anaphoric gender grams are highly compatible with agreement phenomena and can be integrated in agreement systems, even though anaphors are essentially semantic, as they can pick up reference from the context without syntactic antecedents.

Furthermore, anaphoric grams are special in that they tend to form chains (multiple occurrences of the same gram, often in different grammatical relations and in free or bound encoding).

In the previous sections we have seen that feminine gender grams entertain close relationships to other grammatical and lexical categories. Considering the closer neighborhood of the feminine anaphoric gender gram type we may speculate about what might be possible next steps for expanding the gram approach to gender and related phenomena. Aside of masculine singular and both feminine and masculine plural and dual forms, the most promising candidates for gram types are female and male person name markers and feminine and masculine NP-markers. These have been occasionally extracted as errors in the present investigation, so it might be possible to formulate procedural definitions that focus on these phenomena specifically and view them as gram types.

7 Conclusions

Grammatical gender is usually considered to be highly complex and it is traditionally defined in terms of agreement and noun classes, which are both complex phenomena. Thus, one way to explore whether gender might be simpler than commonly believed is to try to approach it without reference to the notions of agreement and noun classes. In this paper feminine anaphoric gender has been approached by way of a procedural definition which, when implemented in a computer program, extracts feminine gender markers from a parallel text corpus. This procedural definition does very well without any reference to agreement or noun classes suggesting that these notions are entirely dispensable at least for one important core domain of gender. It was also found that many anaphoric gender markers have high cue validity which suggests that they are not particularly complex. The notions the procedural definition relies on are those of functional domain and gram type which have proven to be useful for many other grammatical category types, suggesting that gender may be less puzzling among grammatical categories than commonly believed.

While there is a long research tradition of investigating particularly complex gender phenomena, less effort has been devoted to uncover simple gender. Thus, it has gone largely unnoticed in typology that there are many languages with non-pronominal anaphoric gender markers which are intermediate between full noun phrases and pronouns (grammatical anaphors). Non-pronominal anaphoric gender is less stable diachronically than pronominal anaphoric gender and can sometimes be proven to be very young. Gender in grammatical anaphors is therefore important for understanding how gender can develop diachronically. However, the low complexity of anaphoric gender also invites for deliberate manipulation as in the case of the Uduk New Testament where a feminine gender was created by missionaries.

Unlike non-pronominal anaphoric gender, pronominal gender is usually highly mature. This is reflected in the widespread suppletion and neutralization according to grammatical relations in pronominal gender, which are features of complexity synchronically even in languages such as English and Belize Kriol English where gender is commonly believed to be simple.

Finally, this paper has shown that parallel texts are highly useful for the study of grammatical gender. They help shift the focus of attention to the most functional aspects of gender and away from more idiosyncratic properties. Parallel texts also show that gender is not an isolated phenomenon, but has often very similar functions as, for instance, light nouns. Hence, to uncover the functions of grammatical gender it may be useful to consider it together with other linguistic categories, including non-grammaticalized ones, which have similar functions. Grammatical anaphors which are often not recognized as gender markers in the descriptive literature can effectively be recognized as incipient gender markers in parallel texts.

Acknowledgments

I would like to thank Francesca Di Garbo, Östen Dahl, Andrej Kibrik, Robert Östling, Martin Haspelmath, Bruno Olsson and Annemarie Verkerk for many useful suggestions. While writing this paper I was partly funded by the Swedish Research Council (*Vetenskapsrådet*, 421–2011–1444).

Special abbreviations

The following abbreviations are not found in the Leipzig Glossing Rules:

A	transitive subject	MED	medial
ACT	active	O	(direct) object
AGR	agreement	N	noun
ANA	anaphoric	P	monotransitive object
CL	classifier	Poss1	inalienable or
COMP	complementizer		non-reflexive possessor
COMPL	completive aspect	Poss2	alienable or reflexive
CONT	continuative aspect	POT	potential aspect
CONNECT	connective	PP	preposition
DETRANS	detransitive	PRO	pronominal
DIR	directional	R	recipient/indirect object
EMPH	emphatic	RESP	respect
INCOMPL	incompletive aspect	RPOSS	reflexive possessive
IO	indirect object	s/S	intransitive subject

SEQ	sequential		V	verb/vowel
SPEC	specific noun		YOUNG	gender for children or
SS	same subject			young people

References

Aikhenvald, Alexandra Y. 2000. *Classifiers: A typology of noun categorization devices*. Oxford: Oxford University Press.

Anderson, Neil. 1989. Folopa existential verbs. In Karl Franklin (ed.), *Studies in componential analysis*, 83–105. Ukarumpa: Summer Institute of Linguistics.

Andronov, Michail S. 1996. *A grammar of the Malayalam language in historical treatment* (Beiträge zur Kenntnis Südasiatischer Sprachen und Literaturen 1). Wiesbaden: Harrassowitz.

Andronov, Michail S. 2003. *A comparative grammar of the Dravidian languages*. Munich: Lincom.

Årsjö, Britten. 1999. *Words in Ama*. Uppsala: Uppsala University. (MA thesis).

Audring, Jenny. 2009. Gender assignment and gender agreement: Evidence from pronominal gender languages. *Morphology* 18(2). 93–116.

Benton, Joseph. B. 1975. *Glossed text in Chichicapan Zapotec*. SIL Language & Culture Archives. oai:sil.org:59688.

Betts, La Vera. 1981. *Dicionário parintintín-português português-parintintín*. Brasília: Summer Institute of Linguistics.

Bosch, Peter. 1988. Representing and accessing focussed referents. *Language and Cognitive Processes* 3(3). 207–232.

Bradley, David P. 1991. A preliminary syntactic sketch of Concepción Pápalo Cuicatec. In C. Henry Bradley & Barbara E. Hollenbach (eds.), *Studies in the syntax of Mixtecan languages*, vol. 3, 409–506. Dallas: Summer Institute of Linguistics.

Bunn, Gordon. 1974. *Golin grammar* (Workpapers in Papua New Guinea 5). Ukarumpa: Summer Institute of Linguistics.

Bybee, Joan & Östen Dahl. 1989. The creation of tense and aspect systems in the languages of the world. *Studies in Language* 13(1). 51–103.

Capen, Carole Jamieson. 1996. *Diccionario mazateco de Chiquihuitlán Oaxaca*. Tucson: Instituto Lingüístico de Verano.

Contini-Morava, Ellen & Eve Danziger. 2018. Non-canonical gender in Mopan Maya. In Sebastian Fedden, Jenny Audring & Greville Corbett (eds.), *Non-canonical gender systems*, 129–146. Oxford: Oxford University Press.

Corbett, Greville G. 1991. *Gender*. Cambridge: Cambridge University Press.

Corbett, Greville G. 2006. *Agreement.* Cambridge: Cambridge University Press.

Corbett, Greville G. & Sebastian Fedden. 2016. Canonical gender. *Journal of Linguistics* 52(3). 495–531.

Craig, Colette. 1986. Jacaltec noun classifiers: A study in language and culture. In Colette Craig (ed.), *Noun classes and categorization,* 263–293. Amsterdam: John Benjamins.

Croft, William. 2003. *Typology and universals.* 2nd edn. Cambridge: Cambridge University Press.

Dahl, Östen. 2000. Animacy and the notion of semantic gender. In Barbara Unterbeck (ed.), *Gender in grammar and cognition.* Vol. 1: *Animacy and the notion of semantic gender: Approaches to gender,* 99–115. Berlin: Mouton de Gruyter.

Dahl, Östen. 2004. *The growth and maintenance of linguistic complexity.* Amsterdam: John Benjamins.

Dahl, Östen & Bernhard Wälchli. 2016. Perfects and iamitives: Two gram types in one grammatical space. *Letras de Hoje* 51. 325–348.

Day, Christopher. 1973. *The Jacaltec language* (Language Science Monographs 12). Bloomington: Indiana University Press.

de Kondo, Riena W. 1985. *El guahibo hablado: Gramática pedagógica del guahibo, lengua de la orinoquía colombiana.* Vol. 1–2. Lomalinda: Instituto Lingüístico de Verano.

Dobson, Rose M. 2005. *Aspectos da língua Kayabí.* 2nd edn. Brasília: Summer Institute of Linguistics.

Earl, Roberto & Catalina de Earl. 2006. *Diccionario zapoteco del Rincón.* SIL Language & Culture Archives. http://www.sil.org/resources/archives/58129.

England, Nora C. 1983. *A grammar of Mam, a Mayan language* (Texas Linguistics Series). Austin: University of Texas Press.

Evans, Nicholas, Jutta Besold, Hywel Stoakes & Alan Lee (eds.). 2005. *Materials on Golin: Grammar, texts and dictionary.* Melbourne: Department of Linguistics & Applied Linguistics, University of Melbourne.

Fedden, Sebastian. 2007. *A grammar of Mian: A Papuan language of New Guinea.* University of Melbourne. (Doctoral dissertation).

Fung, Pascale & Kenneth Ward Church. 1994. K-vec: A new approach for aligning parallel texts. In *Proceedings of the 15th conference on computational linguistics,* vol. 2, 1096–1102. Kyoto.

Garland, Roger & Susan Garland. 1975. A grammar sketch of Mountain Koiali. In Tom E. Dutton (ed.), *Studies in languages of Central and South-East Papua* (Pacific Linguistics C 29), 413–470. Canberra: Australian National University.

Givón, Talmy. 1981. Typology and functional domains. *Studies in Language* 5(2). 163–193.

Grinevald Craig, Colette. 1977. *The structure of Jacaltec.* Austin: University of Texas Press.

Haspelmath, Martin. 1997. *Indefinite pronouns.* Oxford: Oxford University Press.

Haspelmath, Martin. 1999. Why is grammaticalization irreversible? *Linguistics* 37(6). 1040–1068.

Heeschen, Volker. 1992. *A dictionary of the Yale (Kosarek) language (with sketch grammar and English index).* Berlin: Reimer.

Hintikka, Jaakko & Jack Kulas. 1985. *Anaphora and definite descriptions: Two applications of game-theoretical semantics.* Dordrecht: Reidel.

Hockett, Charles F. 1958. *A course in modern linguistics.* New York: Macmillan.

Hunn, Eugene S., Akesha Baron & Roger Reeck. n.d. Un esbozo de la gramática del zapoteco de los pueblos Mixtepec, Oaxaca, México.

Ishiyama, Osamu. 2008. *Diachronic perspectives on personal pronouns in Japanese.* State University of New York at Buffalo. (Doctoral dissertation).

Jung, Ingrid. 2008. *Gramática del páez o nasa yuwe: Descripción de una lengua indígena de Colombia* (Languages of the World: Materials 469). Munich: LINCOM.

Keels, Jack. 1985. Guayabero: Phonology and morphophonemics. In Ruth M. Brend (ed.), *From phonology to discourse: Studies in six Colombian languages* (Language Data, Amerindian Series 9), 57–87. Dallas: Summer institute of linguistics.

Kibrik, Andrej A. 2011. *Reference in discourse.* Oxford: Oxford University Press.

Killian, Don. 2019. Gender in Uduk. In Francesca Di Garbo, Bruno Olsson & Bernhard Wälchli (eds.), *Grammatical gender and linguistic complexity: Volume I: General issues and specific studies*, 147–168. Berlin: Language Science Press. DOI:10.5281/zenodo.3462764

Kroeker, Menno H. 2001. *Gramática descritiva da língua nambikuara.* Cuiabá: Sociedade Internacional de Lingüística.

Lee, Alan. 2005. Verb morphology. In Nicholas Evans, Jutta Besold, Hywel Stoakes & Alan Lee (eds.), *Materials on Golin: Grammar, texts and dictionary*, 31–53. Melbourne: Department of Linguistics & Applied Linguistics, the University of Melbourne.

Levinson, Stephen C. 1987. Pragmatics and the grammar of anaphora. *Journal of Linguistics* 23(2). 379–434.

Lock, Arjen. 2011. *Abau grammar* (Data Papers on Papua New Guinea Languages 57). Ukarumpa: SIL-PNG Academic Publications.

Lowe, Ivan. 1999. Nambiquara. In Robert M. W. Dixon & Alexandra Y. Aikhenvald (eds.), *The Amazonian languages* (Cambridge Language Surveys), 269–292. Cambridge: Cambridge University Press.

Lowing, Richard & Aretta Lowing. 1975. *Awa dictionary* (Pacific Linguistics C 30). Canberra: The Australian National University.

Luraghi, Silvia. 2011. The origin of the Proto-Indo-European gender system: Typological considerations. *Folia Linguistica* 45(2). 435–464.

Macaulay, Monica. 1996. *A grammar of Chalcatongo Mixtec* (University of California Publications in Linguistics 127). Berkeley: University of California Press.

Machal, Marcelo. 2000. Cuiba (Jiwi). In Esteban Emilio Mosonyi & Jorge Carlos Mosonyi (eds.), *Manual de lenguas indígenas de Venezuela* (Serie Origenes), 224–265. Caracas: Fundación Bigott.

Macri, Martha J. 1983. The noun class systems in Mixtec. In Alice Schlichter, Wallace L. Chafe & Leanne Hinton (eds.), *Studies in Mesoamerican linguistics*, vol. 4, 291–306. Survey of California & Other Indian Languages.

Mellow, Greg. 2013. *A dictionary of Owa: A language of the Solomon Islands.* Berlin: De Gruyter Mouton.

Merchán, Hernanda Ana Joaquina. 2000. Breve presentación de lengua cuiba (variante maibén). In María Stella González de Pérez & María Luisa Rodríguez de Montes (eds.), *Lenguas indígenas de Colombia: Una visión descriptiva*, 585–598. Santafé de Bogotá: Instituto Caro y Cuervo.

Milles, Karin. 2011. Feminist language planning in Sweden. *Current Issues in Language Planning* 12(1). 21–33.

Minor, Eugene E., Dorothy A. Minor & Stephen H. Levinsohn. 1982. *Gramática pedagógica huitoto.* Bogotá: Ministerio de Gobierno.

Mous, Maarten. 1992. *A grammar of Iraqw.* Rijksuniversiteit Leiden. (Doctoral dissertation).

Nichols, Johanna. 1992. *Linguistic diversity in space and time.* Chicago: University of Chicago Press.

Paradis, Carole. 1983. *Description phonologique du guéré.* Abidjan: Université d'Abidjan, Institut de linguistique appliquée.

Payne, Doris L. 1985. *Aspects of the grammar of Yagua: A typological perspective.* University of California, Los Angeles. (Doctoral dissertation).

Plank, Frans & Wolfgang Schellinger. 1997. The uneven distribution of genders over numbers: Greenberg Nos. 37 and 45. *Linguistic Typology* 1(1). 53–101.

Sándalo, Filomena. 1997. *A grammar of Kadiwéu with special reference to the polysynthesis parameter* (MIT Occasional Papers in Linguistics 11). Cambridge: Massachusetts Institute of Technology.

Sanders, Arden G. & Joy Sanders. 1994. Kamasau (Wand Tuan) grammar: Morpheme to discourse. Unpublished document.

Sarvasy, Hannah Sacha. 2014. *A grammar of Nungon: A Papuan language of the Morobe Province, Papua New Guinea.* Cairns: James Cook University. (Doctoral dissertation).

Scott, Graham. 1989. *Fore dictionary* (Pacific Linguistics C 62). Canberra: The Australian National University.

Seifart, Frank. 2018. The semantic reduction of the noun universe and the diachrony of nominal classification. In William B. McGregor & Søren Wichmann (eds.), *The diachrony of classification systems*, 9–32. Amsterdam: John Benjamins.

Siewierska, Anna. 2005. Alignment of verbal person marking. In Martin Haspelmath, Matthew S. Dryer, David Gil & Bernard Comrie (eds.), *The world atlas of language structures*, 406–409. Oxford: Oxford University Press.

Small, Priscilla C. 1990. A syntactic sketch of Coatzospan Mixtec. In C. Henry Bradley & Barbara E. Hollenbach (eds.), *Studies in the syntax of Mixtecan languages 2* (Summer Institute of Linguistics and the University of Texas at Arlington Publications in Linguistics 90), 261–479. Dallas: Summer Institute of Linguistics & the University of Texas at Arlington.

Speck, Charles H. 1972. *The study of Zapotec language and culture.* SIL Language & Culture Archives. oai:sil.org:59283.

Stark, Sharon L. 2011. *Ngigua (Popoloca) pronouns* (SIL-Mexico Branch Electronic Working Papers 12). SIL.

Thurman, Robert C. 1987. *The form and function of Chuave clauses.* SIL Language & Culture Archives.

Tomasello, Michael. 2003. *Constructing a language: A usage-based theory of language acquisition.* Cambridge: Harvard University Press.

Trudgill, Peter. 2011. *Sociolinguistic typology: Social determinants of linguistic complexity.* New York: Oxford University Press.

Trussel, Stephen. 1979. *Kiribati (Gilbertese): Grammar handbook* (Peace Corps: Language Handbook Series). Brattleboro VY School for International Training. http://www.trussel.com/f_kir.htm#Gil.

Vafaeian, Ghazaleh. 2013. Typology of nominal and adjectival suppletion. *Sprachtypologie und Universalienforschung STUF* 66(2). 112–140.

van Driem, Georg. 1987. *A grammar of Limbu.* Berlin: Mouton de Gruyter.

Vincent, Lois E. 2010. *Tairora-English dictionary.* Wycliffe Papua New Guinea Branch.

Wälchli, Bernhard. 2018. The rise of gender in Nalca (Mek, Tanah Papua): The drift towards the canonical gender attractor. In Sebastian Fedden, Jenny Audring & Greville G. Corbett (eds.), *Non-canonical gender systems*, 68–99. Oxford: Oxford University Press.

Wälchli, Bernhard. 2019. The feminine anaphoric gender gram, incipient gender marking, maturity, and extracting anaphoric gender markers from parallel texts. In Francesca Di Garbo, Bruno Olsson & Bernhard Wälchli (eds.), *Grammatical gender and linguistic complexity: Volume II: World-wide comparative studies*, 61–131. Berlin: Language Science Press. DOI:10.5281/zenodo.3462780

Wälchli, Bernhard & Michael Cysouw. 2012. Lexical typology through similarity semantics: Toward a semantic map of motion verbs. *Linguistics* 50(3). 671–710.

Wälchli, Bernhard & Francesca Di Garbo. 2019. The dynamics of gender complexity. In Francesca Di Garbo, Bruno Olsson & Bernhard Wälchli (eds.), *Grammatical gender and linguistic complexity: Volume II: World-wide comparative studies*, 201–364. Berlin: Language Science Press. DOI:10.5281/zenodo.3462784

Zavala, Roberto. 1992. *El kanjobal de San Miguel Acatán* (Colección Lingüística Indígena 6). Mexico City: Universidad Nacional Autonoma de México, Instituto de Investigaciones Filológicas, Seminario de Lenguas Indígenas.

Appendix A: Languages in the sample with anaphoric gender and the automatic extraction from parallel texts

>x<: morphemes, #: word boundary

I. Languages with a non-mature feminine anaphoric gender gram [59 languages]

Table 11: Languages with a mature feminine anaphoric gender gram

Language	Extracted form	Remarks
Esperanto (epo)	sxi, >#sxi<	*sxi-n* ACC, *sxi-a*-AGR POSS
Malayalam (mal)	avall, avallodu, avalle	*avall* NOM, *avall-e* ACC, *avall-odu* INST
Japanese (jpn)	kanojo	*kano-jo* PROX-woman
Wè Northern (wob)	υ, υa'	*υ-a(')* POSS, object *υ(')*, *-'* intransitivizer, also after object pronouns (Paradis 1983)
Uduk (udu) [artificial variety of Bible translation]	yim, ayim	*yim* 'female friend' (noun)
Zome (zom)	tuanu	*tua-nu* DIST-mother, *hih nu* PROX mother
Naga, Angami (njm)	{süpfü}	*sü-pfü* DEM-F
Khmer, Northern (kxm)	เนียง	*niang* young female person
Kiribati (gil)	neierei, nei	*neierei* F.DIST, *Nei* female person name marker
Owa (stn)	{kani}	*kani* 'that woman; wife'
Naasioi (nas)	teni, tenie	*teni-e* ERG
Ankave (aak)	i'	*i'* F
Chuave (cjv)	oparomi	*opa-rom-i* woman-?-DIST
Golin (gvf)	abalini	*abal-ini* woman-REFL
Oksapmin (opm)	uh, uhnong, uhe, {urhe}	*uh* F, *oh* M, *uh-nong* ACC, *uh-e* GEN, *urhe* REFL.GEN (M *orhe*)
Chuj (cac)		*'ix* woman, noun classifier for woman
Jacaltec (jac)	ix	*ix* woman, noun classifier for woman
Akateko (knj)	ix	*ix* woman, noun classifier for woman
Ixil, Nebaj (ixi)	ixoj	*ixoj(e)* woman
Mam, Todos Santos (mvj)	>xuj#<	*xuj* 'old woman', *txin* young woman, *te-* to
Cuicatec, Teutila (cut)		*tạhn* full form, *te* reduced form

Language	Extracted form	Remarks
Cuicatec, Tepeuxila (cux)	tá, tá^n'ā, ta	*tá^n'ā* full form, *tá/ta* reduced form
Mixtec, Atatlahuca (mib)	ña	*ña* F
Mixtec, Ocotepec (mie)	ña	*ña* F
Mixtec, San Miguel (mig)	>-ñ<	*-ña* F
Mixtec, Peñoles (mil)	>-a^n#<	*-a^n* F
Mixtec, Pinotepa Nacional (mio)	ña	*ña* F
Mixtec, Southern Puebla (mit)		*-nè, -ne, -né, -ñá, -ña* F
Mixtec, Coatzospan (miz)		*tún* F (girls), adult respect *ña*
Mixtec, San Juan Colorado (mjc)	ña	*ña* F
Mixtec, Silacayoapan (mks)	ñá	*ñá* F
Mixtec, Yosondúa (mpm)	ña	*ña* F
Mixtec, Tezoatlan (mxb)	>án#<	*án, -án* F
Mixtec, Jamiltepec (mxt)	ña	*ña* F
Mixtec, Diuxi-Tilantongo (xtd)	>-ña<	*-ña,* F *nuu* 'to'
Triqui, Copala (trc)	no'	*no'* F
Triqui, San Martin Itunyoso (trq)	ún'	*ún'* F
Popoloca, San Marcos Tlalcoyalco (pls)		*nčha* 'woman[ANA]', *xan* 'child, child[ANA]'
Mazatec, Chiquihuitlan (maq)	na	*na* F
Zapotec, Ozoltepec (zao)		*nzaa* girl
Zapotec, Quioquitani Quieri (ztq)	me	*me* F
Zapotec, Rincon (zar)	>nu<	*-nu* F

Language	Extracted form	Remarks
Zapotec, Southern Rincon (zsr)	>nu<	*-nu* F
Zapotec, Santo Domingo Albarradas (zas)		*-m* F
Zapotec, Lachixio (zpl)	>nchu#<	*-nchu* F
Zapotec, Amatlan (zpo)	me	*me* F, *xaa* HONOR
Zapotec, Texmelucan (zpz)		*fiñ, ñi, -ñ* F, *mi, -m* RESPECT
Cuiba (cui)	barapowa	*barapowa, bapowa*
Guahibo (guh)	bajarapova	*bajarapova, barapova*
Guayabero (guo)	>ow#<	V-*ow*, N-*ow*, free form *japow*
Kaingang (kgp)	fi	*fi*
Rikbaktsa (rkb)	atatsa, >tatsa#<	*atatsa* 3SG.F, *-tatsa* F
Nambikuara, Southern (nab)	ta¹ka³lxai²na²	*ta¹ka³lx-ai²na²* F-DEM, *ta¹ka³lx-a²* F-DEF
Kayabi (kyz)	ẽẽ, {kĩã}	*ẽẽ* F (M speaker) M, *kyna* F (F speaker), M '*ẽ* (M speaker), and *kĩã* M (F speaker)
Tenharim (pah)	hẽa	*hẽa* F
Muinane (bmr)	diigoco, >go<	*-go* F
Bora (boa)	>lle<	*-lle* 'F'
Huitoto, Minica (hto)	afengo, {aféngona}	*afe-ngo* DIST-F
Huitoto Murui (huu)	>ñaiñ<	*nai-ñaiño* DIST-F, *bi-ñaiño* PROX-F

II. Languages with a mature feminine anaphoric gender gram [128 languages]

See Table 12.

Table 12: Languages with a mature feminine anaphoric gender gram

Language	Extracted form	A	S	P	R	Poss1	Poss2
Kannada (kan)	>alu#<, ake, akege	V-aḷu, avaḷu, ake(yu)	"	avaḷannu, ākeyannu	avaḷige, ākege	avaḷa, ākeya	-
Tamil (tam)	>oɾaḷ#<, அவள், {அவளது}	avaḷ, V-aḷ	"	avaḷ-ai	avaḷ-iṭum/ukku	avaḷ-attu	-
Albanian, Gheg (aln)	ajo, saj	ajo	"	-	-	saj	-
Latvian (lav)	viņai, [-usi]	viņa, tā, (V-usi, V-dama)	"	ja	viņai	viņas	-
Lithuanian (lit)	ji, jai, ją, {>usi#<}	ji, (V-usi, V-dama)	"	ją	jai	jos	-
Breton (bre)	he, dezhi	hi	"	anezhi	dezhi	he	-
Welsh (cym)	hi, iddi, [wrthi]	hi, hithau, iddi	"	hi, hithau	wrthi, iddi	ei+ASP	-
Norwegian, Bokmål (nor)	hun, henne	hon	"	henne	"	hennes	-
Danish (dan)	hun, hende	hon	"	hende	"	hendes	-
Swedish (swe)	hon, henne	hon	"	henne	"	hennes	-
Faroese (fao)	hon, hana, henni	hon	"	henni	hana	hennara	-
Icelandic (isl)	hún, hana, hennar, [henni]	hún	"	henni	hana	hennar	-
English (eng)	her, she	she	"	her	"	"	-
English, Middle (enm)	hir, sche	sche	"	hir	hir	"	-
German, Standard (deu)	sie, ihr	sie	"	"	ihr	ihr-AGR	-
Alemannic (swg)	sie	sie	"	"	ihr	ihr-AGR	-
Afrikaans (afr)	haar	sy	"	haar	"	"	-
Dutch (nld)	haar, zij	zij	"	haar	"	"	-
Saxon, Low (nds)	äa, see, äare	see	"	äa	"	äar-AGR	-
Greek (ell)	της, [αυτήν]	εκείνη	"	την	της	της	-
Greek, Koine (grc)	αυτης, αυτη, αυτην	η, εκεινη, V-ουσα	"	αυτην	αυτη	αυτης	-
Panjabi, Eastern (pan)			V-i	V-i	-	-	-
Romani, Sinte (rmo)	joi, li, late, lat, {lakro}	joi, koi	V-i	lat	late	lakr-AGR	-
Romani, Vlax (rmy)	lake, woi, la	woi	woi, V-i	la	lake	lak-AGR	-
Hindi (hin)			V-i	(V-i)	-	-	-
Marathi (mar)	तिला, ती, तिनं	tine, ti / V-i / -	ti / V-i	ti-lā / V-i / -	ti-cyā		-
Kurdish, Northern (kmr)	wê	wê		wê	wê		-
Latin (lat)	eam	illa, quæ, hæc	"	eam, illam	-	"	-
Romanian (rmo)	ea	ea	"	(o)	ei	"	-
Italian (ita)	ella	ella, essa	"	la	le	"	-
French (fre)	elle	elle	"	la	-	"	-
Catalan-Valencian-Balear (cat)	ella	ella	"	la	-	-	-
Spanish (spa)	ella	ella	"	la	-	-	-
Portuguese (por)	ela	ela	"	a	-	-	-
Russian (rus)	>ла#<, она, её, ей	она, V-ла	"	её	её	её	-
Ukrainian (ukr)	вона, >ла#<, її, неї, [їй]	вона, V-ла	"	її	їй	її	-
Bulgarian (bul)	й, тя, я	тя	"	я	й		-
Slavonic, Old Church (chu)	ей, ю, ея	она	"	ю	ей	ея	-
Croatian (hrv)	joj, ona, {>la#<}	ona, V-la	"	je	joj	joj	-
Czech (ces)	>la#<, jí, {ji, jeji}	ona, V-la	"	ji	jí	její	-
Polish (pol)	>la#<, jej, ja, [ona]	ona, V-la	"	jej	jej	její	-
Avar (ava)	гьей, гьелда, гьелъ	гьель	"	-	гьелда	гьелгьул	-
Chechen (che)		гьей / й-V / -		- / -j-V	-	-	-

Language	Extracted form	A	S	P	R	Poss1	Poss2
Tachelhit (shi)	nttat	t-V, nttat	"	=tt	-	-	-
Kabyle (kab)	{>#tt e<}	te-V	"	=t	-	-	-
Tamasheq (taq)	>tăt<	tă-V	"	=tăt	-	-	N-ta
Bana (bcw)	ngɔta, nza	ghanza / -	V-ta, ghanza	-	ngɔ-ta	N-ta, N nza	-
Gude (gde)	ki, kya	kya		ka ki	-	N-ta	-
Dangaléat (daa)	>iit<, >ti#<, ta	ta / te-V			V-t	(not mother)	-
Hausa (hau)	ta, >ta#<	ta V, ita		V ta	mata	N-ta	-
Mwaghavul (sur)	wura, fira, nwura, [yi]	wura	"	wura	nwura/wura	fira	-
Somali (som)	>eed<, [>say#<]	t-V, V-tay/say, iyada		various	-	N-eed	-
Iraqw (irk)		V-eer, V-VC, V-VVn			-	-	-
Dawro (dwr)	>aaddu#<, izo, izi, iza	iza, V-aaddu		izo	izo	-	-
Gamo (gmv)	>adus#<, izis, {izo}	iza, V-us		izo	izos, izo	izi	-
Gofa (gof)	>u#<, [iyo]	iya, V-asu		iyo	iikko	-	-
Wolaytta (wal)	>su#<, o	a, V-aasu		o	iyyo, o	i	-
Kafa (kbr)	>an#<, >qqa#<	V-an		-?	-?	-?	-
Maltese (mlt)	>ha#<	V-et	"	?-h/-tu	V-ha	N-ha	-
Amharic (amh)	>äčɔ<, >wama#<, >atɔ#<	V-äč		V-at	V-ha	N-wa	-
Jur Modo (bex)	lăko, 'bèni	lăko		ni	zi-ni	bèni	N-ni
Belize Kriol English (bex)	shee	shee	"	her	-	-	-
Hawaiian Pidgin English (hwc)	her, she	she	"	her	-	-	-
Burarra (bvr)	achila, >#ji<, >ny-<	-	jiny(u)-V	jiny(u)-V	achila	acha	-
Galela (gbi)	muna, ami, >#mo<, >mi<, munaka	mo-V, muna	"	-mi-V	munaka	ami	-
Tabaru (tby)	>#mo<, muna, gumuna, 'ami, mi, ngo	mo-V, (gu)muna ?		-mi-V	munaka	ami	-
Tobelo (tbl)	munanga, >#mo<, >#ami<, ngo	mo-V, munanga		-mi-V	munangika	ami	-
Rotokas (roo)	oira, >aev<, oirare	V-o-, (oira)		oira	oira-re	oira	-
Qaqet (byx)	qia, qi, ara, ki, kia	qia		qi	o-	-	-
Kuot (kto)	>ieng#<, iang	i-	m-V / mo / r-V	V-ieng	r- /rai	ieng	-
Yawa (yva)	mo	m-V / mo	"	r-V	"	ama	-
Ama (amm)	isoki	-	V-so-	V-so-	V-so-	-	-
Ambulas (abt)	léku, lat, >lé<	lé	"	lerét	?	léku	-
Iatmul (ian)	>li#<, lila	li, V-li		li	li	-	-
Kwoma (kmo)	siina, sii, siiti, [siita]	sii		siina	"	siiti	-
Kwanga (kwj)	tini	ti		tini		ti	-
Mende (sim)	si, simu, sirin	si(mu)		sirin		sihi	-
Yessan-Mayo (yss)	te, tene, teri	te		tene			-
Abau (aau)	hoko, hoke, sokwe	hok(we)		hoke/ke	-we	hoko	-
Sepik Iwam (iws)	saeya, saiir	saeya		saiir			-
Mufian (aoj)	>kw<, ako'w, >'w<, >ko<	kw(a)-V / ako'w		V-'w	-akw	N-kw/'w	-
Bumbita Arapesh (aon)	okwok, kwape, nakripok, >#k<	kw(a)-V, okwok		V-k	okwudok	okwokwik	-
Bukiyip (ape)	>ok<, >#kw<, >#ku<	kw(a)-V, okwok		V-k	-p-ok	okwokwik	-
Kamasau (kms)	wuso	w-V, <q>		stem inflection	-w	wung	-
Au (avt)	hire, >iwe#<, >#we<, {>iye#<}	hire / w-V		V-p	-we	AGR-ire	-
Olo (ong)	ne, >ene<	ne / n-V		V-(e)ne		pene	-
Yongom (yon)	yu, >uun<, >eent#<	V-een / yu(-mbed)	V-een / yu	V-end- / yu		yu	-
Bimin (bhl)	>u#<, >koum<, >ui#<, ulo, um, {wangei}	V-((e))u		wa-/w-/we-/um-/wam-V		um-	-
Faiwal (fai)	?	?		u-V		-ulum	-
Mian (mpt)	o, baabonea	V--o		wa-V	V-bo	o	-
Ngalum (szb)	u, ua, >du<, >ukhe<, uede	?		?	?	u	-

Language	Extracted form	A	S	P	R	Poss1	Poss2
Telefol (tlf)	>lu#<, tal	V-mulu		u-V	"	umi	"
Bine (bon)	jojige	-	Co-	"	"	-	-
Paumari (pad)	>ˀihi#<	-	V-'i-hi	"	"	-	-
Garifuna (cab)	>#t<	t-V	"	-, tugía	t-un	t-N	"
Wayuu (guc)	shia, sümüin	s/sh-V	"	shia	sü-müin	sü-N	"
Piapoco (pio)	>#u<, úa	u-V	"	úa	u-li	ú-N	"
Yucuna (ycn)	>#ru<, >#ro<	ru-V, V-yo ?		rucá	ro-jló	ru-N	"
Ignaciano (ign)	>#su<	-, su-V, esu		esu	?	su-N	"
Trinitario (trn)	esu, >#s<	-, mue-V		esu		sa-N	"
Asheninka Pajonal (cjo)	oa, >#o<, >aro<	o-V	"	V-ro	V-ro	Ø-N	"
Ashaninka (cni)		o-/Ø-V	"	V-ro	V-ro	Ø-N	"
Caquinte (cot)		o-/Ø-V	"	V-ro	V-ro	o-/Ø-N	"
Asheninka, Pichis (cpu)		o-/Ø-V	"	V-ro	V-ro	o-/Ø-N	"
Machiguenga (mcb)	irorori	o-/Ø-V, iroro(ri)	"	V-ro	V-ro	o-/Ø-N	"
Nomatsiguenga (not)		o-/po-/Ø-V	"	V-ro	V-ro	o-/Ø-N	"
Apurinã (apu)	oa, >#o<, >aro<	o-/Ø-V	"	V-ro	V-ro	o-/Ø-N	"
Yine (pib)	>#t<, wala, {chinro}	t-V, wala	"	V-Lo	V-Lo	t-N	"
Chiquitano (cax)	imo	V-ti		imo	imo	ni-N-x-x-Ø/ IRREG	"
Cacua (cbv)	mi, mit, caántdih, miih	mít, caántboó	mi	mi, caántdih	caántdih	mi	-
Yagua (yad)	>#nanu<	nan- / -	nan- / naada / -	naada / -	nan- / -	-	?
Ticuna (tca)	>#ngi <, >#iya<	?	?	?	?	?	"
Tsimane (cas)	mo', {je}	mo'	?	V-' / mo'	V-'	mo'	"
Cubeo (cub)	ðre, >jaco<, ö, öi	V-(a)co /V- / ð	"	ð-re		ji-N	"
Waimaha (bao)	coo, >go#<, coore	V-Co / cô	"	cô-re		cô	"
Tuyuca (tue)	igo, igore, >go<, >mo#<, >po#<,	V-go/mo / igo	"	coo-re		coo	"
Desano (des)	igo, igore, >yupo#<, >mo#<, >deo#<, {igoya}	V-go/mo / igo	"	igo-re		igo	"
Siriano (sri)	so, sore, >mo#<	V-Co / so	"	igo-re		igo	"
Barasana Eduria (bsn)	iso, isore, >yijo#<	V-Co / iso	"	so-re		so	"
Macuna (myy)	cô, >upo#<, >ñupô#<, >mo#<	V-Co / V- / cô	"	isore		iso	"
Carapana (cbc)	co, >upo#<, côre	V-wô / co	"	cô		cô	"
Tatuyo (tav)	>icoro<		"	(côre) co V		co	"
Piratapuyo (pir)	koô, koôre, >ko#<, >go<, niiiwô, >mo#<	ticoro / V-?	"	ticoro-re	co	ticoro	"
Tucano (tuo)	>mo#<, repao, repao'te, >si'ko#<, {chikona}	V-Co / koô	"	koô-re		koô	"
Koreguaje (coe)	>go<, {>si'co<}	V-mo / repao	"	repao-'te		repao	-
Siona (snn)		V-Co / bago	"	bago-ni		bago	-
Chipaya (cap)	na, >incha#<, nãza, {nãkiś, nãki}	V-incha / V- / nãki	na	"	nãkiś	nãza, ź-N	"

III. Languages with feminine person name markers, wrongly extracted [6 languages]

Language	Extracted form	Remarks
Uab Meto (aoz)	{bi}	*bi* N, with feminine person names
Iraya (iry)	bayi	*bayi* N, with feminine person names
Huave (huv)	{müm}	*müm* 'mother' used with feminine person names
Satere-Mawe (mav)	mana	*mana* N, with feminine person names
Nalca (nlc)	gera	*ge-ra* F-TOP, also with feminine person names

IV. Languages with wrongly extracted demonstrative/definite forms for 'woman' [9 languages]

Language	Extracted form	Remarks
Sabaot (spy)	:cheebyoosyaanaa	*cheebyoosya* 'woman'
Endo (enb)	cheepyoosoonoonēē	*cheepyooso* 'woman'
Mazatec, Ayautla (vmy)	chjunbiu	*chjun* 'woman'
Djambarrpuyngu (djr)	{miyalknhany}	*miyalk* 'woman'
Safeyoka/Wojokeso (apz)	a'musi	*a'mu* 'girl'
Fasu (faa)	{hinamoamo}	*hinamo* 'woman', *-amo* "referent subject"
Umbu-Ungu (ubu)	ambomo	*ambo* 'woman', *-mo* 'the'
South Tairora (omw)	nraakyeva	*nraakye* 'woman', *-ve* DEM
Rawa (rwo)	barega	*bare* 'woman', *-ga* DEF.SG

V. Wrongly extracted forms for 'woman' [1 language]

Language	Extracted form	Remarks
Awa (awb)	{iní, mi}	*iní* 'woman[ABS]'; *mi* 'that'

VI. Wrongly extracted demonstratives and articles (without or with gender) [5 languages]

Language	Extracted form	Remarks
Mountain Koiali (kpx)	{keu}	*ke-u* [that-SUBJECT]
Folopa (ppo)	kale	'the'
Fore (for)	kana	*kana-* 'this mentioned one, the aforementioned'
Kadiweu (kbc)	naɡajo	
Mocoví (moc)	aso'maxare	*a-so'-maxare* F-GOING-PRO

VII. Wrongly extracted general third person forms [2 languages]

Language	Extracted form	Remarks
Zapotec, Miahuatlan (zam)	{xa'}	*xa'* 3 M/F, *mza'* girl
Zapotec, Chichicapan (zpv)	bi	*bi* 3 M/F, *ba* 3.RESPECT

VIII. Entirely wrongly extracted forms

Language	Extracted form	Remarks
Buglere (sab)	{chku}	*chku* arrive.PFV

Appendix B: Languages in the sample without any feminine anaphoric gender gram [629 languages]

Phyla or families and ISO 639-3 codes Languages with only wrongly extracted forms (Appendix A III-VII) are included and underlined.

Creoles and artificial languages

Creoles (12/14): acf, bis, djk, hat, kri, mbf, mfe, pis, rop, srm, srn, tpi

Artificial languages (0/1)

Eurasia

Altaic (10/10): aze, bxr, kaa, kaz, krc, kum, tat, tur, uzb, xal

Basque (1/1): eus

Dravidian (0/3)

Indo-European (10/50): awa, hif, hns, hye, mai, ory, oss, pes, prs, tgk

North Caucasian (1/3): tab

Korean (1/1): kor

Japanese (0/1)

Uralic (7/7): est, fin, hun, kpv, mhr, myv, sme

Africa

Afro-Asiatic (7/24): gnd, hig, meq, mfh, mfi, mif, pbi

Niger-Congo (126/127): acd, adj, ann, anv, atg, bam, bav, bba, bfd, bib, bim, biv, blh, box, bqc, bss, bud, bwq, bwu, cce, cko, cme, csk, cwt, dgi, dnj, dop, dts, dug, dyo, dyu, ewe, fal, fub, fuv, gbo, gej, gkn, gng, gog, gur, gux, guz, hag, hay, heh, izr, jbu, kao, kbp, ken, kez, kik, kin, kki, kkj, kma, kng, knk, kno, kub, kus, las, ldi, lee, lef, lem, lia, maw, mcu, mda, men, mfq, mnf, mnk, mos, muh, myk, mzk, mzm, mzw, ncu, ndz, neb, nfr, nhu, nim, nko, nnw, nso, ntr, nya, nyf, nyy, old, ozm, pkb, rim, sbd, sig, sil, sld, sna, soy, spp, sus, swh, swk, tbz, tem, thk, tik, toh, tum, vag, wmw, wol, vun, xho, xon, xrb, xsm, yal, yam, yor, zul

Nilo-Saharan (14/15): avu, bjv, dik, dip, dje, enb, kyq, lwo, mfz, mur, nus, shk, spy, udu

East Asia and Southeast Asia

> Austroasiatic (2/3): bru, vie
>
> Austronesian (132/134): aai, ace, adz, agn, aia, akb, alp, aoz, ban, bbc, bcx, bdd, bhp, bku, blz, bnp, bpr, bps, btd, bth, bto, bts, btx, bug, buk, bzh, ceb, cha, dad, dob, dww, fij, gfk, gor, haw, hil, hla, hnn, hot, hvn, iba, ifb, ifk, ifu, ilo, ind, iry, itv, jav, jvn, kbm, khz, kne, krj, kud, kwf, kzf, lcl, lcm, leu, lew, lid, ljp, mad, mah, mak, mbb, mbt, mee, mek, mhy, min, mlg, mmo, mmx, mna, mnb, mog, mox, mpx, mqj, mri, msm, mta, mva, mwc, mvp, mwv, nak, nia, nij, npy, nsn, pag, pam, plt, pmf, ppk, prf, pse, ptp, ptu, pwg, rai, rro, sas, sbl, sda, sgb, sgz, smk, sml, smo, snc, sps, sso, sun, swp, sxn, tbc, tbo, tgl, tpz, tte, twu, urk, uvl, war, wuv, xkl, xsi, zlm
>
> Hmong-Mien (1/1): mww
>
> Sino-Tibetan (22/24): acn, ahk, bgr, cfm, cmn, cnh, cnk, cnw, csy, ctd, czt, grt, hlt, kac, kyu, lhu, lif, mhx, mwq, nan, pww, taj

New Guinea and Australia

> Australian (3/4): djr, gvn, wim
>
> East Bird's Head (3/3): mej, mnx, mtj
>
> East Papuan (2/6): sua, yle
>
> Geelvink Bay (1/2): bvz
>
> Karkar-Yuri (1/1): yuj
>
> Arai (Left May) (0/1)
>
> Sepik-Ramu (2/10): msy, sny
>
> Torricelli (0/6)
>
> Trans-New Guinea (79/90): aey, agd, agg, amn, aom, apz, aso, auy, awb, bbr, bef, big, bjr, bmh, bmu, boj, byr, dah, ded, dgz, faa, for, gaw, gdn, ghs, hui, imo, iou, ipi, kgf, kjs, kmh, knv, kpf, kpr, kpw, kpx, ksr, kue, kyc, kyg, mcq, med, mhl, mlh, mlp, mps, mux, naf, nca, nii, nlc, nop, nou, nvm, okv, omv, ppo, rwo, sll, snp, soq, ssd, ssx, sue, tim, ubu, waj, wer, wiu, wnc, wnu, wsk, xla, yby, yli, yut, yuw, zia,
>
> West Papuan (0/3)

North and Mesoamerica

>   Algic (1/1): ojs

>   Eskimo-Aleut (2/2): esk, kal

>   Hokan (1/1): chd

>   Huavean (1/1): huv

>   Iroquoian (1/1): chr

>   Mayan (23/28): acc, acr, agu, caa, cak, chf, cke, ctu, hus, hva, ixl, kek, lac, mam, mop, mvc, poh, toj, ttc, tzj, tzo, tzt, usp

>   Mixe-Zoque (8/8): mco, mir, mto, mxp, mxq, mzl, poi, zos

>   Na-Dene (3/3): caf, crx, gwi

>   Otomanguean (36/63): amu, azg, cco, chq, chz, cle, cnl, cnt, cpa, cso, ctp, cuc, cya, maa, mau, maz, ote, otm, otn, otq, vmy, zab, zac, zad, zai, zam, zat, zav, zaw, zpc, zpi, zpm, zpq, zpu, zpv, zty

>   Totonacan (5/5): tku, toc, too, top, tos

>   Uto-Aztecan (18/18): azz, crn, hch, ncj, ncl, ngu, nhe, nhg, nhi, nhw, npl, ntp, ood, pao, stp, tac, tar, yaq

South America

>   Arauan (0/1)

>   Araucanian (1/1): arn

>   Arawakan (3/17): ame, pab, ter

>   Aymaran (1/1): ayr

>   Barbacoan (4/4): cbi, cof, gum, kwi

>   Cahuapanan (1/1): cbt

>   Camsa (1/1): kbh

>   Candoshi-Shapra (1/1): cbu

>   Carib (7/7): ake, apy, bkq, car, hix, pbc, way

>   Chibchan (8/8): bzd, cjp, con, gym, kvn, sab, tfr, tuf

>   Choco (3/3): emp, noa, sja

>   Guahiban (0/3)

>   Harakmbet (1/1): amr

Jivaroan (3/3): acu, hub, jiv

Macro-Ge (4/7): apn, mbl, txu, xav

Maku (1/2): mbj

Mataco-Guaicuru (2/3): kbc, mzh,

Nambiquaran (0/1)

Paez (1/1): pbb

Panoan (7/7): cao, cbr, cbs, kaq, mcd, shp, yaa

Peba-Yaguan (0/1)

Quechuan (25/25): inb, qub, quf, qug, quh, qul, qup, quw, quy, quz, qvc, qve, qvh, qwh, qvi, qvm, qvn, qvo, qvs, qvw, qvz, qxh, qxn, qxo, qxr

Tacanan (3/3): cav, ese, tna

Ticuna (0/1)

Tol (1/1): jic

Tsimane (0/1)

Tucanoan (0/13)

Tupi (10/12): gnw, gug, gui, gun, gyr, kgk, mav, myu, srq, urb

Urarina (1/1): ura,

Uru-Chipaya (0/1)

Waorani (1/1): auc

Witotoan (0/4)

Yanomam (1/1): wca,

Yuracare (1/1): yuz

Zaparoan (1/1): arl

Chapter 4

On the distribution and complexity of gender and numeral classifiers

Kaius Sinnemäki

University of Helsinki

This paper surveys the occurrence of gender and numeral classifiers in the languages of the world and evaluates statistically whether there is a complexity trade-off between these two linguistic patterns. Complexity is measured as overt coding of the pattern in a language, an approach that has been shown earlier to provide a reliable first estimate for possible trade-offs between typological variables. The data come from a genealogically and areally stratified sample of 360 languages. The relationship between gender and numeral classifiers in this data was researched by constructing Generalized Linear Mixed Models. According to the results a significant inverse relationship occurs between the variables independently of genealogical affiliation and geographical areas. The distributions are explained functionally by economy, that is, the tendency to avoid using multiple patterns in the same functional domain.

Keywords: gender, numeral classifiers, language universals, complexity trade-off, description-based complexity, mixed effects modeling, economy, distinctness, language contact.

1 Introduction

In the past 35 years there has been an increasing amount of cross-linguistic research on gender, and more broadly on noun classification (e.g., Dixon 1982; Corbett 1991; Aikhenvald 2000; Audring 2009; Kilarski 2013; Di Garbo 2014). However, much of this research has been qualitative and not many researchers have focused on noun classification from a statistical typological perspective.

Earlier work on noun classification systems suggested that languages might not have both classifiers and gender as separate categories (e.g., Dixon 1982).

Kaius Sinnemäki. 2019. On the distribution and complexity of gender and numeral classifiers. In Francesca Di Garbo, Bruno Olsson & Bernhard Wälchli (eds.), *Grammatical gender and linguistic complexity: Volume II: World-wide comparative studies*, 133–200. Berlin: Language Science Press. DOI:10.5281/zenodo.3462782

Later work has revisited these claims and more languages have been found which use both gender and classifier systems (e.g., Aikhenvald 2000). For instance, Palikur (Arawakan) has gender and additionally five different classifier systems, including numeral classifiers. The examples in (1) illustrate the co-occurrence of gender and numeral classifiers in noun phrases.

(1) Palikur (Arawakan; Aikhenvald & Green 2011: 411)

    a. *paha-p-ru*   *tino*
        one-NUM.CLF:ANIM-F woman

        'one woman'

    b. *paha-p-ri*   *awayg*
        one-NUM.CLF:ANIM-M man

        'one man'

However, while the co-occurrence of both gender and classifiers is possible in languages, it is relatively rare for a language to have both types of noun classification (Corbett 2013). It seems therefore possible that classifiers and gender occur in roughly complementary distribution across languages. If so, such complementary distribution would amount to evidence on a possible complexity trade-off in the domain of noun classification. While complexity trade-offs have been researched and discussed recently in various grammatical domains, the results have mostly proven to be negative: trade-offs occur far less often than has been thought earlier (e.g., Shosted 2006; Miestamo 2009; Nichols 2009; Sinnemäki 2008; 2011; 2014a,c).

My aim in this paper is to research the relationship between gender and classifiers to find out whether they interact in particular ways across languages in terms of complexity. For the purpose of this paper I sample numeral classifiers because they are the most common type of classifier system in the languages of the world (Aikhenvald 2000: Ch. 4). Data is drawn from a genealogically and areally stratified sample of 360 languages. The data comes partly from the databases of Gil (2013), Corbett (2013), and Nichols (1992) and is supplemented by my own extensive data collection and analysis. To assess statistical tendencies in the data I use generalized mixed effects modeling (see Jaeger et al. 2011 and Bentz & Winter 2013 for recent applications to typological data). Mixed effects modeling provides a way of modeling the effects of genealogical inheritance and areal diffusion as random factors and so doing justice to the observation (e.g. Nichols 2003) that rates of language change may vary across language families and geographical areas.

The rest of the paper is organized as follows. §2 presents my approach to language complexity. §3 describes the analysis of gender and numeral classifiers (§3.1), the statistical methods (§3.2), and the data (§3.3). §4 presents preliminary results (§4.1) as well as the results of the main hypothesis testing (§4.2). §5 discusses explanations and §6 concludes the paper. Appendix 1 and 2 at the end of the paper provide additional information about statistical modeling and about the data and sources.

2 On language complexity

A critical question in language complexity research is what approach should be taken to complexity.[1] In recent cross-linguistic research language complexity has been approached in basically two different ways that are briefly introduced here.

First, it has been argued, most notably by Kusters (2003; 2008), that the notion of complexity should be tied with language usage, hence usage complexity, or difficulty. In this approach the complexity of different structures, such as the agreement classes of gender, are based on their on-line difficulty in language use or possibly on the time it takes to acquire them in first or second language acquisition (Kusters 2003).

Second, many scholars have argued instead that complexity should be kept separate from difficulty (Dahl 2004; Miestamo 2008; Sinnemäki 2011). In this approach, the formulation of complexity is based on the number and variety of the parts of the grammatical description and the interactions between these parts. The main reason for this delimitation of complexity from difficulty is that usage complexity inevitably raises the context-sensitive question "difficult to whom" and the different user-based criteria do not necessarily lead to the same complexity measurement. The speaker, the hearer, the first language acquirer, and the second language learner do not all find the same linguistic patterns easy or difficult (see Miestamo 2008; Sinnemäki 2011 for details). As in my earlier writings in this area, I maintain that a typological approach to complexity is most feasibly done from this perspective, which I call description-based complexity (Sinnemäki 2014b). Description-based complexity should also be applied to local domains instead of attempting to measure overall complexity of language (Sinnemäki 2011).

There are different pros and cons in these two approaches and I refer the reader to Miestamo (2008), Kusters (2008), and Sinnemäki (2011) for earlier debate. One

---

[1]This section is largely based on Sinnemäki (2014b: Section 9.2).

further issue, however, deserves mention here. It has been pointed out that these approaches have not been well-connected to complex systems theory and have rather focused on the enumeration of complexity in terms of constituents or rules (Andrason 2014). What actually makes a system complex in complex systems theory is not the number of parts or rules but a number of different aspects of the system: that it is open, non-linear, emergent and adaptive, to name a few (see Kretzschmar 2015 for further details). My aim in this paper is not the enumeration of complexity as such but to use the notion of linguistic complexity to evaluate what is a central goal in language typology, namely, to find the ways in which linguistic patterns may interact with each other (Bickel 2007). This interaction may be seen as an adaptive process of different linguistic patterns (see §5). In this sense, my approach combines aspects of the complex systems theory with description-based complexity.

Although my aim here is not the enumeration of complexity, it is necessary to say a few words about the basis of measuring complexity. I follow here Gell-Mann and Lloyd's (2004: 387) proposal that complexity be defined as effective complexity of an entity, that is, "the length of a highly compressed description of its regularities" (see also Dahl 2004 for an application of effective complexity to linguistics). Effective complexity is a way of focusing on the set of regularities of a system, that is, on the minimal description of its structure. In other words, complexity may be measured as the compressibility of the system's regularities. When applied to grammatical systems this means that the more patterns a linguistic entity contains, the longer (or the less compressible) description is required to capture these regularities, and hence, the greater is the complexity of that system.

As an example, compare the numeral classifier system in Pnar (Khasian; Austroasiatic) with that of Thai (Kam-Tai; Tai-Kadai). Pnar has three general classifiers used when enumerating count nouns: *ŋut* for classifying people (2a), *tḷli* for classifying non-humans (2b), and *ta* for classifying weeks (2c) (Ring 2015: 124–125, 361–362).[2]

(2) Pnar (Khasian; Austroasiatic; Ring 2015: 362)

    a. *ki=ni*   *tɔʔ ki* *san ŋut*   *ki=kʰɔn jɔŋ ka*
        PL=PROX be 3PL five CLF.HUM PL=child GEN 3SG.F
        'these were her five children'

---

[2]Note that Pnar has gender as well, while Thai does not (see Appendix 2).

b. ɛm ŋɲiaw tḷli   ki=kʰlo kṇtaŋ   ha ʥwaj
   have seven CLF.NHUM PL=forest special/holy LOC Jowai

'there are seven sacred groves here in Jowai'

c. ar ta   jaw ha-den ka tʰɔʔ ja tɛ ka
   two CLF.WK week LOC-back 3SG.F write BEN NVIS 3SG.F

'after two weeks (we) sign it (the agreement)'

A grammatical description of Pnar numeral classifiers and their usage takes no more than a couple of pages including examples. In Thai, however, there are about 80–90 numeral classifiers (although some of them are archaic) (Iwasaki & Ingkaphirom 2005: 74) and much research has been done on their semantics, structure, and acquisition (e.g., Hundius & Kölver 1983; Gandour et al. 1984; Inglis 2003). In addition, numeral classifiers in Thai express a range of functions, namely, individuation, singulative, definiteness, and contrast (Bisang 2009). This kind of interaction between different linguistic systems certainly increases description length, and thus also complexity (Sinnemäki 2014b). In Pnar, no evidence has yet been presented of this type of complexity in the system of numeral classifiers (Ring 2015: 360–368).

From the viewpoint of complexity, it is thus clear that the system of numeral classifiers requires greater length – and is consequently more complex – in Thai as compared to Pnar. Effective complexity can thus be applied to estimating grammatical complexity yet without using compression algorithms but instead linguists' descriptive tools, as in the discussion of numeral classifiers in Pnar and Thai above (see also Miestamo 2008; Sinnemäki 2014b).

In Sinnemäki (2011) I argued that the notion of complexity can be broken down into various types (see also Good 2012). In Sinnemäki (2014b) I further suggested that focusing on the number of parts, or even the sheer presence vs. absence of a linguistic pattern in a language, is a feasible starting point for studying whether particular typological variables may interact with one another in terms of complexity. In that paper I showed that there is an inverse statistical relationship between rigid word order and case marking in core argument marking. In this paper I apply the same approach to the domain of noun classification. My hypothesis is that to determine whether there is a complexity trade-off between gender and numeral classifiers, the most productive place to start from is to analyze the presence vs. absence of these variables in a language.[3] I call this approach

---

[3]Note that when focusing on overt coding the differences between usage complexity and the description-based complexity practically disappear: compared to the presence of a distinction the absence of a distinction is both simpler from the perspective of grammar description and easier from the perspective of the user as well (Sinnemäki 2009: 127–128).

"complexity as overt coding" (Sinnemäki 2014b). I assume that overt coding is more complex than its absence, since overt coding requires a longer minimal description than its absence. To count the number of genders or numeral classifiers would demand more effort and data, but the result might not add much new information concerning their interaction compared to binomial coding of the variables.

3 Method and data

3.1 Definitions

Gender and classifiers are generally considered different types of noun classification. A typical way has been to treat them as opposite ideal types on a continuum, gender being the more grammaticalized, more rule-governed and less semantic in nature, while classifiers have been considered as less grammaticalized, less governed by grammatical rules, and more semantic in nature (Dixon 1982; Serzisko 1982; Corbett 1991; Aikhenvald 2000; Passer 2016b). However, intermediate cases have always existed which are difficult to classify as either classifier or gender systems. Languages such as Miraña (Boran) are particularly striking examples, their noun classification system showing properties of both gender and classifier systems (Seifart 2005). For these reasons the dichotomy between gender and classifiers has been rejected especially in the canonical typology approach (e.g., Corbett & Fedden 2016), which rather uses a variety of factors for defining one canonical type and then determines the ways in which for instance gender and classifiers may conform to or deviate from this canonical type according to various factors. However, rejecting the typological distinction between gender and classifiers may be unnecessary, since intermediate cases can be analyzed as deviations from prototypical ideals for gender and classifiers, the prototypes being different endpoints of the same continuum of grammaticalization (Passer 2016b). In this view, languages like Miraña can be analyzed as similar to the noun class systems in Niger-Congo languages albeit at an earlier or intermediate stage of grammaticalization (Grinevald & Seifart 2004).

For the current purpose I treat gender and numeral classifiers as two separate linguistic patterns and analyze the borderline instances on a case by case basis. As for gender I follow the general tendency in the literature to define it as an agreement class, that is, a language has a gender system only if agreement on other syntactic constituents reflects nouns of different types (e.g., Corbett 1991: 4–5; Nichols 1992: 124–125). This formulation subsumes under gender two broad types of phenomena. First, it includes the Romance-type gender, as in (3), that has only a handful of distinctions in the gender system, most commonly masculine (3a) and feminine (3b).

(3) French (Romance; Indo-European; author)

   a. *un   garçon*
       INDF.M boy

       'a boy'

   b. *une   fille*
       INDF.F girl

       'a girl'

Second, gender here also includes systems of noun classification found in many African and some Papuan languages, often called noun classes. Noun class systems are here defined as a subtype of gender systems that have four or more agreement classes instead of the common two or three based on sex or and/or animacy. These systems may have more than a dozen agreement classes, not always clearly motivated semantically. In Mufian (Torricelli), for instance, different suffixes on the noun and adjective as well as prefixes on the verb reflect the noun class of different types, as in Table 1 (Alungum et al. 1978). Different sets of affixes exist for singular and plural.

Table 1: A set of noun classes in Mufian (Alungum et al. 1978: 93)

Class	Example (sg)	Gloss	noun suffix	adjective suffix	verb prefix
1	*bol*	'pig'	-*l*	-*si*	*l-*
2	*éngél*	'name'	-*ngél*	-*ngili*	*g-*
3	*nalof*	'tooth'	-*f*	-*fi*	*f-*
5	*batéwin*	'child'	-*n*	-*ni*	*n-*
...					
17	*kos*	'course'	-*s*	-*si*	*s-*

A language may also express gender-like distinctions on just the noun but not on any other constituent. For instance, in Petalcingo Tzeltal (Mayan) some nouns may be marked with different noun prefixes, *x-* and *j-* which appear in complementary distribution and if used for person's names, *x-* is used for women's names (4a) and *j-* for men's names (4b) (Shklovsky 2005: 20).[4] Because there is no agreement marking on syntactic constituents reflecting the different noun types, this pattern in Petalcingo Tzeltal and similar instances in other languages (whether the markers are affixes, clitics, or isolating formatives) were not counted as examples of grammatical gender and were left outside of this research.

(4)   Petalcingo Tzeltal (Mayan; Shklovsky 2005: 20)

    a. *me x-Martaj-e   ch^a way   nax   x-k^ot*
        DET x-Marta-CLT two   sleep only ICMP-arrive

       'Marta only stayed two nights.'

    b. *ta   s-pat   s-nah   te   j-Laloj-e*
        PREP POSS:3-back POSS:3-house DET j-Lalo-CLT

       'At the back of Lalo's house.'

As for numeral classifiers, I define them following Gil (2013), which is my main data source on numeral classifiers. Almost all languages use additional linguistic items to assist enumerating nouns of low countability, as in English *two **pints** of beer, three **glasses** of water,* or *five **pounds** of sand*. These additional items are often called mensural classifiers or measure words (e.g., Grinevald 2002: 260–261; Her 2012). Many languages, however, use such additional linguistic items even when enumerating nouns of high countability, such as books, fingers, bananas or the like. Such items are classified as numeral classifiers if they occur with countable nouns when enumerated using numerals. The function of the classifier is then to "divide the inventory of count nouns into semantic classes, each of which is associated with a different classifier" (Gil 2013). An example is given below from Mandarin (Sinitic; Sino-Tibetan). The enumeration of the noun *rén* 'person' in (5a) is obligatorily accompanied by an additional item *ge*, while the enumeration of the noun *fēijī* 'airplane' is accompanied by another additional item, namely *jià* (5b) (Li & Thompson 1981: 104). These items are here called numeral classifiers.[5] Quite typically these items can also occur in constructions with demonstratives, as in (5c), but it seems to be somewhat rarer for them to occur with other constituents (see Aikhenvald 2000: 206–220).

---

[4]The marker *-e* at the end of many noun phrases in Petalcingo Tzeltal is a determiner enclitic (Shklovsky 2012: 127) that apparently participates in marking the definiteness of the noun phrase. Glossing (e.g., of the *x-* and *j-* prefixes) follows the sources. Note that in the source the hat symbol (^) marks the preceding consonant as an ejective.

[5]Her (2012) proposes a mathematical criterion to distinguish numeral classifiers from measure words. A numeral classifier necessarily has value 1, while a measure word does not.

(5) Mandarin (Sinitic; Sino-Tibetan; Li & Thompson 1981: 104–105)

    a. *sān ge rén*
       three CLF person

       'three people'

    b. *wǔ jià fēijī*
       five CLF airplane

       'five airplanes'

    c. *nèi tiáo niú*
       that CLF cow

       'that cow'

Two further issues need to be mentioned in analyzing numeral classifier languages (see Gil 2013). First, not all languages with numeral classifiers use them with all numerals. For instance, the numeral classifiers in Pnar are used only for numerals above one, as can be seen by comparing the examples in (2) above and (6) below (Ring 2015: 108).

(6) Pnar (Khasian; Austroasiatic; Ring 2015: 108)
    ɛm jap ka=wi ka=kṇtʰaj tṃmɛn
    have die F=one F=female old

    'there is one old woman (who) died'

In Abau (Upper Sepik; Sepik) numeral classifiers are used only for a small set of lower numerals from one to three (Lock 2011: 56–57).[6] These kinds of limitations do not make a difference to the analysis here: all languages in which numeral classifiers are limited to low numerals or do not occur with low numerals are analyzed as having a numeral classifier system.

Second, in some languages the set of classifiers is very limited. Marathi (Indo-European), for instance, has one numeral classifier *jaṇ*, which is used with nouns denoting persons. A similar system occurs in some Hindi dialects and in Nepali (Indic; Indo-European; Emeneau 1956: 11–12). Since these languages have only one numeral classifier, they were not analyzed as having a numeral classifier system. In this I follow, for instance, Nichols (1992) and the *Autotyp* database (Bickel et al. 2017).

Following Nichols (1992: 129, 132) and Corbett (1991: 4–5) my main criterion for distinguishing numeral classifiers and gender from one another was agreement. The defining criterion for gender is that gender classes are marked by agreement

---

[6]Note that higher numerals do not exist in Abau at all.

on other syntactic constituents – and importantly that gender marking is not limited to numeral constructions, whereas classifiers are not marked by agreement and numeral classifiers in particular may exist only in conjunction with numerals. However, there are some borderline instances that may be in transition or there may be multiple systems of noun classification in a language. Three such borderline examples are discussed briefly.

The noun classification system in Luganda (Bantoid; Niger-Congo) has more than 12 classes and some are based on shape, much like in typical numeral classifier systems. The classes are further marked on numerals, as in numeral classifier systems. However, "there is agreement, multiple marking in the sentence, marking elsewhere than on or with numerals, and sufficient lexical fixation to justify regarding these systems as noun classes" (Nichols 1992: 136). This system therefore has many properties of gender but also some properties of typical numeral classifier systems. Following Nichols (1992) and Corbett (2013), I analyze such systems as gender.

Some languages use a single set of class markers for multiple purposes. These systems have been accordingly analyzed in different ways. For instance, according to Derbyshire & Payne (1990: 261) Mundurukú (Tupian) has verb-incorporated classifiers, as in (7a). However, in their definition of verb-incorporated classifiers they specifically state that such classifiers "do not occur in noun phrases and do not express concord in the generally accepted sense" (Derbyshire & Payne 1990: 245). These classifiers in Mundurukú occur, nevertheless, also on numerals (7b) and demonstratives (7c), wherefore Munduruku has been classified as a multiple classifier system (Aikhenvald 2000; Passer 2016a). Derbyshire & Payne (1990) consider this system as verb-incorporated because of its historical origins, but because these classifiers in Munduruku are used in environments outside the predicate as well, it is less desirable to analyze this system primarily as a verb-incorporated classifier system. Passer (2016a) analyzes these classifiers originally as nominal classifiers that have spread to an additional host, namely to predicates. Since it is not uncommon for numeral classifiers to attach to demonstratives as well, as in Mandarin (see example 5c), it seems justified to analyze Munduruku as a numeral classifier language.[7]

(7)   Munduruku (Tupian; Derbyshire & Payne 1990: 261)

    a. *bekitkit ako-ba   o'-su-ba-dobuxik*
       child   banana-CLF 3-REF-CLF-find

      'The child found the banana.'

---

[7]Gil (2013) analyzes Munduruku as not having numeral classifiers based on data from Derbyshire & Payne (1990). Here I follow the more recent data and analyses of Passer (2016a).

b. *xepxep-'a wexik-'a*
   two-CLF potato-CLF

   'two potatoes'

c. *ija-ba   ako-ba*
   this-CLF banana-CLF

   'this banana'

Yagua (Pega-Yaguan) is similar to Mundurukú in that it has a single set of classifiers that can be used in multiple environments, namely, with predicates, demonstratives and numerals (Payne 2007). However, these classifiers also attach to nominal modifiers, such as adjectives and have sometimes been thought of as marking agreement (Aikhenvald 2000: 217). In line with these analyses, Yagua has sometimes been analyzed as having both numeral classifiers and gender (Nichols 1992: 136–137). However, according to Payne (2007) these constructions do not exhibit syntactic agreement, at best semantic agreement "between nouns that are in apposition" as in example (8a). Example (8b) illustrates a construction with a numeral and the same classifier -*nu* as in (8a). For this reason, I analyze Yagua as having numeral classifiers (following Gil 2013) but no gender (following Payne 2007).

(8)   Yagua (Peba-Yaguan; Payne 2007: 461)

   a. *wánu wásíyqa-nu   háámu-kii-nu*
      man fat-CLF.ANIM.SG big-long-CLF.ANIM.SG

      'big fat man' (or 'man, a fat animate one, a big long animate one')

   b. *Hásiy sa=wichá-ásiy   ádnq-nu-huy   kiiwá.*
      there 3SG.ANIM=be-PROX1 two-CLF.ANIM.SG-two fish

      'There were two fish.'

The noun classification systems in the sample languages were analyzed following the above criteria. My main hypothesis, based on earlier literature, is that there is an inverse relationship between gender and numeral classifiers. Some preliminary indication for this relationship was provided by Sinnemäki (2014c: 188–189) on the basis of the data in the *World atlas of language structures* (henceforth, *WALS*, Dryer & Haspelmath 2013), but here this hypothesis is approached with a much larger sample and with more rigorous methods (using generalized mixed effects modeling instead of ordinal correlation). The null hypothesis is that there is no relationship between gender and numeral classifiers. In the next section I describe the statistical methods used in this research.

3.2 On statistical methods

One of the central interests in language typology is the interactions among linguistic patterns across languages (Bickel 2007). However, the distribution of linguistic patterns, such as gender or numeral classifiers, can be affected by a number of factors that may be difficult to delineate from one another. It has been customary in language typology to treat such factors, especially inheritance and borrowing, as nuisance factors. Their confounding effects on the typological distributions have been tried to eliminate primarily through (stratified) sampling to draw conclusions on the actual relationship between the structural factors, usually with association or correlation tests. In recent years more advanced multifactorial methods have been applied to typological data as well which allow genealogical and areal factors to be built as factors into the models themselves so that their effects can be tested rather than simply controlled away. Genealogical and areal factors have been modeled as fixed effects using generalized linear modeling (e.g., Cysouw 2010; Sinnemäki 2010) or as random factors using mixed effects modeling (e.g., Bentz & Winter 2013).

Yet it has proven difficult to model particularly the effect of genealogical inheritance on typological distributions because of the large number of small families and language isolates. Isolates are not genealogically related to any known languages. In effect they are language families with just one member; yet such families may constitute roughly one third of the world's language families (Campbell 2016). This high proportion of isolates means that if language family is built into the research design, the number of parameters in the model increases so much that reliable estimates are no longer possible (cf. Sinnemäki 2010: 877–880). Four approaches have been used in recent research to address this issue.

In one of the earlier approaches genealogical inheritance is controlled by restricting the way datapoints are counted. One such way is to group languages into genera – genealogical groups of languages that have approximately the same time-depth to the branches of Indo-European – and then count as datapoints not languages but different values in genera (Dryer 1992; 2000). If three languages are sampled from the same genus, all without gender, then this genus contributes one datapoint to the calculations. If four languages are sampled from another genus in which all but one have gender, then this genus contributes two datapoints (= one with gender and one without gender). While this method is rather crude, it enables the controlling of genealogical inheritance to some degree but it may also leave out important variation at some other level of taxonomic classification than the one chosen (see Bickel 2008).

Another, more recent approach evaluates whether a particular linguistic pattern is statistically preferred in languages within families (Bickel 2013). In case of a binomial variable (e.g., presence vs. absence of gender) a family is either biased towards presence of gender, towards absence of gender, or they are indifferent: in any event a family always contributes just one datapoint to the calculations. This method is related to the controlled genealogical sampling of Dryer (1992; 2000) but it tests biases within families statistically. However, biases can only be estimated when the families are large enough, usually requiring at least five sampled languages from a family. The preferences in large families can then be extrapolated to smaller families and isolates (see Bickel 2013 for details). While this method enables a dynamic approach to language universals, it requires very large samples – the typical samples have contained roughly 400 languages (e.g., Bickel 2013; Bickel et al. 2014).

Linguists have also adapted methods from biology to model correlated changes in genealogical lineages. In this approach lexical data is first used to build a family tree and to estimate branch lengths within the tree. Then typological feature-values are mapped on the trees and finally it is estimated whether a change in one typological feature is correlated with a change in another feature in a particular lineage (e.g., Dunn et al. 2011; Levinson et al. 2011). While this phylogenetic approach is promising, it has been criticized especially for lack of statistical power (e.g., Cysouw 2011).

Researchers have also applied (Generalized) Linear Mixed Models (or GLMM) to typological data (e.g., Cysouw 2010; Jaeger et al. 2011; Bentz & Winter 2013).[8] The idea in mixed effects modeling is that the value of the dependent variable is predicted based on the independent variables and using a particular grouping structure (that is, random structure) in the modeling to adjust the variables of interest. The distributions are therefore affected by both the independent variables (the fixed factors) and random factors. In typological research fixed effects are typically the structural factors, such as numeral classifiers, while language families and geographical areas can be modeled as random factors. Once the effect of the random factors is accounted for, the impact of the fixed factors can be established. Mixed models offer efficient and flexible ways of modeling group level structure both within groups and across groups and they are also suitable for small samples which are typical in typological data (Jaeger et al. 2011: 289–290). For these reasons I use here Generalized Mixed Effects Modeling to construct a

---

[8]Winter (2013) provides a tutorial on mixed effects modeling that was helpful in learning more about mixed effects modeling also in typology. See Breslow & Clayton (1993) and Gelman & Hill (2007) for general introductions to GLMM.

model that statistically evaluates the relationship between gender and numeral classifiers across the languages of the world.[9]

The first step in using GLMMs is to plan the model design and to decide which variable is the response or the dependent variable and which variable is the predictor. The dependent is the variable whose distributions are modeled with the predictor variable(s) and the random structure. When choosing the dependent variable it is not theoretically completely clear whether gender or numeral classifiers should be chosen as the dependent. One argument for choosing gender as the dependent is the fact that classifiers are often thought as the most common source of gender in languages (see Corbett 1991: 136; Seifart 2010: 727–728; Luraghi 2011: 450–452 and references). Greenberg (1978: 78–79) suggests that gender develops from classifying demonstratives which in turn often develop from numeral classifiers (see Harris & Campbell 1995: 341–342 for further evidence for the development of gender from demonstratives). Although he does not present any actual reconstructions, Greenberg (1972: 35–36) suggests that there seems to be a synchronic universal that if a numeral classifier system spreads within a language, it will spread to demonstratives (and often only to them), as seems to have happened in Mandarin (see example 5).

Luraghi (2011: 451) presents the general stages in the development of gender as in (9). While some gender systems develop from classifiers others may develop from case and number agreement (Luraghi 2011: 452). In addition, it may be more likely that gender develops not from numeral classifiers but from an earlier noun classifier system, as has happened in some Australian languages (Plaster & Polinsky 2007).

(9)   Generic nouns > classifiers > pronominal demonstratives > attributive
      demonstratives > determiners > agreement markers

There is thus clear theoretical reason to choose gender as the dependent variable. Diachronically the opposite grammaticalization path, that is, numeral classifiers developing directly from gender has not been attested. However, there are examples such as Bengali which lost its gender and number marking but developed numeral classifiers partly recycling the same morphological material that was used for gender and number earlier (see Aikhenvald 2000: 379 and references). This data suggests that it is possible but rare for a numeral classifier

---

[9]All statistical computing and graphs were done in the R programming environment (R Core Team 2017) using the packages lme4 (Bates, Maechler, et al. 2015), ggplot2 (Wickham 2009), vcd (Meyer et al. 2006; 2015; Zeileis et al. 2007), and pbkrtest (Halekoh & Højsgaard 2014). The maps were generated with a mapping tool developed by Hans-Jörg Bibiko for the *WALS*.

system to arise from an earlier gender system. For these reasons, I model gender as the dependent and numeral classifiers as the independent factor in my main model, but I also used a competing model in which I modeled numeral classifiers as the dependent and gender as the independent variable.

The equation showing the structure of mixed logistic regression is presented in (10) (cf. Gelman & Hill 2007: 279; Bentz & Winter 2013: 8).

(10) $P(y_i = 1) = \text{logit}^{-1}(\alpha_{j,k[i]} + \beta_{j,k[i]}x_i)$

The term α is the intercept for each ith datapoint (= language) and the β is the regression coefficient (the slope) for the predictor (x). In (mixed) logistic regression the intercept is the logarithm of the odds for the dependent variable given the default level of the predictor(s), which in R are chosen alphabetically (Arppe 2008: 128). In my models gender is the dependent variable with two values "absence" and "presence" and its default level is "absence". The predictor in my model is numeral classifiers which has two values "absence" and "presence" and with a default value "absence". The intercept in my model, therefore, is the log odds of gender for languages that have no numeral classifiers. In (mixed) logistic regression the slope for a binary variable is the difference in the log odds of the dependent variable between the different levels of the predictor variable. Here this means that the slope is the difference in log odds for having gender in a language that has numeral classifiers compared to a language that has no numeral classifiers.

In (mixed) logistic regression the dependent variable is categorical and its expected response, the odds $1/(1 - p)$, is transformed via natural logarithm to yield logarithm of the odds. In my model design this means $\log(1/(1 - p))$ for observing gender vs. not observing gender. Alternatively, to obtain predicted *probabilities* for observing gender vs. observing no gender in a language the predictor is transformed via inverse logit function, as in (10). In this equation, $P(y_i = 1)$ is the predicted probability that we observe gender (presence of gender = 1) for each item i and the subindices j and k represent the adjustments of the intercept and slope for each grouping factor (here area and family, see below).

This possibility to adjust the intercept and the slope through each grouping factor is probably the most powerful property of mixed effects modeling. I use geographical area and language family as grouping factors and I let both the intercept and the slope vary between the levels of these grouping factors. A random intercept for family means that each family is allowed to have different intercepts to account for the family-related variability in the distribution of gender. A random slope for the family, on the other hand, means that numeral classifiers are allowed to have a different effect on gender in each family to account for the family-related variability in how numeral classifiers affect gender. The random effects for area work analogously. In addition, the models include a correlation term between the intercepts and slopes of a particular random effect. This correlation term accounts for the variation that may arise from families (or areas) with large adjustment for the intercept (= gender) having also a large coefficient for the slope (= numeral classifiers).

The grouping factors language family and area were coded as follows. For language families I used the highest level of classification in the genealogical taxonomy of the *WALS*. For geographical area I used the ten continents of the *Autotyp* (Bickel et al. 2017), illustrated in Figure 1 with the 2949 languages of the *Autotyp* database.[10]

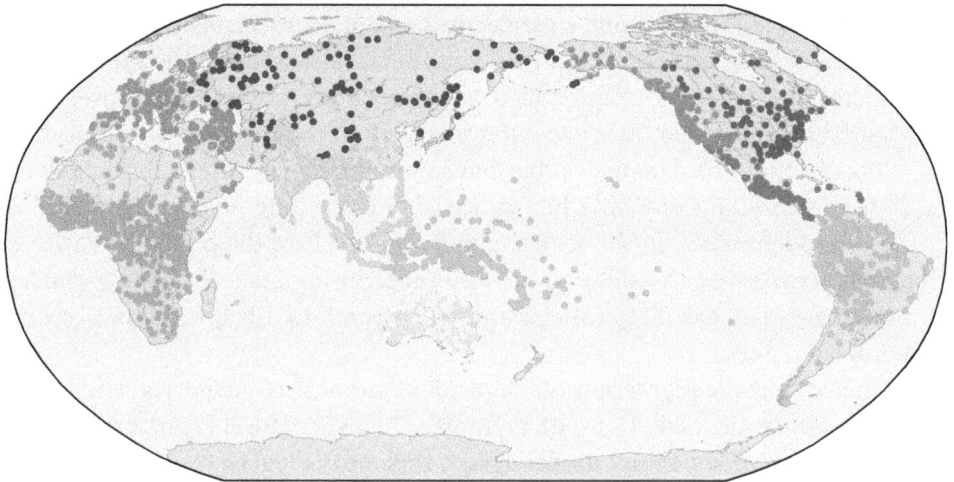

Figure 1: The ten continents of the Autotyp on a world map (Bickel et al. 2017)

For mixed models p-values can be derived by using maximum likelihood ratio tests. This was done by comparing the likelihood ratio of a model with the variable of interest to that of a simpler model without the variable of interest (e.g., Baayen et al. 2008; Barr et al. 2013).

---

[10]The ten continents are: Africa, West and Southwest Eurasia, North-Central Asia, South/Southeast Asia, New Guinea and Oceania, Australia, West North America, East North America, Central America, and South America. The database has information on 2950 languages, but there are no latitudes or longitudes provided for International Sign Language.

3.3 Sampling and data

The main data sources were two chapters in the *WALS*, Corbett (2013) on "Number of genders" and Gil (2013) on "Numeral classifiers". Corbett (2013) has data on 257 languages and Gil (2013) on 400 languages. The cross-section of their data, however, is "only" 133 languages (from 106 genera), which is a relatively small proportion of the two samples and not really adequate for modeling the effect of areal and genealogical factors statistically. Moreover, the languages of Eurasia are overrepresented in the cross-section of the samples: the coverage of genealogical diversity (the share of sampled genera from all genera in a macroarea) is 2–3 times greater in Eurasia than in the other five macroareas.

For these reasons, I analyzed more data based on the same principles as in the two main sources in an attempt to increase the sample sizes especially outside Eurasia. I also reanalyzed Corbett's (2013) data, since he included pronominal gender in his data, whereas I focus solely on noun gender. By pronominal gender I mean pronouns that reflect gender, such as the English third person pronouns *he* and *she*, which as anaphoric pronouns are often analyzed as part of agreement (Corbett 2013). In the minimal case, pronominal gender can provide the only evidence for a gender system in a language, as was done by Corbett (2013). In this paper pronominal gender is excluded in order to make gender and numeral classifiers more comparable to one another, because numeral classifiers co-occur with nouns but not usually (or possibly at all) with pronouns. The main data sources for my own data collection were grammar descriptions, scholarly articles (e.g., Derbyshire & Payne 1990), Nichols' (1992) database on gender and numeral classifiers, and general works on linguistic areas and language families (e.g., Mithun 2001; Janhunen 2003).

The sample contains 360 languages from 252 genera (see Appendix for more information), which is significantly larger compared to what the *WALS* can offer with regard to these variables. I have also attempted to ensure that especially areas that are often less well sampled, such as South America and New Guinea would be sampled to a reasonable degree; in the current paper languages are sampled from roughly 40% of all the genera in those areas. Table 2 provides more detailed information about the sample composition by macroarea. Note that the coverage of genealogical diversity of macroareas outside Eurasia is now much better than in the cross-section of the *WALS* chapters: genealogical coverage of Eurasia is not more than 1.2–1.4 times greater than in the other areas.

Table 2: Number of sampled languages, number of genera, and the genealogical coverage (share of genera sampled) in each macroarea

	Afr.	Eur.	Papunes.	Austr.	N. Am.	S. Am.	Total[a]
Languages	52	69	99	23	58	59	360
Genera (sample/total)	34/81	49/87	61/139	18/44	49/102	43/108	252/544
Genealogical coverage	42%	56%	44%	41%	48%	40%	46%

[a]In Table 2 the total number of genera in the *WALS* are not sums of the macroarea-wise counts, because languages from one genus can be spoken in multiple macroareas and thus be counted multiple times. The total is the total of all genera without macroareal partition.

4 Results

4.1 Preliminary results

The data come from 360 languages (see Appendix 2). Based on the raw numbers there were 122 languages (34%) that had only gender, 81 languages (23%) that had only numeral classifiers, 22 languages (6%) with both gender and numeral classifiers and 135 languages (38%) with neither.[11] All in all, 144 languages had gender (40%) and 103 languages (29%) had numeral classifiers. The geographical distribution of the sample languages on the world map is shown in Figure 2. The three smaller maps in Figure 2 zoom into three areas where gender and/or numeral classifiers are particularly frequent: 1. Central Africa, 2. Southeast Asia, New Guinea, and North Australia, and 3. South America (see also the discussion below on the areal distribution of gender and numeral classifiers). When counting distinct values in genera, gender occurred in 38% of genera and numeral classifiers in 28% of genera. These shares suggest that gender is globally more common than numeral classifiers. In the *WALS*-data, the shares for genera that had gender or numeral classifiers were 40% and 29%, respectively (Corbett 2013; Gil 2013). The differences to my data (38% and 28%, respectively) are very small, and the 2% difference in terms of gender can be explained to some extent by the fact that I sampled only noun gender, whereas Corbett (2013) included pronominal gender in his research.

Aikhenvald (2000: 1) estimates that "[a]lmost all languages have some grammatical means for the linguistic categorization of nouns and nominals". While

---

[11]Note that the frequency of languages that had both gender and numeral classifiers (6%; counting genera) is similar to the frequency of languages with dominant object-subject word order (6%; counting genera; Dryer 2013) which is usually considered to be typologically very rare.

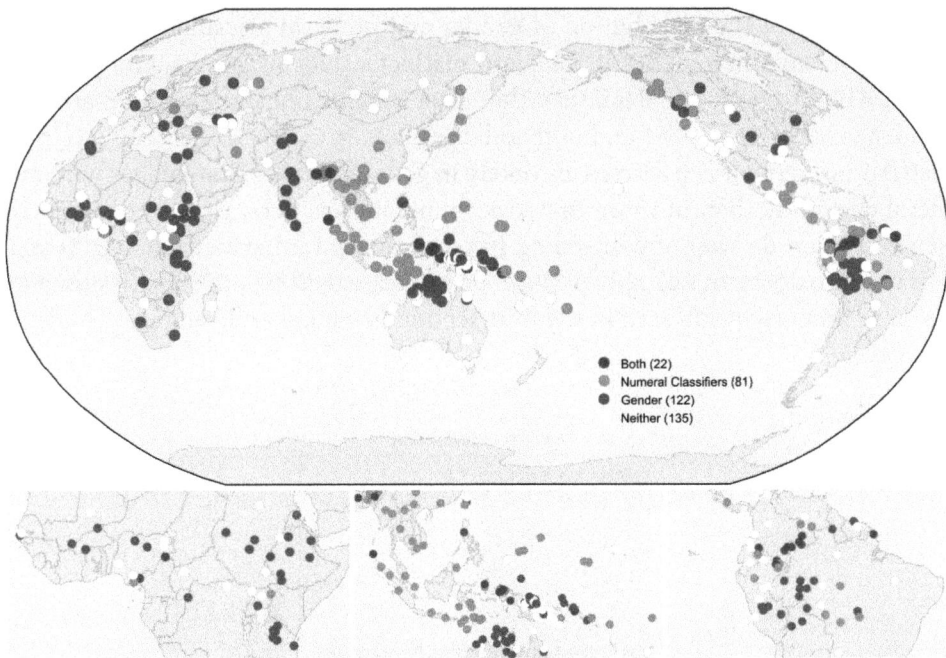

Figure 2: Sample languages on a world map. The three smaller maps at the bottom zoom into central Africa on the left, Southeast Asia and New Guinea in the middle, and the Northern half of South America on the right.

here my focus is not on all types of noun classification, it is worth noting that 63% of the sample languages (n = 225) had either gender or numeral classifiers or both and this may suggest an overall preference for languages to develop some type of noun classification (but since 38% of my sample languages had neither gender nor numeral classifiers, the estimation that almost all languages have some type of noun classification is too strong). If we count how many genera had languages with either type of noun classification, roughly 58% of genera (n = 152) had either gender or numeral classifiers or both, while 42% of genera (n = 111) had neither gender nor numeral classifiers. According to exact binomial test, this distribution is statistically significant (one-tailed p = 0.0067). This result provides evidence that languages prefer to develop either gender or numeral classifiers or both rather than not to develop any type of noun classification. Since my counts do not include possessive classifiers and noun classifiers, it is plausible that if those other types of classifiers had been included, the preference would have been even stronger.

A heatmap of the distribution of gender and numeral classifiers is shown in Figure 3 (counts in genera). If we count distinct values in genera, and perform Fisher's Exact test to the data, then there is a statistically significant inverse dependence between gender and numeral classifiers (p = 0.005). According to this distribution, gender is 2.3 times less likely in genera that have languages with numeral classifiers than in those that lack numeral classifiers. However, counting genera is a crude way of controlling for genealogical inheritance (cf. §3.2) and this test also does not take into account possible areal diffusion. Those issues will be more properly dealt with in the next section using generalized mixed logistic regression.

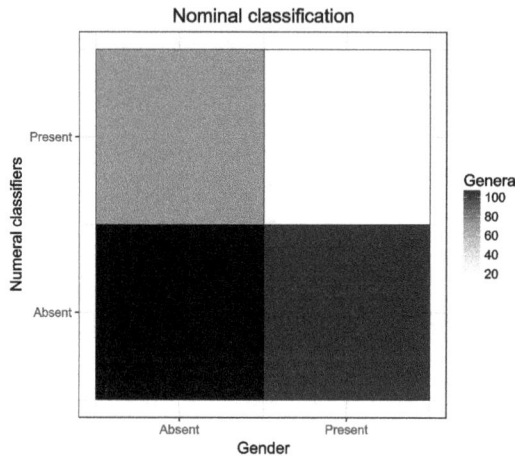

Figure 3: Heatmap of the distribution of gender and numeral classifiers (counts in genera).

The data also allows to estimate genus-internal diversity and stability of gender and numeral classifiers. There were altogether 56 genera with more than one sampled language and in 12 of these (21%) there was diversity in terms of gender (that is, some languages with gender and some without gender). This means that 79% of genera were uniform in either having gender or not having gender and this distribution is statistically significant (exact binomial test; two-tailed p = 0.00002). As for numeral classifiers, there was diversity in 11 genera (20%). This means that 80% of genera were uniform in either having numeral classifiers or not having them and this distribution is statistically significant (exact binomial test; two-tailed; p = 0.000005). If we take these figures as a proxy for the stability of gender and numeral classifiers within genera, both features seem to be relatively stable (see Bickel 2013: 433–434 for similar conclusions for pronominal gender; also Dahl 2004: 196–202).

A few words can also be said concerning the areal distributions of gender and numeral classifiers. As for numeral classifiers, it has been noted by Johanna Nichols and colleagues that they cluster in languages spoken around the Pacific Ocean (e.g., Nichols 1992: 132–133; Nichols & Peterson 1996: 366–367; Nichols 2003: 299). On the basis of the distributions in Figure 2, this claim seems largely true, although some languages in Africa, Europe and Central Asia also have numeral classifiers, while no language in Australia has them (Aikhenvald 2000: 121–124).[12] Here I use GLMM to evaluate Nichols' claim whereby numeral classifiers are more likely to occur in languages spoken in the Circum-Pacific. Following Bickel & Nichols (2006) I define Circum-Pacific as encompassing the Americas, Oceania (including New Guinea and Australia), Southeast Asia, and the Northeastern Coast of Asia. Following Nichols (2003), I include mainland and island Southeast Asia in this area. I then compare the distribution of numeral classifiers in this large area against the rest of the world (that is, Africa and Eurasia except for Southeast Asia and Northeastern Coast of Asia). Figure 4 presents the sample languages inside and outside the Circum-Pacific area on a world map. An association plot of the distribution of numeral classifiers inside and outside the Circum-Pacific area is shown in the left panel of Figure 5.

I modeled numeral classifiers as the dependent, area as a binomial predictor (whether a language is spoken inside or outside the Circum-Pacific area), and the *WALS* families as a random intercept. According to the mixed logistic regression, languages spoken in the Circum-Pacific area were significantly more likely to have numeral classifiers than languages spoken outside this area (logit estimates: 2.2 ± 1.0 (standard errors); χ^2 (1) = 5.7; p = 0.02). As an alternative approach I used stocks (the highest level of genealogical classification in the *Autotyp*) as a random intercept. According to this model design, languages spoken in the Circum-Pacific area were again significantly more likely to have numeral classi-

---

[12]The observation that there are no numeral classifiers in Australian languages may be related to their numeral systems in general. The existence of numeral classifiers presupposes that a language has a numeral system (Aikhenvald 2000: 99). However, many Australian languages have numbers only for the low numerals (e.g., from one to three), but these do not necessarily form a separate part of speech (see Aikhenvald 2000: 100 and references there). The reason why there are no numeral classifiers in Australia may thus be related to the fact that in many languages in this area numerals either do not exist at all as a separate part of speech or numbers are expressed through other larger parts of speech. However, other types of classifiers, such as noun classifiers, are common in Australian languages (Aikhenvald 2000: 82; see also Plaster & Polinsky 2007).

fiers than languages spoken outside this area (logit estimates: 3.3 ± 1.5 (standard errors); χ^2 (1) = 8.3; p = 0.004). When interpreting the coefficients as odds ratios in this model, languages spoken in the Circum-Pacific region were 27 times more likely to have numeral classifiers than languages spoken outside this region.

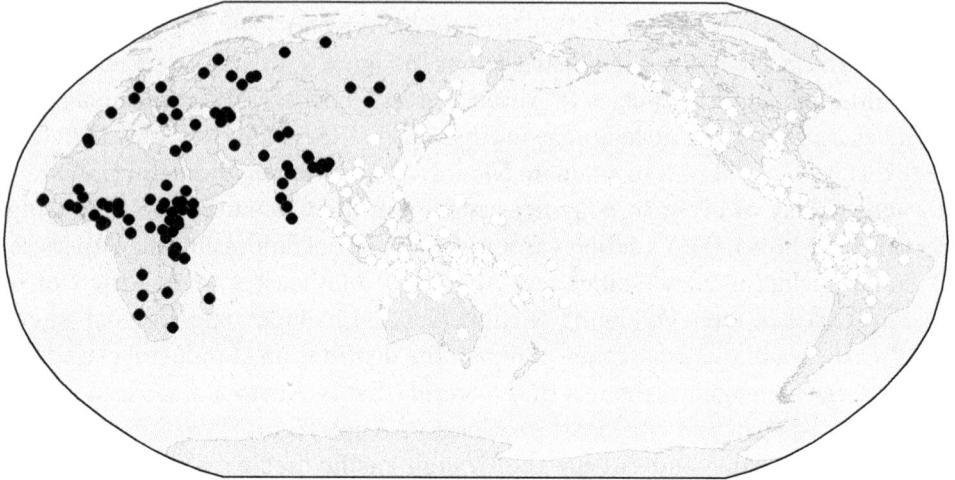

Figure 4: Sample languages on a world map according to area (white = Circum-Pacific area, black = the rest)

The areal distribution of gender has not been in focus very often, but what has been said about it in the literature (simplifying a little) is that gender is not too frequent in the Americas and in the Austronesian languages, whereas it tends to cluster especially in Africa, Europe, Caucasus and the Indian Peninsula as well as in Australia (Corbett 1991: 1–2; Nichols 1992: 130–132; Corbett 2013).[13] This distribution sounds like the opposite to that of numeral classifiers. I therefore compared the distribution of gender in the Circum-Pacific area against the rest of the world as above in the case of numeral classifiers, first modeling *WALS-family* as random intercept. An association plot of this distribution is shown in the right panel of Figure 5.

According to the mixed logistic regression, languages spoken in the Circum-Pacific area were less likely to have gender than languages spoken outside this area (logit estimates: −1.2 ± 0.6 (standard errors); χ^2 (1) = 5.3; p = 0.02). As an

---

[13] Nichols (1992: 130–132) proposes that most gender-languages occur in hotbeds, that is, areas in which gender occurs in most languages of the area, but they come from diverse families and occur in diverse forms. Because my focus is not on the formal aspects of gender marking, her proposal cannot be statistically tested in this paper.

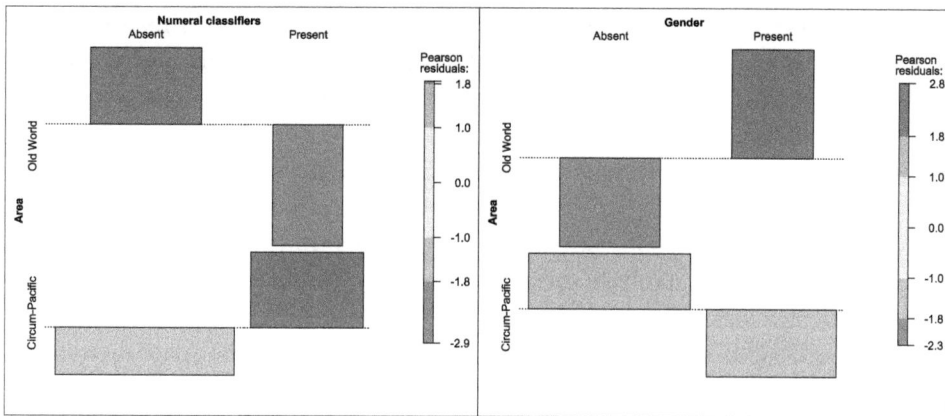

Figure 5: Association plots of the distribution of numeral classifiers (left panel) and gender (right panel) inside and outside the Circum-Pacific. Positive Pearson residuals (blue color) indicate that the cell values were greater than expected and negative Pearson residuals (red) indicate that the cell values were smaller than expected.

alternative approach I used stocks (the highest level of genealogical classification in the *Autotyp*) as a random intercept. According to this model design, languages spoken in the Circum-Pacific area were significantly more likely to have numeral classifiers than languages spoken outside this area (logit estimates: −1.6 ± 0.6 (standard errors); χ^2 (1) = 8.8; p = 0.003). When interpreting the coefficients as odds ratios in this model, languages spoken in the Circum-Pacific were about five times less likely to have gender than languages spoken outside this region.

The conclusion from these distributions is that there is an inverse relationship between gender and numeral classifiers in the languages of the world. On the other hand, there is a roughly complementary areal distribution of gender and numeral classifiers so that numeral classifiers are more likely to occur in the Circum-Pacific region than outside it, whereas gender has the opposite distribution. One consequence of these results could be that the inverse relationship between gender and numeral classifiers is simply an outcome of their biased areal distributions. However, as will be shown in the following section, gender has this inverse relationship to numeral classifiers independently of geographical areas.

4.2 Testing the main hypothesis

The hypothesis that an inverse relationship exists between gender and numeral classifiers was tested with generalized mixed effects models. I constructed a model using the *WALS* families as a grouping factor for genealogical affiliation and the ten continents from the *Autotyp* as the grouping factor for areas. This is my main model and it is also a maximal model that has all the theoretically motivated random intercepts and slopes included. In recent research, it has been suggested that maximal models are preferred in mixed models and especially that models without random slopes may produce spurious results (Schielzeth & Forstmeier 2009; Barr et al. 2013).

According to the mixed logistic regression, languages with numeral classifiers were significantly less likely to have gender than those with no numeral classifiers (logit estimates: −2.1 ± 1.1 (standard errors); χ^2 (1) = 7.7; p = 0.0056). The negative coefficient and the highly significant p-value suggest that the hypothesis is confirmed. A closer inspection of the random effects in Table 3 confirms that the random structure is feasible: the correlation terms between the random intercept and the random slopes for both family and continent are not too large (0.41 and −0.09, respectively).

Table 3: Random effects for the maximal model

Groups	Name	Variance	Std. Dev.	Corr
family	(Intercept)	2.35	1.53	
	classifiers=present	1.48	1.22	0.41
continent	(Intercept)	0.63	0.80	
	classifiers=present	0.53	0.73	−0.09

I further tested the validity of the result with a parametric bootstrap method (Halekoh & Højsgaard 2014). This method returns the fraction of those simulated likelihood ratio test values that are larger or equal to the observed likelihood ratio test value. Using 2 000 simulations the parametric bootstrap derived p-value was 0.0398. Although this p-value is larger than the one derived from the χ^2-distribution (p = 0.0056), it still confirms that the inverse relationship between gender and numeral classifiers is significant and holds independent of geographical area and language families. When interpreting the coefficients as odds ratios, we can conclude that gender is about eight times less likely to occur in a language when that language already has a numeral classifier compared to languages without numeral classifiers. To put it in another way, there is a statistical implicational universal in languages that if a language has numeral classifiers, then it is likely not to have gender but if a language does not have numeral classifiers then it is likely to have gender. The results were then tested by using an alternative genealogical classification and three alternative areal configurations.

These tests and their results are presented in Appendix 1. In all these additional models the result was the same as here: an inverse and significant relationship occurred between gender and numeral classifiers.

I then fitted a competing model choosing numeral classifiers as the dependent and gender as the predictor. I modeled the random structure as in the model above. *WALS*-families were used to model genealogical affiliation and the ten *Autotyp* continents were used to model geographical areas. According to the mixed logistic regression, languages with gender were *more* likely to have numeral classifiers than languages with no gender (logit estimates: 1.0 ± 2.2 (standard errors), but this relationship was not statistically significant (χ^2 (1) = 0.21; p = 0.64). But the random structure of this competing model suggests that the model may be too complex to fit to the data. The correlation between the random intercepts and slopes for both family and continent are –1.0 and the variances for family are extremely large (93 for the random intercept and 21 for the random slope). These problems with the random structure may explain why the relationship between numeral classifiers and gender was positive and not negative as expected (cf. Appendix 1). To further double-check this I refitted the competing model but using the six macroareas of the *WALS* as the geographical area-factor (see Appendix 1 for the distribution of these macroareas on a map). According to this model, languages with gender were *less* likely to have numeral classifiers than languages with no gender (logit estimates: –1.8 ± 2.5 (standard errors), but this inverse relationship was not statistically significant (χ^2 (1) = 0.0; p = 1.0). I then refitted the competing model using the 24 areas of the *Autotyp* as the geographical area-factor (see Appendix 1 for the distribution of the 24 areas on a map). According to this model, languages with gender were again less likely to have numeral classifiers than languages with no gender (logit estimates: –4.0 ± 3.4 (standard errors) and this inverse relationship was statistically significant (χ^2 (1) = 4.8; p = 0.028).

All in all the results of the competing models were very variable and depended on the areal configuration used, whereas the results of the main model (and the additional models in Appendix 1) were consistent regardless of how genealogical affiliation and geographical areas were coded. I interpret these results to mean that numeral classifiers are more likely to have an effect on gender rather than the other way round, which is exactly what has been suggested in the literature (§3.2).

The results of the mixed effects logistic models suggest that there is a statistically significant complexity trade-off between gender and numeral classifiers. This result was also independent of how geographical area and language family were coded. However, because the data contained many counterexamples against the trade-off the generalization is not an absolute universal. Many languages, for instance, had neither gender nor numeral classifiers, and therefore the generalization must be understood as a probabilistic universal.[14]

5 Discussion

The distribution of gender and numeral classifiers and the complexity trade-off between them raise questions that require explanations. Three issues in particular require attention. Why is there a trade-off between gender and numeral classifiers? Why are their areal distributions so biased? Why are languages more likely to have some noun classification system rather than no noun classification at all? Within the limits of this paper I confine myself to providing some preliminary thoughts on possible explanations.

The central question here is why there is a complexity trade-off between gender and numeral classifiers. Two relevant issues are discussed here. First, from a functional point of view gender and numeral classifiers tread the same functional domain, that is, they encode semantically-pragmatically closely related functions across languages (Miestamo 2007: 293). These functions have to do primarily with individuation and reference-identification (or "reference-tracking"), although other functions are also shared across gender and numeral classifier systems (Contini-Morava & Kilarski 2013: 293–294). Because gender and numeral classifier systems share these similar functions, the inverse correlation between these variables can be explained functionally by economy and distinctness. The rationale for this explanation is the following. Economy and distinctness are functional motivations that relate to the amount of linguistic structure, economy for keeping it minimal, and distinctness for preserving distinctions in linguistic structure. Now, if a language has already developed a system of noun classification (e.g., gender), it is inefficient and redundant for that language to develop another type of nominal classification (e.g., numeral classifiers) to serve a similar set of functions (e.g., Hawkins 2004; Sinnemäki 2014b). The small likelihood of developing multiple systems of noun classification is, therefore, a matter of the Zipfian principle of least effort or economy and its interaction with distinctness: linguistic structures are kept minimal without losing distinctness.

---

[14]For instance, all or almost all languages in Quechuan, Otomanguean, Uto-Aztecan, and Trans-New Guinea language families had neither gender nor numeral classifiers, whereas some languages in the Arawakan, Tucanoan, and West Papuan families had both gender and numeral classifiers (e.g., Palikur in (1)).

The second issue is diachronic in nature. If a language loses its noun classification system, it may redevelop another type via reanalysis. For instance, gender markers have been lost in many Iranian and Indic languages, but many of these languages have developed numeral classifiers. In Bengali this resulted in reinterpreting the old feminine forms in terms of numeral classifiers. In Africa, Ogonoid (also called Kegboid) languages, such as Kana (Ogonoid; Niger-Congo), lost their noun class system and instead developed numeral classifiers, which are very rare in Africa. Overall, noun classification may thus be a rather stable feature in language although the particular classification system may be lost. (See Aikhenvald 2000: 379–381 and references.)

While multiple systems of noun classification are possible, they are rare (see §4.1). One reason for languages to develop more than one system of noun classification is language contact. For instance, Santali (Munda; Austroasiatic) has two gender systems as well as numeral classifiers. One gender system is native to Santali and it distinguishes animate from inanimate, while the other system is borrowed from Indo-Aryan and it distinguishes male from non-male (Ghosh 2008: 39). In (11), the noun *Kali-idol* triggers object gender agreement on the verb, which is marked by the third person object clitic *-e* that is reserved for animate beings, but it also requires the use of the a numeral classifier *-taŋ*.

(11) Santali (Austroasiatic; Ghosh 2008: 39)
 uni   mit'-taŋ kəli-boŋga benao-akad-e-a-e
 3SG.M one-CLF Kali-idol   make-PRF.A-3SG.OBJ-FIN-3SG.SBJ
 'He has made a Kali idol.'

Numeral classifier systems can also be borrowed, as seems to have happened in Malto (Dravidian). Malto presumably borrowed numeral classifiers from Magahi (Indic; Indo-European) and elaborated the system subsequently (Emeneau 1980: 117–118). Besides the numeral classifier system Magahi also has a gender system (Steever 1998). These are illustrated in (12).

(12) Malto (Dravidian; Steever 1998: 363, 372)

 a. *tīni   jen maler*
   three CLF man.PL
   'Three men'

 b. *rājah   awḍah*
   king.M.NOM say.PST.3SG.M
   'The king said'

Language contact is also one reason for why multiple systems of noun classi-fication get reduced. For instance, Retuara (Tucanoan) has lost its classifier sys-tem and retained only a gender system because of language contact with Yucuna (Arawakan; see Aikhenvald 2000: 386 and references).

The kinds of "compensating" mechanisms discussed above, motivated by econ-omy and distinctness and manifest in diachronic change, may be found in other areas of grammar as well (e.g., Sinnemäki 2014b). Ultimately economy and dis-tinctness are grounded in language processing and are like the two sides of the same coin. As a processing principle economy is a matter of 'minimize all you can', which means that all unnecessary distinctions can be dispensed so that distinctness is not lost (Bornkessel-Schlesewsky & Schlesewsky 2009). In terms of language change, complexity trade-offs may be seen as adaptive pro-cesses where linguistic structure adapts to preferences in language processing (Sinnemäki 2014a; Bickel et al. 2015). In noun classification this adaptation shows up in the fact that while the majority of the world's languages have a system of noun classification (§4.1), there is a tendency in languages not to develop more than one such system.

This leads us to another important question raised by the results, namely, why the presence of noun classification is preferred over its absence across languages (§4.1). One relevant issue in this regard is the discussion on language complexity that has taken place during the past 15 years. Many researchers have argued that gender is relatively devoid of meaning (not marking real-world categories), adds unnecessary complexity to language, and therefore tends to be lost in situations that involve heavy language contact by adult learners (e.g., McWhorter 2001: 129; Kusters 2003: 25; Trudgill 2011: 155–166). It has also been claimed that classifier systems are at a corresponding level of complexity compared to gender systems (Riddle 2008: 136–141, 147–148). Although numeral classifiers tend to mark real-world categories – and in this sense are more semantically based – they have been analyzed in the same way as gender, adding unnecessary complexity to language (e.g., McWhorter 2007: 22). Some quantitative evidence for the loss of gender complexity comes from pidgins, which tend to lose especially agreement categories, such as gender (Roberts & Bresnan 2008). Against this background it is surprising that there seems to be a preference for languages to develop this kind of grammatical marking, be it gender or numeral classifiers, if it really is unnecessary for human communication.

One possibility for this preference may be functional. The shared functions of gender and numeral classifiers deal primarily with individuation and reference-identification, but gender shares further functions with other types of classifiers as well, including the derivational expansion of the lexicon (Contini-Morava & Kilarski 2013; see also Riddle 2008: 136–141). These functions may be central enough in communication that there is a general preference in languages to develop some type of noun classification to serve these functions. On the contrary, especially gender marking may sometimes lead to tracking failure and ambiguity and there are also grounds to believe that the referential functions of gender (and possibly also those of classifiers) are important only in languages which have many classes in their noun classification system (Trudgill 2011: 158–159). In this sense it is unclear whether the above functions of noun classification are important enough to attract and sustain noun classification in languages.

Another possible explanation is based on the simple fact that noun classification groups nouns into classes. Even languages that do not have noun classification may have some other forms of grouping nouns into subcategories. One such example is declensional type (or inflectional class), which is a way of classifying nouns into groups depending on how they inflect for grammatical categories such as number and case (e.g., Kramer 2015: 67–68). Dahl (2000: 583–584) makes the strong point that sometimes inflectional classes actually look like gender distinctions and some of them could be analyzed as gender. Thus, noun classification and inflectional classes share the fact that they group nouns into subcategories. This leads me to the following preliminary conclusion for why there is a preference to develop noun classification in the languages of the world: languages prefer to classify nouns into subcategories and languages reach this goal in different ways by using gender, classifiers, inflectional classes, or some other means.

The third question that the results raised is why the areal distributions of gender and numeral classifiers were so biased. Since the origin and/or distribution of gender and classifiers have been discussed in multiple publications (e.g., Corbett 1991, Corbett 2013; Nichols 1992, Nichols 2003; Aikhenvald 2000; Luraghi 2011; Gil 2013; Passer 2016b), I will only provide some observations here.

There is increasing evidence suggesting that classifiers spread through language contact more easily than gender does and therefore serve as strong areal markers (Seifart 2010: 730). In addition, what tends to diffuse is often the pattern of classifiers and not the actual markers (in terms of Matras 2009: 234–237); it is rather the native words that are employed for the purpose of an incipient classifier system. Gender systems do not spread so easily because agreement systems are less easily borrowed, although parts of the systems may be borrowed (Aikhenvald 2000: 386–388). Since the pattern of numeral classifiers may be relatively easy to spread, whereas the pattern of gender tends not to spread easily, it is probably no coincidence that gender is considered more stable (that is, more likely to be genealogically inherited) than numeral classifiers (e.g., Nichols 2003: 299–303). This observation is confirmed by Dediu & Cysouw (2013) who compared eight stability metrics recently developed for estimating the stability of typological parameters. Based on their comparisons, gender (more specifically number of gender; data from the *WALS*) appears to be more stable than numeral classifiers according to the metrics (p. 13, Table 7).

On the other hand, the greater diffusability and instability of numeral classifiers may be related to the way noun classification systems develop. Numeral classifiers tend to develop ultimately from lexical sources, from generic nouns, such as 'man' and 'woman', whereas gender tends to develop either from an earlier classifier system or from a morphosyntactic source, namely, case or number agreement (Luraghi 2011). In other words, when a language begins to develop noun classification, it most commonly starts with a classifier system that may then, in some cases, further develop into a noun class or a gender system. The latter systems require longer time and more steps in their development and are, therefore, more "mature" in terms of Dahl (2004). The fact that gender does not spread so easily is probably related to its greater dependence on the language-specific agreement system, whereas the idea of classifiers can spread much more easily from one language to another, possibly regardless of the language-specific system.

This last point leads us to consider the macroareal distributions of gender and numeral classifiers. As was observed in §4.1, numeral classifiers cluster in the Circum-Pacific, while gender clusters in the Old World.

However, if we focus on the frequency distribution of gender and numeral classifiers separately inside and outside the Circum-Pacific, a different picture emerges. The barplot in Figure 6 shows that the frequency distributions of these two types of noun classification are almost identical in the Circum-Pacific. In the Old World, on the contrary, gender is much more frequent than numeral classifiers. In other words, what stands out in the frequency distributions is the smaller than expected frequency of numeral classifiers in the Old World and the higher than expected frequency of gender in the Old World. Thus, if we focus on the distributions of noun classification overall, there is evidence that it is the distributions in the Old World that are biased rather than those in the Circum-Pacific.

Here I can only speculate possible reasons for these distributions. One possible explanation for the greater frequency of gender in the Old World is the following. As was discussed above, gender can develop from classifiers or from case or number agreement. If we assume that there has been a roughly equal probability of developing gender from classifiers in both the Circum-Pacific and in the Old World, then the higher frequency of gender must be explained by gender having developed in the Old World more probably from case or number agreement compared to the Circum-Pacific. However, this explanation cannot really account for why the frequency of numeral classifiers is so much lower than expected in the Old World. If gender would develop more likely from case or number agreement than from classifiers in the Old World, this may explain the higher frequency of gender in that area, but not the lower than expected frequency of numeral classifiers.

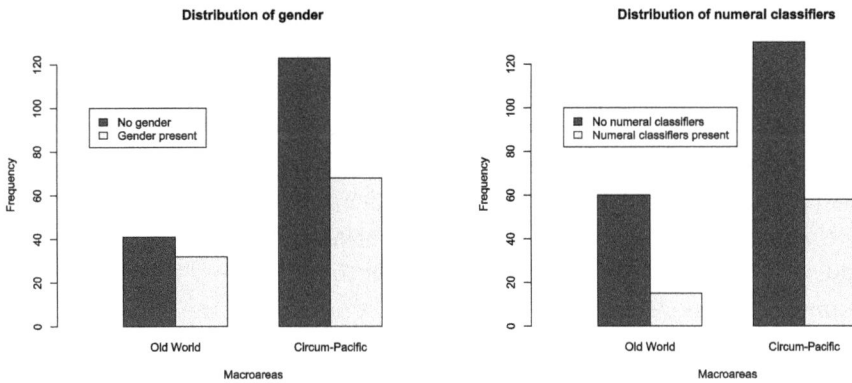

Figure 6: Barplots of gender (on the left) and numeral classifiers (on the right) inside and outside the Circum-Pacific region (counts in genera)

Another possibility is to assume that the probability of developing gender from case or number agreement was roughly similar in the Circum-Pacific and in the Old World. The higher frequency of gender in the Old World could then only be explained by gender being developed more likely from classifiers in the Old World compared to the Circum-Pacific. This explanation could account for the higher than expected frequency of gender in the Old World and also the lower than expected frequency of numeral classifiers in the Old World – provided that we assume that when a numeral classifiers system changes into gender that change is complete and the old system of numeral classifiers is practically lost.

This possibility crucially depends on the hypothesized grammaticalization path from classifiers to gender (see §3.2). Although many researchers have suggested this path as one possibility for gender to develop, Passer (2016b: 346) found no evidence for this process in his in-depth study. He suggests that the reason for the lack of evidence may be the following: when a classifier system turns into a gender system, this change requires large changes in the grammar of the language that go beyond noun classification, including the development of obligatory inflectional agreement. Such large changes in grammars would require that many languages change their morphological type in the process. Numeral classifiers tend to occur especially in analytic languages, but changing morphological type to synthetic is unlikely and rare in the languages of the world. The reasons for the biased areal distributions must, therefore, be sought from elsewhere. (Passer 2016b.)

Another reason for the biased areal distributions of gender and numeral classifiers may be related to structural stability (cf. §4.1 and Dahl 2004: 196–202). Gender and numeral classifiers may simply be stable over very long periods of time, numeral classifiers being further reinforced by neighboring languages in the Circum-Pacific area and gender being reinforced by neighboring languages outside this area. This may be part of the story, since these variables are not the only ones that mark off Circum-Pacific area from the rest of the world. Bickel & Nichols (2006) show that this area is typologically marked off from the rest of the world by about 40% of the 86 linguistic variables they surveyed. In addition, Dediu & Cysouw (2013: 13) observed that both gender and numeral classifiers are among the more stable features when compared to the other selected *WALS* features. This stability may be related to language type, as was implied above: although the morphological type of languages may sometimes change, it is unlikely that so extensive changes would be mere epiphenomena of changes in noun classification. Languages are more likely to stick to their morphological type and change some aspects of their linguistic patterns or lose those patterns but not change those patterns completely from one type to another (Passer 2016b: 346). It is more cautious but probably more to the point to say that the kind of noun classification attracted by analytic/isolating languages is (numeral) classifiers and those attracted by languages with inflection is gender (cf. Corbett 1991: 137).

6 Conclusion

In this paper I have researched the interaction between gender and numeral classifiers in a representative sample of the world's languages. The data suggested that there is a strong inverse relationship between gender and numeral classifiers.

This interaction adds to our knowledge of statistical language universals and bespeaks for the existence of complexity trade-offs in well-circumscribed areas of grammar. Previous research has not revealed many instances of complexity trade-offs (e.g., Shosted 2006; Maddieson 2006; Miestamo 2009). Those that have been found, such as the one between case marking and rigid word order (Siewierska 1998; Sinnemäki 2008, Sinnemäki 2011, Sinnemäki 2014b), have overwhelmingly occurred between functionally related variables that, for instance, tread the same functional domain (such as argument marking). It is possible that new complexity trade-offs will be found among typological variables, but my contention is that they will be found among variables that are functionally related and may therefore also be diachronically connected to one another.

Although the current data suggests a new complexity trade-off this result does not provide evidence for the claim that all languages are equally complex. As I have demonstrated elsewhere (Sinnemäki 2014c) correlational evidence based on typological feature-data cannot either validate or falsify this claim.

I have said very little about the typological distribution of noun classifiers and possessive classifiers. Numeral classifiers are just one subtype of classifiers, so to form a more precise picture of how gender interacts with classifiers in general it would be necessary to survey at least these two types of classifiers in the future as well.

Acknowledgments

I would like to thank the audiences of the workshops *Grammatical gender and linguistic complexity* held at the University of Stockholm 20–21 November 2015 and *Gender and Classifiers: Diachronic and Synchronic Variation* at the University of Surrey 28–29 January 2016 for helpful comments. I especially thank Jenny Audring, Greville Corbett, Marcin Kilarski, Don Killian, Johanna Nichols, Maria Polinsky, Adam Schembri, and Marc Tang for their comments. I am grateful to Richard Futrell and Sean Roberts for advice with mixed effects modeling. For financial support I am grateful to the Helsinki Collegium for Advanced Studies and to the Academy of Finland (grant no. 296212).

Special abbreviations

The following abbreviations are not found in the Leipzig Glossing Rules:

A	active	HUM	human	POSS	possessor marking
ANIM	animate	ICMP	incompletive	PREP	preposition
CLF	classifier	NHUM	non-human	PRF	perfect
CLT	clitic	NUM	numeral	REF	referential
FIN	finite	NVIS	non-visible	WK	week

Appendix 1: Supporting material about mixed effects modeling

The results of the mixed effect modeling indicated that gender correlated inversely with numeral classifiers irrespective of variation related to language families and geographical areas. Here I discuss the model specifications in greater detail and present also a few additional tests that replicate the results.

One important issue that often surfaces in relation to generalized mixed effects modeling is the convergence of models. A common problem in fitting the models is that they do not always converge. In generalized linear mixed effects modeling an iterative algorithm is used to produce the model parameters. This iteration stops when the difference between successive iterations is smaller than a predetermined tolerance. If so, the model is said to converge, otherwise it is said not to converge. In R the tolerance is set to 1e−8 by default, which means that in practice the model fit cannot be improved with further iterations. See Hardin & Hilbe (2007: 2, 9, 10, 31) and Kimball et al. (submitted: 3−4) for more details and references to more technical papers.

When the model does not converge, there are three options available: simplify the models, increase the number of iterations, or use a different optimizer. Based on my experience with generalized linear mixed models using binomial response factors it is hardly ever the case that increasing the number of iterations leads to convergence. The most common alternative in linguistics has been to simplify the models and remove one or more of the random slopes (or the correlation parameters between the random intercept and random slope for some effect). However, there is ongoing debate among researchers whether it is justified to leave out any aspect of the random structure. The simulations of Barr et al. (2013) suggest that it is best to work with maximal models, whereas, for instance, Baayen (2008), Baayen et al. (2008: 395), Bates, Kliegl, et al. (2015), and Gries (2015) argue that it is fully justified to ask whether all of the random structure is necessary. The statistical literature, on the other hand, suggests that estimating random effects with likelihood ratio test (anova) is not a valid approach for building mixed effects models (see Kimball et al. submitted: 8 and references there). For this latter reason I did not use model simplification for the purpose of improving convergence. (Kimball et al. submitted.)

However, there are situations that may be somewhat problematic if maximal random structure is used. Sometimes the correlation parameter between the random intercept and the random slope for a particular effect is close to or even equals ±1.0. This circumstance means that there is not enough data to fit both a random intercept and a random slope for a particular effect (Baayen et al. 2008; Bates, Kliegl, et al. 2015). In these situations I followed the recommendations of Barr et al. (2013) and chose to keep the maximal model. There are two reasons for this. First, simplifying the models by removing the correlation between random effects or by removing a random slope usually only increases the likelihood ratio of the fixed term (here numeral classifiers) and makes its p-value smaller. In all the models below, the fixed effect was significant even with the maximal model, so simplifying the models would not have changed the situation. Second, since languages change at different rates across families and areas (cf. Nichols 2003), it is crucial to include random slopes for both families and areas. Yet owing to the high number of families it may not be usually possible to include more than one random factor for genealogical affiliation especially in Generalized Linear Mixed Models. For instance, Atkinson (2011) modeled both genera and families as random factors but only as random intercepts not as random slopes (or as nested factors, which could have been done). Thus mixed models may not be able to account for the internal structure of language families for which other approaches are called for, such as the Family Bias Theory of Bickel (2013) or phylogenetic regression (e.g., Dunn et al. 2011).

Convergence can be improved also by using a different optimizer. The R package lme4 (Bates, Maechler, et al. 2015) uses two optimizers, BOBYQA and Nelder-Mead, to estimate the random effects in generalized linear mixed effects modeling. My models did not always converge with the default settings, that is, when using both these optimizers. My solution was to use only one optimizer at a time. I used BOBYQA for most of the models (it is also faster in practice) and Nelder-Mead only when using BOBYQA did not work: these choices resulted in model convergence in all situations. A more general solution to the convergence error is offered by Bayesian mixed effects modeling (see e.g. Kimball et al. submitted), but I chose to use the frequentist approach here because of its greater familiarity in linguistics.

In the mixed effects modeling I let the intercepts and the slopes vary between the *WALS* families and between the continents as defined in the *Autotyp*. But there are other genealogical classifications that could have been used and the world can also be divided into geographical areas based on different criteria. The classifications I chose capture variation at one particular level of configuration, so it is informative to try out alternative configurations as well. For instance, the ten continents used in the *Autotyp* may conceal variation that occurs in finer-grained areas or in larger macro-areas. For this reason I retested the hypothesis by using an alternative genealogical classification as well as two alternative

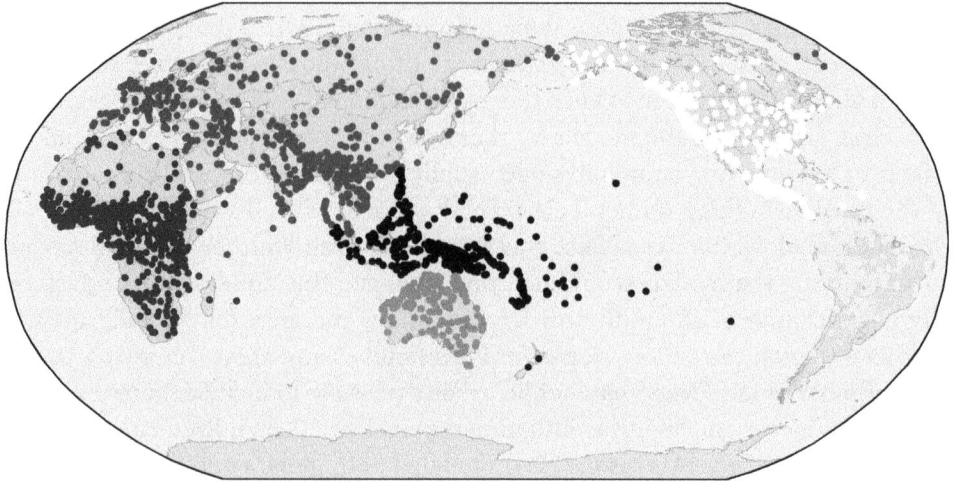

Figure 7: Six macroareas of the *WALS* on the world map

areal configurations. As an alternative genealogical classification I used stocks, the highest level of classification in the *Autotyp* database (Bickel et al. 2017). As alternative areal configurations I used the six macroareas in the *WALS* and the 24 areas in the *Autotyp*. The six macroareas of the *WALS* are illustrated on a world map in Figure 7 (using the 2679 languages of that database) and the 24 areas of the *Autotyp* are illustrated in Figure 8 (using 2949 languages of that database).[15] These combinations of the genealogical and areal classifications produced five additional models listed in Table 4.

The results of these additional models are summarized in Table 4. As the fourth column suggests, in all the additional models there was an inverse relationship between gender and numeral classifiers. As the rightmost column suggests, this relationship was significant in all the models. These results further replicate those reported in §4.2.

---

[15]See Hammarström & Donohue (2014) for a macroareal definition that is different from those used in the *WALS*. Most areal breakdowns in language typology are based on geography, but it would be possible to use also areal breakdowns based on other criteria, such as social structure (Burton et al. 1996). However, typological research has yet to discuss and employ such approaches.

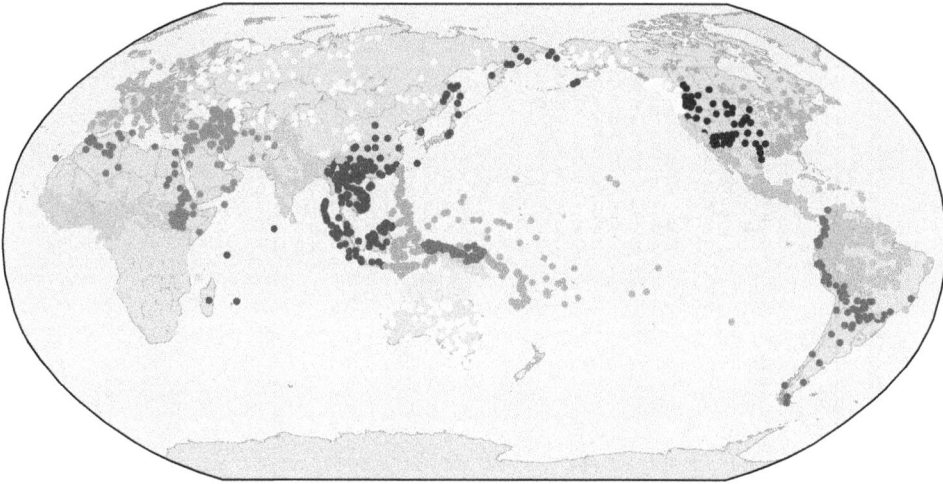

Figure 8: The 24 areas of the *Autotyp* on a world map

Table 4: Five additional models, the design of their random effect structure, and the results of the mixed effects modeling

Model	Areal configuration	Genealogical classification	logit estimates + std. error	$\chi^2(1)$	p-value
W24	24 areas	*WALS*-families	−2.1 ± 1.1	9.3	0.002
W6	6 macroareas	*WALS*-families	−1.9 ± 0.9	4.1	0.042
A10	10 continents	*Autotyp*-stocks	−3.4 ± 2.4	8.3	0.004
A24	24 areas	*Autotyp*-stocks	−3.1 ± 2.3	9.2	0.002
A6	6 macroareas	*Autotyp*-stocks	−3.1 ± 1.9	4.7	0.030

Appendix 2: The sample and sources

The table below provides information about the 360 sample languages, including genealogical classification, macroareal classification, the data on numeral classifiers and gender, and sources. A more detailed database on noun gender is in preparation to *Journal of Cross-Linguistic Databases*.

Table 5

Macroarea	Family	Genus	Language	Cl	Gd	Sources (classifiers)	Sources (gender)
Africa	Afro-Asiatic	Berber	Berber (Middle Atlas)	–	+	Penchoen 1973: 24–25	Penchoen 1973: 12–13, 21–22, 25–27, 39–40, 54–55
Africa	Afro-Asiatic	Biu-Mandara	Margi	–	–	Gil 2013	Hoffman 1963: 46, 72–75, 85–87
Africa	Afro-Asiatic	Central Cushitic	Kemant	–	+	Appleyard 1975: 329, passim	Appleyard 1975: 319–322, 332–333
Africa	Afro-Asiatic	Dizoid	Dizi	–	+	Gil 2013	Corbett 2013; Nichols 1992: 295
Africa	Afro-Asiatic	E. Cushitic	Arbore	–	+	Gil 2013	Corbett 2013; Hayward 1984: 131–132
Africa	Afro-Asiatic	E. Cushitic	Oromo (Harar)	–	+	Gil 2013	Corbett 2013; Owens 1985: 65
Africa	Afro-Asiatic	E. Cushitic	Qafar	–	+	Bliese 1981: 185–186	Bliese 1981: 180–182, 186–188
Africa	Afro-Asiatic	S. Cushitic	Alagwa	–	+	Gil 2013	Corbett 2013; Mous 2008: 147–149
Africa	Afro-Asiatic	S. Cushitic	Iraqw	–	+	Gil 2013	Corbett 2013; Mous 1992: 41
Africa	Afro-Asiatic	Semitic	Amharic	–	+	Gil 2013	Corbett 2013; Leslau 1995: 33–34
Africa	Afro-Asiatic	Semitic	Arabic (Egyptian)	–	+	Gil 2013	Corbett 2013; Hanna 1967: 12–18
Africa	Afro-Asiatic	Semitic	Arabic (Moroccan)	–	+	Gil 2013	Harrell 1962: 40, 45–46, 95–97
Africa	Afro-Asiatic	Semitic	Tigré	–	+	Elias 2005: 110–112	Corbett 2013; Elias 2005: 210–216
Africa	Afro-Asiatic	W. Chadic	Hausa	–	+	Gil 2013	Corbett 2013; Schuh 1976: 47
Africa	Afro-Asiatic	W. Chadic	Miya	–	+	Gil 2013	Corbett 2013; Schuh 1989: 171–173
Africa	Austronesian	Barito	Malagasy	–	–	Gil 2013	Corbett 2013
Africa	Central Sudanic	Moru-Ma'di	Lugbara	+	–	Gil 2013	Nichols 1992: 295
Africa	Eastern Sudanic	Kuliak	So	–	+	Gil 2013	Carlin 1993: 73
Africa	Eastern Sudanic	Nilotic	Datooga	–	–	Gil 2013	Kiessling 2007: passim
Africa	Eastern Sudanic	Nilotic	Lango	–	–	Gil 2013	Corbett 2013
Africa	Eastern Sudanic	Nilotic	Maasai	–	+	Gil 2013	Payne 1998: 160
Africa	Eastern Sudanic	Nubian	Nubian (Dongolese)	–	–	Gil 2013	Corbett 2013
Africa	Eastern Sudanic	Surmic	Murle	–	+	Arensen 1982: 100	Corbett 2013
Africa	Fur	Fur	Fur	–	+	Gil 2013	Jakobi 1990: 84, 99–115
Africa	Gumuz	Gumuz	Gumuz	–	–	Ahland 2012: 131–135	Ahland 2012: 95–96
Africa	Hadza	Hadza	Hadza	–	+	Edenmyr 2004: passim	Sands 2013: 108–110
Africa	Kadu	Kadugli	Krongo	–	+	Reh 1985: 309–310	Reh 1985: 126–127
Africa	Khoe-Kwadi	Khoe-Kwadi	Khoekhoe	–	+	Gil 2013	Corbett 2013; Hagman 1973: 81–88
Africa	Koman	Koman	Uduk	–	+	Killian 2015: 129–132	Killian 2015: 67–68
Africa	Kordofanian	Rashad	Orig	–	+	Gil 2013	Nichols 1992: 295
Africa	Kx'a	Ju Kung	Ju|'hoan	–	–	Gil 2013	Corbett 2013; Dickens 1992: 12–16
Africa	Mande	W. Mande	Mandinka (Gambian)	+	–	Nichols 1992: 295	Nichols 1992: 295
Africa	Niger-Congo	Bantoid	Ejagham	+	–	Watters 1981: 309–313	Watters 1981: 291–293, 318–321, 328–331, 434–440
Africa	Niger-Congo	Bantoid	Lingala	–	+	Meeuwis 1998: 23–24	Corbett 2013; Kamwangamalu 1989: 110–111
Africa	Niger-Congo	Bantoid	Luganda	–	+	Gil 2013	Nichols 1992: 295
Africa	Niger-Congo	Bantoid	Luvale	–	+	Horton 1949: 36–37, 166–167	Horton 1949: 36–37, 166–167
Africa	Niger-Congo	Bantoid	Shona	–	+	Fortune 1985: 108–109, 127	Corbett 2013; Fortune 1985: 107–126
Africa	Niger-Congo	Bantoid	Swahili	–	+	Gil 2013	Corbett 2013; own knowledge
Africa	Niger-Congo	Bantoid	Zulu	–	+	Gil 2013	Corbett 2013; Canonici 1995: 21
Africa	Niger-Congo	Cross River	Kana	+	–	Gil 2013	Aikhenvald 2000: 110–111
Africa	Niger-Congo	Defoid	Yoruba	–	–	Gil 2013	Corbett 2013

Macroarea	Family	Genus	Language	Cl	Gd	Sources (classifiers)	Sources (gender)
Africa	Niger-Congo	Gbaya-Manza-Ngbaka	Gbeya Bossangoa	–	–	Gil 2013	Samarin 1966: 98
Africa	Niger-Congo	Gur	Dagaare	–	+	Gil 2013	Grimm 2012: 45–48
Africa	Niger-Congo	Gur	Koromfe	–	+	Gil 2013	Corbett 2013; Rennison 1997: 206–233
Africa	Niger-Congo	Gur	Supyire	–	+	Gil 2013	Corbett 2013; Carlson 1994: 75
Africa	Niger-Congo	Igboid	Igbo	–	–	Gil 2013	Corbett 2013
Africa	Niger-Congo	N. Atlantic	Diola-Fogny	–	+	Sapir 1965: 74	Sapir 1965: 24–25, 61–62
Africa	Niger-Congo	N. Atlantic	Fula (Cameroonian)	+	+	Nichols 1992: 295	Nichols 1992: 295
Africa	Niger-Congo	Ubangi	Zande	–	+	Gore 1926: 42–45	Corbett 2013; Gore 1926: 20–23
Africa	Saharan	W. Saharan	Kanuri	–	–	Gil 2013	Corbett 2013
Africa	Sandawe	Sandawe	Sandawe	–	+	Gil 2013	Nichols 1992: 295; Eaton 2010: 14–17
Africa	Songhay	Songhay	Koyra Chiini	–	–	Gil 2013	Heath 1999: 55
Africa	Bunuban	Bunuban	Gooniyandi	–	–	Gil 2013	Corbett 2013
Australia	Gaagudju	Gaagudju	Gaagudju	–	+	Gil 2013	Harvey 2002: 144–157
Australia	Garrwan	Garrwan	Garrwa	–	–	Gil 2013	Mushin 2012: 38, 190
Australia	Gunwinyguan	Nunggubuyu	Nunggubuyu	–	+	Gil 2013	Corbett 2013; Heath 1983: 131–132
Australia	Iwaidjan	Iwaidjan	Mawng	–	+	Gil 2013	Corbett 2013; Capell & Hinch 1970: 73–77
Australia	Mangarrayi-Maran	Alawa	Alawa	–	+	Sharpe 1972: passim	Sharpe 1972: 66, 79–80
Australia	Mangarrayi-Maran	Mangarrayi	Mangarrayi	–	+	Gil 2013	Corbett 2013; Nichols 1992: 297
Australia	Mangarrayi-Maran	Warndarang	Warndarang	–	+	Gil 2013	Nichols 1992: 299; Heath 1980: 22–23
Australia	Mirndi	Djingili	Djingili	–	+	Gil 2013	Pensalfini 1997: 247–248, 253–259
Australia	Mirndi	Jaminjungan	Jaminjung	–	–	Gil 2013	Schultze-Berndt 2000: passim
Australia	Mirndi	Wambayan	Wambaya	–	+	Nordlinger 1998: 72–80	Nordlinger 1998: 59–70
Australia	N. Daly	Malakmalak	Malakmalak	–	+	Gil 2013	Birk 1976: 30–31
Australia	Pama-Nyungan	N. Pama-Nyungan	Dyirbal	–	+	Gil 2013	Corbett 2013; Dixon 1972: 44
Australia	Pama-Nyungan	N. Pama-Nyungan	Uradhi	–	–	Gil 2013	Corbett 2013
Australia	Pama-Nyungan	N. Pama-Nyungan	Yidiny	–	–	Gil 2013	Corbett 2013
Australia	Pama-Nyungan	S-E. Pama-Nyungan	Ngiyambaa	–	+	Gil 2013	Corbett 2013
Australia	Pama-Nyungan	W. Pama-Nyungan	Martuthunira	–	–	Gil 2013	Dench 1998: 20
Australia	Pama-Nyungan	W. Pama-Nyungan	Yingkarta	–	–	Gil 2013	Corbett 2013; Osborne 1974: 51–52
Australia	Tiwian	Tiwian	Tiwi	–	+	Gil 2013	McGregor 2004: 146–149
Australia	Worrorran	Worrorran	Gunin	–	+	Gil 2013	Nichols 1992: 299
Australia	Worrorran	Worrorran	Ungarinjin	–	–	Gil 2013	Clendon 2000: 95
Australia	Worrorran	Worrorran	Worora	–	+	Gil 2013	Corbett 2013; Merlan 1994: 61–63, 241–242
Australia	Yangmanic	Yangmanic	Wardaman	–	+	Merlan 1994: 120	Corbett 2013
Eurasia	Afro-Asiatic	Semitic	Hebrew (Modern)	–	+	Gil 2013	Corbett 2013; Glinert 1989: 51–52, 91, 104, 117–120, 185–198
Eurasia	Ainu	Ainu	Ainu	+	–	Gil 2013	Corbett 2013
Eurasia	Altaic	Mongolic	Buriat	–	–	Gil 2013	Skribnik 2003: 110–111, 117–120
Eurasia	Altaic	Mongolic	Khalkha	–	–	Gil 2013	Corbett 2013
Eurasia	Altaic	Tungusic	Evenki	–	–	Gil 2013	Corbett 2013
Eurasia	Altaic	Tungusic	Nanai	–	–	Gil 2013	Nichols 1992: 297
Eurasia	Altaic	Turkic	Chuvash	+	–	Gil 2013	Corbett 2013
Eurasia	Altaic	Turkic	Tatar	+	–	Gil 2013	Poppe 1968: 29–57
Eurasia	Altaic	Turkic	Turkish	+	–	Gil 2013	Corbett 2013
Eurasia	Altaic	Turkic	Tuvan	–	–	Gil 2013	Nichols 1992: 297
Eurasia	Austroasiatic	Aslian	Semelai	+	–	Gil 2013	Corbett 2013

Macroarea	Family	Genus	Language	Cl	Gd	Sources (classifiers)	Sources (gender)
Eurasia	Austroasiatic	Khasian	Pnar	+	+	Ring 2015: 124–125, 357–369	Ring 2015: 101, 107–108
Eurasia	Austroasiatic	Khmer	Khmer	+	–	Gil 2013	Corbett 2013
Eurasia	Austroasiatic	Munda	Korku	–	+	Gil 2013	Bhattacharya 1976: passim
Eurasia	Austroasiatic	Munda	Santali	+	+	Gil 2013	Ghosh 2008: 11–12, 32–33, 39–40, 44–45
Eurasia	Austroasiatic	Nicobarese	Nicobarese (Car)	+	–	Gil 2013	Corbett 2013; Braine 1970: 103–108
Eurasia	Austroasiatic	Palaung-Khmuic	Khmu'	+	–	Gil 2013	Corbett 2013; Premsrirat 1987: 30, 32–33
Eurasia	Austroasiatic	Viet-Muong	Vietnamese	+	–	Gil 2013	Corbett 2013
Eurasia	Austronesian	Malayo-Sumbawan	Acehnese	+	–	Durie 1985: 137–139	Durie 1985: 29
Eurasia	Austronesian	Malayo-Sumbawan	Cham (E.)	+	–	Gil 2013	Thurgood 2005: passim
Eurasia	Basque	Basque	Basque	–	–	Gil 2013	Corbett 2013
Eurasia	Burushaski	Burushaski	Burushaski	–	+	Gil 2013	Corbett 2013; Munshi 2006: 161–167
Eurasia	Chukotko-Kamchatkan	N. Chukotko-Kamchatkan	Chukchi	–	–	Gil 2013	Corbett 2013
Eurasia	Dravidian	N. Dravidian	Brahui	–	–	Gil 2013	Corbett 2013
Eurasia	Dravidian	S. Dravidian	Kannada	–	+	Gil 2013	Corbett 2013; Sridhar 1990: 221–222
Eurasia	Dravidian	S. Dravidian	Tamil	–	+	Schiffman 1999: 48–50	Corbett 2013; Schiffman 1999: 57–58
Eurasia	Hmong-Mien	Hmong-Mien	Hmong Daw	+	–	Gil 2013	Nichols 1992: 297
Eurasia	Indo-European	Albanian	Albanian	–	+	Gil 2013	Matasović 2012: 17, 18, 29
Eurasia	Indo-European	Armenian	Armenian (E.)	–	–	Gil 2013	Corbett 2013
Eurasia	Indo-European	Baltic	Latvian	–	+	Gil 2013	Corbett 2013; Kalnača 2014: 66–73
Eurasia	Indo-European	Germanic	English	–	–	Gil 2013	Corbett 2013; own knowledge
Eurasia	Indo-European	Germanic	German	–	+	Gil 2013	Corbett 2013; own knowledge
Eurasia	Indo-European	Indic	Assamese	–	–	Gil 2013	Goswami & Tamuli 2003: 415
Eurasia	Indo-European	Indic	Bengali	–	–	Gil 2013	Klaiman 2009: 425
Eurasia	Indo-European	Indic	Hindi	–	+	Gil 2013	Corbett 2013; McGregor 1986: 1–22
Eurasia	Indo-European	Indic	Marathi	–	+	Gil 2013	Corbett 2013; Pandharipande 2003: 702–707
Eurasia	Indo-European	Indic	Sinhala	–	+	Gil 2013	Henadeerage 2002: passim; Chandralal 2010: 79–82, 228–229
Eurasia	Indo-European	Indic	Waigali	–	+	Gil 2013	Nichols 1992: 297
Eurasia	Indo-European	Iranian	Persian	–	–	Gil 2013	Corbett 2013
Eurasia	Indo-European	Romance	French	+	+	Gil 2013	Corbett 2013; own knowledge
Eurasia	Indo-European	Slavic	Bulgarian	–	+	Gil 2013	Nicolova 2017: 86–89
Eurasia	Indo-European	Slavic	Russian	–	+	Gil 2013	Corbett 2013; Wade 2011: 54
Eurasia	Japanese	Japanese	Japanese	+	–	Gil 2013	Kaiser et al. 2001: passim
Eurasia	Kartvelian	Kartvelian	Georgian	–	–	Gil 2013	Corbett 2013
Eurasia	Korean	Korean	Korean	+	–	Gil 2013	Nichols 1992: 297
Eurasia	Nakh-Daghestanian	Avar-Andic-Tsezic	Avar	+	+	Gil 2013	Charachidzé 1981: 29–30; van den Berg 2005: 155–156
Eurasia	Nakh-Daghestanian	Avar-Andic-Tsezic	Bagvalal	–	+	Gil 2013	Corbett 2006: 749–750
Eurasia	Nakh-Daghestanian	Avar-Andic-Tsezic	Hunzib	–	+	Gil 2013	Corbett 2013; van den Berg 2004: 1367
Eurasia	Nakh-Daghestanian	Lak-Dargwa	Dargwa	–	+	Gil 2013	van den Berg 2005: 156–158
Eurasia	Nakh-Daghestanian	Lezgic	Lezgian	–	–	Gil 2013	Corbett 2013
Eurasia	Nakh-Daghestanian	Nakh	Chechen	–	+	Gil 2013	Nichols 1994: 37
Eurasia	Nakh-Daghestanian	Nakh	Ingush	–	+	Gil 2013	Corbett 2013; Nichols 2011: 141–142
Eurasia	Nivkh	Nivkh	Nivkh	+	–	Gil 2013	Corbett 2013
Eurasia	NW Caucasian	NW Caucasian	Abkhaz	+	+	Gil 2013	Corbett 2013; Spruit 1986: 108
Eurasia	Sino-Tibetan	Bodic	Gurung	–	–	Nichols 1992: 297	Nichols 1992: 297
Eurasia	Sino-Tibetan	Bodo-Garo	Garo	+	–	Gil 2013	Burling 1961: passim

Macroarea	Family	Genus	Language	Cl	Gd	Sources (classifiers)	Sources (gender)
Eurasia	Sino-Tibetan	Burmese-Lolo	Burmese	+	−	Gil 2013	Corbett 2013
Eurasia	Sino-Tibetan	Burmese-Lolo	Lahu	+	−	Gil 2013	Corbett 2013
Eurasia	Sino-Tibetan	Chinese	Cantonese	+	−	Gil 2013	Corbett 2013
Eurasia	Sino-Tibetan	Chinese	Mandarin	+	−	Gil 2013	Corbett 2013
Eurasia	Sino-Tibetan	Mahakiranti	Chepang	−	−	Gil 2013	Caughley 1982: 42, 50, 51, 55
Eurasia	Tai-Kadai	Kadai	Lachi	+	−	Gil 2013	Kosaka 2000: 68–77
Eurasia	Tai-Kadai	Kam-Tai	Thai	+	−	Gil 2013	Corbett 2013
Eurasia	Uralic	Finnic	Finnish	−	−	Gil 2013	Corbett 2013
Eurasia	Uralic	Mordvin	Mordvin (Erzya)	−	−	Gil 2013	Zaicz 1998: 191–197
Eurasia	Uralic	Permic	Komi-Zyrian	−	−	Gil 2013	Nichols 1992: 295
Eurasia	Uralic	Samoyedic	Nenets	−	−	Gil 2013	Corbett 2013
Eurasia	Uralic	Ugric	Hungarian	+	−	Gil 2013	Corbett 2013
Eurasia	Yukaghir	Yukaghir	Yukaghir (Kolyma)	−	−	Gil 2013	Corbett 2013
N. America	Algic	Algonquian	Cree (Plains)	−	+	Gil 2013	Corbett 2013; Wolfart 1973: 20–24, 33–38
N. America	Algic	Yurok	Yurok	+	−	Nichols 1992: 299	Corbett 2013
N. America	Atakapa	Atakapa	Atakapa	−	−	Gil 2013	Swanton 1929: 125, 136–140
N. America	Chibchan	Talamanca	Teribe	−	−	Gil 2013	Quesada & Skopeteas 2010: passim
N. America	Chimakuan	Chimakuan	Quileute	+	+	Gil 2013	Nichols 1992: 299
N. America	Chitimacha	Chitimacha	Chitimacha	−	−	Gil 2013	Granberry 2004: 52–53, 78–85
N. America	Chumash	Chumash	Chumash (Barbareño)	−	−	Gil 2013	Wash 2001: passim
N. America	Chumash	Chumash	Chumash (Ineseño)	−	−	Gil 2013	Applegate 1972: passim
N. America	Eskimo-Aleut	Eskimo	Yup'ik (C.)	−	−	Reed et al. 1977: 201–207	Corbett 2013
N. America	Haida	Haida	Haida	+	−	Gil 2013	Corbett 2013
N. America	Hokan	Chimariko	Chimariko	−	−	Gil 2013	Corbett 2013
N. America	Hokan	Yuman	Diegueño (Mesa Grande)	−	−	Nichols 1992: 299	Nichols 1992: 299
N. America	Hokan	Yuman	Maricopa	−	−	Gil 2013	Corbett 2013
N. America	Iroquoian	N. Iroquoian	Seneca	−	+	Gil 2013	Corbett 2013; Chafe 1967: 13–22
N. America	Karok	Karok	Karok	−	−	Gil 2013	Corbett 2013
N. America	Keresan	Keresan	Acoma	−	−	Gil 2013	Corbett 2013
N. America	Kiowa-Tanoan	Kiowa-Tanoan	Kiowa	−	+	Gil 2013	Sutton 2010: 59–67
N. America	Kutenai	Kutenai	Kutenai	−	−	Gil 2013	Corbett 2013
N. America	Mayan	Mayan	Jacaltec	+	−	Gil 2013; Craig 1986: 244	Day 1973: passim
N. America	Mayan	Mayan	Tzeltal	+	−	Gil 2013	Kaufman 1963: 171–172
N. America	Mayan	Mayan	Tzutujil	+	−	Nichols 1992: 301	Nichols 1992: 301
N. America	Mayan	Mayan	Yucatec	+	−	Gil 2013	Brody 2004: 66, 69
N. America	Misumalpan	Misumalpan	Miskito	−	−	Gil 2013	Heath 1913: 56
N. America	Muskogean	Muskogean	Choctaw	−	−	Gil 2013	Davies 1986: passim
N. America	Na-Dene	Athapaskan	Navajo	−	−	Gil 2013	Nichols 1992: 299
N. America	Tlingit	Tlingit	Tlingit	+	−	Gil 2013	Boas 1917: passim
N. America	Oregon Coast	Coosan	Coos (Hanis)	−	−	Gil 2013	Corbett 2013
N. America	Otomanguean	Chichimec	Chichimeca-Jonaz	−	−	Gil 2013	de Suárez 1984: 23–30
N. America	Otomanguean	Mixtecan	Mixtec (Chalcatongo)	−	−	Gil 2013	Corbett 2013; Macaulay 1996: 81–85
N. America	Otomanguean	Otomian	Otomi (Mezquital)	−	−	Gil 2013	Hess 1968: passim
N. America	Otomanguean	Zapotecan	Zapotec (Coatlán)	−	−	Hess 1968: passim	Beam de Azcona 2004: passim
N. America	Penutian	Chinookan	Chinook (Upper)	−	+	Beam de Azcona 2004: passim	Hymes 1955: 72–75, 214
N. America	Penutian	Klamath-Modoc	Klamath	−	−	Gil 2013	Mithun 2001: 448–451
N. America	Penutian	Maiduan	Maidu (NE)	−	−	Gil 2013	Nichols 1992: 299

Macroarea	Family	Genus	Language	Cl	Gd	Sources (classifiers)	Sources (gender)
N. America	Penutian	Miwok	Miwok (S. Sierra)	–	–	Gil 2013	Corbett 2013
N. America	Penutian	Sahaptian	Sahaptin (Umatilla)	+	–	Nichols 1992: 299	Nichols 1992: 299
N. America	Penutian	Tsimshianic	Gitksan	+	–	Nichols 1992: 299	Hunt 1993: passim
N. America	Penutian	Tsimshianic	Tsimshian (Coast)	+	–	Gil 2013	Corbett 2013
N. America	Penutian	Yokuts	Yawelmani	–	–	Gil 2013	Nichols 1992: 299
N. America	Salinan	Salinan	Salinan	–	–	Gil 2013	Nichols 1992: 299
N. America	Salishan	Central Salish	Halkomelem (Island)	+	+	Gerdts & Hinkson 2004: 254–266	Gerdts 2013: 417–418; Gerdts 2010: 176–177
N. America	Salishan	Interior Salish	Thompson	+	–	Gil 2013	Corbett 2013
N. America	Siouan	Core Siouan	Lakhota	–	+	Gil 2013	Van Valin 1977: 36–37
N. America	Siouan	Core Siouan	Mandan	–	–	Gil 2013	Kennard 1936: passim
N. America	Takelma	Takelma	Takelma	–	–	Gil 2013	Nichols 1992: 299
N. America	Tequistlatecan	Tequistlatecan	Chontal (Huamelultec Oaxaca)	+	–	Nichols 1992: 301	Waterhouse 1967: 356–358
N. America	Tol	Tol	Tol	–	–	Gil 2013	Corbett 2013
N. America	Totonacan	Totonacan	Tepehua (Tlachichilco)	+	–	Nichols 1992: 301	Nichols 1992: 301
N. America	Tunica	Tunica	Tunica	–	+	Gil 2013	Corbett 2013; Haas 1940: 36–38, 62, 64–65, 102–110
N. America	Uto-Aztecan	Aztecan	Nahuatl (Tetelcingo)	–	–	Gil 2013	Corbett 2013
N. America	Uto-Aztecan	Aztecan	Pipil	–	–	Gil 2013	Corbett 2013
N. America	Uto-Aztecan	California Uto-Aztecan	Luiseño	–	–	Gil 2013	Elliott 1999: 23–28
N. America	Uto-Aztecan	Numic	Paiute (S.)	–	–	Gil 2013	Nichols 1992: 299
N. America	Uto-Aztecan	Tepiman	O'odham	–	–	Gil 2013	Nichols 1992: 299
N. America	Uto-Aztecan	Tepiman	Tepehuan (SE)	–	+	Gil 2013	Willett 1991: 83–84
N. America	Wappo-Yukian	Wappo	Wappo	–	–	Gil 2013	Nichols 1992: 299
N. America	Yuchi	Yuchi	Yuchi	–	+	Gil 2013	Nichols 1992: 301
N. America	Zuni	Zuni	Zuni	–	–	Gil 2013	Corbett 2013
Papunesia	Atayalic	Atayalic	Atayal	+	–	Gil 2013	Rau 1992: passim
Papunesia	Austronesian	C. Malayo-Polynesian	Kambera	+	–	Gil 2013	Corbett 2013
Papunesia	Austronesian	C. Malayo-Polynesian	Ke'o	–	–	Gil 2013	Baird 2002: passim
Papunesia	Austronesian	C. Malayo-Polynesian	Leti	+	–	Gil 2013	van Engelenhoven & Williams-van Klinken 2005: passim
Papunesia	Austronesian	C. Malayo-Polynesian	Sawu	+	–	Gil 2013	Corbett 2013
Papunesia	Austronesian	C. Malayo-Polynesian	Tetun	+	–	Gil 2013	Morris 1984:xiv
Papunesia	Austronesian	Celebic	Tukang Besi	–	–	Gil 2013	Corbett 2013
Papunesia	Austronesian	Chamorro	Chamorro	+	–	Nichols 1992: 137, 299; Topping 1973: 164–166	Topping 1973: passim; Nichols 1992: 299
Papunesia	Austronesian	E. Formosan	Amis	–	–	Gil 2013	Wu 2006: 79
Papunesia	Austronesian	Greater C. Philippine	Tagalog	–	+	Gil 2013	Corbett 2013; Schachter & Otanes 1972: 197–198
Papunesia	Austronesian	Javanese	Javanese	+	–	Gil 2013	Oakes 2009: passim
Papunesia	Austronesian	Malayo-Sumbawan	Balinese	–	–	Gil 2013	Artawa 2013: passim
Papunesia	Austronesian	Malayo-Sumbawan	Indonesian	+	–	Gil 2013	Corbett 2013
Papunesia	Austronesian	Malayo-Sumbawan	Minangkabau	+	–	Gil 2013	Crouch 2009: 60–63
Papunesia	Austronesian	N. Borneo	Begak-Ida'an	–	–	Gil 2013	Goudswaard 2005: 88, 101–102
Papunesia	Austronesian	NW Sumatra-Barrier Islands	Batak (Karo)	+	–	Gil 2013	Corbett 2013
Papunesia	Austronesian	Oceanic	Drehu	–	–	Gil 2013	Nichols 1992: 299
Papunesia	Austronesian	Oceanic	Erromangan	–	–	Gil 2013	Corbett 2013

Macroarea	Family	Genus	Language	Cl	Gd	Sources (classifiers)	Sources (gender)
Papunesia	Austronesian	Oceanic	Fijian	−	−	Gil 2013	Corbett 2013
Papunesia	Austronesian	Oceanic	Futuna-Aniwa	−	−	Gil 2013	Dougherty 1983: passim
Papunesia	Austronesian	Oceanic	Hawaiian	−	−	Gil 2013	Corbett 2013
Papunesia	Austronesian	Oceanic	Iaai	+	−	Gil 2013	Corbett 2013
Papunesia	Austronesian	Oceanic	Kilivila	+	−	Gil 2013	Corbett 2013
Papunesia	Austronesian	Oceanic	Mokilese	+	−	Gil 2013	Corbett 2013
Papunesia	Austronesian	Oceanic	Pileni	+	−	Gil 2013	Corbett 2013
Papunesia	Austronesian	Oceanic	Pohnpeian	+	−	Gil 2013	Rehg & Sohl 1981: passim; Nichols 1992: 299
Papunesia	Austronesian	Oceanic	Rapanui	−	−	Gil 2013	Corbett 2013
Papunesia	Austronesian	Oceanic	Tawala	−	−	Gil 2013	Nichols 1992: 297
Papunesia	Austronesian	Oceanic	Teop	−	+	Mosel & Spriggs 2000: 328–329	Svärd (2019 [in Volume I])
Papunesia	Austronesian	Oceanic	Tongan	+	−	Gil 2013	Otsuka 2000: 49
Papunesia	Austronesian	Oceanic	Toqabaqita	+	−	Gil 2013	Lichtenberk 2008: passim
Papunesia	Austronesian	Oceanic	Tuvaluan	+	−	Gil 2013	Corbett 2013
Papunesia	Austronesian	Oceanic	Ulithian	+	−	Lynch 2002: passim	Lynch 2002: passim
Papunesia	Austronesian	Paiwan	Paiwan	−	−	Tang 2004: 380–382	Corbett 2013
Papunesia	Austronesian	Palauan	Palauan	+	−	Georgopoulos 1985: passim	Georgopoulos 1985: passim
Papunesia	Austronesian	S. Halmahera - W. New Guinea	Taba	+	−	Gil 2013	Corbett 2013
Papunesia	Austronesian	S. Sulawesi	Makassar	+	−	Gil 2013; Jukes 2006: 205	Jukes 2006: passim
Papunesia	Austronesian	Sama-Bajaw	Bajau (Sama)	+	−	Jun 2005: 387	Jun 2005: 387
Papunesia	Austronesian	Yapese	Yapese	+	−	Gil 2013	Jensen 1977: passim
Papunesia	Baining-Taulil	Taulil	Mali	−	+	Gil 2013	Stebbins & Tayul 2012: 12–15
Papunesia	Baining-Taulil	Taulil	Taulil	−	+	Gil 2013	Terrill 2002: 69–70
Papunesia	Border	Border	Imonda	−	−	Gil 2013	Corbett 2013
Papunesia	Dagan	Dagan	Daga	−	−	Murane 1974: 75–81, 91	Corbett 2013
Papunesia	E. Bougainville	E. Bougainville	Motuna	−	+	Terrill 2002: 74–75	Terrill 2002: 74–75
Papunesia	E. Bougainville	E. Bougainville	Nasioi	−	+	Nichols 1992: 299; Foley 1986: 83–85	Nichols 1992: 299; Terrill 2002: 75–76; Hurd & Hurd 1966: passim
Papunesia	Kiwaian	Kiwaian	Kiwai	+	−	Gil 2013	Brown 2009: 14
Papunesia	Kuot	Kuot	Kuot	−	+	Lindström 2002: 132, 200	Lindström 2002: 130, 176–177
Papunesia	Left May	Left May	Ama	−	+	Arsjö 1999: 79	Svärd (2019 [in Volume I])
Papunesia	Lower Sepik-Ramu	Lower Sepik	Yimas	−	+	Gil 2013	Corbett 2013; Phillips 1993: 175–178
Papunesia	Sentani	Sentani	Sentani	−	−	Gil 2013	Corbett 2013
Papunesia	Sepik	Middle Sepik	Ambulas	−	+	Gil 2013	Wilson 1980: 53, 63, 67
Papunesia	Sepik	Middle Sepik	Iatmul	−	+	Jendraschek 2012: 137–140	Jendraschek 2012: 124–128
Papunesia	Sepik	Ram	Awtuw	−	+	Gil 2013	Feldman 1986: 41, 45, 108–109
Papunesia	Sepik	Sepik Hill	Alamblak	−	+	Gil 2013	Corbett 2013; Bruce 1984: 74–75, 81, 96–98, 149
Papunesia	Sepik	Tama Sepik	Yessan-Mayo	−	−	Gil 2013	Foreman 1974: 27–28, 34–42, 56
Papunesia	Sepik	Upper Sepik	Abau	+	+	Lock 2011: 56–59	Lock 2011: 85–89
Papunesia	Sepik	Upper Sepik	Iwam	−	−	Laycock & Z'graggen 1975: 742–743	Laycock & Z'graggen 1975: 742–743
Papunesia	Skou	W. Skou	Dumo	−	+	Gil 2013	Ross 1980: 83–86, 94
Papunesia	Skou	Warapu	Barupu	−	+	Corris 2005: 115–116	Svärd (2019 [in Volume I])
Papunesia	Solomons E. Papuan	Lavukaleve	Lavukaleve	−	+	Terrill 2003: passim	Corbett 2013; Terrill 2003: 53–56, 243
Papunesia	Sulka	Sulka	Sulka	−	−	Gil 2013	Tharp 1996: 79, 85, 90
Papunesia	Timor-Alor-Pantar	Greater Alor	Adang	+	−	Haan 2001: 292–304	Haan 2001: passim

Macroarea	Family	Genus	Language	Cl	Gd	Sources (classifiers)	Sources (gender)
Papunesia	Timor-Alor-Pantar	Greater Alor	Klon	+	−	Baird 2008: 62–64	Baird 2008: 62–64
Papunesia	Timor-Alor-Pantar	Greater Alor	Teiwa	+	−	Klamer 2017: 36	Klamer 2017: 33
Papunesia	Timor-Alor-Pantar	Makasae-Fataluku-Oirata	Makasae	+	+	Huber 2008: 13, 23–24	Huber 2008: 13, 23–24
Papunesia	Tor-Orya	Tor	Berik	−	−	Westrum 1988: 139, 155–156, passim	Westrum 1988: 150, 153
Papunesia	Torricelli	Kombio-Arapesh	Arapesh (Mountain)	+	−	Nichols 1992: 297	Nichols 1992: 297
Papunesia	Torricelli	Kombio-Arapesh	Mufian	−	+	Alungum et al. 1978: 104	Alungum et al. 1978: 92–93
Papunesia	Torricelli	Urim	Urim	−	−	Hemmilä & Luoma 1987: 82–84, 139–140	Hemmilä & Luoma 1987: passim
Papunesia	Torricelli	Wapei-Palei	Olo	−	+	Staley 2007: 17, 19	Staley 2007: 9–10, 17–18
Papunesia	Torricelli	Wapei-Palei	Au	−	+	Scorza 1985: 231–232, 238–239, 259	Svärd (2019 [in Volume I])
Papunesia	Angan	Angan	Tainae	−	+	Carlson 1991: 7, 116–118	Carlson 1991: 7, 23–34
Papunesia	Trans-New Guinea	Awju-Dumut	Kombai	−	−	Gil 2013	de Vries 1993: 21, 34–42
Papunesia	Trans-New Guinea	Binanderean	Korafe	−	−	Gil 2013	Farr 1993: passim
Papunesia	Trans-New Guinea	Binanderean	Suena	−	−	Gil 2013	Corbett 2013
Papunesia	Trans-New Guinea	Dani	Dani (Lower Grand Valley)	−	−	Bromley 1981: passim	Bromley 1981: passim
Papunesia	Trans-New Guinea	E. Highlands	Hua	−	−	Gil 2013	Haiman 1980: 47, 219
Papunesia	Trans-New Guinea	Engan	Huli	−	−	Lomas 1988: 196–197	Lomas 1988: 184–185
Papunesia	Trans-New Guinea	Engan	Kewa	−	−	Gil 2013	Corbett 2013
Papunesia	Trans-New Guinea	Finisterre-Huon	Awara	−	−	Quigley 2016: 16–19; Aikhenvald 2000: 124	Quigley 2016: passim
Papunesia	Trans-New Guinea	Finisterre-Huon	Käte	−	−	Gil 2013	Nichols 1992: 297
Papunesia	Trans-New Guinea	Koiarian	Koiari	−	−	Gil 2013	Dutton 1996: 39–41
Papunesia	Trans-New Guinea	Madang	Amele	−	−	Gil 2013	Corbett 2013
Papunesia	Trans-New Guinea	Madang	Kobon	−	−	Gil 2013	Corbett 2013
Papunesia	Trans-New Guinea	Madang	Usan	−	−	Reesink 1987: passim	Reesink 1987: passim
Papunesia	Trans-New Guinea	Mek	Nalca	−	+	Svärd 2013: 31–33	Svärd (2019 [in Volume I])
Papunesia	Trans-New Guinea	Mek	Una	−	−	Louwerse 1988: 77–78	Corbett 2013
Papunesia	Trans-New Guinea	Ok	Mian	+	+	Fedden 2011: 144–148	Fedden 2011: 169–171
Papunesia	Trans-New Guinea	Ok	Telefol	+	+	Gil 2013	Nichols 1992: 299
Papunesia	Trans-New Guinea	Wissel Lakes-Kemandoga	Ekari	−	+	Doble 1987: 75	Doble 1987: 89, 94
Papunesia	W. Bougainville	W. Bougainville	Konua	−	−	Gil 2013	Müller 1954: 14, 21–25
Papunesia	W. Bougainville	W. Bougainville	Rotokas	+	+	Robinson 2011: 125–127	Svärd (2019 [in Volume I])
Papunesia	W. Papuan	Hatam	Hatam	−	−	Gil 2013	Corbett 2013
Papunesia	W. Papuan	Kebar	Mpur	+	+	Klamer 2014: 109–110; Reesink 1996: 10	Reesink 1996: 2–3
Papunesia	W. Papuan	N. Halmaheran	Tidore	+	+	Gil 2013	Corbett 2013; van van Staden 2006: passim
Papunesia	W. Papuan	N-C. Bird's Head	Abun	+	−	Gil 2013	Berry & Berry 2000: passim
Papunesia	W. Papuan	N-C. Bird's Head	Maybrat	+	+	Gil 2013; Derbyshire & Payne 1990: 249–252	Corbett 2013; Dol 1999: 68, 98
Papunesia	W. Papuan	W. Bird's Head	Tehit	+	+	Gil 2013	Hesse 2000: 25–26
Papunesia	Yale	Yale	Nagatman	−	+	Campbell & Campbell 1987: 14	Campbell & Campbell 1987: 18–22, 44–49
S. America	Arauan	Arauan	Culina	−	+	Gil 2013	Derbyshire & Payne 1990: 249–251
S. America	Arauan	Arauan	Deni	−	+	Gil 2013; Derbyshire & Payne 1990: 249–252	Moran & Moran 1977: 40–41
S. America	Arauan	Arauan	Jamamadi	−	−	Gil 2013; Derbyshire & Payne 1990: 249–250	Campbell 1985: 1
S. America	Arauan	Arauan	Jarawara	−	+	Aikhenvald 2000: passim	Dixon 1995: 264–265
S. America	Arauan	Arauan	Paumari	−	+	Gil 2013	Corbett 2013; Aikhenvald 2010: 237

Macroarea	Family	Genus	Language	Cl	Gd	Sources (classifiers)	Sources (gender)
S. America	Araucanian	Araucanian	Mapudungun	–	–	Gil 2013	Corbett 2013
S. America	Arawakan	Alto-Orinoco	Baniwa	+	+	Aikhenvald 2007: 479–487	Aikhenvald 2007: 476–479
S. America	Arawakan	Bolivia-Parana	Teréna	–	–	Gil 2013	Derbyshire & Payne 1990: 252
S. America	Arawakan	C. Arawakan	Parecís	+	–	Gil 2013	Brandao 2014: 4
S. America	Arawakan	C. Arawakan	Waurá	+	–	Gil 2013	Payne 1991: 377
S. America	Arawakan	Caribbean Arawakan	Arawak	–	+	Gil 2013	Pet 1987: 23, 28–29
S. America	Arawakan	E. Arawakan	Palikur	+	+	Gil 2013; Aikhenvald 2000: 192–198	Derbyshire & Payne 1990: 262–263; Aikhenvald 2000: 192–198
S. America	Arawakan	Inland Northern Arawakan	Baré	–	+	Gil 2013	Aikhenvald 2007: 850–852
S. America	Arawakan	Inland Northern Arawakan	Warekena	+	+	Gil 2013	Aikhenvald & Dixon 1998: 298–299
S. America	Arawakan	Pre-Andine Arawakan	Ashéninka Perené	–	+	Mihas 2010: 184–185	Mihas 2010: 121–122
S. America	Arawakan	Pre-Andine Arawakan	Nomatsiguenga	–	+	Derbyshire & Payne 1990: 262	Derbyshire & Payne 1990: 262
S. America	Arawakan	Purus	Apurinã	–	+	Gil 2013	Corbett 2013; da Silva Facundes 2000: 145–148, 222–232, 348–349
S. America	Arawakan	Purus	Piro	–	+	Gil 2013	Derbyshire & Payne 1990: 248
S. America	Aymaran	Aymaran	Jaqaru	–	–	Gil 2013	Corbett 2013
S. America	Barbacoan	Barbacoan	Awa Pit	–	–	Curnow 1997: 86, 93–94	Corbett 2013
S. America	Cahuapanan	Cahuapanan	Chayahuita	+	–	Gil 2013	Hart 1988: 258–272
S. America	Cariban	Cariban	Hixkaryana	–	–	Gil 2013	Corbett 2013; Derbyshire 1985: 6–7
S. America	Cariban	Cariban	Macushi	–	+	Abbott 1991: 89	Abbott 1991: 105
S. America	Cariban	Cariban	Panare	–	–	Gil 2013	Derbyshire & Payne 1990: 263–264
S. America	Cayuvava	Cayuvava	Cayuvava	–	–	Gil 2013	Corbett 2013
S. America	Chapacura-Wanham	Chapacura-Wanham	Wari'	+	–	Gil 2013	Corbett 2013; Everett & Kern 1997: 2–3
S. America	Chibchan	Arhuacic	Ika	–	+	Gil 2013	Corbett 2013
S. America	Chibchan	Chibcha-Duit	Muisca	–	–	Gil 2013	Corbett 2013
S. America	Choco	Choco	Epena Pedee	–	+	Gil 2013	Adelaar & Muysken 2004: 81–108
S. America	Harakmbet	Harakmbet	Amarakaeri	–	+	Gil 2013	Tripp 1995: 213
S. America	Huitotoan	Boran	Bora	+	+	Gil 2013	Thiesen 1996: 27, 33, 36–37, 46–47
S. America	Huitotoan	Huitoto	Ocaina	+	–	Gil 2013	Derbyshire & Payne 1990: 257
S. America	Jivaroan	Jivaroan	Jivaro	–	–	Gil 2013	Saad 2014: 32
S. America	Kwaza	Kwaza	Kwazá	+	–	Gil 2013	van der Voort 2004: 24, 105
S. America	Macro-Ge	Ge-Kaingang	Canela-Krahô	–	–	Gil 2013	Corbett 2013
S. America	Máku	Máku	Máku	–	+	Gil 2013	Aikhenvald & Dixon 1999: 362
S. America	Mosetenan	Mosetenan	Mosetén	–	+	Gil 2013	Corbett 2013; Sakel 2002: 288–302
S. America	Movima	Movima	Movima	–	–	Haude 2006: 10, 113–114	Haude 2006: 148–149
S. America	Mura	Mura	Pirahã	–	–	Gil 2013	Corbett 2013; Everett 1986: 281
S. America	Nadahup	Nadahup	Hup	+	–	Gil 2013	Epps 2008: 191–195, 241–244
S. America	other	Creoles & Pidgins	Ndyuka	–	–	Gil 2013	Corbett 2013
S. America	Panoan	Panoan	Capanahua	–	–	Gil 2013	Loos 1969: passim
S. America	Panoan	Panoan	Shipibo-Konibo	–	–	Gil 2013	Corbett 2013
S. America	Peba-Yaguan	Peba-Yaguan	Yagua	+	–	Gil 2013	Payne 2007: 457, 460–462
S. America	Quechuan	Quechuan	Quechua (Huallaga)	–	–	Gil 2013	Weber 1989: passim
S. America	Quechuan	Quechuan	Quechua (Imbabura)	–	–	Gil 2013	Corbett 2013
S. America	Sáliban	Piaroa	Piaroa	+	–	Gil 2013	Krute 1989: passim
S. America	Trumai	Trumai	Trumai	–	+	Guirardello 1999: 68–75	Guirardello 1999: 48–55
S. America	Tucanoan	Tucanoan	Barasano	+	+	Jones & Jones 1991: 49–50, 59–60	Jones & Jones 1991: 31, 73–75
S. America	Tucanoan	Tucanoan	Orejón	+	+	Gil 2013	Velie 1975: 24–27
S. America	Tucanoan	Tucanoan	Siona	+	+	Gil 2013; Derbyshire & Payne 1990: 256	Wheeler 1970: 2, 91–95, 140–141; Derbyshire & Payne 1990: 256

Macroarea	Family	Genus	Language	Cl	Gd	Sources (classifiers)	Sources (gender)
S. America	Tucanoan	Tucanoan	Tucano	+	+	Gil 2013	Derbyshire & Payne 1990: 255–256; Ramírez 1997: 207–208
S. America	Tucanoan	Tucanoan	Tuyuca	+	+	Gil 2013; Derbyshire & Payne 1990: 354	Bowles 2008: 19, 21–22
S. America	Tupian	Monde	Gavião	-	-	Gil 2013; Derbyshire & Payne 1990: 246, 248	Moore 1984: passim
S. America	Tupian	Mundurukú	Mundurukú	+	-	Passer 2016a: passim; Gil 2013	Passer 2016a: passim; Derbyshire & Payne 1990: 261
S. America	Tupian	Tupi-Guarani	Guaraní	-	-	Gil 2013	Corbett 2013
S. America	Waorani	Waorani	Waorani	+	-	Gil 2013	Derbyshire & Payne 1990: 259; Peeke 1973: 125–128
S. America	Yanomam	Yanomam	Sanuma	+	-	Gil 2013; Derbyshire & Payne 1990: 246–248	Borgman 1990: 144–149, 197–198
S. America	Zaparoan	Zaparoan	Arabela	-	-	Gil 2013; Derbyshire & Payne 1990: 256–257	Rich 1999: 22–23, 35–36

References

Abbott, Miriam. 1991. Macushi. In Desmond C. Derbyshire & Geoffrey K. Pullum (eds.), *Handbook of Amazonian languages*, vol. 3, 23–160. Berlin: Mouton de Gruyter.

Adelaar, Willem F. H. & Pieter C. Muysken. 2004. *The languages of the Andes.* Cambridge: Cambridge University Press.

Ahland, Colleen Anne. 2012. *A grammar of Northern and Southern Gumuz.* University of Oregon. (Doctoral dissertation).

Aikhenvald, Alexandra Y. 2000. *Classifiers: A typology of noun categorization devices.* Oxford: Oxford University Press.

Aikhenvald, Alexandra Y. 2007. Reciprocals and reflexives in North-Arawak languages of the Upper Rio Negro. In Vladimir. P. Nedjalkov, Emma Š. Geniušienė & Zlatka Guentchéva (eds.), *Reciprocal constructions*, 845–855. Amsterdam: John Benjamins.

Aikhenvald, Alexandra Y. 2010. Gender, noun class and language obsolescence: The case of Paumarí. In Eithne B. Carlin & Simon van de Kerke (eds.), *Linguistics and archaeology in the Americas: The historization of language and society*, 235–252. Leiden: Brill.

Aikhenvald, Alexandra Y. & Robert M. W. Dixon. 1998. Dependencies between grammatical systems. *Language* 74(1). 56–80.

Aikhenvald, Alexandra Y. & Robert M. W. Dixon. 1999. Other small families and isolates. In R. M. W. Dixon & Alexandra Y. Aikhenvald (eds.), *The Amazonian languages*, 341–384. Cambridge: Cambridge University Press.

Aikhenvald, Alexandra Y. & Diana Green. 2011. Palikur and the typology of classifiers. In Alexandra Y. Aikhenvald & Robert M. W. Dixon (eds.), *Language at large: Essays on syntax and semantics*, 394–450. Leiden: Brill.

Alungum, John, Robert J. Conrad & Joshua Lukas. 1978. Some Muhiang grammatical notes. In Richard Loving (ed.), *Miscellaneous papers on Dobu and Arapesh* (Workpapers in Papua New Guinea Languages 25), 89–130. Ukarumpa: Summer Institute of Linguistics.

Andrason, Alexander. 2014. Language complexity: An insight from complex-system theory. *International Journal of Language and Linguistics* 2(2). 74–89.

Applegate, Richard B. 1972. *Ineseño Chumash grammar.* University of California, Berkeley. (Doctoral dissertation).

Appleyard, David L. 1975. A descriptive outline of Kemant. *Bulletin of the School of Oriental and African Studies* 38. 316–350.

Arensen, Jonathan E. 1982. *Murle grammar* (Occasional papers in the study of Sudanese languages 2). Juba: Summer Institute of Linguistics & University of Juba.

Arppe, Antti. 2008. *Univariate, bivariate, and multivariate methods in corpus-based lexicography: A study of synonymy.* University of Helsinki. (Doctoral dissertation).

Årsjö, Britten. 1999. *Words in Ama.* Uppsala: Uppsala University. (MA thesis).

Artawa, Ketut. 2013. The basic verb construction in Balinese. In Alexander Adelaar (ed.), *Voice variation in Austronesian languages of Indonesia* (NUSA 54), 5–27. Jakarta: Atma Jaya Catholic University of Indonesia.

Atkinson, Quentin D. 2011. Phonemic diversity supports a serial founder effect model of language expansion from Africa. *Science* 332(6027). 346–349.

Audring, Jenny. 2009. *Reinventing pronoun gender.* Vrije Universiteit, Amsterdam. (Doctoral dissertation).

Baayen, R. Harald. 2008. *Analyzing linguistic data: A practical introduction to statistics using R.* Cambridge: Cambridge University Press.

Baayen, R. Harald, Doug J. Davidson & Douglas M. Bates. 2008. Mixed-effects modeling with crossed random effects for subjects and items. *Journal of Memory and Language* 59(4). 390–412.

Baird, Louise. 2002. *A grammar of Kéo: An Austronesian language of Eastern Nusantara.* Australian National University. (Doctoral dissertation).

Baird, Louise. 2008. *A grammar of Klon: A non-Austronesian language of Alor, Indonesia* (Pacific Linguistics 596). Canberra: Australian National University.

Barr, Dale J., Roger Levy, Christoph Scheepers & Harry J. Tily. 2013. Random effects structure for confirmatory hypothesis testing: Keep it maximal. *Journal of Memory and Language* 68(3). 255–278.

Bates, Douglas, Reinhold Kliegl, Shravan Vasishth & R. Harald Baayen. 2015. Parsimonious mixed models. arXiv:1506.04967.

Bates, Douglas, Martin Maechler, Ben Bolker & Steve Walker. 2015. Fitting linear mixed-effects models using lme4. *Journal of Statistical Software* 67(1). 1–48.

Beam de Azcona, Rosemary Grace. 2004. *A Coatlan-Loxicha Zapotec grammar (Mexico).* University of California, Berkeley. (Doctoral dissertation).

Bentz, Christian & Bodo Winter. 2013. Languages with more second language learners tend to lose nominal case. *Language Dynamics and Change* 3. 1–27.

Berry, Keith & Christine Berry. 2000. Abun. In Ger P. Reesink (ed.), *Studies in Irian languages, Part II* (NUSA 47), 35–44. Jakarta: Universitas Katolik Indonesia Atma Jaya.

Bhattacharya, Sudhibhushan. 1976. Gender in the Munda languages. In Philip N. Jenner, Laurence C. Thompson & Stanley Starosta (eds.), *Austroasiatic studies, part I* (Oceanic Linguistics Special Publications 13), 189–211. Honolulu: University of Hawaii Press.

Bickel, Balthasar. 2007. Typology in the 21st century: Major current developments. *Linguistic Typology* 11(1). 239–251.

Bickel, Balthasar. 2008. A refined sampling procedure for genealogical control. *Language Typology and Universals* 61(3). 221–233.

Bickel, Balthasar. 2013. Distributional biases in language families. In Balthasar Bickel, Lenore A. Grenoble, David A. Peterson & Alan Timberlake (eds.), *Language typology and historical contingency: In honor of Johanna Nichols*, 415–444. Amsterdam: John Benjamins.

Bickel, Balthasar & Johanna Nichols. 2006. Oceania, the Pacific Rim, and the theory of linguistic areas. In *Proceedings of the 32nd annual meeting of the Berkeley Linguistics Society*, vol. 32, 3–15. Berkeley: Berkeley Linguistics Society. http://journals.linguisticsociety.org/proceedings/index.php/BLS/issue/view/120.

Bickel, Balthasar, Johanna Nichols, Taras Zakharko, Alena Witzlack-Makarevich, Kristine Hildebrandt, Michael Rießler, Lennart Bierkandt, Fernando Zúñiga & John B. Lowe. 2017. *The AUTOTYP typological databases*. https://github.com/autotyp/autotyp-data/tree/0.1.0. Version 0.1.0.

Bickel, Balthasar, Alena Witzlack-Makarevich, Kamal K. Choudhary, Matthias Schlesewsky & Ina Bornkessel-Schlesewsky. 2015. The neurophysiology of language processing shapes the evolution of grammar: Evidence from case marking. *PLoS ONE* 10(8). e0132819.

Bickel, Balthasar, Alena Witzlack-Makarevich & Taras Zakharko. 2014. Typological evidence against universal effects of referential scales on case alignment. In Ina Bornkessel-Schlesewsky, Andrej Malchukov & Marc Richards (eds.), *Scales and hierarchies: A cross-disciplinary perspective on referential hierarchies*, 7–44. Berlin: Mouton De Gruyter.

Birk, David B. W. 1976. *The Malakmalak language, Daly River (Western Arnhem Land)* (Pacific Linguistics B 45). Canberra: Australian National University.

Bisang, Walter. 2009. On the evolution of complexity: Sometimes less is more in East and mainland Southeast Asia. In Geoffrey Sampson, David Gil & Peter Trudgill (eds.), *Language complexity as an evolving variable*, 34–49. Oxford: Oxford University Press.

Bliese, Loren F. 1981. *A generative grammar of Afar* (Summer Institute of Linguistics Publications 65). Dallas, TX: The Summer Institute of Linguistics & the University of Texas at Arlington.

Boas, Franz. 1917. *Grammatical notes on the language of the Tlingit Indians* (University of Pennsylvania University Museum Anthropological Publications 8.1). Philadelphia: University of Pennsylvania.

Borgman, Donald M. 1990. Sanuma. In Desmond C. Derbyshire & Geoffrey K. Pullum (eds.), *Handbook of Amazonian languages*, vol. 2, 15–248. Berlin: Mouton de Gruyter.

Bornkessel-Schlesewsky, Ina & Matthias Schlesewsky. 2009. Minimality as vacuous distinctness: Evidence from cross-linguistic sentence comprehension. *Lingua* 119(10). 1541–1559.

Bowles, Joshua Wayne. 2008. *Agreement in Tuyuca*. University of Utah. (MA thesis).

Braine, Jean Critchfield. 1970. *Nicobarese grammar (Car dialect)*. University of California, Berkeley. (Doctoral dissertation).

Brandao, Ana. 2014. *A reference grammar of Paresi-Haliti (Arawak)*. University of Texas at Austin. (Doctoral dissertation).

Breslow, Norman E. & David G. Clayton. 1993. Approximate inference in generalized linear mixed models. *Journal of the American Statistical Association* 88(421). 9–25.

Brody, Michal. 2004. *The fixed word, the moving tongue: Variation in written Yucatec Maya and the meandering evolution toward unified norms*. University of Texas at Austin. (Doctoral dissertation).

Bromley, H. Myron. 1981. *A grammar of Lower Grand Valley Dani* (Pacific Linguistics C 63). Canberra: Australian National University.

Brown, Jessica. 2009. *A brief sketch of Urama grammar with special consideration of particles marking agency, aspect and modality*. University of North Dakota. (MA thesis).

Bruce, Leslie P. 1984. *The Alamblak language of Papua New Guinea (East Sepik)* (Pacific Linguistics C 81). Canberra: Department of Linguistics, Research School of Pacific Studies, Australian National University.

Burling, Robbins. 1961. *A Garo grammar* (Deccan College Monograph Series 25). Pune: Deccan College Postgraduate & Research Institute.

Burton, Michael L., Carmella C. Moore, John W. M. Whiting & A. Kimball Romney. 1996. Regions based on social structure. *Current Anthropology* 37(1). 87–123.

Campbell, Barbara. 1985. Jamamadi noun phrase. In David Lee Fortune (ed.), *Porto Velho workpapers*, 130–165. Barsília: Summer Institute of Linguistics.

Campbell, Carl & Judy Campbell. 1987. Yade grammar essentials. Unpublished Manuscript.

Campbell, Lyle. 2016. Language isolates and their history, or, what's weird, anyway? In *Proceedings of the 36th annual meeting of the Berkeley Linguistics Society*, vol. 36, 16–31. Berkeley: Berkeley Linguistics Society. http://escholarship. org/uc/item/79c9q87s.

Canonici, Noverino N. 1995. *Zulu grammatical structure*. Durban: Zulu language & literature, University of Natal.

Capell, Arthur & Heather H. Hinch. 1970. *Maung grammar: Texts and vocabulary*. The Hague: Mouton.

Carlin, Eithne. 1993. *The So language*. Cologne: Institut für Afrikanistik, Universität zu Köln.

Carlson, Robert. 1994. *A grammar of Supyire*. Berlin: Mouton de Gruyter.

Carlson, Terry. 1991. Tainae grammar essentials. Ukarumpa. Unpublished Manuscript.

Caughley, Ross Charles. 1982. *The syntax and morphology of the verb in Chepang* (Pacific Linguistics B 84). Canberra: Australian National University.

Chafe, Wallace. 1967. *Seneca morphology and dictionary*. Washington: Smithsonian Press.

Chandralai, Dileep. 2010. *Sinhala*. Amsterdam: John Benjamins.

Charachidzé, Georges. 1981. *Grammaire de la langue avar (langue du Caucase Nord-Est)* (Documents de linguistique quantitative 38). Paris: Farvard.

Clendon, Mark. 2000. *Topics in Worora grammar*. University of Adeleide. (Doctoral dissertation).

Contini-Morava, Ellen & Marcin Kilarski. 2013. Functions of nominal classification. *Language Sciences* 40. 263–299.

Corbett, Greville G. 1991. *Gender*. Cambridge: Cambridge University Press.

Corbett, Greville G. 2006. *Agreement*. Cambridge: Cambridge University Press.

Corbett, Greville G. 2013. Number of genders. In Matthew S. Dryer & Martin Haspelmath (eds.), *The world atlas of language structures online*. Leipzig: Max Planck Institute for Evolutionary Anthropology. http://wals.info/chapter/30.

Corbett, Greville G. & Sebastian Fedden. 2016. Canonical gender. *Journal of Linguistics* 52(3). 495–531.

Corris, Miriam. 2005. *A grammar of Barupu: A language of Papua New Guinea*. Sydney: University of Sydney. (Doctoral dissertation).

Craig, Colette. 1986. Jacaltec noun classifiers: A study in language and culture. In Colette Craig (ed.), *Noun classes and categorization*, 263–293. Amsterdam: John Benjamins.

Crouch, Sophie Elizabeth. 2009. *Voice and verb morphology in Minangkabau, a language of West Sumatra, Indonesia.* The University of Western Australia. (MA thesis).

Curnow, Timothy J. 1997. *A grammar of Awa Pit (Cuaiquer): An indigenous language of South-western Colombia.* Australian National University. (Doctoral dissertation).

Cysouw, Michael. 2010. Dealing with diversity: Towards an explanation of NP-internal word order frequencies. *Linguistic Typology* 14(2-3). 253–286.

Cysouw, Michael. 2011. Understanding transition probabilities. *Linguistic Typology* 15(2). 415–431.

da Silva Facundes, Sidney. 2000. *The language of the Apurinã people of Brazil (Maipure/Arawak).* State University of New York, Buffalo. (Doctoral dissertation).

Dahl, Östen. 2000. Elementary gender distinctions. In Matti Rissanen, Terttu Nevalainen & Mirja Saari (eds.), *Gender in grammar and cognition. Vol. 2: Elementary gender distinctions: Manifestations of gender* (Trends in Linguistics. Studies and Monographs 124), 577–593. Berlin: de Gruyter.

Dahl, Östen. 2004. *The growth and maintenance of linguistic complexity.* Amsterdam: John Benjamins.

Davies, William D. 1986. *Choctaw verb agreement and universal grammar.* Dordrecht: Reidel.

Day, Christopher. 1973. *The Jacaltec language* (Language Science Monographs 12). Bloomington: Indiana University Press.

de Suárez, Yolanda Lastra. 1984. Chichimeco Jonaz. In Munro S. Edmonson (ed.), *Supplement to the handbook of Middle American Indians: Linguistics,* vol. 2, 20–42. Austin: University of Texas Press.

de Vries, Lourens. 1993. *Forms and functions in Kombai, an Awyu language of Irian Jaya* (Pacific linguistics B 108). Canberra: Australian National University.

Dediu, Dan & Michael Cysouw. 2013. Some structural aspects of language are more stable than others: A comparison of seven methods. *PLoS ONE* 8(1). https://doi.org/10.1371/journal.pone.0055009.

Dench, Alan. 1998. *Yingkarta.* Munich: Lincom.

Derbyshire, Desmond C. 1985. *Hixkaryana and linguistic typology.* Dallas: Summer Institute of Linguistics.

Derbyshire, Desmond C. & Doris L. Payne. 1990. Noun classification systems of Amazonian languages. In Doris L. Payne (ed.), *Amazonian linguistics: Studies in Lowland South American languages,* 243–272. Austin: University of Texas Press.

Di Garbo, Francesca. 2014. *Gender and its interaction with number and evaluative morphology: An intra- and intergenealogical typological survey of Africa.* Stockholm University. (Doctoral dissertation).

Dickens, Patrick. 1992. Juǀ'hoan grammar. Unpublished manuscript.

Dixon, Robert M. W. 1972. *The Dyirbal language of North Queensland.* Cambridge: Cambridge University Press.

Dixon, Robert M. W. 1982. *'Where Have all the adjectives gone?' and other essays in semantics and syntax.* Berlin: Mouton de Gruyter.

Dixon, Robert M. W. 1995. Fusional development of gender marking in Jarawara possessed nouns. *International Journal of American Linguistics* 61(3). 263–294.

Doble, Marion. 1987. A description of some features of Ekari language structure. *Oceanic Linguistics* 26. 55–113.

Dol, Philomena. 1999. *A grammar of Maybrat: A language of the Bird's Head, Irian Jaya, Indonesia.* University of Leiden. (Doctoral dissertation).

Dougherty, Janet W. D. 1983. *Futuna-Aniwa: An introduction to a Polynesian outlier language.* Berkeley: University of California Press.

Dryer, Matthew S. 1992. The Greenbergian word order correlations. *Language* 68(1). 81–138.

Dryer, Matthew S. 2000. Counting genera vs. counting languages. *Linguistic Typology* 4(3). 334–356.

Dryer, Matthew S. 2013. Order of subject, object and verb. In Matthew S. Dryer & Martin Haspelmath (eds.), *The world atlas of language structures online.* Leipzig: Max Planck Institute for Evolutionary Anthropology. https : / / wals . info / chapter/81.

Dryer, Matthew S. & Martin Haspelmath (eds.). 2013. *The world atlas of language structures online.* Leipzig: Max Planck Institute for Evolutionary Anthropology. http://wals.info/.

Dunn, Michael, Simon J. Greenhill, Stephen C. Levinson & Russell D. Gray. 2011. Evolved structure of language shows lineage-specific trends in word-order universals. *Nature* 473(7345). 79–82.

Durie, Mark. 1985. *A grammar of Acehnese on the basis of a dialect of North Aceh* (Verhandelingen van het Koninklijk Institut voor Taal-, Land- en Volkenkunde 112). Dordrecht & Cinnaminson: Foris Publications.

Dutton, Tom E. 1996. *Koiari.* Munich: Lincom Europa.

Eaton, Helen. 2010. *A Sandawe grammar.* Dallas, TX: SIL International.

Edenmyr, Niklas. 2004. The semantics of Hadza gender assignment: A few notes on the field. *Africa & Asia: Göteborg working papers on Asian and African languages and literatures* 4. 3–19.

Elias, David Lyndon. 2005. *Tigre of Habab: Short grammar and texts from the Rigbat people.* Harvard University. (Doctoral dissertation).

Elliott, Eric Bryant. 1999. *Dictionary of Rincón Luiseño.* University of California, San Diego. (Doctoral dissertation).

Emeneau, Murray B. 1956. India as a linguistic area. *Language* 32(1). 3–16.

Emeneau, Murray B. 1980. *Language and linguistic area: Essays.* Stanford: Stanford University Press.

Epps, Patience. 2008. *A grammar of Hup.* Berlin: Mouton de Gruyter.

Everett, Daniel L. 1986. Pirahã. In Desmond C. Derbyshire & Geoffrey K. Pullum (eds.), *Handbook of Amazonian languages,* vol. 1, 200–325. Berlin: Mouton de Gruyter.

Everett, Daniel L. & Barbara Kern. 1997. *Wari'.* London: Routledge.

Farr, Cynthia. 1993. The switch-reference clause chaining phenomenon from a Korafe perspective. *Language and Linguistics in Melanesia* 24. 159–190.

Fedden, Sebastian. 2011. *A grammar of Mian.* Berlin: Mouton de Gruyter.

Feldman, Harry. 1986. *A grammar of Awtuw* (Pacific linguistics B 94). Canberra: Australian National University.

Foley, William A. 1986. *The Papuan languages of New Guinea.* Cambridge: Cambridge University Press.

Foreman, Velma. 1974. *Grammar of Yessan-Mayo* (Language Data, Asian-Pacific Series 4). Ukarumpa: Summer Institute of Linguistics.

Fortune, George. 1985. *Shona grammatical constructions.* Harare: Mercury Press.

Gandour, Jack, Soranee Holasuit Petty, Rochana Dardarananda, Sumalee Dechongkit & Sunee Mukngoen. 1984. The acquisition of numeral classifiers in Thai. *Linguistics* 22(4). 455–479.

Gell-Mann, Murray & Seth Lloyd. 2004. Effective complexity. In Murray Gell-Mann & Constantino Tsallis (eds.), *Nonextensive entropy: Interdisciplinary applications,* 387–398. Oxford: Oxford University Press.

Gelman, Andrew & Jennifer Hill. 2007. *Data analysis using regression and multilevel/hierarchical models.* Cambridge: Cambridge University Press.

Georgopoulos, Carol Perkins. 1985. *The syntax of variable binding in Palauan.* University of California, San Diego. (Doctoral dissertation).

Gerdts, Donna B. 2010. Agreement in Halkomelem complex auxiliaries. In *Papers for the Forty-fourth and Forty-fifth International Conferences on Salish and Neighbouring Languages* (UBCWPL 27), 175–189.

Gerdts, Donna B. 2013. The purview effect: Feminine gender on inanimates in Halkomelem Salish. In Chundra Cathcart, I-Hsuan Chen, Greg Finley, Shinae Kang, Clare S. Sandy & Elise Stickles (eds.), *Proceedings of the 37th annual meet-*

ing of the Berkeley Linguistics Society, 417–426. Berkeley: Berkeley Linguistics
Society.

Gerdts, Donna B. & Mercedes O. Hinkson. 2004. Salish numeral classifiers: A
lexical means to a grammatical end. *STUF – Language Typology and Universals*
57(2-3). 247–279.

Ghosh, Arun. 2008. Santali. In Gregory S. Anderson (ed.), *The Munda languages*,
11–98. Abingdon: Routledge.

Gil, David. 2013. Numeral classifiers. In Matthew S. Dryer & Martin Haspelmath
(eds.), *The world atlas of language structures online*. Leipzig: Max Planck Institute for Evolutionary Anthropology. http://wals.info/chapter/55.

Glinert, Lewis. 1989. *The grammar of modern Hebrew*. Cambridge: Cambridge University Press.

Good, Jeff. 2012. Typologizing grammatical complexities, or: Why creoles may
be paradigmatically simple but syntagmatically average. *Journal of Pidgin and
Creole Languages* 27(1). 1–47.

Gore, Edward Cline. 1926. *A Zande grammar*. London: Sheldon Press.

Goswami, G. C. & Jyotiprakash Tamuli. 2003. Asamiya. In George Cardona &
Dhanesh Jain (eds.), *The Indo-Aryan languages*, 391–443. London: Routledge.

Goudswaard, Nelleke Elisabeth. 2005. *The Begak (Ida'an) language of Sabah*. Free
University of Amsterdam. (Doctoral dissertation).

Granberry, Julian. 2004. *Modern Chitimacha (Sitimaxa)*. Munich: Lincom Europa.

Greenberg, Joseph H. 1972. Numeral classifiers and substantival number: Problems in the genesis of a linguistic type. In *Working papers on language universals*, vol. 9, 1–39. Stanford: Stanford University, California Committee on
Linguistics.

Greenberg, Joseph H. 1978. How does a language acquire gender markers? In
Joseph H. Greenberg, Charles Ferguson & Edith Moravcsik (eds.), *Universals
of human language*. Vol. 3: *How does a language acquire gender markers?: Word
structure*, 47–82. Stanford: Stanford University Press.

Gries, Stefan Th. 2015. The most under-used statistical method in corpus linguistics: Multi-level (and mixed-effects) models. *Corpora* 10(1). 95–125.

Grimm, Scott. 2012. *Number and individuation*. Stanford University. (Doctoral
dissertation).

Grinevald, Colette. 2002. Making sense of nominal classification systems: Noun
classifiers and the grammaticalization variable. In Ilse Wischer & Gabriele
Diewald (eds.), *New reflections on grammaticalization*, 259–275. Amsterdam:
John Benjamins.

Grinevald, Colette & Frank Seifart. 2004. Noun classes in African and Amazonian languages: Towards a comparison. *Linguistic Typology* 8(2). 243–285.

Guirardello, Raquel. 1999. *A reference grammar of Trumai.* Rice University. (Doctoral dissertation).

Haan, Johnson Welem. 2001. *The grammar of Adang: A Papuan language spoken on the Island of Alor East Nusa Tenggara, Indonesia.* University of Sydney. (Doctoral dissertation).

Haas, Mary R. 1940. Tunica. In *Handbook of American Indian Languages*, vol. 4, 1–143. New York: Augustin.

Hagman, Roy Stephen. 1973. *Nama Hottentot grammar.* Columbia University. (Doctoral dissertation).

Haiman, John. 1980. *Hua: A Papuan language of the Eastern Highlands of New Guinea.* Amsterdam: John Benjamins.

Halekoh, Ulrich & Søren Højsgaard. 2014. A Kenward-Roger approximation and parametric bootstrap methods for tests in linear mixed models: The R package pbkrtest. *Journal of Statistical Software* 58(10). 1–30.

Hammarström, Harald & Mark Donohue. 2014. Some principles on the use of macro-areas in typological comparison. *Language Dynamics and Change* 4(1). 167–187.

Hanna, H. Morcos. 1967. *The phrase structure of Egyptian Colloquial Arabic.* The Hague: Mouton.

Hardin, James W. & Joseph W. Hilbe. 2007. *Generalized linear models and extensions.* 2nd edn. College Station, TX: Stata Press.

Harrell, Richard S. 1962. *A short reference grammar of Moroccan Arabic.* Washington: Georgetown University Press.

Harris, Alice C. & Lyle Campbell. 1995. *Historical syntax in cross-linguistic perspective.* Cambridge: Cambridge University Press.

Hart, Helen. 1988. *Diccionario Chayahuita-Castellano.* Yarinacocha: Instituto Lingüístico de Verano.

Harvey, Mark. 2002. *A grammar of Gaagudju.* Berlin: Mouton de Gruyter.

Haude, Katharina. 2006. *A grammar of Movima.* Nijmegen University. (Doctoral dissertation).

Hawkins, John A. 2004. *Efficiency and complexity in grammars.* Oxford: Oxford University Press.

Hayward, Dick. 1984. *The Arbore language: A first investigation (including a vocabulary).* Hamburg: Helmut Buske Verlag.

Heath, G. R. 1913. Notes on Miskuto grammar and on other Indian languages of Eastern Nicaragua. *American Anthropologist* 15(1). 48–62.

Heath, Jeffrey. 1980. *Basic materials in Warndarang: Grammar, texts and dictionary* (Pacific linguistics B 72). Canberra: Australian National University.

Heath, Jeffrey. 1983. Referential tracking in Nunggubuyu (Australia). In John Haiman & Pamela Munro (eds.), *Switch reference and universal grammar*, 129–149. Amsterdam: John Benjamins.

Heath, Jeffrey. 1999. *A grammar of Koyra Chiini: The Songhay of Timbuktu.* Berlin: Mouton de Gruyter.

Hemmilä, Ritva & Pirkko Luoma. 1987. Urim grammar. Ukarumpa. Unpublished manuscript.

Henadeerage, Deepthi Kumara. 2002. *Topics in Sinhala syntax.* Australian National University. (Doctoral dissertation).

Her, One-Soon. 2012. Distinguishing classifiers and measure words: A mathematical perspective and implications. *Lingua* 122(14). 1668–1691.

Hess, H. Harwood. 1968. *The syntactic structure of Mezquital Otomi.* The Hague: Mouton.

Hesse, Ronald. 2000. Tehit. In Ger P. Reesink (ed.), *Studies in Irian languages, part II* (NUSA 47), 25–33. Jakarta: Universitas Katolik Indonesia Atma Jaya.

Hoffman, Carl. 1963. *A grammar of the Margi language.* London: Oxford University Press.

Horton, A. E. 1949. *A grammar of Luvale.* Johannesburg: Witwatersrand University Press.

Huber, Juliette. 2008. *First steps towards a grammar of Makasae.* Munich: Lincom.

Hundius, Harald & Ulrike Kölver. 1983. Syntax and semantics of numeral classifiers in Thai. *Studies in Language* 7(2). 165–214.

Hunt, Katharine Dorothy. 1993. *Clause structure, agreement and case in Gitksan.* The University of British Columbia. (Doctoral dissertation).

Hurd, Conrad & Phyllis W. Hurd. 1966. *Nasioi language course.* Port Moresby: Summer Institute of Linguistics, Department of Information & Extension Services.

Hymes, Dell Hathaway. 1955. *The language of the Kathlamet Chinook.* Indiana University. (Doctoral dissertation).

Inglis, Douglas. 2003. Conceptual structure of numeral classifiers in Thai. In Eugene H. Casad & Gary B. Palmer (eds.), *Cognitive linguistics and non-Indo-European languages*, 223–246. Berlin: Mouton De Gruyter.

Iwasaki, Shoichi & Preeya Ingkaphirom. 2005. *A reference grammar of Thai.* Cambridge: Cambridge University Press.

Jaeger, T. Florian, Peter Graff, William Croft & Daniel Pontillo. 2011. Mixed effect models for genetic and areal dependencies in linguistic typology. *Linguistic Typology* 15(2). 281–319.

Jakobi, Angelika. 1990. *A Fur grammar: Phonology, morphophonology, and morphology.* Hamburg: Helmut Buske Verlag.

Janhunen, Juha (ed.). 2003. *The Mongolic languages.* London: Routledge.

Jendraschek, Gerd. 2012. *A grammar of Iatmul.* Regensburg: Universtiy of Regensburg. (Habilitation).

Jensen, John Thayer. 1977. *Yapese reference grammar.* Honolulu: University Press of Hawaii.

Jones, Wendell & Paula Jones. 1991. *Barasano syntax* (Publications in Linguistics 101). Dallas: Summer Institute of Linguistics & The University of Texas at Arlington.

Jukes, Anthony. 2006. *Makassarese (basa Mangkasara'): A description of an Austronesian language of South Sulawesi.* University of Melbourne. (Doctoral dissertation).

Jun, Akamine. 2005. Sama (Bajau). In Alexander Adelaar & Nikolaus P. Himmelmann (eds.), *The Austronesian languages of Asia and Madagascar*, 377–396. London: Routledge.

Kaiser, Stefan, Yasuko Ichikawa, Noriko Kobayashi & Hilofumi Yamamoto. 2001. *Japanese: A comprehensive grammar.* London: Routledge.

Kalnača, Anna. 2014. *A typological perspective on Latvian grammar.* Berlin: Mouton de Gruyter.

Kamwangamalu, Nkonko Mudipanu. 1989. *Code-mixing across languages: Structure, functions, and constraints.* University of Illinois at Urbana-Champaign. (Doctoral dissertation).

Kaufman, Terrence S. 1963. *Tzeltal grammar.* University of California, Berkeley. (Doctoral dissertation).

Kennard, Edward. 1936. Mandan grammar. *International Journal of American Linguistics* 9(1). 1–43.

Kiessling, Roland. 2007. The "marked nominative" in Datooga. *Journal of African Languages and Linguistics* 28(2). 149–191.

Kilarski, Marcin. 2013. *Nominal classification: A history of its study from the classical period to the present.* Amsterdam: John Benjamins.

Killian, Don. 2015. *Topics in Uduk phonology and morphosyntax.* University of Helsinki. (Doctoral dissertation).

Kimball, Amelia E., Kailen Shantz, Christopher Eager & Joseph Roy. submitted. Beyond maximal random effects for logistic regression: Moving past convergence problems. Submitted manuscript. Available at https://arxiv.org/pdf/1611. 00083.pdf.

Klaiman, M. H. 2009. Bengali. In Bernard Comrie (ed.), *The world's major languages*, 2nd edn., 417–436. London: Routledge.

Klamer, Marian. 2014. Numeral classifiers in the Papuan languages of Alor and Pantar: A comparative perspective. In Marian Klamer & František Kratochvíl (eds.), *Number and quantity in East Nusantara*, 103–122. Canberra: Pacific Linguistics.

Klamer, Marian. 2017. The Alor-Pantar languages: Linguistic context, history and typology. In Marian Klamer (ed.), *The Alor-Pantar languages: History and typology*, 2nd edn. (Studies in Linguistic Diversity 3), 1–48. Berlin: Language Science Press.

Kosaka, Ryuichi. 2000. *A descriptive study of the Lachi language: Syntactic description, historical reconstruction and genetic relation*. Tokyo University of Foreign Studies. (Doctoral dissertation).

Kramer, Ruth. 2015. *The Morphosyntax of gender*. Oxford: Oxford University Press.

Kretzschmar, William A., Jr. 2015. *Language and complex systems*. Cambridge: Cambridge University Press.

Krute, Laurence Dana. 1989. *Piaroa nominal morphosemantics*. Columbia University. (Doctoral dissertation).

Kusters, Wouter. 2003. *Linguistic complexity: The influence of social change on verbal inflections*. University of Leiden. (Doctoral dissertation). Utrecht: LOT.

Kusters, Wouter. 2008. Complexity in linguistic theory, language learning and language change. In Matti Miestamo, Kaius Sinnemäki & Fred Karlsson (eds.), *Language complexity: Typology, contact, change*, 3–22. Amsterdam: John Benjamins.

Laycock, Donald C. & John Z'graggen. 1975. The Sepik-Ramu phylum. In Stephen A. Wurm (ed.), *Papuan languages and the New Guinea linguistic scene*, vol. 1, 731–763. Canberra: Australian National University.

Leslau, Wolf. 1995. *Reference grammar of Amharic*. Wiesbaden: Harassowitz.

Levinson, Stephen C., Simon J. Greenhill, Russell D. Gray & Michael Dunn. 2011. Universal typological dependencies should be detectable in the history of language families. *Linguistic Typology* 15(2). 509–534.

Li, Charles N. & Sandra A. Thompson. 1981. *Mandarin Chinese: A functional reference grammar*. Berkeley: University of California Press.

Lichtenberk, Frantisek. 2008. *A grammar of Toqabaqita*. Vol. 1. Berlin: Mouton de Gruyter.

Lindström, Eva. 2002. *Topics in the grammar of Kuot: A non-Austronesian language of New Ireland, Papua New Guinea.* Stockholm: Stockholm University. (Doctoral dissertation).

Lock, Arjen. 2011. *Abau grammar* (Data Papers on Papua New Guinea Languages 57). Ukarumpa: SIL-PNG Academic Publications.

Lomas, G. C. J. 1988. *The Huli language of Papua New Guinea.* Macquarie University. (Doctoral dissertation).

Loos, Eugene. 1969. *The phonology of Capanahua and its grammatical basis.* Norman: University of Oklahoma.

Louwerse, John. 1988. *The Morphosyntax of Una in relation to discourse structure* (Pacific linguistics B 100). Canberra: Australian National University.

Luraghi, Silvia. 2011. The origin of the Proto-Indo-European gender system: Typological considerations. *Folia Linguistica* 45(2). 435–464.

Lynch, John. 2002. Ulithian. In John Lynch, Malcolm Ross & Terry Crowley (eds.), *The Oceanic languages,* 792–803. Richmond: Curzon.

Macaulay, Monica. 1996. *A grammar of Chalcatongo Mixtec* (University of California Publications in Linguistics 127). Berkeley: University of California Press.

Maddieson, Ian. 2006. Correlating phonological complexity: Data and validation. *Linguistic Typology* 10(1). 106–123.

Matasović, Ranko. 2012. A grammatical sketch of Albanian for students of Indo-European. http://mudrac.ffzg.unizg.hr/~rmatasov/Albanian.pdf. Unpublished manuscript.

Matras, Yaron. 2009. *Language contact.* Cambridge: Cambridge University Press.

McGregor, Ronald S. 1986. *Outline of Hindi grammar, with exercises.* 3rd edn. Oxford: Oxford University Press.

McGregor, William B. 2004. *The languages of the Kimberley, Western Australia.* Abingdon: Routledge.

McWhorter, John. 2001. The world's simplest grammars are creole grammars. *Linguistic Typology* 5(2-3). 125–166.

McWhorter, John. 2007. *Language interrupted: Signs of non-native acquisition in standard language grammars.* New York: Oxford University Press.

Meeuwis, Michael. 1998. *Lingala.* Munich: Lincom.

Merlan, Francesca C. 1994. *A grammar of Wardaman, a language of the Northern Territory of Australia.* Berlin: Mouton de Gruyter.

Meyer, David, Achim Zeileis & Kurt Hornik. 2006. The strucplot framework: Visualizing multi-way contingency tables with vcd. *Journal of Statistical Software* 17(3). 1–48.

Meyer, David, Achim Zeileis & Kurt Hornik. 2015. *vcd: Visualizing categorical data*. R package version 1.4-1.

Miestamo, Matti. 2007. Symmetric and asymmetric encoding of functional domains, with remarks on typological markedness. In Matti Miestamo & Bernhard Wälchli (eds.), *New challenges in typology: Broadening the horizons and redefining the foundations*, 293–314. Berlin: Mouton De Gruyter.

Miestamo, Matti. 2008. Grammatical complexity in a cross-linguistic perspective. In Matti Miestamo, Kaius Sinnemäki & Fred Karlsson (eds.), *Language complexity: Typology, contact, change*, 23–41. Amsterdam: John Benjamins.

Miestamo, Matti. 2009. Implicational hierarchies and grammatical complexity. In Geoffrey Sampson, David Gil & Peter Trudgill (eds.), *Language complexity as an evolving variable*, 80–97. Oxford: Oxford University Press.

Mihas, Elena. 2010. *Essentials of Ashéninka Perené grammar*. The University of Wisconsin-Milwaukee. (Doctoral dissertation).

Mithun, Marianne. 2001. *The languages of native North America*. Cambridge: Cambridge University Press.

Moore, Denny. 1984. *Syntax of the language of the Gavião Indians of Rondônia, Brazil*. The City University of New York. (Doctoral dissertation).

Moran, Paul & Dorothy Moran. 1977. Notas sobre morfología verbal dení. *Serie Lingüística* 7. 29–71.

Morris, Cliff. 1984. *Tetun-English dictionary* (Pacific linguistics C 83). Canberra: Australian National University.

Mosel, Ulrike & Ruth Spriggs. 2000. Gender in Teop (Bougainville, Papua New Guinea). In Barbara Unterbeck (ed.), *Gender in grammar and cognition I: Approaches to gender* (Trends in Linguistics. Studies and Monographs 124), 321–349. Berlin: Mouton de Gruyter.

Mous, Maarten. 1992. *A grammar of Iraqw*. Rijksuniversiteit Leiden. (Doctoral dissertation).

Mous, Maarten. 2008. Number as an exponent of gender in Cushitic. In Zygmunt Frajzyngier & Erin Shay (eds.), *Interaction of morphology and syntax: Case studies in Afroasiatic*, 137–160. Amsterdam: John Benjamins.

Müller, Adam. 1954. *Grammar and vocabulary of the Konua language* (Microbibliotheca Anthropos 12). Fosieux: Anthropos.

Munshi, Sadaf. 2006. *Jammu and Kashmir Burushaski: Language, language contact, and change*. University of Texas at Austin. (Doctoral dissertation).

Murane, Elizabeth. 1974. *Daga grammar, from morpheme to discourse*. Norman: Summer Institute of Linguistics of the University of Oklahoma.

Mushin, Ilona. 2012. *A grammar of (Western) Garrwa*. Berlin: Mouton de Gruyter.

Nichols, Johanna. 1992. *Linguistic diversity in space and time*. Chicago: University of Chicago Press.

Nichols, Johanna. 1994. Chechen. In Rieks Smeets (ed.), *The indigenous languages of the Caucasus*, 1–77. Delmar: Caravan Books.

Nichols, Johanna. 2003. Diversity and stability in language. In Brian D. Joseph & Richard D. Janda (eds.), *The handbook of historical linguistics*, 283–310. Oxford: Blackwell.

Nichols, Johanna. 2009. Linguistic complexity: A comprehensive definition and survey. In Geoffrey Sampson, David Gil & Peter Trudgill (eds.), *Language complexity as an evolving variable*, 110–125. Oxford: Oxford University Press.

Nichols, Johanna. 2011. *Ingush grammar*. Berkeley: University of California Press.

Nichols, Johanna & David A. Peterson. 1996. The Amerind personal pronoun. *Language* 72(2). 336–371.

Nicolova, Ruselina. 2017. *Bulgarian grammar*. Berlin: Frank & Timme. Translated by Christo Stamenov.

Nordlinger, Rachel. 1998. *A grammar of Wambaya, Northern Territory (Australia)* (Pacific linguistics C 140). Canberra: Australian National University.

Oakes, Michael P. 2009. Javanese. In Bernard Comrie (ed.), *The world's major languages*, 819–832. London: Routledge.

Osborne, C. R. 1974. *The Tiwi language: Grammar, myths and dictionary of the Tiwi language spoken on Melville and Bathurst Islands, Northern Australia*. Canberra: Australian Institute of Aboriginal Studies.

Otsuka, Yuko. 2000. *Ergativity in Tongan*. University of Oxford. (Doctoral dissertation).

Owens, Jonathan. 1985. *A grammar of Harar Oromo (Northeastern Ethiopia)* (Kuschitische Sprachstudien 4). Hamburg: Helmut Buske Verlag.

Pandharipande, Rajeshwari. 2003. Marathi. In George Cordona & Dhanesh Jain (eds.), *The Indo-Aryan languages*, 698–728. London: Routledge.

Passer, Matthias Benjamin. 2016a. (What) do verb classifiers classify? *Lingua* 174(1). 16–44.

Passer, Matthias Benjamin. 2016b. *The typology and diachrony of nominal classification*. Utrecht: University of Amsterdam. (Doctoral dissertation).

Payne, David L. 1991. A classification of Maipuran (Arawakan) languages based on shared lexical retentions. In Desmond C. Derbyshire & Geoffrey K. Pullum (eds.), *Handbook of Amazonian languages*, vol. 3, 355–500. Berlin: Mouton de Gruyter.

Payne, Doris L. 1998. Maasai gender in typological perspective. *Studies in African Linguistics* 27(2). 159–175.

Payne, Doris L. 2007. Source of the Yagua nominal classification system. *International Journal of American Linguistics* 73(4). 447–474.

Peeke, M. Catherine. 1973. *Preliminary grammar of Auca*. Norman: Summer Institute of Linguistics.

Penchoen, Thomas. 1973. *Tamazight of the Ayt Ndhir* (Afroasiatic Dialects 1). Los Angeles: Undena Publishing.

Pensalfini, Robert. 1997. *Jingulu grammar, dictionary, and texts*. Massachusetts Institute of Technology. (Doctoral dissertation).

Pet, Willen Jan Agricola. 1987. *Lokono Dian, the Arawak language of Suriname: A sketch of its grammatical structure and lexicon*. Cornell University. (Doctoral dissertation).

Phillips, Colin. 1993. Conditions on agreement in Yimas. In Jonathan D. Bobaljik & Colin Phillips (eds.), *Papers on case & agreement I* (MIT Working Papers in Linguistics 18), 173–213. Cambridge: MIT.

Plaster, Keith & Maria Polinsky. 2007. Women are not dangerous things: Gender and categorization. *Harvard Working Papers in Linguistics* 12. 1–44.

Poppe, Nicholas. 1968. *Tatar manual: Descriptive grammar and texts with Tatar-English-glossary*. Bloomington: Indiana University Press.

Premsrirat, Suwilai. 1987. *A Khmu grammar* (Pacific Linguistics A 75). Canberra: Australian National University.

Quesada, J. Diego & Stavros Skopeteas. 2010. The discourse function of inverse voice: An experimental study in Teribe (Chibchan). *Journal of Pragmatics* 42(9). 2579–2600.

Quigley, Susan R. 2016. *The Awara verbal system*. University of North Dakota. (MA thesis).

R Core Team. 2017. *R: A language and environment for statistical computing*. R Foundation for Statistical Computing. Vienna. http://www.R-project.org/.

Ramirez, Henri. 1997. *A fala tukano dos Ye'pâ-Masa, tomo I: Gramática*. Manaus: CEDEM.

Rau, Der-Hwa Victoria. 1992. *A grammar of Atayal*. Cornell University. (Doctoral dissertation).

Reed, Irene, Osahito Miyaoka, Steven Jacobson, Paschal Afcan & Michael Krauss. 1977. *Yup'ik Eskimo grammar*. Fairbanks: Alaska Native Language Center, University of Alaska.

Reesink, Ger P. 1987. *Structures and their functions in Usan: A Papuan language of Papua New Guinea*. Amsterdam: John Benjamins.

Reesink, Ger P. 1996. Morpho-syntactic features of the Bird's Head languages. In Ger P. Reesink (ed.), *Studies in Irian languages* (NUSA 40), 1–20. Jakarta: Universitas Katolik Indonesia Atma Jaya.

Reh, Mechthild. 1985. *Die Krongo-Sprache (Nìinò Mó-Dì): Beschreibung, Texte, Wörterverzeichnis.* Vol. 12. Berlin: Reimer.

Rehg, Kenneth L. & Damian G. Sohl. 1981. *Ponapean reference grammar.* Honolulu: University of Hawaii Press.

Rennison, John R. 1997. *Koromfe.* London: Routledge.

Rich, Rolland G. 1999. *Diccionario arabela-castellano.* Peru: Instituto Lingüístico de Verano.

Riddle, Elizabeth M. 2008. Complexity in isolating languages: Lexical elaboration versus grammatical economy. In Matti Miestamo, Kaius Sinnemäki & Fred Karlsson (eds.), *Language complexity: Typology, contact, change*, 133–151. Amsterdam: John Benjamins.

Ring, Hiram. 2015. *A grammar of Pnar.* Singapore: Nanyang Technological University. (Doctoral dissertation).

Roberts, Sarah J. & Joan Bresnan. 2008. Retained inflectional morphology in Pidgins: A typological study. *Linguistic Typology* 12(2). 269–302.

Robinson, Stuart Payton. 2011. *Split intransitivity in Rotokas, a Papuan language of Bougainville.* Nijmegen: Radboud Universiteit. (Doctoral dissertation).

Ross, Malcolm. 1980. Some elements of Vanimo, a New Guinea tone language. In *Papers in New Guinea linguistics 20* (Pacific Linguistics A 56), 77–109. Canberra: Australian National University.

Saad, George. 2014. *A grammar sketch of Shuar: With a focus on the verb phrase.* Radbound University Nijmegen. (MA thesis).

Sakel, Jeanette. 2002. Gender agreement in Mosetén. In Mily Crevels, Simon van de Kerke, Sérgio Meira & Hein van der Voort (eds.), *Current studies on South American languages*, 287–305. Leiden: Research School of Asian, African, & Amerindian Studies (CNWS).

Samarin, William J. 1966. *The Gbeya language: Grammar, texts, and vocabularies* (Publications in linguistics 44). Berkeley: University of California Press.

Sands, Bonny. 2013. Morphology: Hadza. In Rainer Vossen (ed.), *The Khoesan languages*, 107–123. London: Routledge.

Sapir, J. David. 1965. *A grammar of Diola-Fogny: A language spoken in the Basse-Casamance region of Senegal.* Vol. 3. Ibadan: Cambridge University Press in association with The West African Languages Survey & The Institute of African Studies.

Schachter, Paul & Fe T. Otanes. 1972. *Tagalog reference grammar.* Berkeley: University of California Press. Reprinted in 1983.

Schielzeth, Holger & Wolfang Forstmeier. 2009. Conclusions beyond support: Overconfident estimates in mixed models. *Behavioral Ecology* 20(2). 416–420.

Schiffman, Harold F. 1999. *A reference grammar of spoken Tamil.* Cambridge: Cambridge University Press.

Schuh, Russell G. 1976. *Spoken Hausa.* Ithaca: Spoken Language Services.

Schuh, Russell G. 1989. Gender and number in Miya. In Zygmunt Frajzyngier (ed.), *Current progress in Chadic linguistics,* 171–181. Amsterdam: John Benjamins.

Schultze-Berndt, Eva. 2000. *Simple and complex verbs in Jaminjung: A study of event categorization in an Australian language.* Katholieke Universiteit Nijmegen. (Doctoral dissertation).

Scorza, David. 1985. A sketch of Au morphology and syntax. In *Papers in New Guinea linguistics 22* (Pacific Linguistics A 63), 215–273. Canberra: Australian National University.

Seifart, Frank. 2005. *The structure and use of shape-based noun classes in Miraña.* Nijmegen: Radboud Universiteit Nijmegen. (Doctoral dissertation).

Seifart, Frank. 2010. Nominal classification. *Language and Linguistics Compass* 4(8). 719–736.

Serzisko, Fritz. 1982. Gender, noun class and numeral classification: A scale of classificatory techniques. In René Dirven & Günter Radden (eds.), *Issues in the theory of universal grammar,* 95–123. Tübingen: Narr.

Sharpe, Margaret C. 1972. *Alawa phonology and grammar.* Canberra: Australian Institute of Aboriginal Studies.

Shklovsky, Kirill. 2005. Person marking in Petalcingo Tzeltal. Reed College BA thesis.

Shklovsky, Kirill. 2012. *Tseltal clause structure.* Massachusetts Institute of Technology. (Doctoral dissertation). https://dspace.mit.edu/handle/1721.1/77801.

Shosted, Ryan K. 2006. Correlating complexity: A typological approach. *Linguistic Typology* 10(1). 1–40.

Siewierska, Anna. 1998. Variation in major constituent order: A global and a European perspective. In Anna Siewierska (ed.), *Constituent order in the languages of Europe,* 475–551. Berlin: Mouton De Gruyter.

Sinnemäki, Kaius. 2008. Complexity trade-offs in core argument marking. In Matti Miestamo, Kaius Sinnemäki & Fred Karlsson (eds.), *Language complexity: Typology, contact, change,* 67–88. Amsterdam: John Benjamins.

Sinnemäki, Kaius. 2009. Complexity in core argument marking and population size. In Geoffrey Sampson, David Gil & Peter Trudgill (eds.), *Language complexity as an evolving variable*, 126–140. Oxford: Oxford University Press.

Sinnemäki, Kaius. 2010. Word order in zero-marking languages. *Studies in Language* 34(4). 869–912.

Sinnemäki, Kaius. 2014a. Cognitive processing, language typology, and variation. *WIREs Cognitive Science* 5(4). 477–487.

Sinnemäki, Kaius. 2014b. Complexity trade-offs: A case study. In Frederick J. Newmeyer & Laurel B. Preston (eds.), *Measuring grammatical complexity*, 179–201. Oxford: Oxford University Press.

Sinnemäki, Kaius. 2014c. Global optimization and complexity trade-offs. *Poznan Studies in Contemporary Linguistics* 50(2). 179–195.

Sinnemäki, Kaius. 2011. *Language universals and linguistic complexity*. University of Helsinki. (Doctoral dissertation).

Skribnik, Elena. 2003. Buryat. In Juha Janhunen (ed.), *The Mongolic languages*, 102–128. London: Routledge.

Spruit, Arie. 1986. *Abkhaz studies*. Rijksuniversiteit Leiden. (Doctoral dissertation).

Sridhar, Shikaripur N. 1990. *Kannada*. London: Routledge.

Staley, William E. 2007. *Reference management in Olo: A cognitive perspective* (SIL e-Books 5). SIL International.

Stebbins, Tonya & Julius Tayul. 2012. *Mali (Baining) dictionary*. Canberra: Australian National University.

Steever, Sanford B. 1998. Malto. In Sanford B. Steever (ed.), *The Dravidian languages*, 359–387. London: Routledge.

Sutton, Logan. 2010. Noun class and number in Kiowa-Tanoan: Comparative-historical research and respecting speakers' rights in fieldwork. In Andrea L. Berez, Jean Mulder & Daisy Rosenblum (eds.), *Fieldwork and linguistic analysis in indigenous languages of the Americas*, 57–89. Honolulu: University of Hawaii Press.

Svärd, Erik. 2013. *Selected topics in the grammar of Nalca*. Stockholm University. (BA-thesis). http://www.diva-portal.org/smash/get/diva2:631006/FULLTEXT02.pdf, accessed 2013-11-9.

Svärd, Erik. 2019. Gender in New Guinea. In Francesca Di Garbo, Bruno Olsson & Bernhard Wälchli (eds.), *Grammatical gender and linguistic complexity: Volume I: General issues and specific studies*, 225–276. Berlin: Language Science Press. DOI:10.5281/zenodo.3462770

Swanton, John R. 1929. A sketch of the Atakapa language. *International Journal of American Linguistics* 5(2-4). 121–149.

Tang, Chih-Chen Jane. 2004. Two types of classifier languages: A typological study of classification markers in Paiwan noun phrases. *Language and Linguistics* 5(2). 377–407.

Terrill, Angela. 2002. Systems of nominal classification in East Papuan languages. *Oceanic Linguistics* 41(1). 63–88.

Terrill, Angela. 2003. *A grammar of Lavukaleve*. Berlin: Mouton de Gruyter.

Tharp, Doug. 1996. Sulka grammar essentials. In John M. Clifton (ed.), *Two non-Austronesian grammars from the islands*, 77–179. Ukarumpa: Summer Institute of Linguistics.

Thiesen, Wesley. 1996. *Gramatica del idioma bora* (Serie Lingüistica Peruana 38). Yarinacocha: Instituto Lingüístico de Verano.

Thurgood, Graham. 2005. Phan Rang Cham. In Alexander Adelaar & Nikolaus P. Himmelmann (eds.), *The Austronesian languages of Asia and Madagascar*, 489–512. London: Routledge.

Topping, Donald M. 1973. *Chamorro reference grammar*. Honolulu: The University Press of Hawaii.

Tripp, Robert. 1995. *Diccionario amarakaeri-castellano*. Yarinacocha: Ministerio de Educación & Instituto Lingüístico de Verano.

Trudgill, Peter. 2011. *Sociolinguistic typology: Social determinants of linguistic complexity*. New York: Oxford University Press.

van den Berg, Helma. 2004. Hunzib (North-East Caucasian). In Geert Booij, Christian Lehmann, Joachim Mugdan & Stavros Skopeteas (eds.), *Morphology: An international handbook on inflection and word-formation*, vol. 2, 1367–1375. Berlin: Walter de Gruyter.

van den Berg, Helma. 2005. The East Caucasian language family. *Lingua* 115. 147–190.

van der Voort, Hein. 2004. *A grammar of Kwaza*. Berlin: De Gruyter.

Van Valin, Robert D. 1977. *Aspects of Lakhota syntax: A study of Lakhota (Teton Dakota) syntax and its implications for universal grammar*. University of California, Berkeley. (Doctoral dissertation).

van Engelenhoven, Aone & Catharina Williams-van Klinken. 2005. Tetun and Leti. In Alexander Adelaar & Nikolaus P. Himmelmann (eds.), *The Austronesian languages of Asia and Madagascar*, 735–768. London: Routledge.

van Staden, Miriam. 2006. The body and its parts in Tidore, a Papuan language of Eastern Indonesia. *Language Sciences* 28. 323–343.

Velie, Daniel. 1975. *Bosquejo de la fonologia y gramatica del idioma orejon (coto).* Lima: Instituto Lingüístico de Verano.

Wade, Terence. 2011. *A comprehensive Russian grammar.* 3rd edn. Oxford: Wiley-Blackwell.

Wash, Suzanne. 2001. *Adverbial clauses: Barbareño Chumash narrative discourse.* University of California, Santa Barbara. (Doctoral dissertation).

Waterhouse, Viola. 1967. Huamelultec Chontal. In Robert Wauchope (ed.), *Handbook of Middle American Indians*, 349–367. London: University of Texas Press.

Watters, John Robert. 1981. *A phonology and morphology of Ejagham – with notes on dialect variation.* University of California, Los Angeles. (Doctoral dissertation).

Weber, David John. 1989. *A grammar of Huallaga (Huánaco) Quechua* (University of California publications in linguistics 112). Berkeley: University of California Press.

Westrum, Peter N. 1988. A grammatical sketch of Berik. *Irian: Bulletin of Irian Jaya* 16. 133–181.

Wheeler, Alva Lee. 1970. *Grammar of the Siona language, Colombia, South America.* University of California, Berkeley. (Doctoral dissertation).

Wickham, H. 2009. *Ggplot2: Elegant graphics for data analysis.* New York: Springer-Verlag.

Willett, Thomas Leslie. 1991. *A reference grammar of Southeastern Tepehuan.* Dallas: Summer Institute of Linguistics & The University of Texas at Arlington.

Wilson, Particia R. 1980. *Ambulas grammar* (Workpapers in Papua New Guinea Languages 26). Ukarumpa: Summer Institute of Linguistics.

Winter, Bodo. 2013. Linear models and linear mixed effects models in R with linguistic applications. http://arxiv.org/pdf/1308.5499.pdf. arXiv:1308.5499.

Wolfart, H. Christoph. 1973. *Plains Cree: A grammatical study* (Transactions of the American Philosophical Society, New Series 63.5). Philadelphia: American Philosophical Society.

Wu, Jing-Ian Joy. 2006. *Verb classification, case marking, and grammatical relations in Amis.* Buffalo State University of New York. (Doctoral dissertation).

Zaicz, Gábor. 1998. Mordva. In Daniel Abondolo (ed.), *The Uralic languages*, 184–218. London: Routledge.

Zeileis, Achim, David Meyer & Kurt Hornik. 2007. Residual-based shadings for visualizing (conditional) independence. *Journal of Computational and Graphical Statistics* 16(3). 507–525.

Chapter 5

The dynamics of gender complexity

Bernhard Wälchli

Francesca Di Garbo
Stockholm University

In this chapter we view grammatical gender as a category type that emerges, evolves and disappears in languages as a result of diachronic processes and whose complexity grows and diminishes through time (§1–§2). Traditional approaches to grammatical gender focus on two properties that already presuppose a high degree of maturity of gender systems: noun classes and agreement. Here we conceive of gender rather as a category type with a semantic core of animacy and/or sex reflecting classes of referents, which have a propensity to turn into classes of noun lexemes. When growing and retracting, gender characteristically follows the animacy or individuation hierarchy. However, this hierarchical patterning breaks down when animacy leaks into the inanimate domain led astray by many different associative pathways, which is why lexical organization according to noun classes has to be invoked to maintain some sort of order (§3). Gender manifests itself in the form of marking on noun-associated words, often within the local domain of noun phrases. Here we put gender marking into the wider context of nominal morphology (non-lexical markers within the noun phrase), which often originate in independent use in headless noun phrases and are extended to headed noun phrases only in a subsequent development (§4). As more mature manifestations of gender get organized in the form of noun classes, they typically follow certain pathways of development that can be subsumed under the formula "From X to Y" (§5–§6). Agreement is fuzzy as its prototypical non-noun targets gradually develop by way of decategorialization from nouns, and controllers and targets are not always simple words, but can be complex (consist of syntactic formal groups) and controllers can be entirely contextual (§7). Gender should not be considered in isolation as it is – more often than not – parasitic on other grammatical category types, notably number, case, and person, with which it cumulates and which contribute to its high degree of complexity (§8). Number is particularly tightly intertwined with gender in pluralia tantum and other phenomena related to lexical plurality (§9). As gender is

Bernhard Wälchli & Francesca Di Garbo. 2019. The dynamics of gender complexity. In Francesca Di Garbo, Bruno Olsson & Bernhard Wälchli (eds.), *Grammatical gender and linguistic complexity: Volume II: World-wide comparative studies*, 201–364. Berlin: Language Science Press. DOI:10.5281/zenodo.3462784 organized in form of systems, its diachronic evolution cannot be captured in terms of individual diachronic processes. When gender systems evolve, there is virtually always co-evolution of connected events. Hence the study of system evolution is indispensable for understanding the complexity of gender (§10). However, the evolution of gender also displays characteristic areal and genealogical patterns and is sensitive to external factors of language ecology (§11).

Keywords: gender, complexity, animacy, historical linguistics, agreement, number, pluralia tantum, system emergence, areal linguistics, language ecology.

1 Introduction

This chapter has no ambition to provide a comprehensive survey of the very rich literature that exists on grammatical gender, for which we refer to Corbett (1991; 2006; 2014), Aikhenvald (2000; 2016), Kilarski (2013), Heine (1982), and Seifart (2010), to mention just a few. Furthermore, no attempts are made here to strictly delimit gender from classifiers; rather, grammatical gender is our focus of interest. Moreover, this chapter does not relate grammatical gender to gender studies. Having stated what this chapter is NOT about, let us now proceed to explain its focus of interest.

This chapter represents a DYNAMIC APPROACH to the understanding of grammatical gender (henceforth simply called *gender*). This means that we view gender as something that emerges, evolves and disappears in languages as a result of diachronic processes. Greenberg (1978) has been an important source of inspiration for the kind of diachronic and dynamic approach we propose here. In addition to the diachronic perspective, we are also interested in assessing the complexity of gender. While in many languages gender is complex, which is why Corbett (1991: 1) calls it "the most puzzling of the grammatical categories", different degrees of gender complexity are attested in different languages. There are also languages with simpler kinds of gender.

In this chapter we are interested in why gender can grow quite complex in some languages and remain rather simple or turn simple again in other languages. Thus, even as far as complexity is concerned, we adopt a dynamic approach. We view gender as a MATURE PHENOMENON. According to Dahl (2004: 2), a mature phenomenon is a phenomenon that presupposes a non-trivial prehistory. Since we are also interested in how gender comes into being in the first place, we cannot define the object of study too narrowly, as otherwise there is a risk that we will miss much of the non-trivial prehistory. Our approach to linguistic complexity, in general as well as in the domain of gender, is outlined in §2. In the following, we provide a roadmap for the topics discussed in the chapter and how they relate to the general purposes of this two-volume work.

At least since Hockett's (1958: 231) succinct definition – "Genders are classes of nouns reflected in the behavior of associated words", adopted by Corbett (1991) – it has been common to define gender in terms of NOUN CLASSES and AGREEMENT. We argue here that noun classes and agreement are both mature phenomena.

The prototypical function of nouns is to express referents (Croft 2005: 438; Baker 2003). Hence, there are two different things that can be meant by noun classes: classes of noun lexemes and classes of referents. These are manifest in Dahl's (2000a: 107) notions LEXICAL GENDER, classes of noun lexemes, and referential gender, for which we use the name REFERENT-BASED GENDER suggested by Nichols (2019 [in Volume I]), classes of referents. Most approaches to gender take for granted that lexical gender is the primary object of interest, as, for instance, reflected in Corbett & Fedden's (2016: 9) Canonical Gender Principle: *in a canonical gender system, each noun has a single gender value.* It is not a priori clear why it should be useful for a language to partition noun lexemes into classes, but it is immediately understandable why speakers may be inclined to classify real world objects into classes. If we adopt a dynamic approach to gender, it is thus a reasonable assumption that referent-based gender is primary and that lexical gender is a later development that does not really have any clear purpose, but is somehow hard to avoid once words bearing gender markers are constantly associated with nouns and constantly collocate with nouns. The relationship of gender and reference is discussed in §3.

Many researchers agree that gender always has a SEMANTIC CORE: ANIMACY and/or SEX (Dahl 2000a: 101; Corbett 1991: 68; Luraghi 2011). However, somewhat strangely, this semantic core is usually not considered part of the definition of gender. The male-female sex distinction is clearly connected to animacy, as it is not applicable strictly semantically to inanimates. Animacy is thus crucial for the organization of gender. Animacy is a hierarchy rather than a simple dichotomy. Hierarchies are principles of organization that can considerably limit the complexity of a phenomenon. Hence, an important question for us to consider is how the ANIMACY HIERARCHY relates to the complexity of gender. As far as reference and lexicon are concerned, it makes more sense to organize referents according to a semantic core, and notably according to the animacy hierarchy, than noun lexemes. In languages where nouns carry grammatical markers, the DECLENSION CLASSES that structure grammatical allomorphs need not adhere to any semantic principle. This can be taken as evidence that classes of referents are crucial for the understanding of gender. The hierarchical patterning of gender is also discussed in §3.

Like other grammatical category types, gender is expressed by grammatical markers, viz. GENDER MARKERS. Unlike declension classes, these are not directly realized on nouns that condition the choice of class (Güldemann & Fiedler 2019 [in Volume I], use the term "deriflection"), but on NOUN-ASSOCIATED FORMS (adnominal modifiers, verbal argument indexes, or anaphoric pronouns, to mention just the most important ones). Many noun-associated forms are parts of the NP, so gender marking has to do with the wider question of what kind of non-lexical marking exists within noun phrases and how this marking emerges. There are languages that get along perfectly well without any NOMINAL MORPHOLOGY (non-lexical markers within the noun phrase). Nominal morphology is obviously a mature phenomenon. However, unlike its sub-phenomenon gender within noun phrases, nominal morphology need not necessarily distinguish classes. It can be the same marker all over, as in the English prop-word *one* for independent adjectives (adjectives without overt nominal head), as in *the big one*. Lehmann (1982), Moravcsik (1994), and others have emphasized the importance of independent noun-associated elements (such as free relative clauses, pronominal demonstratives and numerals) for the development of markers on attributive modifiers. From a developmental perspective on gender, it is important to put gender into the broader context of how nominal morphology emerges and spreads across various kinds of elements in the noun phrase. This is what we discuss in §4.

Conceiving of NOUN CLASSES in a dynamic perspective means to view them as phenomena undergoing change, which can be expressed by the formula "FROM X TO Y". As already mentioned above, noun classes typically change from referent-based to predominantly lexical, and sometimes back to referent-based gender again (as in English). Several types of changes in noun classes have in common that there is an increase of complexity, notably the development of several types of gender assignment, the development from semantic to opaque assignment (gender assignment characterized by numerous exceptions), and the generalization of noun classes to all nouns. The dynamics of gender assignment and its evolution are what we focus on in §5 and §6.

The word *complex* is ambiguous. Most of the time we are talking about complexity in this chapter we mean by it (i) non-trivial in structure, so that an exhaustive description cannot be short. But "complex" can also mean (ii) consisting of several elements and (iii) consisting of different, but related phenomena. In discussing agreement, meanings (ii) and (iii) will be as important as meaning (i) and it is important to discuss how they relate to each other. Since Corbett's (2006) influential monograph, AGREEMENT has often been conceived of as a morphosyntactic feature, which emphasizes the morphological realization on word-forms and the syntactic nature of the link between controller and target. Given that there is not only intra-sentential, but also inter-sentential agreement, we hold that agreement is less uniform than commonly believed. It can be both syntactic and semantic. However, controllers and targets are not just morphological units, but often consist of several words (complex controllers and complex targets), and hence syntactic rather than morphological units. Controllers can be latent and are then neither morphological nor syntactic, but entirely contextual elements. It is often claimed that agreement always expresses coreferentiality, but coreference is actually only one of several specific relationships that may hold between controller and target. While controllers are typically nouns and targets noun-associated words, there are also nominal gender targets, and it can be shown that agreement often emerges step-by-step when nouns DECATEGORIALIZE (lose their nominal properties). To put agreement into a dynamic perspective means to recognize that agreement is not a uniform phenomenon, but rather a family of similar phenomena with complex diachronic relationships among them. We therefore suggest a broad definition of agreement, since a narrow definition is not easily compatible with a dynamic approach. This is the topic of §7.

Every definition of gender faces the problem that there is not just one, but several other grammatical category types that gender interacts with. Many researchers have recognized the close relationship to CLASSIFIERS, and it has even become common to view gender and classifiers as one set of phenomena, for which various cover terms have been proposed, such as nominal classification (Seifart 2010) and nomifiers (Haspelmath 2018). At least since Dixon (1982: 160), it has been common to argue that gender is characterized by a smallish number of classes (usually between two and ten, but sometimes up to twenty) and by obligatory grouping of all nouns into noun classes. A possible dynamic interpretation would be that gender is just a more advanced stage in the grammaticalization of nominal classification than classifiers (Passer 2016b). However, there is much reason to believe that many gender categories never went through a classifier stage (Nichols 1992: 142). While it is undeniable that some phenomena are intermediate between genders and classifiers, a major problem of the unified account is that gender does not entertain close relationships only to classifiers, but also to a range of other grammatical category types; for instance, with indexation (Croft 2003, Croft 2013; see §7.1) and with person name markers (markers indicating that an element is the name of a person). It has been repeatedly observed that a majority of languages with gender exhibit CUMULATION with NUMBER, and cumulation of gender and CASE and of gender and PERSON is also very common. This trend is so far-reaching that we think it is reasonable to include "cumulation with number, case and/or person" into the definition of gender (notably since such cumulation is often lacking in classifiers). In fact, to the extent that it is known how gender systems evolve, cumulation with number or case often exists from the very beginning. One reason for this is that animacy is a typical conditioning factor for the choice of number and/or case (for instance, in differential object or other differential case marking). From a condition on number or case, animacy can further develop into a gender feature (a fully paradigmaticized grammatical category type expressed by systematic morphological marking) that still maintains cumulative exponence with the grammatical categories it originates from. This suggests that gender can be mature and hence complex from the very beginning and just appropriates the complexity of other mature grammatical categories it is connected with. Thus, when we say that gender is mature this does not necessarily entail that there is a non-trivial prehistory of gender, it can be a non-trivial prehistory of another grammatical category. Cumulation of gender with number, person, and case is discussed in §8.

Beyond the patterns of cumulative exponence that make gender closely interact with the encoding of number, case, and person, PLURALIA TANTUM nouns, that is, nouns that only exist in the plural, and other phenomena related to LEXICAL PLURALITY, whereby plural nouns form lexical classes, may also pose delimitation problems to the definition of gender as an independent grammatical category type. A common approach is to do away with this delimitation problem by saying that pluralia tantum cannot be a gender because their special behavior stems from them being lexically specified for number, which is a separate morphosyntactic category. This way of thinking derives from the assumption that gender and number are different morphosyntactic features. However, there is growing evidence that there are languages with two largely independent CONCURRENT GENDER SYSTEMS which cannot be subsumed under one gender feature (Fedden & Corbett 2017; Corbett et al. 2017; Svärd 2019 [in Volume I]; Liljegren 2019 [in Volume I]). If there is not just one gender feature, why then should we assume a priori that gender and number features must always be neatly distinct? There is evidence from a dynamic perspective that pluralia tantum can develop into gender classes diachronically, which is an argument for a close relationship between gender and lexical plurality (Dryer 2019, Olsson 2019, both in Volume I of this work). The relationship between gender and pluralia tantum is discussed in §9.

Gender is often called a "SYSTEM", but few approaches are explicit in what this label implies. A system is minimally an opposition between at least two markers, but mature gender systems are more complex than that. They are highly organized language-specific complexes with both paradigmatic and syntagmatic components that play an important role in the architecture of grammar. Although systems can exhibit considerable complexity, there is reason to believe that they are also mechanisms to keep complexity within manageable limits. For the dynamic approach it is important to view systems as phenomena that emerge and evolve. Hence, rise, expansion, reduction and loss of gender must be viewed as processes of system evolution. This is the topic of §10.

However, the structure of gender does not only have language-internal implications. Gender exhibits specific GENEALOGICAL AND AREAL PATTERNS. It has repeatedly been observed that gender is quite stable diachronically, but gender seems to be more stable in a language if the contact languages also have gender systems of the same kind. A further question is whether there are any external factors in the ECOLOGY OF LANGUAGES that condition whether languages have gender and what kind of gender systems. This and related questions are addressed in §11.

Having provided a roadmap for the main topics discussed in this chapter, we are now in a position to propose a tentative definition of gender that takes the dynamic approach into account.

> Gender is a grammatical category type with a semantic core of animacy and/or sex reflecting classes of referents, which have a propensity to turn into classes of noun lexemes. It is overtly marked on noun-associated forms. It typically exhibits cumulative exponence with number, case, and/or person. Gender is organized in the form of systems.

The building blocks of this dynamic definition of gender are discussed in the remainder of this chapter and based on the following outline. §2 considers the relationship between gender and complexity. §3 explores the relationship of gender with reference and animacy. §4 discusses gender in the broader context of nominal morphology. §5 and §6 deal with noun classification and gender assignment. §7 reconsiders the notion of gender agreement. §8 investigates the relationship between gender, number, case and person while §9 focuses on pluralia tantum. §10 explores the extent to which gender is subject to system evolution. §11 addresses gender in its genealogical and areal context and discusses the relevance of external factors in the ecology of languages. §12 summarizes the results and concludes the chapter.

Since *gender* is not the only term to keep track of, we have compiled an appendix with short definitions of terms at the end of this chapter. All definitions have the perspective of gender and/or complexity and their primary purpose is to facilitate the understanding of this chapter rather than being universally applicable in linguistics.

2 Complexity and gender

In §2.1 we provide an overview of current approaches to the notion of linguistic complexity. §2.2 then discusses the relationship between complexity and gender, as well as the existing metrics of gender complexity.

2.1 Understanding and measuring complexity

Over the last couple of decades, the debate on linguistic complexity has focused primarily on three overarching topics:

(i) what counts as linguistic complexity,

(ii) what to measure when quantifying complexity,

(iii) and what relevance this has for understanding languages overall.

These topics, and their relevance to the understanding of grammatical gender, are tackled in the two volumes of this work, and, more specifically, in the chapters by Audring, Nichols and Sinnemäki. Audring (2019 [in Volume I]) provides a theoretical account of gender system complexity by comparing the notion of linguistic complexity with canonicity and difficulty. Nichols (2019 [in Volume I]) tests and falsifies the hypothesis that languages with gender are more complex overall. Sinnemäki (2019 [this volume]) investigates whether there is a complexity trade-off between the distribution of gender systems and that of numeral classifiers across the languages of the world. A fourth contribution, Di Garbo & Miestamo (2019 [this volume]), approaches gender system complexity from a diachronic perspective by investigating disappearing and/or emerging patterns of gender agreement and their complexity features.

Starting with the first topic – what counts as linguistic complexity – all four contributions define complexity in ABSOLUTE terms, that is as an objective property of grammatical domains rather than as a subjective feature of language use (what is also known as *relative complexity*). This issue has been extensively debated in the literature. While some influential cross-linguistic studies in the field (Kusters 2003; 2008) deal with complexity as a measure of difficulty in language learning and use, the dominant approach in the functionally-oriented literature has been that linguistic complexity is best viewed as a property of language systems, rather than as a measure of ease of acquisition and use. This is essentially because we do not yet have a full account of language processing difficulties in different domains of grammar and across different modes of language acquisition. Important contributions in establishing the roadmap for such an approach to the theoretical and empirical study of linguistic complexity are the two volumes edited by Miestamo et al. (2008) and Sampson et al. (2009).

The second issue that has been central in the debate on language complexity is what to measure when quantifying complexity. Nichols (2019 [in Volume I]) sees two main answers to this question: (i) INVENTORY or (COMPOSITIONAL) COMPLEXITY, that is, the number of distinctions in a grammatical system (e.g., the number of tones, tenses, genders), and (ii) DESCRIPTIVE COMPLEXITY (or Kolmogorov complexity), defined as the information required to describe a system (the longer the description, the more complex the system). While Nichols sees inventory and descriptive complexity as independent of one another and argues that descriptive complexity "is a better measure" that "captures well the non-transparency relevant to learnability and prone to be shaped by sociolinguistics", an integrated approach is proposed by Miestamo (2008), and followed by Audring (2019 [in Volume I]) and Di Garbo & Miestamo (2019 [this volume]). Under this approach, linguistic complexity is defined in terms of overall description length, which can be measured on the basis of two principles, the Principle of Fewer Distinctions and the Principle of One-Meaning–One-Form.

The PRINCIPLE OF FEWER DISTINCTIONS is a measure of inventory complexity and states that the fewer distinctions are made within a grammatical domain the less complex the domain (the fewer the tones, tense or gender distinctions, the less complex the tone, tense or gender system overall). The PRINCIPLE OF ONE-MEANING–ONE-FORM is a measure of transparency whereby the less complex grammatical phenomenon is one where there is a one-to-one correspondence between meaning and form.

Under the Principle of One-Meaning–One-Form, cumulative morphemes (simultaneously expressing more than one grammatical meaning) or multiple exponents (where one grammatical meaning is distributed over several morphemes) are more complex than morphemes that are only associated with one grammatical meaning. Working specifically on the measurability of gender system complexity, Di Garbo (2014; 2016) expands this approach by proposing a third complexity principle, the PRINCIPLE OF INDEPENDENCE, which targets interactions between grammatical domains and their effect on the overall complexity of individual domains. Under the Principle of Independence, a marker that cumulates the encoding of gender and number distinctions features higher gender complexity than a non-cumulative marker, because the marking of gender distinctions is dependent on the number value of nouns. In the gender complexity measure proposed by Audring (2019 [in Volume I]), the Principle of Fewer Distinctions and the Principle of One-Meaning–One-Form are referred to as Principle of Economy and Principle of Transparency, while the same label as Di Garbo (2014; 2016) is kept for the Principle of Independence.

The third and final issue that has been frequently addressed in the literature on linguistic complexity is the relevance that complexity measures may have to understanding languages overall. Is it at all possible to design complexity metrics that allow us to estimate whether one language is generally more complex than another? And, provided that this is the case, how can such metrics be used? McWhorter (2001) proposes to measure overall grammatical complexity on the basis of a pool of features ranging from phonology to syntax. However, the features suggested by McWhorter (2001) aim to capture the peculiarities of one specific language profile, the creole profile, and to demonstrate that creole languages are overall less complex than non-creoles. The question thus remains whether the ambition to measure linguistic complexity overall is a feasible, and even meaningful, enterprise even beyond the creole/non-creole dichotomy. This question is approached in work by Miestamo (2008), Nichols (2009), and Sinnemäki (2014b), who argue that measures of global linguistic complexity are both theoretically and empirically unfeasible. Even assuming that the daunting task of formulating an exhaustive inventory of complexity features that are truly representative of overall grammatical complexity could be accomplished, it is still hard to establish empirically how each of these features contributes to overall complexity in comparison to others. For instance, it would be impossible to truly establish whether the presence of grammatical gender implies higher complexity than the presence of, say, grammaticalized tone distinctions, or the other way round, both within and across languages. Miestamo (2008) refers to this as the problem of comparability, and argues that one way to overcome this problem is to restrict the quantitative and qualitative typological study of linguistic complexity to individual grammatical domains, and eventually compare domain-specific data with each other in search of potential complexity trade-offs between individual grammatical domains and their functional explanations. All contributions to this two-volume work approach the complexity of gender systems in the spirit of this suggestion, and even those chapters that explicitly focus on comparisons and relationships between the complexity of gender and other domains of grammar bring support to the idea that domain-specificity is a key to understanding the distribution of linguistic complexity within and across languages.

The chapter by Nichols (2019 [in Volume I]) shows that testing whether the presence of grammatical gender makes languages more complex overall produces negative results. Sinnemäki (2019 [this volume]) demonstrates that comparing gender and classifier systems in terms of complexity distributions may be useful to unravel functional trade-offs in the domain of nominal classification, whereby the presence of grammatical gender in a language disfavors the occurrence of numeral classifiers and vice versa.

2.2 Gender complexity metrics and the principles behind them

Gender complexity metrics have been proposed by Audring (2014; 2017) and Di Garbo (2014; 2016). In their approaches, gender is considered to be a grammatical domain of its own, and its complexity is assessed on the basis of the three principles introduced in §2.1: (i) Economy, or the Principle of Fewer Distinctions, (ii) Transparency, or the Principle of One-Meaning–One-Form and (iii) (the Principle of) Independence. See Audring (2019 [in Volume I]) and Di Garbo & Miestamo (2019 [this volume]) for a more detailed treatment of the three principles.

Di Garbo's (2014; 2016) metric is an index of six features, each ranging between zero and one, that is applied to a dataset of 84 African languages with gender. The features are Number of gender values (GV), Nature of assignment rules (AR), Number of indexing targets (IND) (all three Fewer Distinctions), Cumulative exponence of gender and number (CUM) (One-Meaning–One-Form and Independence), Manipulation of gender assignment triggered by number/countability (M1), and Manipulation of gender assignment triggered by size (M2) (both Independence). The first three features of the metric are based on the proposal by Audring (2014). Features CUM, M1, and M2 are meant to measure the impact that interactions of gender and number, and gender and evaluative morphology, have on the overall complexity of gender. The features by Di Garbo (2014; 2016) are designed such that a simpler gender system can always take the value zero (only two genders, only semantic assignment, only one indexing target, non-cumulative exponence and no manipulation of gender). However, all languages in Di Garbo's sample have higher total values than 0.0, and many have 1.0, which can be interpreted such that gender tends to be complex at least in African languages. The metric has been applied by Liljegren (2019 [in Volume I]) to the languages of the Greater Hindu Kush area. He identifies two languages with value 0.0, Khowar and Kalasha (together making up the Chitral subgroup), both of which have developed animacy-based gender distinctions quite recently. All other gender languages in Liljegren's sample have Medium or High gender complexity.

Based on the same three principles, Audring (2017) develops a metric consisting of 23 features, which all can take the values *simple* and *complex*. The metric is illustrated only for one language, German (Indo-European, Germanic), whose gender system turns out to score less than expected (only 9 of 23 features complex). This is most likely due to the fact that many simple gender features have been overlooked in the literature, while the metrics proposed by Audring allows to capture them. This metric is further elaborored upon by Audring (2019 [in Volume I]) in the context of a broader discussion of the relationships between complexity, canonicity, and difficulty.

3 Referent-based gender and the limited hierarchical patterning of gender

3.1 Introduction

In this section we are going to argue that REFERENT-BASED GENDER (classes of referents) is more basic from a developmental perspective than LEXICAL GENDER (classes of noun lexemes). Referents are typically classified in terms of animacy, and animacy is organized in form of a hierarchy. Nichols (2019 [in Volume I]) suggests that hierarchical patterning is a decomplexifying mechanism. The question thus arises as to why hierarchical patterning in gender does not limit complexity. In this section we will argue that hierarchical patterning in gender is rooted in referent-based gender and that gender typically originates as referent-based gender in the top segment of the animacy or individuation hierarchy (§3.2). However, as referent-based gender travels down the animacy hierarchy, there are two things that happen that render it less transparent. First, some or several animal gender values (animate, or, masculine and/or feminine) are expanded to inanimate objects by means of various factors often of a metonymic or metaphoric character, such as agentivity, discourse salience, uniqueness, power, purview, and possession (discussed in §3.3 and §3.4). These cannot be neatly arranged on a single scale and hence hierarchical patterning fails to apply to them. Second, if gender has travelled down the animacy hierarchy, it gets increasingly more associated with nouns and is aligned with the conceptual structure of nouns, which means that it turns into lexical gender (§3.5). Noun lexemes, however, are not subject to hierarchical patterning in the same way as referents, and hence there is no hierarchical mechanism that can efficiently limit the complexity of lexical gender, even though the semantic core originating in referent-based gender is maintained. In order to prevent complete disorder, gender must thus resort to lexical patterning, instead of hierarchical patterning, and lexical patterning has a much higher degree of freedom than hierarchical patterning, which entails that complexity is less effectively limited in lexical gender. However, when lexical gender develops, referential-based gender does not disappear, but interacts with it, and lexical and referential-based gender are sometimes so similar that they are difficult to distinguish (§3.6). Both lexical and referent-based gender allow for reconceptualization of referents, which is why gender is not suitable for reference tracking (§3.7).

3.2 The animacy/individuation hierarchy

Dahl (2000a) follows Aksenov (1984) and Corbett (1991) in claiming that all gender systems have a semantic core. He uses the animacy hierarchy in (1)

(1) Animacy hierarchy
     human > higher animals > lower animals > inanimate

to further specify that core. Above some cutoff point on the animacy hierarchy, gender is semantically assigned; below the cutoff point, gender is non-semantic (formal or arbitrary). If the animate pole is further subdivided, the major criterion is sex. From the point of view of complexity, this means that gender tends to be simple on the animate pole of the hierarchy and complex on the inanimate pole of the hierarchy, even though often the same gender values are used both above and below the cutoff point: "inanimate nouns are quite often assigned to genders whose semantically determined core consists of animates" (Dahl 2000a: 102–103) and "gender distinctions often cut through the animal kingdom" (Dahl 2000a: 100). A neat example is Walman (Nuclear Torricelli, West Palai; see Dryer 2019 [in Volume I]), where nouns denoting humans and some larger animals are either masculine or feminine, depending on the sex of the referent, whereas nouns denoting most animals, especially non-mammals, appear to have relatively arbitrary gender, but are assigned to the same two genders masculine and feminine.

Various forms of the animacy hierarchy can be found in the literature. Croft (2003: 130) uses the so-called extended animacy hierarchy (2), which, according to him, combines three distinct, but related hierarchies: person, referentiality, and animacy (3). Here and elsewhere we replace "proper names" by *person names*, since names of animals, things, and places are usually disregarded in discussions of animacy.

(2) Extended animacy hierarchy (Croft 2003: 130, following Dixon 1979: 85 and Silverstein 1976):
first/second person pronouns > third person pronoun > person names > human common nouns > nonhuman animate common nouns > inanimate common nouns

(3) Component hierarchies of the extended animacy hierarchy
Person: first, second > third (proximate > obviative)
Referentiality: pronoun > person name > common noun
Animacy: human > higher animals > lower animals > inanimate

As pointed out by Croft (2003: 166), different hierarchies often interact. He illustrates this with examples from Eastern Panjabi[1] (Indo-European, Indo-Aryan) for differential object marking, which combines the factors animacy and referentiality. Eastern Panjabi objects are overtly coded with *(-)nū̃* unless the object is both inanimate and non-definite (specific or non-specific). This suggests that the component hierarchy "Referentiality" actually falls into two different sub-hierarchies: Part-of-speech (pronoun > person name > common noun) and Definiteness (unique > definite > specific/referential > non-specific/non-referential).

Siemund (2008) surveys pronominal gender in varieties of English and other languages. He comes to the conclusion that pronominal gender in English crucially depends on the degree of individuation of the entries referred to. He adduces Sasse's Individuation Hierarchy (1) to account for this, a further variant of the animacy hierarchy.

person names	humans	animals	inanimate tangible objects	abstracts	mass nouns
humans			non-humans		
animates			inanimates		
count nouns				mass nouns	

Figure 1: Individuation hierarchy according to Sasse (1993: 659), as adapted by Karatsareas (2014: 90)

The individuation hierarchy is more elaborate than Croft's extended animacy hierarchy in that it contains two further sub-hierarchies: countability (count noun > mass noun) and concreteness (concrete/tangible > abstract).

---

[1]Here and elsewhere in this chapter, we use mostly the language names in Glottolog in Hammarström et al. (2018). Thus, here "Punjabi" is replaced by "Eastern Panjabi". If Glottolog names are not used, these are given in brackets.

Individuation is relevant in varieties of English in various ways. Diachronically, Siemund & Dolberg (2011: 527) show that "gender change appears to have started with nouns ranking low in terms of individuation" in English in the transformation of a German-like complex gender system to a pronominal gender system. In West Somerset English there is a mass/count distinction (*the bread* – *it*, *the loaf* – *he*). For further examples from other languages, see Siemund (2008: 175–217).

3.3 The animacy hierarchy does not structure the connections between inanimate referents and animacy

The extended animacy hierarchy does not provide any guidelines for the domain of inanimates and the individuation hierarchy offers only three very general groupings: tangible objects, abstracts and mass nouns. However, there are various semantic connections that can link inanimate referents with animates, notably the following: agentivity, salience, purview, uniqueness, power, and possession. Possession will be addressed in §3.4, the others in this section. In these semantic domains, there are often metaphorical or metonymic connections between inanimate referents and animacy. These cannot easily be arranged on a single scale of animacy and individuation. But they all provide pathways for expansion from animate genders to the inanimate domain.

(i) *Agentivity.* Agents are usually conceived of as animate. Inanimate referents can leak into animate genders when they are construed as agents. In Zande (Atlantic-Congo, Ubangi), nouns referring to inanimate things usually control inanimate gender, but can take animate gender when animacy is imputed on them, as in (4):

(4) Zande (Atlantic-Congo, Ubangi; Gore 1926: 32)
    Ime ki   sa ti-ru   (/ti-e)   ni   kure.
    water and.then turn REFL-ANIM (/REFL-INAN) with blood.
    'And the water turned itself into blood.'

In various languages with gender, nouns for natural phenomena are treated as animates. In his description of gender in Walman, Dryer (2019 [in Volume I]) mentions that the quasi-animate natural phenomena *onyul* 'earthquake', *knum* 'whirlpool, riptide', *snar* 'moon', and *nganu* 'sun' are masculine (unlike all other inanimates, which are feminine). *Nganu* does not only mean 'sun', but also 'day', and is masculine in both meanings, hereby demonstrating that the gender of this noun, even though motivated by animacy and probably originating from referent-based gender, has become lexical gender.

Agentivity can come in different forms. It can be more syntactic, as in (4) where an inanimate referent is construed as an actor, or it can be more derivational, when an inanimate referent is construed as an agentive noun. Mopán Maya has masculine and feminine person name markers extended to common nouns, and one of their major functions is to form analytic agentive nouns: *ix p'o'* [GM.F wash] 'washerwoman' ("Ms wash"), *aj jook'* [GM.M fish] 'fisherman' ("Mr fish") (Contini-Morava & Danziger 2018: 140). Gender markers can be used to suggest unexpected agentivity of inanimate objects as in (5).

(5) Mopán Maya (Mayan, Yucatecan; Contini-Morava & Danziger 2018: 141)
Ox-tuul-oo'   *aj*   *kuch-b'äk' a*
three-NUM.CLF.ANIM-3UNDERGOER.PL GM.M carry-meat ART
xoolte'   *leek-oo'*   *a*   *b'e'.*
walking_stick 3.EMPH-3UNDERGOER.PL ART DEM.4
'Those aforementioned walking sticks became three (living) meat-carriermen.'

(ii) *Salience.* Pawley (2004) shows that "animated pronouns" are a prominent feature in Tasmanian Vernacular English. That there is some degree of animation can also be seen from examples where other animate words besides pronouns, such as *fella*, are used, as in (6). "The entity must be referential (specific or definite). Other factors include its importance in the discourse (as a main topic, background element, etc.), its sequential position in the discourse, and its inherent salience" (Pawley 2004: 114). For portable goods other than vehicles, *he* expresses an attitude of detachment and *she* (emotional) attachment. Plants, animals, and male genitals are *he*, everything else is *she*.

(6) Tasmanian Vernacular English (Pawley 2004: 126): attitude of detachment
[Salesman is showing carpets to two customers] ***That fella** he's a poly,* **he**'s two fifty.

The classical study on animated pronouns in English is Mathiot & Roberts (1978), who observed similar patterns in spoken English in two parts of the USA, Los Angeles County and Buffalo NY. However, for portable goods there is a polarity effect: men use predominantly *she* and women *he* (Pawley 2004: 134).

(iii) *Purview.* The notion of purview has been introduced by Gerdts (2013) for Halkomelem (Salishan, Central Salish). Halkomelem has a sex-based semantic gender system marked on determiners and demonstratives, where female singular humans take feminine gender and all other nouns masculine gender. However, feminine optionally appears on hundreds of inanimate nouns when they are in the feminine PURVIEW (Gerdts 2013). This includes objects that belong to or relate to a female, are perceived as being feminine in size, shape, or function, or are spoken about by a female.

In Comaltepec Chinantec (Otomanguean, Chinantecan), gender "can be rhetorically upgraded to express a closer association than the normal gender assignment would indicate" (Anderson 1989: 57). In (7), the word for 'paper', which is usually inanimate, is animate in order to mark a more intimate status as a product "of someone's personal labor and attention" (Anderson 1989: 57).

(7) Comaltepec Chinantec (Otomanguean, Chinantecan; Anderson 1989: 57)

$mi^{\ddot{\text{i}}LM}$-r   **$hmi^L gi\acute{u}{:}n^L$-b** hiu^{LH} $ma^H hi^L$
request.3PL-3 **many.ANIM**-AFFIRMATION DIM   paper

'S/he asks for many papers.'

(iv) *Uniqueness.* In the Irish-Canadian author Emma Donoghue's (2010) novel *Room*, a mother and son are captured in a backyard shed that the boy never leaves until they manage to escape when the boy is five. In the boy's language things in Room with unique reference are *he* and *she*. In Room English, feminine and masculine gender are inseparably tied to uniqueness and referentiality. In Room, *Blanket* is feminine: *we put Blanket over [TV] and just listen through the gray of **her*** (p. 11). However, things outside Room are all different and not unique: *it's not fleecy gray like Blanket, it's rougher* (p. 166), *Officer Oh tries to put the blanket over my head, I push **it** off* (p. 177). It may be argued that this example is artificial, but it is still a doculect of English, and the example shows that a particular use of referent-based gender may be contextual and need not necessarily apply to a whole language as a system.

In narrative discourse, inanimates are often personified as unique referents. One of the arguments adduced by Leeding (1989: 232) that gender assignment in Anindilyakwa (Gunwinyguan) is semantically motivated is that masculine and feminine words often are connected in traditional Dreamtime stories as dramatis personae, e.g. *yi-ningwimwapwalhpwa akwa thi-wirrawilya* 'M-Bat and F-Rainbow'. This suggests that they at least in some of their typical uses are conceived of as unique, which may have favored the extension of masculine and feminine to inanimates.

(v) *Power.* Straus & Brightman (1982) have argued that the seemingly arbitrary distribution of animate and inanimate gender for inanimate referents in Algonquian languages is motivated by power. Animate nouns are all in some sense "powerful" (Straus & Brightman 1982: 135). In Cheyenne (Algic, Algonquian, Cheyenne), some body parts (finger/toe, thumb, fingernail, claw, eyebrow, knee, kidney, and brain) are animate, but not when indicated on a drawing or discussed as abstractions, and there is a good story for each of them why exactly these are powerful (Straus & Brightman 1982: 128–130). Cheyenne *moʔeško* 'finger, toe', for instance, is animate because fingers are used symbolically as weapons and as channels of power in cursing, but there is also an inanimate noun *moʔeško* 'ring'. Power has cultural implications. However, whether ascribed to language or culture, the classification of nouns is complex and on some level due to convention. "For example, nouns labeling mechanical items introduced by Whites are largely inanimate in Ojibwa while they are often animate in Menomini" [Menominee] (Straus & Brightman 1982: 133). This suggests that referent-based animate gender of inanimates, originally motivated by the factor power, has largely turned into lexical gender in Algonquian languages.

3.4 Inherited gender

A further semantic connection between animate and non-animate referents is possession, which is even more difficult to include in the animacy hierarchy. In INHERITED GENDER, surveyed by Evans (1994) for Australian languages, the gender of a noun or NP is determined by the gender of its possessor. Inherited gender is usually referent-based rather than lexical gender, and this is stated explicitly by Olsson (2017: 186) for Coastal Marind (Anim, Marindic). In Coastal Marind, a few nouns, including *igih* 'name' in (8), inherit the gender of the referent to which they are attached.

(8) Coastal Marind (Anim, Marindic; Olsson 2017: 187)

igih   ta/tu/ta/ti   ka-ha-b
name **what:I/what:II/what.III/what.IV** PRS.NEUT-INT-ACT[3SG.A]

'What is his/her/its name?' more literally: 'What is the he-name, she-name, it-name?'

Note that the possessive pronoun in the English translation is misleading. The interrogative pronoun simply takes the gender that the speaker assumes to be the class of the referent (male name for gender I, female or nouns denoting animals for class II, thing of a noun in class III or IV for class III and IV; Olsson 2017: 187–188). For inherited gender in New Guinea, see also Fedden (2011: 177).

In Halkomelem, inherited gender is part of the extension of feminine to inanimates by purview. In example (9), the instrument *šəptən* 'knife' can be feminine if possessed by a female, but must be masculine when possessed by a male:

(9) Halkomelem (Salishan, Central Salish; Gerdts 2013)

Niʔ ʔəncə kʷθə/łə   šəptən-s   θeẏ ɋemiʔ?
AUX where DET/DET.F knife-3.POSS DEM.F girl

'Where is that girl's knife?'

In North America, inherited gender is also attested in Tunica (isolate), where body parts inherit gender (Swanton 1921: 23).

It is important to emphasize that inherited gender is not always referent-based gender. In Jarawara (Arawan, Madi) inalienable possession, the gender of the NP is determined by the gender of the possessor. The Arawan languages have complex lexical gender assignment. It is thus not surprising that even inherited gender in Jarawara is more complex than in Halkomelem, where there is virtually no lexical gender anywhere in the language. In Jarawara, it is the lexical gender of the possessor that is inherited, not the gender of the referent. Pronouns are feminine irrespective of referent-based gender (Dixon 2000: 489).[2] Hence, the NP in (10) is feminine and triggers feminine agreement on the predicate, whatever the sex of the referents. As we will see in §7.3, this is a kind of gender resolution. However, some inalienable nouns also have derivational gender suffixes, whose gender is determined in a different and rather complex way, but also by the lexical gender of the possessor. A first person inclusive possessor, as in (10), always

---

[2] Jarawara is not the only language where pronouns all trigger a specific gender. In Uduk (Koman; Killian 2019 [in Volume I]) pronouns are always in class 1.

triggers masculine derivational gender. This is an instance of a nominal target (see §7.6), where a derivational affix of a noun can be an agreement target.

(10) Jarawara (Arawan, Madi; Dixon 2000: 490)
      Ee   *man-o*   *koma-ke.*
      1PL.INCL.INALIEN arm-DERIV.M be.sore-DECL.F
      'Our (inclusive) arms are sore.'

In Australian languages it is common to mix inherited gender and intrinsic lexical gender. In Mawng (Iwaidjan Proper), some nouns for body parts, such as *ngijalk* 'body', always have inherited gender, whereas *ngaralk* 'tongue' (class IV), *murlu* 'nose' (class III) and *algij* 'liver' (class V) can have lexical gender (Capell & Hinch 1970; Evans 1994: 5). In Tiwi (isolate), body part nouns take the gender of their possessor, except for genitals that take the gender of the opposite sex (Evans 1994: 2). The opposite choice for genitals can be explained by purview. Genitals relate to the other sex. Opposite choice is also attested for the Amwi variety of War-Jaintia (Austroasiatic, Khasian; Weidert 1975): *ʔu kdɛ* 'DET.M vagina', *kə khlɛ* 'DET.F penis'. However, inverted inherited gender, i.e. gender opposite to that of the referent of the possessor, is generalized in Amwi War. Body parts, tools and household items take the gender opposite to the person they are associated with. Inverted inherited gender in Amwi War exhibits the same fluidity as non-inverted inherited gender in Halkomelem, and this suggests that we have to deal with referent-based gender rather than with lexical gender here: *ʔu khlia kə* [DET.M head 3.SG.F] 'her head' (personal pronouns preposed to nouns are gender markers of that noun, possessors are postposed to their heads in NPs), *kə klia-w* [DET.F head-3.SG.M] 'his head'. Only tools and clothes only associated with one sex are not fluid, in the same way as genitals: *kə cin* 'jeans (only for men)'.

Inherited gender and gender by purview is a kind of associated gender. The most famous case of associated gender in the literature is Dyirbal. Corbett (1991: 16) uses the term concept association for the well-known Dyirbal examples where 'fishing line' and 'fish spear' are gender I (animate) because of their association with 'fish' (but see Plaster & Polinsky 2007 for an alternative explanation). In the light of the many examples of association by referent surveyed in this section it seems to us that the term "concept association" is problematic. Association in gender is mainly association with referents and not association with concepts. Of course, as in other cases where referent-based gender turns into lexical gender, association of referents can eventually turn into association of concepts.

Not only are the semantic connections discussed in §3.3 and this section often metonymical or metaphorical in character, some of them also provide pathways for how cultural beliefs can make their way into language structure. This holds in particular for purview and power. If we conceive of gender as referent-based originally, it does not necessarily express cultural beliefs from its very origin. There are many languages with semantic gender assignment where there is no associated gender of the kind that is attested in Dyirbal and Algonquian languages. There is no reason to believe that communities speaking languages without associated gender are poorer in their cultural beliefs. It is thus possible to view the "culturalization" of gender as a trait of maturity. Languages with many cultural properties embedded in grammatical gender presuppose gender categories with non-trivial prehistories.

3.5 Lexical gender originates from referent-based gender

In §3.2 and §3.3 we have considered cases where referent-based animate gender leaks to inanimate referents. In this section we will now consider instances of referent-based gender marking that have further developed into lexical gender as gender has travelled down the animacy hierarchy from personal pronouns and person names to NPs headed by common nouns.

Russian and other Slavic languages have developed a lexical animacy distinction in addition to the three-way masculine-feminine-neuter lexical gender system inherited from Indo-European. Slavic animacy subgenders originate from differential object marking. Due to sound change, nominative and accusative singular came to be morphologically indistinguishable in the major masculine declension class, which is why forms of the genitive singular started being used in object function (Meillet 1897; Huntley 1980: 206), and the genitive form was then also used in non-object function following prepositions. In Old Russian of the 13th and 14th centuries, genitive singular forms had generally replaced accusative forms for personal pronouns and person names (Dietze 1973: 263). According to Dietze (1973: 265), socioeconomically subordinate and dependent persons, such as children, servants, slaves, and messengers, go with the inanimate category; *mužъ* 'man' is animate in the meaning 'husband' but inanimate as the subjects of a prince, and *vinogradъ* 'vineyard' is animate when used metaphorically for the world populated with people, as in (11). Hence, animacy gender on masculine singular common nouns was referent-based in Old Russian.

(11)   Old Russian (Indo-European, Slavic; Dietze 1973: 267)
       gospodi   *bože...*   *posěti*   *svoego*
       lord.VOC.SG god.VOC.SG... visit(PFV).IMP.2SG own.GEN.SG.M

> *vinograda*
> vineyard(M/ANIM).GEN.SG
> 'O Lord God...visit your vineyard'

Animate forms with animals start appearing in the 16th century, and in the 17th century, animate forms for animals were generalized (Dietze 1973: 270). (12) from Modern Russian illustrates that animate gender has become lexical. Even though the Modern Russian animacy distinction is clearly semantically motivated, it is entrenched in the lexicon and some modern dictionaries now indicate whether a noun is animate or inanimate. In (12) *konkurent* 'competitor' is animate (takes genitive singular in object function) and *Uzbekistan* is inanimate (takes nominative singular in object function), although they both have the same referent.

(12) Russian (Indo-European, Slavic): lexically entrenched animacy distinction
      Kazaxstan-Ø   rassmatrivaet   Uzbekistan-Ø   kak
      K.(INAN/M)-NOM.SG view(IPFV).PRS.3SG U.(INAN/M)-NOM.SG how/as
      konkurent-a.
      competitor(ANIM/M)-GEN.SG
      'Kazakhstan views Uzbekistan as a competitor.'

Gender marked on NP-markers may develop from person name markers. Person name markers have a tendency to be expanded. Varieties of Catalan have the person name markers masculine *en* (< *don* < Latin *dominus*) and feminine *na* (< *dona* < Latin *domina*). In Balearic Catalan, these markers can be expanded to names of animals (*en Pluto* for a male dog), and to folk names of clouds and celestial bodies: *en Catalí* 'Venus at dawn' (Caro Reina 2018: 195–197). This is arguably not lexical gender, since common nouns are not involved, but referent-based gender having traveled down the animacy hierarchy. Person name markers are very common in Austronesian languages, where they are sometimes extended to some older kinship terms, such as 'father' and 'mother', which are often unique, or titles.[3] Like many other Austronesian languages, Tagalog (Central Philippine) makes a distinction between noun phrase markers for common nouns (topic *ang*,

---

[3]It should be noted here that uniqueness does not have the same effect in gender as in definiteness, where it has also been claimed to play an important role (Russell 1905; Lyons 1999). Definite articles are used in the first place with concepts that are not unique out of context, but which happen to be unique in a particular situation. Person name markers, however, express uniqueness on items that are unique in any context and are extended first of all to expressions that are typically construed as unique.

non-topic *nang*, oblique *sa*) and for person names (topic *si*, non-topic *ni*, oblique *kay*). Person name markers can also be used with older kinship terms (*ate* 'eldest sister', *kuya* 'eldest brother', *ina/nanay* 'mother', *ama/tatay* 'father' and some others); the difference is that this use is optional. They can be used with nouns designating occupations when expressing titles: *si Abogado Cruz* 'Lawyer Cruz' (Schachter & Otanes 1972: 94). In several Oceanic languages, person name markers have been extended to some common nouns and turned into lexical gender. In Nakanai, the person name marker is used with about 70% of the names of species of fish, birds and insects and a majority of loanwords (Johnston 1980: 166–167). For Teop, see Svärd (2019 [in Volume I]) and the references given there; for Owa and Kahua, see §6.4; and for Austronesian in general, see Handschuh (2018).

In the Mek languages in New Guinea it can be observed how lexical gender can develop from a referent-based gender uniqueness vs. non-uniqueness distinction, where uniqueness looks very much like an extended person name marking. The more conservative Mek languages Una and Eipo [=Eipomek] have a uniqueness distinction, and Nalca, which is more progressive and closely related to Eipo, has developed a gender system with four lexical gender classes with rather simple gender assignment principles (Wälchli 2018).

Una has only an opposition between *bi-* unique and *a-* non-unique. *Bi-* is mainly used with person names and kinship terms older than ego – thus the cutoff point on the animacy hierarchy is between older and younger kin – but also with highly individuated non-kinship human nouns and sometimes even animals and things. Thus, in the Una New Testament, *bi-* occurs, for instance, with *ner* 'woman' where it means 'queen', with *Mi* 'child, son' only when it is the 'Son of God' (capitalization in orthography has a function similar to the uniqueness marker), and with *Uram* 'voice, word' only when it is 'God's voice'. (13) illustrates its use with a person name as opposed to *a-* with common nouns. Note that Una also can mark person names with preposed third person pronouns not distinguishing gender (*Er Jesus* 'he Jesus') and that the two strategies can be combined, as exemplified in (13).

(13) Una (Nuclear Trans-New Guinea, Mek; New Testament 41009020)
      Ba, sun-ci   a   mi   a-si   Er Yesus dam bo-ya-nmai
      but they-ERG this child N.UNI-ACC 3SG Jesus near carry-come-PST.3PL

      ura, a   mi   wek-am-we   isa   a-ryi   Er Yesus
      after this child enter-previously-PST.3SG ghost N.UNI-ERG 3SG Jesus

      bi-si   asing eib-mou   ura, a   mi   a-si   tomob-oka
      UNI-ACC eye   see-PST.3PL after this child N.UNI-ACC erect-CVB

oublob-mou.

crush-PST.3SG

'And they brought this child to Jesus. And when the ghost who had entered the child saw Jesus, the spirit immediately convulsed the child...'

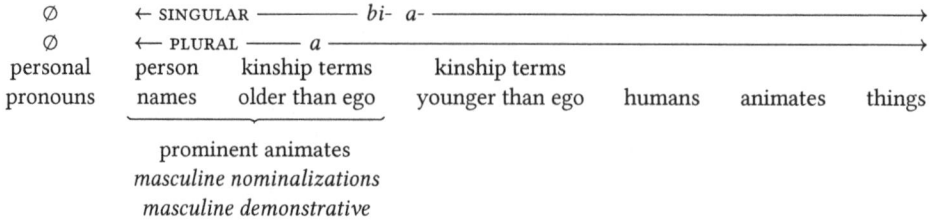

∅	← SINGULAR —————— *bi-* *a-* ———————————————————————→
∅	←— PLURAL ——— *a* ————————————————————————————————→

personal pronouns	person names	kinship terms older than ego	kinship terms younger than ego	humans	animates	things

prominent animates
masculine nominalizations
masculine demonstrative

Figure 2: Una *bi-* unique and *a-* non-unique and the animacy hierarchy

The Una gender system can thus largely be characterized by the animacy hierarchy in Figure 2. There are two anomalies (in italics in Figure 2). There is a masculine singular nominalizing suffix *-nyi*, often used in indigenous names, and nominalizations suffixed by *-nyi* are always unique *bi-*.[4] The same marker *-nyi* can also be added to the demonstrative *a-*, which then together with *bi-* unique can serve as a masculine grammatical anaphor (but is different from the third person pronoun which does not distinguish gender). These anomalies are the germs for a further development of the Una unique marker *bi-* towards a lexical masculine gender *be-* in Nalca (see Wälchli 2018 for the details).

In a wide range of languages from different places in the world, noun markers, whether they distinguish gender or not, are so called PRONOMINAL ARTICLES (Himmelmann 2001: 838), which means that noun markers have the same form as personal pronouns (mainly third person pronouns, but occasionally also second and first person) and have developed from personal pronouns (unlike Romance, where both articles and personal pronouns independently originate from demonstratives). For the development of pronominal articles from personal pronouns in Kxoe (Khoe-Kwadi, Khoe), see Heine & Reh (1984: 231–234). Interestingly, many languages with pronominal articles with gender, such as the Khoekhoe language Nama (Khoe-Kwadi, Khoe), Khasi (Khasian, Austroasiatic), Mian and Oksapmin (Ok-Oksapmin, Nuclear Trans-New Guinea), Abau (Sepik), Kayabi and Tenharim (Tupian, Tupi-Guarani), use pronominal articles with proper names (except in vocatives and non-referential use where a person is given a name), in contrast to articles from other origins, which are rarely used with proper names. This

---

[4]We will return to Mek nominalizations in §7.3 in the discussion of complex controllers.

suggests that person names may play an important role when pronouns extend to articles, and a reasonable hypothesis is that pronominal gender can expand to nouns by travelling down the animacy hierarchy, among other things via person names. Evidence that pronominal articles travel down the animacy hierarchy comes from languages where pronominal articles are less grammaticalized and restricted to human or animate referents. In Oksapmin (Loughnane 2009: 178–184), pronominal articles occur with specific human referents, but usually not with things or animals, where the definite article (of demonstrative origin) is used (14).

(14) Oksapmin (Nuclear Trans-New Guinea, Ok-Oksapmin; Loughnane 2009: 180)

robin **ux**=*nuŋ* *bəp ulxe* *ap* *jox*
Robyn 3SG.F=OBJ SO 3SG.F.REFL.POSS house DEF/DEM

o=m-de-pti
leave=PROX.OBJ-make-IPFV.PL.PRS

'After that, we left Robyn at the house.'

The Oksapmin definite article (a demonstrative) may co-occur with the pronominal article and the order is then noun-definite.article-pronominal.article: *nap jox ux* [younger.sister DEF/DEM 3SG.F] 'the younger sister' (Loughnane 2009: 128). In Oksapmin, pronominal articles can be used with animals, when a specific animal is opposed to another one, or for mythical animals with human-like characteristics. Pronominal articles can also occur with forces of nature. There does not seem to be any lexical gender in Oksapmin. Feminine is restricted to female human referents. Oksapmin thus provides support for the hypothesis that, if expressing gender, pronominal articles mark referent-based gender at first, and can later turn into markers of lexical gender, if their extension to inanimate nouns is more advanced.

3.6 The relationship between referent-based and lexical gender

The preceding sections might have evoked the idea that referent-based and lexical gender are strictly opposed to each other, but this is actually not the case. To the extent that lexical concepts denote sets of referents that are homogeneous with respect to the referent-based properties distinguished in gender, there is no mismatch.

The best-known mismatches are so-called HYBRID NOUNS, such as German *Mädchen*, which is neuter as a lexical noun (due to its diminutive suffix *-chen*, which morphologically assigns neuter gender to the lexeme), but refers to female beings. In cases of conflict, lexical gender is more likely in local than in distant agreement, where semantic agreement (referent-based gender) prevails, which is Corbett's well-known Agreement Hierarchy (15).

(15) The Agreement Hierarchy (Corbett 1991: 226)
      attributive < predicate < relative pronoun < personal pronoun
      ein nettes [N] *Mädchen* (N), *das* [N] *ich kenne. Sie* [F]...
      'a nice girl whom I know. She...'

We assume here that lexical gender is the special case and referent-based gender is the rule. Lexical gender need only be invoked if gender in a language cannot be captured in terms of the animacy or individuation hierarchy. If a language distinguishes marking associated with person names as opposed to common nouns, such as Tagalog, discussed in §3.5, there is no need to invoke lexical gender.

Now, many languages with lexical gender still have choices of gender values that are reminiscent of referent-based gender. Thus, Swedish (Indo-European, Germanic) makes a distinction between the mass noun *öl* 'beer' (neuter gender) and *en öl* 'one.CM beer' (common gender) when it is countable as a glass or a bottle of beer. This distinction is well in-line with the individuation hierarchy, but it is also lexical, since most Swedish nouns denoting liquids do not follow the same pattern.

Plains Cree (Algic, Algonquian, Cree) *mistik* means 'tree' when animate and 'stick' when inanimate (Wolfart 1973: 22; similarly in Cheyenne, see Straus & Brightman 1982: 128). This is again in accordance with the animacy/individuation hierarchy. However, it can hardly be avoided to specify this distinction in a lexical description of Cree and Cheyenne.

If lexical gender develops from referent-based gender, as we assume here, it has to be expected that there are many such cases where the transition from referent-based to lexical gender is tangible. This does not mean that the direction of diachronic change will always be referent-based > lexical. (It is not unlikely that the Swedish, Danish and Norwegian use of counting 'beer' in common – or masculine – gender is an innovation.) However, hybrid nouns re-instantiating the animacy/individuation hierarchy testify to the relevance of referent-based categorization in gender even in languages with predominantly lexical gender.

Audring (2009) shows that pronominal gender systems (where gender is restricted to pronouns) are generally semantically organized; Wälchli 2019 [this volume]), in a typological study based on parallel texts, argues that gender in anaphoric use can be addressed in terms of semantic core only, and Bosch (1988: 227) claims that the descriptive content of gender is activated in contrastive use in implicit or explicit focus. While the development of referent-based to lexical gender can entail loss of transparency (see §6.3), transparency can also be reintroduced, especially in certain anaphoric uses, such as contrastive focus constructions and reference tracking after long stretches of discourse (in line with Corbett's Agreement Hierarchy). Seifart (2018: 24) discusses the case of nouns denoting animals in the Miraña variety of Bora (Boran) that have undergone re-classification to a transparent class. Based on Bosch's (1988) findings, Seifart (2018) argues that contrastive use and other contexts, where the descriptive content of gender is activated, is more frequent with animate than with inanimate nouns. As a consequence, animate nouns are more likely to undergo re-classification to a transparent class. The preference of animate referents for transparent gender is well in line with Dahl's (2000a) findings about the interaction of gender and animacy discussed in §3.2 above.

While there are languages with referent-based gender only (such as Una), there are probably no languages that only have lexical gender and no referent-based gender. Languages and language varieties with referent-based gender only are not restricted to emergence of gender, but also occur where gender is in decline. Modern English is a good example of a language with referent-based gender which developed from an earlier stage with predominantly lexical gender. Notably in cases of intensive language contact, gender systems tend to be reorganized based on animacy, as shown, for instance, by Karatsareas (2014) for varieties of Koineic Greek in Asia Minor (see also Di Garbo & Miestamo 2019 [this volume]).

In many languages, definiteness and referentiality play important roles for whether or not gender is marked. Greenberg (1978) shows how important the definiteness hierarchy is for the evolution of gender systems along the cycle of the definite article (0 demonstrative > I definite article > II non-generic article > III general noun marker). In several languages, gender markers or noun classifiers are missing when nouns are used in predicative function, where they are non-referential (see Fedden 2011: 110–111 for Mian and Grinevald Craig 1977: 330 for Jacaltec [=Popti']).

3.7 Gender and reference tracking

Above we have emphasized the importance of reference for gender, especially from a developmental perspective. One important thing that remains is to show that this does not entail that gender is suitable for reference tracking (see Kibrik 2011: 355 against Heath 1975 and Foley & Van Valin 1984, chap. 7). Much of the complex ways in which gender deals with reference originates from the fact that it is more important for gender how objects are categorized than what they refer to. Here we will show that this holds both for lexical and referent-based gender. Let us consider lexical gender first.

It is directly understandable why lexical gender is not particularly suitable for reference tracking, since classes of noun lexemes are easily affected by reconceptualization of referents in discourse (also called recategorization). The best known case is probably Cornish's (1987: 256) example from French (see also Croft 2013: 121), where *le potage* 'soup(M) (refined term)' is later referred to by another interlocutor by the anaphor *elle* (F), implicitly associated with *la soupe* 'soup(M) (common term)'.

Similarly, in (16) from Meskwaki (Algic, Eastern Great Lakes Algonquian), where gender is marked on verbal pronominal indexes and free pronouns, a referent is first implicitly construed as 'game (venison)' and later as 'birds'. *Mi:čipe:h-i* [game-INAN.SG] is animate when indefinite, but animate *mi:čipe:h-a* [game-ANIM.SG] when definite "by convention" (Thomason 2003: 380). Here, "by convention" simply means that we are dealing with lexical gender. As in the French example with the soup, the noun is not explicitly mentioned, but only latently present in association with the inanimate form of the indefinite pronoun *ke:ko:h-i* [something-INAN.SG]. The speaker then further specifies the referent as 'birds', a noun that is always animate in Meskwaki, whether indefinite or definite, and therefore the next verb 'he put them' agrees for animate object. This and other examples in Thomason (2003) show that gender does not necessarily remain constant in cases of coreference. However, person, in (16) obviative, is more constant in this respect.

(16) Meskwaki (Algic, Eastern Great Lakes Algonquian; Thomason 2003: 380)
Ke:ko:h-i
something-INAN.SG
ne:hto:-čini,
whenever.3.ANIM.SG.PROX.killed.it-3.INAN.SG.OBV.ITER
wi:škeno:he:h-ahi   *nekotah-meko*
little.bird-ANIM.PL.OBV somewhere-EMPH
e:h-as-a:či   *i:na*   *kwi:yese:h-a.*
3.ANIM.SG.PROX.put-3.ANIM.PL.OBV that.SG.PROX boy-ANIM.SG.PROX

'Whenever he killed anything, birds, that boy put them in a certain place.'

However, keeping markers constant with the same reference does not only fail with lexical gender. This is because a different position on the animacy hierarchy does not always entail a different referent, as can be seen in (17) from Tagalog, where the proper name *Maria* and the common noun *ina* 'mother' have the same referent, but take different topic markers, since the former is a person name and the latter a common noun.

(17) Tagalog (Austronesian, Central Philippine; New Testament 40013055)

    Hindi ba si   *Maria ang*   *kanya-ng*   *ina...*

    not   Q   PN.TOP Maria CM.TOP POSS.3SG-LNK mother

    'Is not Maria his mother?'

In gender systems where person names play an important role, such as Uduk (Koman), Nalca and Owa (Austronesian, Oceanic; Mellow 2013), coreference does not play any major role in agreement. For Uduk, see Killian (2019 [in Volume I]). Note also the gender recategorization in (5) from Mopán Maya in the context of a change of agentivity in the referent.

Following Kibrik (2011: 334–360), Nichols (2019 [in Volume I]) argues that the usefulness of gender in reference tracking is marginal. She argues that gender, unlike person, never refers. If a category is referential, like person, it is the category itself that refers, and not the word that carries that category. Gender can be referent-based (and very often is, as shown in this section), but not referential.

3.8 Conclusion

We can conclude that hierarchical patterning plays an important role for limiting the complexity of gender, but the potential for hierarchical patterning is strongly limited in gender. It is a powerful decomplexifying mechanism only for the top segment of the animacy hierarchy. In this section we have discussed several cases where it can be shown or at least be made plausible that gender originates as referent-based gender in the top segment of the animacy hierarchy. Referent-based gender then tends to leak into inanimate referents due to such factors as agentivity, salience, purview, uniqueness, and possession, which have the potential of linking certain inanimate referents with animacy. These connections cannot easily be arranged on the animacy hierarchy and, as a consequence, hierarchical patterning breaks down. The only alternative, then, to restitute order is to organize gender in terms of lexical nouns, and the outcome of this development is lexical gender. Lexical gender cannot easily be organized in hierarchical terms, which means that gender turns into a category that is fully dependent on the part-of-speech nouns. This leads us to the next section, where nominal morphology is discussed.

4 Gender as a special case of the accumulation of nominal morphology

4.1 Introduction

Many gender markers occur within the noun phrase. According to the Canonical Approach, local agreement (i.e., agreement within the noun phrase) is most canonical (Corbett 2006: 21; Audring 2019 [in Volume I]). In this section we will look at gender markers in the wider context of non-lexical markers within the noun phrase, for which we use the term NOMINAL MORPHOLOGY.

In the simplest possible noun phrase grammar, the head noun and its modifiers are unmarked. However, the elements of noun phrases tend to accrue markers in languages of most different kinds, and presence of nominal morphology is obviously more complex than its absence. Even if there is a set with only one marker, an inventory of one is still larger than an inventory of zero. Nominal morphology can consist of uniform markers not distinguishing gender, such as the suffix *-pela* in (18) from Tok Pisin (Pacific Creole English; from English *fellow*), or gender-number markers, as the plural proclitic *ki=* in Pnar (Austroasiatic, Khasian) in (19) (opposed to *u=* masculine singular, *ka=* feminine singular, and *i=* diminutive/neuter singular), or the feminine gender marker *n(a)* in Bari (Nilotic, Eastern Nilotic) in (20) (opposed to *l(ɔ)* masculine). Accumulation of nominal morphology, including gender marking, does not seem to correlate with high overall morphological complexity (see Nichols 2019 [in Volume I]). As the clitics in Pnar illustrate, nominal morphology need not consist of affixes. Two of the languages used here for illustration, Tok Pisin and Pnar, have low overall morphological complexity.

(18)   Tok Pisin (Pacific Creole English; Verhaar 1995: 417)
    Dis-pela   kantri   Nimrot i bos-im i gat   tri-pela   bik-pela
    this-NOMIN country Nimrot 3 rule-TR 3 have three-NOMIN big-NOMIN
    taun.
    town
    'This country (that) Nimrod ruled over had three big towns.'

(19)   Pnar (Austroasiatic, Khasian; Ring 2015: 339)
    ki=ni   ki=so   ŋut   ki=kʰlawaṭ (ki) wa   jap jɔŋ   u=daloj
    PL=this PL=four CLF.HUM PL=warrior PL   NMLZ die GEN M=Daloj
    'those four warriors of the Daloi who died'

(20)   Bari (Nilotic, Eastern Nilotic; Spagnolo 1933: 396)

"Āso *narakwan* *n-io'* *na* jɔndya *nan nɪ.*"

well wife/female F-POSS.1SG REL.F bring.DETR 1SG here

'Well, my wife whom I brought here.'

(18)–(20) illustrate the attributive use of modifiers with their markers. However, nominal morphology can also occur independently without a noun head. For instance, English adjectives in NPs without nominal heads, which take a prop-word *one(s)* (*the big one(s)*; Jespersen 1949: 245–271), and so called free or headless relative clauses (*she who will read this chapter*). In all cases of NPs with modifiers without noun heads, we will speak here of INDEPENDENT use, a term suggested to us by Martin Haspelmath. Instead of attributive markers we will speak of ADNOMINAL markers, since we need a term that also includes markers accompanying the head noun where there is no attribute in the NP. We will therefore speak of independent adjectives (*the big one*) and independent relative clauses (*he who came*) as opposed to adnominal adjectives (*the big house*) and adnominal relative clauses (*the man who came*).

Given the importance of agreement in traditional approaches to gender, the focus of investigation in the typology of gender has been mainly on adnominal markers. However, there is reason to believe that markers on independent elements (in NPs without head noun) are very important for the development of nominal morphology (including gender markers). For the dynamic approach adopted in this chapter it is therefore essential to consider nominal morphology on independent elements to the same extent as markers on NP attributes. The approach adopted in this section is thus more comprehensive than the study of gender usually is in two ways: (i) markers on independent NP-elements (in NPs lacking head nouns) are included as much as markers on NP attributes, and (ii) sets of markers with one member, such as Tok Pisin *-pela* in (18), which do not partition nouns into noun classes and where there is thus no gender agreement, are also included.

In many languages, nominal morphology first develops in independent use and may then eventually expand to attributive use. English relative clauses illustrate this point neatly. When Middle English had lost gender in relative pronouns – Old English *se* M, *seo* F, *þæt* N were replaced by indeclinable *that* in the 13th century – a human/general gender distinction *who/that* was reintroduced in Standard English[5] from independent relative clauses, probably first with such non-canonical antecedents as personal pronouns as in (21) (Fischer et al. 2000: 91–93).

---

[5]Herrmann (2005) shows that virtually all British English dialects are less constrained.

(21) Middle English (Indo-European, Germanic; Wooing Lord 275.18; Fischer
      et al. 2000)
      *hwam mai **he** luue treweliche **hwa** ne luues his broðer*
      'whom can he love truly, who(ever) does not love his brother'

In this section we will discuss the following four hypotheses, which are all
closely connected:

(a) Nominal morphology – including gender markers – tends to develop in
    independent use and therefore there are usually not more markers in at-
    tributive than in independent use.

(b) Many languages have more than one set of markers (see also Dahl 2000b),
    such as Standard English three genders in pronouns and human/non-
    human in relative clauses.

(c) Relative clauses can play an important role in the development of gender.

(d) The nature of a set of markers has properties from the function where
    it originates. For instance, distinctions originating from interrogative pro-
    nouns are typically human vs. non-human or animate vs. non-animate.

Hypothesis (a) is inspired by Lehmann (1982) and Heine & Reh (1984: 233;
based on Kxoe) and is akin to a universal proposed by Edith Moravcsik: "No
noun phrase constituent carries more gender, number, and/or case inflection
in adnominal use than it does in pronominal use" (Moravcsik 1994; Universals
Archive no. 1733; our term for "pronominal" is independent). (d) is inspired by
Croft (1994), who argues that different kinds of classifiers and noun classes tend
to express different functions. Numeral classifiers tend to express animacy and
shape. Noun classifiers and gender tend to express animacy and sex. Possessive
classifiers (at least in Oceanic) tend to express edibility.

4.2 A notation system for adnominal and independent marking

In this section we introduce a simple notation system for markers, which is illustrated in Table 1 for English. For each attributive, head, or independent content
element in the NP (henceforth in this section simply called *element*), the set of
markers used is represented by the number of markers opposed to each other
(for the sake of simplicity we count singular values only). Where there are several different sets with the same number of values, these are distinguished with

lower case letters of the alphabet. Thus, "3" in the English independent NP slot stands for *he/she/it*, "2a" in the relative clause slot (Rel) stands for *who/that*,[6] and "1b" stands for the prop-word *one(s)* in independent adjectives and independent interrogatives (*which one(s)?*). English has two other sets with two values in independent question words (*who/what* as opposed to the adnominal question word *which*, which can also occur independently with the prop-word *which one*), and in independent indefinites (*someone, -body* vs. *something*),[7] and there are at least four different sets with one value (definite article *the*, prop-word *one*, complementizer [Cmpl] *that*, and genitive *'s*). We distinguish two kind of possessors. "Gen" is used for noun possessors and "Poss" for pronominal possessors (adnominal *my*, independent *mine*).

Table 1: English nominal morphology. 1a: *the* (indefinite *a/an*), 3: *he/she/it*, 1b: *one(s)*, 2a: (*he/she*) *who/that, which*, 1c *that*, 1d *'s, mine*, 2b *who/what*, 2c *-one,-body/-thing*.

	NP	Dem	Num	Adj	Rel	Cmpl	Gen	Poss	Int	Indef
ADNOMINAL	1a	0	0	0	2a	1c	1d	0	0	0
INDEPENDENT	3	0/1b	0	1b	(3+)2a	1c	1d	1d	2b/0/1b	2c

Human/non-human distinctions restricted to relative clauses tend to be disregarded when gender is discussed. Estonian (Uralic, Finnic), which is not usually considered a gender language, has extended the animacy distinction from free relative clauses in Finnic to attributive relative clauses (*kes* 'who', *mis* 'what'), whereas Finnish retains an omni-purpose attributive relative pronoun *joka* and makes the animacy distinction only in free relative clauses (*kuka* 'who', *mikä* 'what'). The approach applied here can be used to get a better grip on nominal morphology falling into classes (sets where the number of markers is larger than one).

The notion of *gender system* might suggest that nominal morphology in a language tends to be uniform in a language with gender or that there are at least not two different sets of markers with a number of items higher than one. English alone shows that this is not the case. However, we do not want to argue that English has more than one gender system or that Estonian has gender.

Even though one might be inclined to believe that interrogative pronouns

---

[6]Non-restrictive *which* is not a value of its own and is not counted, and adverbial contexts such as *where* are disregarded here for the sake of simplicity.

[7]*-one* in indefinite pronouns is by the way the source for the prop-word in independent adjectives (see Rissanen 1997).

'who?' vs. 'what?' are very obvious potential sources for animacy-based gender distinctions, interrogative pronouns do not seem to have developed into a full-fledged gender system anywhere as far as we know. This is perhaps because relative pronouns, which can develop from interrogatives and give rise to NP-internal agreement as in English, are largely restricted to European languages (see, e.g., Comrie & Kuteva 2013). There is thus good reason to exclude interrogative-based animacy distinctions in relative clauses from the definition of gender, as well as animacy-based distinctions in indefinite pronouns. However, it is still useful to have a more comprehensive approach to nominal morphology side-by-side with the gender system approach, since interrogative-based relative clauses are, among other things, instructive for how independent markers can interact with adnominal markers, and this may be relevant for gender as well.

In dealing with nominal morphology in general, we need not be concerned with the question to what extent gender builds uniform systems. Many languages, such as English, have more than one set of markers at the same time. It makes sense to have this more general perspective alongside the more focused gender system perspective.

From the point of view of complexity in NP structure, gender agreement is part of a broader phenomenon of marker accumulation. This is why it is important to also consider sets with one marker, as Tok Pisin *-pela* in (18). Given the frequent origin of markers on adnominal elements from markers on independent elements, markers on independent elements cannot be disregarded. For Tok Pisin, there is actually some evidence that *-pela* has originated in independent use. In Australian Kriol, which is related to Tok Pisin, modifiers can be extended with *wan* ('one') and *pala*. In Fitzroy Australian Kriol, *dijan* 'this one' and *tharran* 'that one' are obligatory in independent use, whereas *dis* 'this' and *det* 'that' frequently occur in attributive use (Hudson 1985: 79). In Tok Pisin, the demonstrative *dispela* is not attested without *-pela* in Verhaar (1995). Thus, both sets of single markers in Tok Pisin and sets of two markers in English and Estonian relative clauses suggest that there is a typical developmental pathway from markers in independent elements to markers in adnominal elements, and this suggests that it might be useful to pay more attention to independent elements in studies of gender as well.

In mature gender systems we expect the same kind of markers pervasively entrenched in all adnominal and independent forms – this is what is usually called a gender system with maximum utilization of available distinctive features. The main expected difference is the kind of elements affected. In German, for instance, noun possessors and numerals above two are not affected. There is the expected animacy distinction in interrogative pronouns, which has also expanded to independent relative clauses (2a), but which has not affected adnominal marking (see Table 2).

Table 2: German nominal morphology

	NP	Dem	Num 2+	Adj	Rel	Cmpl	Gen	Poss	Int	Indef
ADN	3/0	3	0	3	3	1a	1b	3	3	3
IND	3	3	0	3	3/2a	1a	1b/3	3	2a	2b

4.3 Nominal morphology in emergent gender systems

In order to see clear differences between adnominal and independent marking, it may be more promising to look at emergent gender systems, and we will therefore now consider some languages from different families, some of which have figured prominently in the literature on the origin of gender.

Coatzospan Mixtec (Otomanguean; Small 1990: 415) has seven classes for third person pronouns, which occur as stressed free forms and clitics (Table 3), but it is not clear whether the set of genders is a strictly closed class, since some generic nouns also have clitic forms, but, based on the seven rows in Table 3, we label the gender set "7" in Table 4.

Table 3: Coatzospan Mixtec third person pronouns

	Free form	Proclitic form[a]	Enclitic form[b]
Adult	*ñaha*	*ña*	*ña*
Masculine respect	*shtaha*	*shta*	*shta*
Younger masc. man speak.	*naha*	*na*	*na*
Younger masc. woman speak.	*chéhnū*	*chénū*	*chí*
Younger feminine	*táhnū*	*tánū, tá*	*tún*
Animal/spherical object	*kɨtɨ*	*kɨtɨ*	*ti*
Other inanimate		*é*	*i, Ø*

[a]Proclitic pronouns occur, among other things, in relative clauses.
[b]Enclitic forms are used as subjects and objects of verbs.

Table 4: Coatzospan Mixtec nominal morphology. 1a: *é* complementizer; 1b: *iñá* 'thing'; 2: *sh(o)ó* 'who, which (anim.)', *ne(é)* 'what, which (inan.)'

	NP	Dem	Num	Adj	Rel	Cmpl	Poss	Int
ADN	0	0	0	0	1a/7		0	2
IND	7	0	0	7	7	1a	1b	2
PRED				0				

Example (22) consists of two NPs in apposition with two proclitics. There are heavy constraints in Coatzospan Mixtec on the number of modifiers per NP head. Apposition of NPs is the only option for combining a stressed demonstrative with a relative clause, but the order of NPs in appositional sequences can be freely reversed.

(22)   Coatzospan Mixtec (Otomanguean, Mixtec; Small 1990: 366)
      tánū tsīkan tánū kíshi   iku
      F   that   F   COMPL:come yesterday
      'that girl who came yesterday'

Attributive relative clauses need not display gender. The marker *é*, which also occurs in complement clauses (probably from *iñá* 'thing'; de Hollenbach 1995), is always possible and is obligatory, if there is no proclitic pronoun. de Hollenbach (1995), who surveys relative and complement clause formation in Mixtec and Trique languages, argues that the general relativizer and complementizer marker originates in the headless relative function and can be shown to derive from a noun meaning 'thing' in many Mixtec languages. The development is not equally advanced in all Mixtec languages. In Ayutla Mixtec, for instance, the complementizer *ña* (< *ñaha* 'thing') is not obligatory in relative clauses.

Given the nominal origin of the markers, the question may arise as to whether relative clauses headed by proclitic pronouns as in (22) could be considered intermediate between headless and strict relative clauses. Such a proposal has been made by Epps (2012) for Hup [=Hupdë] (Nadahup), and Wälchli (2019 [this volume]) argues that many languages have GRAMMATICAL ANAPHORS, which are intermediate between personal pronouns and full noun phrases. In Hup, relative clause heads range from lexical nouns over bound nouns (cannot occur alone in an NP) and classifying nouns to the general dependent suffix *-Vp*, which is why Epps (2012) comes to the conclusion that headedness is best considered to be a gradient phenomenon. There are many bound and classifying nouns in Hup, which is symbolized by "nnn" in Table 5. Classifiers only very rarely attach to several elements in a row. Thus, example (23) is best considered a sequence of three noun phrases in apposition.

(23)   Hup (Nadahup; Epps 2008: 278)
       núp=(g'æt) pihít=g'æt   tih=pŏg=(g'æt)
       this=LEAF   banana=LEAF 3SG=big=LEAF
       'this big banana leaf'

Table 5: Hup nominal morphology. 1a: *tih* (23); 1b: *-Vp*, 1c: *-n'ĭh*, 1d: *-nĭh*, 2: 'who' vs. 'what'

	NP	Dem	Num	Adj	Rel	Cmpl	Poss	Int
ADN	0	0	0	0	0		1d	1e
INTERMED	1a	nnn	nnn	(nnn)	nnn		1d	nnn
INDEPENDENT	1a	0	1a	1a	1b/1c	1c	1d	2

According to Epps (2008: 279), Hup can be considered an incipient classifier system. More advanced classifier systems, such as Kilivila (Austronesian, Oceanic), look very much like an expansion of the intermediate area between adnominal and independent use to all functions. In languages with large sets of classifiers, such as Kilivila, it is difficult to apply the notion of independent use. Senft (1986: 81) lists 176 classifiers, of which he could find 92 in actual speech. Only few of them occur frequently and only few of them have translation equivalents with independent forms in languages without classifiers. Numerals for maths, for instance, take either the masculine/people or thing classifier (Senft 1986: 84). However, because demonstratives, numerals and one set of adjectives (24) always take classifiers we have decided to use "nnn" for large set for both adnominal and independent use in Table 6.[8] Many classifiers are REPEATERS (the noun and the classifier have the same form) or shortened forms of nouns (Senft 1993: 104).

---

[8] Nauru (Austronesian, Oceanic; Kayser 1993), which has figured prominently in (Dixon 1982: 167), is another Austronesian language with a system similar to Kilivila with many classes, even though not closely related to Kilivila within Oceanic.

(24) Kilivila (Austronesian, Oceanic; Senft 1985: 379)
      M-to-na   tau to-paisewa e-tatai ke-veaka   kuliga ke-vau.
      DEM-M-DEM man M-work   3SG-cut WOODEN-big rudder WOODEN-new

      'This industrious man cuts a big new rudder.'

Table 6: Kilivila nominal morphology

	NP	Dem	Num	Adj	Rel	Cmpl	Poss	Int	Indef
ADN	0	nnn	nnn	0/nnn	nnn		4	1/nnn	nnn
IND	1/2	nnn	nnn	0/nnn	nnn	0	4	2/nnn	nnn

Bora and Miraña – which can be considered two different varieties of the same language – differ from Hup mainly in that class markers are much more frequently used adnominally and in that there is a set of six general class markers (three in the singular: masculine, feminine, and inanimate). Demonstratives, numerals, adjectives and relative clauses in the NP can take either the general class marker, masculine in (25), or the specific class marker, FLAT&ROUND in (25). Seifart (2005: 88–100) lists 66 specific class markers and 53 repeaters for Miraña. Many nouns, such as 'turtle' in (25), have class markers inherently as part of the lexeme ("nnn" underlined in Table 7, underlined stands for non-inflectional use of the marker). Given the lack of concord, as in (24), noun phrases with several elements can be considered sequences of appositions (see also Passer 2016b).

Table 7: Bora nominal morphology

	NP	Dem	Num	Adj	Rel	Cmpl	Poss	Int
ADN	0/nnn	3/nnn	3/nnn	3/nnn	3/nnn		0	2a
INTERMED	nnn	nnn	nnn	nnn	nnn		nnn	nnn
INDEPENDENT	3/1a	3	3	3	3	1b	1b	2b/3

(25) Miraña Bora (Boran; Seifart 2005: 169)
      aj:-di/ɛ:-hɨ   mɯ́ɨhɯ-hɨ/mɯ́ɨhɯ-:bɛ   kɯ́:mɯ-hɨ
      DIST-M/FLAT&ROUND be.big-FLAT&ROUND/M turtle-FLAT&ROUND

      'that big turtle'

Like in Mixtec languages, the marker used in complement clauses (22) is the general class marker for inanimate ("1b" in Table 7) -nè/ɲè 'thing'. It is also used in independent possessors. Note that the whole question in (26) is embedded and -nεε 'INAN/thing' marks it as a complement clause.

(26)   Bora (Boran; Thiesen & Weber 2012: 364)
       tsʰaᴴʔ ò kpá:hákʰ ɨ̀-tʰtɨ́ [mɨ́-ʔà tsaˢ:]-nὲέ
       not   I know-NEG   who-PL come-INAN
       'I do not know who (or what animals) come', lit. 'that who(PL) come'

In possession, class marking is limited to the intermediate domain. Posses-sive pronouns with the inanimate class marker can suffix a specific class marker (Thiesen & Weber 2012: 179).[9]

We have seen above for Mixtec, Hup, and Bora how appositions of noun phrases can contribute to the introduction of markers in adnominal position. Ba-sically there are three possibilities for how attributes and the noun can be con-nected in the NP: (a) the attribute modifies the noun, which is then its head noun, (b) the noun and attribute are appositions, and (c) there is a HEADEDNESS REVER-SAL (a semantic modifier of a phrase is its formal head). Headedness reversal is not equally common for all types of attributes, but is well-known from numerals. In Russian, for instance, numerals higher than four are historically nominalized and the noun counted is in the genitive plural: p'at' čas-ov [five hour-GEN.PL] 'five hours' (literally 'five of hours'). For our purposes it is especially relevant to consider headedness reversals in relative clauses, viz. the so-called head-internal relative clauses or "circum-nominal" relative clauses (Lehmann 1984: 109–121). A gender language with head-internal relative clauses is Mian. Mian has four gender classes (masculine, feminine, neuter 1 and neuter 2; Table 8).

Table 8: Mian nominal morphology

	NP	Dem	Num	Adj	Rel	Cmpl	Poss	Int
ADN	4	4	0/4	0/4	4/0		0	2
IND	4	4	4	4	4	1a	1b+4	2
PRED	0			0			1b	

_____

[9] Aside from third person pronouns with general class markers, there is also an even more gen-eral third person pronoun ("1a") which is used for coreference, glossed as "self" in Thiesen & Weber (2012: 360). This is a further parallel between Bora and Coatzospan Mixtec.

The genders of Mian are distinguished in third person pronouns, which also occur as articles at the end of noun phrases if the noun is used referentially. Adnominal demonstratives replace the article. Attributive adjectives and numerals are not usually followed by gender clitics, but gender clitics may occur with them. Since head-internal relative clauses are noun phrases, they have final enclitic articles, as illustrated in (27). There are also unmarked prenominal relative clauses.

(27) Mian (Nuclear Trans-New Guinea, Ok-Oksapmin; Fedden 2011: 506)

    nĩ   *senso=e*   *Jemeni daak=o*   *walo-Ø-ob=e*

    we.EXCL chainsaw=SG.N1 PN   down=N2 buy.PFV-REAL-1PL.SBJ=N1.SG

    ayam=o=be

    good=PRED=DECL

    'The chainsaw we've bought down in Germany is good.'

Mian head-internal relative clauses are sentential nominalizations with the gender-distinguishing article as nominalizer. The same construction can also be used as temporal adverbial clause, but then always has a "neuter 2"-class article (maybe because time nouns are neuter 2).[10]

The Ngan'gityemerri variety of Nangikurrunggurr (Southern Daly; Reid 1990) is another language prominently figuring in the literature on the origin of gender. It is like Hup rather than Bora in that class markers on modifiers are optional, and not all nouns belong to a class. Demonstratives and possessive pronouns can stand alone in free use ("0"), but adjectives cannot head noun phrases on their own. Personal pronouns make a masculine/feminine distinction ("2a"), but are mainly used as possessive pronouns (28), since subject and object are indexed on verbs, where gender is not marked ("1"; see Table 9). As in Coatzospan Mixtec, gender markers can occur as free words, as proclitics and as postnominal markers, here suffixes, but only a small number of classes have reduced forms. Eight classes have proclitics: M *wa=*, F *wurr=*, group of people *awa=*, animal/meat *a=*, vegetable *mi=*, dogs *wu=*, tree/things *yerr=*, and *yeli=* bamboo spears. Class suffixation is restricted to the interrogative *tyen-* 'what kind of' ("nb"), and the negative particle *minbe-* ("nc"), with which the suffix forms a kind of negative indefinite pronoun. *Tyen-* 'what kind of' has a class -*da* 'country/place', which does not occur in proclitics. Free interrogative pronouns make a human/non-human distinction ("2b"): *kene* 'who', *tyagani* 'what'.

The same set of markers that are used as proclitics occur as prefixes for deriving nouns ("n̲"), except bamboo spears, which has the freeform classifier

---

[10]Mian has further a system of six classificatory prefixes on verbs of object manipulation, which is not considered here (see Fedden 2010: 459; Fedden 2011: 185).

Table 9: Ngan'gityemerri Nangikurrunggurr nominal morphology

	NP	Dem	Num	Adj	Rel	Poss	Int	Neg.indef
ADN	0/n/nn	0/n/nn	0/n/nn	0/n/nn	n	0/n/nn	0?/n/nn?	nc
INTERMED	n/nn	n/nn	n/nn	n/nn	n	n/nn	n/nb	nc
INDEPENDENT	1/2a	0	?	n	n	0	2b	nc
PRED				n/0				

yawurr instead. In four classes (animal/meat *a/e-*, vegetable *mi-*, canines *wu-*, tree/things *yerr/yed-*), the clitics have turned into prefixes in some lexicalized forms, and a prefix is also *da/de-* for bodyparts, which is no agreement class. Class marker proclitics can also be prefixed to sentences, so-called GENDERED CLAUSES, such as *a=yenim-walal-pi* [ANIM=3SG.AUX-shake-head] 'clickbeetle' (lit. animal-it shakes its head), *a=dudu-meny-tyamu* [ANIM=swollen-3SG:do-cheek] 'blanket lizard' (lit. animal-it has swollen cheeks) (Reid 1997: 210). Unlike some other Australian languages, such as Bininj Kun-Wok (Gunwinyguan), where gendered clauses are highly limited in productivity, gendered clauses are fully productive in Ngan'gityemerri, as in (28). Note that the relative clause in (28) actually consists of four clauses with different subjects. The antecedent is possessee of the first, local oblique of the second, subject of the third, and local oblique of the fourth clause. Despite its syntactic complexity, its function is derivational. It serves to express a concept, viz. escalators.

(28) Ngan'gityemerri Nangikurrunggurr (Southern Daly; Reid 1990: 380; Reid 1997: 205)
yentyi-ngirrki-tye   *yerr=[watypela*   *nem,*
3SG.take-1DU.EXCL.do-PST INAN/TREE=whitefella 3SG.M

wannim-derri-tyerr, yentyin-yirrimbin, wannim-fel wun-ambirri]
3PL.go.PRS-back-halt 3SG.take-3SG.go   3PL.go-jump there-ahead

'He took the two of us onto that thing of whitefella's, that they stand still on, and it takes them and they jump off ahead there at the top (i.e., escalators).'

All examples of non-lexicalized relative clauses given by Reid have either masculine or inanimate class proclitics. There is a special relative locational marker *ngan-*, but relative clauses do not seem to be used as complement clauses. Ngan'gityemerri has similar sets of markers for different elements, but they have not really grown together into one uniform gender system.

Let us now return to Bari and Pnar, which were exemplified at the beginning of this section. Bari is an Eastern Nilotic language, and the East Nilotic languages have innovated gender agreement with Bari being the language that has the least developed system (Heine & Vossen 1983: 257). Masculine (*lɔ*) and feminine (*na*) gender is distinguished on demonstratives, one type of adjectives, relative clauses, possessive pronouns and noun possessors (except inalienable kin), and the interrogative adjective. Interrogative pronouns, however, have a human/non-human distinction (*ŋa* 'who', *nyɔ* 'what') ("2b"; see Table 10).

Table 10: Bari nominal morphology

	NP	Dem	Num	Adj	Rel	Cmpl	Poss	Int
ADN	0/2	2	0	0/2	2		2/0	2
IND	1	2	0	0?/2	2	0	2	2b
PRED				0/2				

In Acoli, which is a Western Nilotic language, we can trace the origin of the gender system in a marker set consisting of a single marker. Acoli *là-*, PL *lɔ̂-* is a derivational prefix 'person, individual, one who...' without distinction of sex, and has the function of introducing gendered clauses which are a kind of headless relative clause: *là-ít-ɛ́ ò-tɔɔ̀* [NMLZ-ear-POSS.3SG 3SG.PST-die/become.useless] 'a deaf person' (Crazzolara 1955: 37). This construction seems to have evolved from N N compounds with *là-* as an erstwhile light noun 'person' (which is not a noun anymore in Acoli), as in *là-bòŋò lëɛ̀m* [NMLZ-NEG property] 'one without goods'. The prefix *là-* also forms nouns for members of a nation or tribe in Acoli: *Là-pàtíkô* 'man of Patiko' (Crazzolara 1955: 42). Shilluk, another Western Nilotic language, has a similar feminine element *nya: nya Lul* 'a woman/girl of Lul' (Kohnen 1933: 17). In Acoli, *ny(a)à* means 'daughter' and is much more restricted in its use in compounds. According to Heine & Vossen (1983: 263), the "Eastern Nilotic gender markers *lɔ* M, *na* F are likely to go back to lexical items which formed head nouns in genitive constructions". However, it is important to emphasize that it is attributive possessive construction with non-anchored possessors (possessed expressions without a referential possessor; see Koptjevskaja-Tamm 2005), such as for the expression of membership to a tribe, that we are talking about. Acoli has a different construction for predicative possession with anchored possessors. The non-anchored possessor construction became productive and expanded to possession in general in Bari (but not to inalienable kin), and from gendered clauses, in a similar way as in Ngan'gityemerri, it expanded to relative clauses.

The development probably started with a set with one member **lɔ* M. Feminine **na* joined in later and originally only had the non-anchored possessor function. If, as we assume, Acoli represents the original situation and Bari a secondary development, then this development demonstrates how important it is to include nominal morphology with one member in marker sets if gender is considered from a developmental perspective.

Pnar (Ring 2015) has gender marking third person pronouns and corresponding proclitic noun markers (pronominal articles; *u=* masculine singular, *ka=* feminine singular, and *i=* diminutive/neuter singular, *ki=* plural, "3" because there are three singular classes).[11] There are also three numeral classifiers ("3b") used with numerals above 'one': human *ŋut*, non-human *tḷli*, and weeks *ta* (see also Sinnemäki 2019 [this volume]). Possessors are partly unmarked and partly marked with preposed *jɔŋ* ("1b"), which is obligatory if the possessor occurs without head noun. Relative clauses are nominalized with the preposed marker *wa* ("1a"), which also occurs – together with the gender proclitic – in independent adjectives. Pnar is one of very few languages that lacks an animacy distinction in interrogative pronouns, but the interrogative pronoun *ji* 'who/what' and the interrogative adjective *wɔn* or *nu* is combined with the class proclitic. If the gender of the individual or item asked about is known, the appropriate class proclitic is used, otherwise any class proclitic is possible, but *i=ji* is most common then (Ring 2015: 235). However, there is an animacy distinction in an unexpected place, viz. one of two types of adjectives. Type 1 does not take the nominalizer in attributive position ("0"; *ki=sistar tṃmɛn* [PL=nun old] 'the old nuns'; Ring 2015: 173), but Type 2 requires the nominalizer only when the head noun is human ("2"; see Table 11, example (29)):

(29)   Pnar (Austroasiatic, Khasian; Ring 2015: 177): Type 2 adjective

   a.   *u=ksaw (wa) hɛʔ*
        M=dog NMLZ be.big
        'the big dog'

   b.   *u=bru   wa   hɛʔ*
        M=person NMLZ be.big
        'the big man'

Relative clauses always take the preposed nominalizer *wa* ("1a"). Independent relative clauses require a preposed gender marker. Relative clauses with or without a gender proclitic also function as noun complements (19). Interestingly, the

---

[11]The personal pronoun in the accusative has different forms.

Table 11: Pnar nominal morphology

	NP	Dem	Num(2+)	Adj	Rel	Cmpl	Poss	Int
ADN	3	3	3b/3+3b	0/2	(3+)1a	3+1a	0/1b/3+1b	3
IND	3	3	3+3b	3+1a	3+1a	0	3+1b	3
PRED				0/3				

gender proclitics also serve for forming various kinds of verbal nouns (*ka=* re-sultative/F, *i=* inchoative action/DIM, *u=* purposive nominals/M, Ring 2015: 71), as can also be seen in (30): *ka=sɔrkar* 'government' and *u=pɲɛmkam* 'for using'.

(30) *ka=sɔrkar da   pɳ=miʔ   kɔ   ki=aɲ [wa m̩ hɔj*
      F=govern REAL CAUS-bring.out 3SG.F.NOM PL=rule NMLZ NEG be.fitting
      u=pɳ-ɛmkam   plastik]
      NF=CAUS-need plastic
      'The government brought rules that it's not good to use plastic.'

4.4 Nominal morphology in a gender system in decline

Finally, after having considered examples from emerging class systems, let us now look at an instance of a language variety where gender is in decline and which is a counterexample to Moravcsik's suggested universal that there are never more gender distinctions in attributive than in independent function. We are not making any predictions here about what typically happens in cases of gender loss. However, the example discussed here shows that distinctions in independent use can be lost first, which can result in a system where gender is distinguished only in attributive, but not in independent use.

Whereas Standard Latvian (Indo-European, Baltic) and most Latvian dialects have a fairly canonical gender system with two values, masculine and feminine, Northwestern Latvian dialects [=Tamian], are in various stages of gender loss, which is partly due to Finnic (Livonian and Estonian) substrate (see Wälchli 2017 and Di Garbo & Miestamo 2019 [this volume]). Like Pnar, the Baltic languages Lithuanian and Latvian are exotic in that they lack an animacy distinction in interrogative pronouns (Nau 1999; Lindström 1995). In the dialect of Dundaga, feminine agreement is retained only in attributive function. In all other uses, both independent and predicative, only the masculine form is used. This is illustrated in example (31) with attributive and independent uses of the adjective.

(31) Dundaga Latvian (Indo-European, Baltic; Dravniece 2008: 87; Wälchli
2017)

Vel' bi   *[visâːʒ*   *âːd*   *gurc̄]*   –
still be.PST all.sorts.NOM.PL.F skin.GEN.SG belt(F).NOM.PL

plattak   *un šoûrak,*   *mẹl̂ʼː,*   *brũnʼ*
thicker.NOM.PL.M and thinner.NOM.PL.M black.NOM.PL.M brown.NOM.PL.M

un ʒẹl̂tẹnʼ.
and yellow.NOM.PL.M

'Moreover, there were all kinds of belts: thicker ones and thinner ones,
black ones, brown ones and yellow ones.'

Masculine marking is also generalized in actor nominals, which most typically
occur in predicative function: *oûdʼẹs* [weave.AGN.NOM.SG.M] 'weaver (of a woman
or man)'. See Table 12.

Table 12: Latvian and Dundaga Latvian nominal morphology

Standard Latvian	NP	Dem	Num	Adj	Rel	Cmpl	Poss	Int
ADN	0	2	2	2	1/2	1	2/1	2
IND	2	2	2	2	1/2	1	2/1	1
PRED	2			2				
Dundaga Latvian	NP	Dem	Num	Adj	Rel	Cmpl	Poss	Int
ADN	0	1	2	2	1	1	2/1	2
IND	1	1	1	1	1	1	1	1
PRED	1/2			1				

4.5 Conclusion

Let us now return to the four hypotheses stated at the beginning of this section.
Most elements in the few languages surveyed here are in accordance with hypothesis (a) that there are not more adnominal markers than independent ones.
However, it is important to point out that the hypothesis does not take into account the intermediate area between independent and adnominal use which is
important in classifier languages. Large sets typically develop in the intermediate zone between independent and attributive use as we have seen in the discussion of Hup. This probably holds true also for Bora (synchronically most clearly

in possessives), Kilivila, Mixtec, and Ngan'gityemerri, where the development is more advanced. This means that nominal morphology typically originates in independent or in intermediate function and may eventually expand to attributive use, but not the other way round. It may then occur that a new set in independent use has fewer distinctions than one already entrenched in attributive use, which is the case in German relative clauses, where a human/non-human set originating in interrogative pronouns competes with the three-way masculine/feminine/neuter distinction in relative pronouns. A special case is the Pnar human/non-human distinction emerging in attributive adjectives from the opposition of the presence of the nominalizer *wa* with humans (the same construction as with independent adjectives) versus its absence with non-humans. Finally, Dundaga Latvian shows that in contexts of gender loss the independent function can be innovative in introducing the absence of gender whereas gender is retained in the attributive function.

In this section we have shifted the perspective away from gender systems to sets of markers which need not form systems and entirely different sets may occur in different elements and functions (Hypothesis b). This makes it easier for us to see the many cases where there is arguably more than one set of markers in the same language, which holds for English, Coatzospan Mixtec, Bora, Mian, Ngan'gityemerri, and Pnar. In several cases an animacy distinction originating in interrogative pronouns is involved (English, Coatzospan Mixtec, Bora, Mian, and Ngan'gityemerri). This shows that the question as to what makes a gender system is not a trivial one. Even if marker sets originating from interrogative pronouns are excluded, which is probably reasonable to do, since interrogatives do not seem to be attested as origins for full-fledged gender systems, many languages have more than one marker set (see also Dahl 2000b, who comes to similar conclusions).

We have also argued that relative clauses are important for the emergence of gender (Hypothesis c). Several languages with emergent gender systems have been found to have relative clauses originating from gendered clauses with markers having developed from light nouns. This holds notably for Ngan'gityemerri and Bari. In Mian, a type of relative clauses consists of gender-marked NPs for another reason, namely due to headedness reversal in head-internal relative clauses. This means that relative clauses play an important role in the emergence of gender systems for a number of different reasons.

Can we say in which element and function a gender system originates from its synchronic characteristics (Hypothesis d)? There are at least some trends pointing in that direction. In sets with many markers, some of which express shape, numerals are usually involved. But maybe more importantly, sets with many markers originate in the intermediate zone between independent and attributive function. In systems where edibility plays a role, possessors are involved. This does not only hold for possessive classifiers in Kilivila, but also for Ngan'gityemerri, where class markers originate from generic nouns. Adjectives and relative clauses have a predilection for marker sets with just one single member. Interrogative pronouns are a frequent source for marker sets with two markers distinguishing animacy. If there is a sex distinction, either anaphoric NP expressions or person name markers or non-anchored possession for the expression of origin (Eastern Nilotic) are usually involved. Independent and intermediate NP sets sometimes make a respect/non-respect distinction as in some Mixtec languages. This suggests that gender does not originate as a full-fledged system, but is shaped by discourse functions in particular local domains.

As soon as independent functions of noun phrase constituents are considered, it is difficult not to have the impression that gender and classifiers lurk behind every corner. To paraphrase Sinnemäki (2019 [this volume]), whose statement is based on a much more respectable sample, languages are more likely to have some noun classification system rather than no noun classification system. Or, in order to say it with Gabelentz (1891), in language, there is always a trade-off between the drive for economy (*Bequemlichkeitstrieb*) and the drive for explicitness (*Deutlichkeitstrieb*). Nominal morphology marking explicitness often develops as a compensation for excessive economy (omission of nominal heads in independent use).

5 Gender assignment

In this section, we discuss systems of gender assignment and consider possible diachronic developments in this domain. §5.1 is concerned with the split between semantic and formal assignment principles, and addresses some shortcomings of this binary typology. §5.2 treats flexibility in gender assignment, and how this phenomenon relates to complexity and the maturity of gender systems.

5.1 Types of gender assignment systems

Corbett (2013) argues that the systems of gender assignment attested in the languages of the world can be subsumed under two main types:

- SEMANTIC ASSIGNMENT, whereby gender assignment is predicted by the meaning of nouns. Semantic assignment systems are further divided into two subcategories: STRICT SEMANTIC ASSIGNMENT SYSTEMS, where semantic patterns are predictive of the gender assignment of virtually all nouns, and PREDOMINANTLY SEMANTIC ASSIGNMENT SYSTEMS, where for a minority of nouns no clear semantic pattern of gender assignment can be identified. Kannada (Dravidian) is cited as an example of a language with strict semantic assignment: nouns denoting males are masculine, nouns denoting females are feminine, while all remaining nouns are neuter. Bininj Kun-Wok is classified as a language with predominantly semantic gender assignment: gender assignment is largely predictable for most nouns, but certain nouns with similar meanings may be arbitrarily split across two or more genders. For instance, lower animates can be either masculine or feminine, and no clear pattern motivates this distribution. Even though discussed, the two subtypes are not treated independently in the classification and coding system proposed by Corbett (2013).

- SEMANTIC AND FORMAL ASSIGNMENT, whereby for some nouns gender assignment is predicted by their meaning, while for other nouns it is based on formal (phonological and/or morphological) criteria. Semantic and phonological gender assignment is attested in the East Cushitic language Afar. In Afar, nouns denoting males are masculine and nouns denoting females are feminine. For nouns that do not denote sexually distinguishable entities, gender assignment is based on stress patterns: nouns whose unmarked case forms (used, among other things, for direct object; Parker & Hayward 1985: 225) end in a stressed vowel are feminine, and all other nouns are masculine. An example of a language with semantic and morphological assignment is Russian. In Russian, sex is a predictor of gender assignment for nouns denoting males and females. For the rest of the nominal lexicon, gender assignment is predicted by inflectional class. Inflectional classes are in turn defined based on the different patterns of case and number marking that nouns can take.

Corbett's classification of systems of gender assignment is widely accepted in the literature. Yet at least three of the contributions to this work call the classification into question and argue that a bipartite typology does not fully capture the diversity of the gender assignment systems attested among the world's languages. These are Svärd (2019 [in Volume I]) on grammatical gender in New Guinea, Killian (2019 [in Volume I]) on the gender system of Uduk, and the chapter by Dahl (2019 [in Volume I]) on the language ecology of grammatical gender systems. The rationale behind this reappraisal is the same across all three contributions. Both in languages with semantic assignment and in languages with semantic and formal assignment, there are often rather copious portions of the nominal lexicon for which gender assignment cannot be inferred from the meaning of the noun, nor from its formal (phonological and/or morphological) appearance.[12]

While, as mentioned above, Corbett (2013) recognizes that languages with semantic assignment may have residual areas of the nominal lexicon that are not in the scope of the semantic rules which are elsewhere productive, this observation is not operationalized further in his typology. This in turns means that the incidence of arbitrary or opaque mechanisms of gender assignment in the sample used by Corbett (2013) cannot be estimated based on the existing coding. Svärd (2019 [in Volume I]) proposes a revised version of Corbett's typology, where opacity of assignment is one of the criteria at stake, and tests it on a sample of twenty Papuan languages. The analysis shows that introducing a systematic distinction between *Transparent semantic assignment systems, Semantic and formal systems,* and *Semantic and opaque systems* provides a more accurate representation of the systems attested in the languages of his sample. While sixteen out of the twenty languages count as displaying semantic assignment systems when using Corbett's classification, these figures drop by half (eight out of twenty) when purely semantic systems are distinguished from systems displaying both semantically predictable and opaque gender assignment.[13] Similarly, the gender assignment system of Uduk is described by Killian (2019 [in Volume I]) as partly semantic, partly formal, and largely opaque, since for many nouns in the language it is not possible to retrieve any clear-cut connection with semantic and formal assignment criteria. Finally, Dahl (2019 [in Volume I]) suggests that the notion of opacity should be taken into account when studying the diachrony and evolution of gender systems, under the assumption that non-transparent patterns of gender assignment are an indication of highly mature, grammaticalized gender. While the issue of opaque or arbitrary gender assignment is often mentioned in descriptions of individual languages and has occasionally been brought to attention in the general linguistics debate (see for instance Dahl 2000a), this topic has not yet been addressed in large-scale comparative studies of gender systems. In §6.3 we discuss how opaque gender assignment may emerge from, and relate to, semantic gender assignment.

---

[12]For a recent discussion of semantic transparency and opacity in the diachrony of nominal classification systems, see also Seifart (2018). Opacity is also discussed by Passer (2016b).

[13]Svärd does not exclude the possibility that a language may display a combination of transparent semantic, opaque, and formal assignment, or just opaque assignment. However none of these types is attested in his sample.

Another influential generalization in Corbett's typology of gender assignment systems is that while purely semantic systems are possible and relatively common across languages, purely formal systems of gender assignment are not attested. No matter how important morphological and phonological (or, in principle, opaque or arbitrary) patterns of gender assignment are in a language, there will always be at least a handful of nouns for which gender assignment can be predicted on semantic grounds. This semantic core has been shown to usually target the upper nominal end of the animacy hierarchy, that is nouns denoting humans and (higher) animates, with the cutoff points between these categories varying across languages (Dahl 2000a; see also §3). Killian (2019 [in Volume I]) argues that in the Koman language Uduk, the cutoff point for semantic gender assignment can be higher than 'human'.[14] In Uduk, personal pronouns have inherent gender and are always in class 1; proper names denoting humans (but not place names), on the other hand, are always in class 2. Both personal pronouns and proper names precede human nouns on the animacy hierarchy (1st person > 2nd person > 3rd person > proper names > kinship terms > other humans > animate nouns > inanimate nouns). Below this clearly identifiable cutoff point, semantic predictability in the Uduk gender system is extremely limited.

Di Garbo (2014; 2016) distinguishes between semantic and formal assignment rules and proposes that gender systems with only one type of rule (only semantic) are less complex than systems with both semantic and formal assignment. The relationship between types of assignment rules and the implications for the complexity of gender systems are, however, not discussed in Di Garbo's work. We return to these issues in §6.3 and §6.4, where the relationships between semantic and opaque, and semantic and formal gender assignment are discussed chiefly from a diachronic point of view.

5.2 Flexible gender and the nature of gender assignment

Grammatical gender is traditionally defined as an inherent property of nouns, whereby each noun is lexically associated with only one gender value. Corbett & Fedden (2016: 9) formalize this assumption into the Canonical Gender Principle: in a canonical gender system, each noun has a single gender value. Yet, a moderate to strong degree of flexibility in the patterns of gender assignment that can be productively associated with nominal roots is not uncommon across the languages of the world. In Italian (Indo-European, Romance), many nomi-

---

[14] A similar system is arguably found in Teop (Austronesian; Oceanic). See Dahl (2000b: note 3, 591–592) for details.

nal stems denoting humans and higher animates have a masculine or feminine variant depending on the sex of the denoted entity, cf. *parrucchiere* 'male hairdresser' and *parrucchiera* 'female hairdresser', where the suffixes *-iere* and *-iera* are productive derivational affixes for the overt marking of gender distinctions. Masculine/feminine doublets for one and the same nominal stem also exist outside the domain of animate nouns. For instance, nouns of trees and the respective fruits often belong to opposite genders, as in *pero* 'pear (tree)' and *pera* 'pear (fruit)'. In a language like Italian, gender assignment is thus exploited as a noun formation strategy, whose interpretation rests either on natural gender distinctions or on other kinds of semantic associations that establish taxonomic relationships or contrasts between entities within a given lexico-semantic field (such as, for instance, names of trees and fruits). For an overview of the relationship between gender assignment and word formation rules, see Contini-Morava & Kilarski (2013). The role of gender assignment in establishing contrasts between semantically interrelated entities is also discussed in §6.3. Gender doublets (as well as triplets and quadruplets) for the same nominal roots are also discussed by (Olsson 2019 [in Volume I], §2.1) for Coastal Marind.

While in all the cases mentioned above the gender contrasts are used to encode different classes of referents within a given lexico-semantic field (male vs. female entities, or types of trees vs. types of fruit), there are languages in which flexibility in gender assignment is used not only for this purpose, but also to express variation in a range of semantic properties associated with one and the same (type of) referent. Consider the examples (32)–(35).

(32)   Gitonga (Atlantic-Congo, East Bantu; Carter 2002: 21)

      a. ***mu**-sankwa*
         CL1-boy
         'boy'

      b. ***tu**-sankwa*
         CL12-boy
         'small boy'

(33)   Wamey (Atlantic-Congo, North-Central Atlantic; Santos Sachot 1996: 160)

      a. *i-ñí*
         CL5-elephant
         'elephant'

b. **bə-ŷí**
CL18-elephant
'big elephant'

(34) Tachelhit (Afro-Asiatic, Berber; Penchoen 1973: 12)

a. **aq-nmuš**
[M]SG-pot
'pot'

b. **t-aq-nmuš-t**
F-SG-pot-F
'small pot'

(35) Tachelhit (Afro-Asiatic, Berber; Penchoen 1973: 12)

a. **t-aɣ-nžay-t**
F-SG-spoon-F
'spoon'

b. **aɣ-nža**
[M]SG-spoon
'big spoon, ladle'

All four examples illustrate instances of switches in gender assignment that are used to encode variation in the size of the noun referent, from default to smaller than default (diminutive) in (32) and (34) and from default to bigger than default (augmentative) (33) and (35). Some crucial differences exist between the gender systems of Gitonga and Wamey as opposed to that of Tachelhit, as well as between their use of flexible gender assignment. Gitonga and Wamey have non-sex-based gender systems with more than five gender distinctions and dedicated diminutive and augmentative genders. Tachelhit has a sex-based gender system with two gender distinctions and no dedicated diminutive and augmentative genders. In this language, switches between the masculine and feminine gender are used to encode size-related types of contrasts. Based on a sample of 84 African languages with gender, Di Garbo (2014) finds that the relationship between type of gender system (in terms of number of distinctions and sex-based vs. non-sex-based assignment) and type of attested size-related gender shifts is rather robust in African languages. Languages with non-sex-based gender and rich inventories of gender distinctions are likely to have dedicated diminutive and augmentative genders, while languages with sex-based systems and a smaller number of gender distinctions encode the diminutive-augmentative contrast based on the sex-based contrast. In addition to size-related patterns of flexible gender assignment, Di Garbo (2014) finds that gender switches can also be used to modify the countability of nouns; for instance, to form collectives from nouns with regular singular and plural forms or to derive singulative nouns from nouns with collective meanings. Consider the examples:

(36)   Eegimaa (Atlantic-Congo, North-Central Atlantic; Sagna 2011: 243)

    a.   *e-vval*

        CL3-stone

        'stone'

    b.   *si-vval*

        CL4-stone

        'stones'

    c.   *ba-vval*

        CL5-stone

        'pile of stones'

(37)   Nafusi (Afro-Asiatic, Berber; Beguinot 1942: 32)

    a.   *ettefàḥ*

        apples(M)

        'apples' (collective)

    b.   *t-attefàḥ-t*

        F-apples-F

        'one apple'

In Eegimaa [=Banjal], the regular gender marker for the plural of the noun for 'stone' is *si-* (as exemplified in (36)). However, the noun can be marked by the gender marker *ba-* when the speaker wants to refer to a collection of stones. In Nafusi (37), the masculine, collective noun for 'apples' switches to the feminine gender when speakers want to refer to just one apple. The relationship between gender and the lexicalization of number values is further discussed in §9.

Besides Africa, New Guinea stands out as another documented hotbed of patterns of flexible gender assignment (see also Singer 2018 for an account of flexibility of gender assignment in the Northern Australian language Mawng). These types of systems and their uses have been surveyed by Aikhenvald (2012) and Svärd (2019 [in Volume I]), while Dryer (2019 [in Volume I]) digs into the specifics of the morphosyntax and semantics of the diminutive in Walman, a feature value that in some respects resembles a gender but in other respects does not. Some of the properties of the New Guinean systems, such as the contextual nature of the gender shift and the preferential association between masculine gender and big size and feminine gender and small size, closely match the patterns attested in African languages, and suggest that at least some generalizations about flexible patterns of gender assignment can be made independently of linguistic areas and families. Other properties, such as the existence of dedicated diminutive genders or diminutives reminiscent of gender in languages with sex-based gender, as in the Papuan languages Motuna [Siwai] (South Bougainville) and Walman, seem to be much rarer in African languages, where dedicated diminutive genders are most commonly found in languages with non-sex based gender.

Two questions that can be asked on the nature of flexible gender assignment and that are particularly relevant to the topics discussed in this section are: (i) how does the presence of flexible assignment contribute to the overall complexity of a gender system? and (ii) how can flexible gender assignment be accounted for from a diachronic point of view, that is, from the perspective of the emergence and evolution of gender systems?

The first question has been addressed in work by Di Garbo (2014; 2016), who considers the presence of flexible gender assignment (which she calls manipulation of gender assignment) as a factor that increases the overall complexity of gender systems. This choice is motivated by the fact that in the majority of the languages of her sample, the possibility of manipulating gender assignment as a function of reference construal adds to the lexically specified, inherent, gender of a noun. The noun for 'boy' in Gitonga (32) is inherently a gender 1/2 noun and can be assigned to gender 12 when a diminutive construal is intended. The co-presence of inherent and contextual patterns of gender assignment increases the description length of gender assignment rules and thus the overall complexity of a gender system (see our discussion of gender complexity metrics in §2.1). One could argue that not every noun in languages with grammatical gender has an inherently specified gender value. Aikhenvald (2012: 42), for instance, reports that in the Papuan language Manambu (Ndu) only nouns with animate referents have lexical (masculine and feminine) gender, whereas gender assignment with inanimate nouns is entirely referent-based, with the masculine being associated with the encoding of large size and/or long shape and the feminine with small size and/or round shape. Yet, even in a language like Manambu the existence of context-dependent mechanisms of gender assignment combines with the fact that, at least for some nouns (animate nouns) grammatical gender is an inherent, lexically specified feature. Thus, similarly to Gitonga, the co-occurrence of inherent and contextual gender assignment adds to the overall complexity of assignment rules.

Radically contextual gender assignment has been recently documented for Hamar [=Hamer-Banna] (South Omotic) by Petrollino (2016). In Hamar, neither gender nor number marking is obligatory and their occurrence depends on the speakers' choice. Patterns of gender and number agreement are only activated if nouns are overtly marked as masculine, feminine or plural. Nouns in the general form (that is, devoid of overt gender and number marking) do not trigger agreement. In addition, apart from a few kinship terms that have fixed, lexical gender, "any noun in Hamar can be inflected for masculine and feminine grammatical gender, and plural number" (Petrollino 2016: 77). In general, while higher animates display stronger associations between gender marking and the encoding of natural gender distinctions, for lower animates gender marking can also be used to encode variation in size (feminine = augmentative, masculine = diminutive, that is, the opposite of what commonly found in other African languages) and countability (feminine = collective), which becomes systematic with inanimate nouns. Hamar is a rather intriguing instance of a gender system with almost entirely contextual patterns of assignment and non-obligatory gender marking, two properties that would seem to challenge some widely accepted claims about the typology of gender, notably that gender is a lexical property of nouns with obligatory morphosyntactic realization through patterns of agreement. Yet, with respect to the nature of assignment rules, the fact that for a few nouns gender assignment is still fixed suggests that patterns of flexible gender assignment, no matter how radical, would always imply at least some instances of lexically specified gender, and that in sex-based gender systems, lexically specified gender is likely to pattern with humans and higher animates.

Coming to our second question, how to account for flexibility from a diachronic point of view, one could be tempted to assume that highly flexible gender assignment is bound to be more frequent in non-mature gender systems, where a lower degree of grammaticalization prompts stronger referential ties in gender marking, and the gender of a noun is largely determined by the speaker's construal of its referent. While this is a hypothesis that awaits systematic empirical testing, some observations can be made based on already available data.

For instance, we know for a fact that context-based, flexible gender assignment is well attested in highly grammaticalized gender systems such as those of the Bantu and North-Central Atlantic languages, which often have dedicated diminutive and augmentative genders. Since the Atlantic-Congo gender systems are mature systems, reconstructed in the proto-language and characterized by considerably opaque patterns of assignment, the existence of flexible assignment in these languages would seem to contradict the idea that its presence presupposes young and highly referential gender systems. Interestingly, though, studies of the Bantu gender systems have shown that the dedicated diminutive and augmentative genders (along with the locative genders) are less stable than other gender distinctions and more likely to be replaced by analytic types of evaluative constructions (Creissels 1999; Güldemann 1999; Di Garbo 2014; Verkerk 2014). This could suggest that dedicated diminutive and augmentative genders are less prototypical types of gender distinctions, and therefore likely to disappear or be replaced by other constructions when the system of gender marking undergoes erosion.

Moving on to sex-based gender systems and the use of the masculine/feminine contrast to encode variation in size, countability and/or appreciation/amelioration, one open question is whether the emergence of these patterns of encoding precedes or follows the grammaticalization of a sex-based type of opposition, or whether all these meanings emerge at once, provided that a contrast between two classificatory markers emerge. This issue has been addressed by Mettouchi (2000) for the gender systems of the Berber languages. Mettouchi suggests that the diminutive and singulative meanings of what synchronically is the feminine gender marker *t* developed before the sex-based meaning. According to this proposal, the original function of the marker was purely contrastive. The marker *t* was used to single out an entity with respect to a reference point with which a hierarchical, part-whole type of relationship would be established. The feminine meaning emerged at a later stage and with animate nouns where the pattern of contrast got reinterpreted in terms of natural gender contrast. It remains to be seen whether a diachronic development of this type can be posited for other language families with similar gender systems and uses of flexible assignment.

6 The evolution of noun classes

6.1 Introduction

In accordance with the dynamic approach taken in this chapter, we think that it is crucial to emphasize the diachronic dimension of properties of noun classes. Diachronic developments can be addressed by means of cross-linguistic comparative concepts as much as synchronic systems. Here we will formulate diachronic cross-linguistic concepts using the formula *From X to Y*. This is all prepared by §3 where we already applied this approach to the developmental path that links referent-based gender to lexical gender, which can be described as:

(i) From classes of referents to classes of (noun) lexemes (§3)

In this section we will discuss a number of developments in the domain of noun classes. These can be described as follows:

(ii) From one-to-one assignment to many-to-one assignment (§6.2)

(iii) From semantic to opaque assignment (§6.3)

(iv) From semantic to formal assignment (from "covert" to "overt" gender) (§6.4)

(v) From default genders to gender values with semantic content (§6.5)

(vi) From classes of single items to classes of larger sets (§6.6)

6.2 From one-to-one assignment to many-to-one assignment

Mature gender systems usually have a limited number of classes. But not all gender systems with two genders are complex. Complex gender systems with a limited number of classes can actually have two different kinds of origins, which seem entirely opposite at first glance. They can develop from many classes or they can develop from two classes. Here we argue that what these two seemingly opposite developments have in common is that there is a shift from ONE-TO-ONE ASSIGNMENT, where every assignment rule applies to another gender value, to MANY-TO-ONE ASSIGNMENT, where the same gender value is the outcome of several assignment rules. This is complexification according to the Principle of One-Meaning–One-Form (§2), as it entails a loss of transparency.

In this section we will consider Dyirbal (Pama-Nyungan) and Khasi, which both have many-to-one assignment. For Dyirbal it has been argued that its four genders have originated from many more classes. Khasi has three genders and they have developed from an entirely transparent pronominal two-gender system with referent-based semantic gender. Despite the entirely opposite range of number of original classes, both developments instantiate the same diachronic comparative concept *from one-to-one assignment to many-to-one assignment*.

Plaster & Polinsky (2007) propose that the four-gender system of Dyirbal (Dixon 1972) has developed from a noun classifier system such as the one described for the rather distantly related language Yidiñ with about twenty classifiers (Dixon 1977), "through the collapse of a larger number of classifiers into a smaller number of genders" (Plaster & Polinsky 2007: 14).[15] Yidiñ and some other Australian languages have classifiers that functionally correspond to the classifiers posited by Plaster & Polinsky (2007) for an earlier, not-attested stage of Dyirbal (see Table 13).

Table 13: Merger of classes to Dyirbal noun classes according to Plaster & Polinsky (2007)

Dyirbal genders and their semantic core	Corresponding classifiers in Yidiñ
I -*l*: male humans, non-human animates	*bama waguḍa* 'male', *miɲa* '(edible) non-human animate'
II -*n* : female humans, birds, stinging things, inanimate nouns related to fresh water or fire	*bama buɲa* 'female', *ḍaruy* 'bird', *buṛi* 'fire, sparks, charcoal, a light, etc.', *bana* 'drinkable liquid', *ḍama* 'stinging animals and plants'
III -*m*: edible (non-meat) inanimates	*mayi* 'edible plant'
IV -Ø: everything else	*wira* 'inanimate nouns', no classifier

According to Plaster & Polinsky (2007), some of the complexities in Dyirbal can be explained by the earlier classifier system that must have been similar to that in Yidiñ. In Yidiñ, a dog "could never be called *miɲa*" (Dixon 1977: 490). Accordingly, in Dyirbal, 'dog' is not in class I, but in class II. For a more limited case of coalescence of homophonous partial repeaters in Boran, see Seifart (2018: 22).

Many-to-one assignment can also develop when masculine and feminine anaphoric pronouns expand and become noun phrase markers for all inanimate nouns, as has happened in Khasi. Rabel-Heymann (1977) proposes 20 semantic sub-classes for feminine, and 14 for masculine nouns. However, the many-to-one assignment does not stop there, since many sub-classes have exceptions. These can even affect compounds. Usually, Khasi compounds have the gender of their head. But although *ka sim* [F bird] and most birds are feminine, some compounds

---

[15] According to Dixon (1977: 496) it is most likely that both Dyirbal noun classes and Yidiñ classifiers have developed from a smallish set of half-a-dozen or so classifiers.

with *sim* 'bird' are masculine, e.g.: *'u sim so' pho* 'woodpecker', put differently, have their own COMPOUND GENDER, where gender of the compound is different from the gender of the head. There are also a number of homophones different only in gender, such as *ka ja* 'rice', *'u ja* 'vegetable' and *ka dpey* 'hearth', *'u dpey* 'ashes' (Rabel-Heymann 1977: 271), which demonstrate that gender assignment cannot be phonological here. An example of a sub-class with exceptions is natural forces and landscape features, where 37 feminine items contrast with six masculine exceptions: *'u khnñʋ'* 'earthquake', *'u prthat* 'thunder', *'u bnaay* 'moon', *'u khlʋor* 'star', *'u l'o'* 'cloud' and *'u slap* 'rain' (Rabel-Heymann 1977: 265).

6.3 From semantic to opaque assignment

According to Svärd (2019 [in Volume I]), opaque gender is characterized by rules that are "not general or have numerous exceptions" (see also §5.1). He finds that 8 of 20 languages of New Guinea in his sample have semantic and opaque gender assignment (as opposed to 8 with transparent semantic and 4 with semantic and formal assignment). Killian (2019 [in Volume I]) describes Uduk as a gender system with largely arbitrary assignment, and Dahl (2019 [in Volume I]) holds that "opaque" or "arbitrary" gender assignment is "a possibility that has been downplayed in recent decades". Opaque gender assignment is not entirely without rules, but, however the rules are formulated (and there may be conflicting solutions), there are many rules and they make reference to many semantic groups and parts of semantic groups or even to individual nouns. Opaque gender assignment systems do not necessarily lack formal criteria entirely, but non-formal rules (semantic or item-wise) prevail.

Before considering the phenomenon any further, an admonition to caution is in order. There is a risk of adopting extreme positions, on the one hand, by postulating general principles of conceptual underpinning or formal assignment on the basis of a discussion of few examples or, on the other hand, by denying the reality of any assignment rules by emphasizing particular exceptions to trends. Plaster & Polinsky (2007) criticize attempts to explain gender assignment in Dyirbal as semantic by invoking such principles as association in myth or belief, domain of experience, and important property, because they cannot be falsified. "[T]he rules do not apply in any systematic way and, as they are, seem to act more as after-the-fact generalizations than operational principles" (Plaster & Polinsky 2007: 6). They further argue that young children acquiring the language do not have access to the necessary information for motivating gender assignment in such manners. However, their own approach of explaining the gender of some Dyirbal nouns by phonological assignment is not free of after-the-fact generalizations either. Their five proposed phonological rules only account for one or two examples each, in some cases with as many or more counterexamples, and leave many nouns unexplained.

Here complexity may be useful as a methodological tool. It can be argued, for instance, that if a proposal is not shorter than another one in terms of description length, it cannot be considered adequate. For some languages, such as Dyirbal, it may be difficult to account for gender assignment in a straightforward manner and often it cannot be excluded that certain generalizations are real (researchers will disagree about them). However, different solutions will share the conclusion that gender assignment in a language such as Dyirbal is complex in terms of description length.

There are many unrelated languages in all major parts of the world with opaque gender assignment and some of them have developed grammatical gender quite recently, such as Khasi. Hence the question arises as to whether there is anything systematic about these exceptions. We suggest here that these expections can be summarized as the Principle of Contrast (38), which is an observation rather than an explanation.

(38)   Principle of Contrast in opaque gender systems
       While nouns in a semantic field often have a preferred gender, some
       salient nouns in the field tend to contrast with them and take an opposite
       gender.

Table 14 lists eleven unrelated languages with opaque masculine-feminine gender and how they treat the gender of 'sun' and 'moon'. Difference of gender is in majority, but the null-hypothesis that same gender is equally common cannot be rejected statistically.[16]

One difficulty with contrast is that it is unpredictable where exactly there is an opposition in the semantic field (and how semantic fields are delimited). In Paumari (Arawan), a language which "shows a high degree of semantic opacity" (Aikhenvald 2010: 44), masculine 'sun' and 'moon' are arguably opposed to feminine 'sky' (Aikhenvald 2010: 44).

Donohue's (2004: 334–342) description of Skou (Sko) emphasizes the relevance of gender oppositions and he launches the term "dynamic oppositions". Oppositions, such as female vs. male, small vs. large, squat-and-round vs. long-and-thin, natural vs. technological, etc., while global, can undergo local reversals, and

---

[16]It is important not to include languages with formal assignment, where the difference in gender need not be accounted for by semantics.

Table 14: Gender of 'sun' and 'moon' in opaque masculine-feminine gender systems

Different gender	Same gender
'sun' M vs. 'moon' F: Abau, Skou	both M: Paumari, Rotokas (North Bougainville)
'sun' F vs. 'moon' M: Bari, Dyirbal, Ket, Khasi, Mian	both F: Manambu, Tunica

"there are different, and contradictory, rationales behind the assignment of feminine and non-feminine gender" (2004: 341). Donohue provides possible explanations for many individual cases of gender choices. For instance, according to Donohue, *tang* 'canoe' (feminine), is an extension of land (feminine) and human society (feminine) into the changing, destructive, environment of the sea (masculine). However, what matters for our discussion here is that there are many local gender oppositions which all taken together form a complex pattern, whatever the explanation may be in individual cases.

Dynamic oppositions can especially be observed when two animate genders, typically masculine and feminine, expand below the cutoff point on the animacy hierarchy where gender can no longer be controlled by hierarchical patterning (see §3). Female and male purview (§3.3 iii) will not always be congruent with semantic fields in their entirety, and the metonymic and metaphorical associations at work (which are cross-field rather than intra-field) can be of many different kinds. As a consequence, the expanding masculine and feminine classes have a predilection for sharing semantic fields when taking over them. One reason is that size and shape oppositions, which are frequently observable in opaque masculine-feminine gender systems (see §5; Svärd 2019 [in Volume I], and Aikhenvald 2016, chap. 3), easily lend themselves to intra-field oppositions.

Another reason is that cross-domain (metaphorical) associations often have the form of contrasted pairs. According to Capell & Hinch (1970: 49), sun and moon in Australia are always female and male respectively in mythology, even where the local language has no noun classes. However, such oppositions need not always be sensitive to the kind of grammatical gender oppositions at work, which accounts for its unpredictability. In Tunica, where both 'sun' and 'moon' are feminine, there is still a local opposition, but one of age which is irrelevant for gender: the moon is personified as a granny and the sun as a young woman (Haas 1940: 57).

As discussed by Seifart (2018: 21), increase in opacity can be also due to histori-cal "accidents" when the prototypical referents of a noun change. In Miraña, 'axe' takes the classifier *-hɨ* for 'flat and round', since axes were earlier made of stone and round. Similar developments are also attested with pluralia tantum nouns, whose semantically motivated association with plurality may be lost when a noun no longer refers to a multiplicity of entities, but to just one entity, possibly consisting of smaller parts, as in Konso (Afro-Asiatic, East Cushitic) *filaa* 'comb' (more on lexical plurality and its relation with gender in §9). As mentioned in §3, opacity can also decrease, for instance, when nouns denoting animals shift to a transparent class in contemporary Miraña Bora (Seifart 2018: 24).

Generally, it may be assumed that animate reference, distant targets and ana-phoric use is an attractor for transparent gender, whereas inanimate reference, local targets and non-anaphoric use is an attractor for opaque gender. This is con-sistent with Audring's (2009) finding that all pronominal gender systems (where gender is restricted to pronouns) are semantically organized. Not unexpectedly, gender in Uduk (Killian 2019 [in Volume I]), which is highly non-transparent, is local (adjacent) and non-anaphoric. Among the non-transparent gender lan-guages in Svärd's sample from New Guinea, Ama, with only verbal agreement, is probably the most unexpected case. However, gender agreement in Ama goes with absolutive arguments, which entails frequent use with inanimate referents. Interestingly, in a language with two concurrent gender systems, such as Pau-mari (Aikhenvald 2010), both systems can be opaque, which adds to their com-plexity.

We conclude that unpredictable exceptions are the essence of opaque gender assignment. They come into being, among other things, because cross-domain extensions have the form of local, in Donohue's (2004) terms, "dynamic", oppo-sitions and by historical accidents (Seifart 2018). Hence in many-to-one assign-ment in opaque gender, many does not only mean many semantic fields behaving differently, but also local oppositions within semantic fields without any overar-ching principle. Hence opaque gender assignment is complex, and its complexity may develop rapidly. However, this complexity is not due to the absence of any principles at work, so one could say that its complexity and unpredictability is, to some extent, systematic.

6.4 From semantic to formal gender assignment and from "covert" to "overt" marking of gender

In many languages with gender, the gender of nouns correlates to a large extent with some morphological or phonological characteristics of nouns. The terms "overt marking" or "formal gender assignment" (Corbett 1991, chap. 3, as well as §5 in this chapter) applied to these phenomena suggest that the morphological or phonological marking is the cause and the assigned gender is the effect. From a diachronic perspective, however, the relationship usually goes the other way round.

There are at least three well-known ways in which overt gender marking can develop:

(i) As shown by Greenberg (1978) with a focus on African languages, free demonstratives or definite articles indicating gender can fuse with their head noun. For the fused markers, Greenberg further proposes a development from definite article via non-generic article to class affix.

(ii) When gender markers evolve from repeaters, as in Boran (Grinevald & Seifart 2004: 278–279) or Ngan'gityemerri (Reid 1997), fused repeaters become gender markers on noun-associated words and can become derivational affixes on nouns. The grammatical and derivational markers will then exhibit a large amount of parallelism given their common source.

(iii) In languages with many declension classes, most of them will not originally be associated with a gender. In ancient Indo-European languages, only the non-neuter vs. neuter distinction is entrenched in declension classes. The more recent masculine-feminine distinction only correlates with few declension classes (Delbrück 1883: 116–117). However, in many modern Indo-European languages, such as Slavic and Baltic, declension classes strongly correlating with gender have almost completely replaced all other declension classes.

When declension classes disappear, morphological assignment can turn into phonological assignment, which can entail considerable restructuring, as has happened, for instance, in the development from Latin to French (Polinsky & Van Everbroeck 2003) or in Wolof (Atlantic-Congo, North-Central Atlantic; Becher 2001: 46). In Rendille (Afro-Asiatic, East Cushitic), pitch accent on the final mora in the majority of feminine nouns as opposed to masculines with pitch accent on the penultimate mora is due to a lost feminine suffix -et (Oomen 1981: 46; Corbett 1991: 102). Malkiel (1957–1958) introduces the term HYPERCHARACTERIZATION for the addition of a marker that overtly indicates a category, and a large amount of his examples are about gender in Romance, such as Modern Spanish *cuchara* 'spoon(F)' with the addition of -a formed from covert Old Spanish *cuchar* 'spoon(F)'. Newman (1979: 202) argues for Hausa (Afro-Asiatic, West Chadic) that phonological characterization of feminine nouns has developed by massive application of hypercharacterization. Hypercharacterization is often not transparent in morphology synchronically. Hypercharacterization is thus a pathway from morphological to phonological gender assignment.

Phonological assignment can also originate directly from SANDHI without detour via morphological assignment, as in Nalca (Wälchli 2018). Owa (Austronesian, Oceanic; Mellow 2013: 26) is another example. While the neighboring language Kahua has four classes distinguished by articles (*o* male person names and kinship terms, *ka* female person names and kinship terms, *i* places, and *na* default), as can be deduced from the Kahua Bible translation, Owa has in addition an *e*-class for five kinship terms beginning with *e-*: *ema(-na)* 'father(-POSS.3SG)', *ena(-na)* 'mother(-POSS.3SG)', *ewa(-na)* 'older sibling(-POSS.3SG)', *esi(-na)* 'younger sibling(-POSS.3SG)' and *epu(-na)* 'maternal uncle(-POSS.3SG)'. Borrowed names and words beginning with *e-* are not *e*-class, which shows that phonological assignment is not productive. While the *e*-class is also semantically coherent (kinship terms), kinship terms not beginning with *e-* are masculine, feminine or default. Perhaps *e-* is a relic of an older general person name *a*-class. The closely related language Arosi, also spoken on the Island of Makira, has an article *a* for male and female person names and kinship terms: *a ina-mu* [PERS.NAME mother-POSS.2SG] 'your mother' (Capell 1982: 14, 40). Nalca and Owa have in common that gender markers have developed from an extension of person name markers and that the classes of nouns with phonological assignment have very few members.

Güldemann & Fiedler (2019 [in Volume I]) argue that "overt gender" marking on nouns has to be kept strictly distinct from gender, and they term it "deriflection (classes)" as opposed to gender. Some other researchers make the same distinction, but not always using the same terminology. For instance, Evans (2003: 181–221) for Bininj Kun-Wok strictly distinguishes between derivational markers on nouns (he calls this "noun classes"; this is deriflection classes according to Güldemann & Fiedler) and inflectional agreement markers on modifiers (he calls this "gender", as do Güldemann & Fiedler).

Other grammatical categories, such as number, do not have a restriction that the category has to exhibit syntactic DISPLACEMENT (has to be realized on another word). This is, of course, a consequence of how gender is defined and that other grammatical categories are defined in different ways. For instance, nominal number can be realized both on the head noun of a noun phrase, or, syntactically, on another word in the noun phrase or clause. Here we will argue that the special definition for gender makes sense, even though it differs from how most other grammatical categories are defined, because it is only displacement that turns gender into a grammatical category. If not displaced, a gender marker is derivational. Gender on nouns changes the meaning of the noun in such a way that it looks more like derivation than inflection. That is, the change in meaning is too large for it to stay within the limits of a lexeme. In this context, Bybee's (1985) notion of RELEVANCE is useful. According to Bybee (1985: 13), a "meaning element is *relevant* to another meaning element *if the semantic content of the first directly affects or modifies the semantic content of the second*" (emphasis in original source). Animacy and sex, which are the semantic core of gender, are directly relevant to nouns. As a consequence, markers expressing meanings related to gender realized on nouns will typically yield derivation rather than inflection, since, as Bybee (1985: 17) puts it, "relevant categories produce derived words that are more distinct in meaning from their bases than the ones produced by less relevant categories, the combinations of relevant notions tend to be lexicalized". For all parts of speech other than nouns, however, gender is not relevant. In Bybee's (1985) scale of relevance categories realized on verbs, gender is the most inflectional and least lexical expression type, which means that gender markers tend to be more distant from the verb stem than markers of other categories.

In this context it is interesting to investigate what happens when function words bearing gender marking, such as articles or demonstratives, fuse with the noun controlling gender. If grammatical gender has to be displaced, it will cease to be grammatical as soon as fusion takes place. This issue is not yet very well investigated typologically, but there are some indications that the prediction holds true at least as a trend. In Bulgarian (Indo-European, Slavic), the definite article is a second position clitic, but behaves differently depending on whether or not it is fused with the controller (Enger & Corbett 2012: 315). If the clitic is realized on another word preceding the noun, such as an adjective, the article expresses the gender of the noun (39a/c). If the clitic is realized on the noun itself, however, its form can be influenced by the declension class of the noun as in (39b/d). According to Dost & Gribanova (2006: 134) the clitic is phonologically clearly an affix when realized on the noun. Inflectional affixes on nouns can lead to complexities in declension classes (see Güldemann & Fiedler 2019 [in Volume I], their term is deriflection), but do not constitute additional genders. However, Bulgarian is specific in that the declension class affixes on nouns and the displaced gender markers on attributes have the same function within noun phrases.

(39)   Bulgarian (Indo-European, Slavic; Enger & Corbett 2012: 315)

    a.   *dobri-jat*   *bašt-a*
        good-DEF.SG.M father(M)-SG

        'the good father'

b. *bašt-a-ta*
father(M)-SG-DEF.SG.{F}
'the father'

c. *dobri-jat   čič-o*
good-DEF.SG.M uncle(M)-SG
'the good uncle'

d. *čič-o-to*
uncle(M)-SG-DEF.SG.{N}
'the uncle'

For similar phenomena in Norwegian dialects see Enger & Corbett (2012), where the situation, however, is complicated by the fact that feminine gender is in decline.

Fusion of an article with its head noun is a syntagmatic process. There is a paradigmatic parallel to this if inflectional markers on gender targets are extended to inflectional marking on nouns, which has happened in Latvian. Indo-European has different inflectional suffixes on nouns and pronouns. In Baltic, the pronominal suffixes are extended to adjectives and in Latvian even to nouns in some case-number forms, especially in the dative singular. This entails that the dative singular nominal suffix in Latvian correlates 100% with gender (Nau 2011). Not only do masculine nouns of the ā-declension (usually feminine) have masculine agreement, they also take the masculine ending of the dative singular -*am* rather than the feminine ending -*ai*: *puik-am* [boy(M)-DAT.SG] 'to the boy' vs. *mās-ai* [sister(F)-DAT.SG] 'to the sister'. As in Norwegian, there can be further complications when gender in such a system is in decline (Wälchli 2017).

Since derivational phenomena connected to gender are beyond the scope of Hockett's classical definition of gender, they are often completely disregarded. An exception is Contini-Morava & Kilarski (2013), who argue, among other things, that "[n]oun class markers and classifiers can be used to expand the referential power of the lexicon either by creating new lexical items or by presenting referents from different perspectives" (Contini-Morava & Kilarski 2013: 263). It is unclear to us whether this means that languages without noun classes and classifiers have less referential power in their lexicon. However, we would like to emphasize here that it also might be argued that gender, especially in languages without formal assignment, can mean that the lexicon can have fewer elements. As mentioned in §6.3 above, Khasi sometimes has a remarkable lexical underdifferentiation just because gender disambiguates as in *ka brɪw* [F human.being] 'woman' vs. *'u brɪw* [M human.being] 'man' (Rabel-Heymann 1977: 270). However, as pointed out by Dahl (2019 [in Volume I]) it is not always quite easy to distinguish between formal and non-formal gender assignment. From a discourse perspective there is nothing particularly covert about gender in Khasi, since articles distinguishing gender are very frequent. Their status as independent word is not entirely clear either, and at least in the closely related language Pnar, the articles are clearly clitics (Ring 2015).

Sometimes decisions whether a language has formal or non-formal gender assignment are quite arbitrary. Algonquian languages are usually considered to have semantic gender assignment (Corbett 1991: 24), which is, however, quite opaque despite its motivation by power, see §3.3 (v). However, the plural marker on the noun clearly distinguishes between animate and inanimate, which is a morphological distinction. In Meskwaki, even the singular is clearly distinguished in noun inflection (see Table 15).

Table 15: Meskwaki noun inflection (Thomason 2003: 10)

	Animate	Inanimate
singular proximate	*-a*	*-i*
singular obviative	*-ani*	*-i*
plural proximate	*-aki*	*-ani*
plural obviative	*-ahi*	*-ani*

Gender in Algonquian can thus be said to be both semantically and morphologically assigned, as there are separate morphological paradigms for animate and inanimate nouns, but it is usually assumed that semantic assignment in Algonquian is so pervasive that morphology is secondary.

6.5 The development of non-noun controllers and neutral genders

It is often argued that noun class systems differ from classifiers in that all nouns must have a gender. As we will see in §8.3, this property of gender systems is closely connected with degree of formalization, which goes hand-in-hand with cumulation of gender with number and/or case. From a developmental perspective, this means that obligatorification of gender is not necessarily a gradual internal development within the category of gender, but is connected to the fact that the development of gender tends to be parasitic on other category types, notably number and case, which are already highly grammaticalized by the time gender starts emerging. As a consequence, there are hardly any attested developments from non-obligatory to obligatory gender. However, this does not mean that all gender systems where all nouns have a gender value are equally mature. Some languages have large default classes, which may be an indication of a non-mature gender system. Such a language is Nalca, where most nouns have default noun gender (see Wälchli 2018).

If all nouns are gender controllers, this usually implies that there are at least some gender targets where there is a forced choice of gender values. This even holds if there are no noun controllers, which means that the gender system must account for non-nominal controllers. This is the major topic of this section.

Many languages have some kind of NEUTRAL agreement form used for agreement with "non-prototypical" controllers, such as infinitive phrases, clauses, interjections and other quoted phrases, where the term "non-prototypical" does not say anything else than that the controller is not a noun. A potential solution is to say that non-noun genders are default genders. However, this is problematic, as argued by Corbett (1991: 214) in languages such as Spanish or Lithuanian, where there is a unique neutral agreement form dedicated to agreement with non-prototypical controllers (*ello* 'it, that', *lo curioso de esta situación* 'the curious thing about that situation; Corbett 1991: 214–215). Both in Spanish and Lithuanian, the unique neutral agreement form is a relic of the neuter gender, that remains after all nouns triggering neuter in Latin and Baltic switched to another gender. So it is arguably at least diachronically a default.

"Default" is usually thought of as last resort, or, as Corbett & Fraser (1999: 71) put it, "the default is the last thing you get to do". However, neutral agreement can be expansive, which is not easily compatible with default as last resort. This is the case in the so-called "pancake" sentences in Scandinavian languages (see Faarlund 1977 and Enger 2004 for Norwegian). In Swedish and Norwegian, predicative adjectives usually agree with the subject in number and, in the singular, in gender. In (40) there is no such agreement. But (40) cannot be an instance of last resort default, since there is a subject to agree with. If default is conceived of as last resort, then it is strange that such a default can be extended.

(40) Swedish (Indo-European, Germanic)
    Pannkakor   *är*   **gott.**
    pancake(CM).PL be:PRS good.N.SG

    'Pancakes are good.'

Sentences such as (40) have the connotation of an event, in this case 'to eat pancakes is good'. In fact, Faarlund (1977) argues that we have to deal with reduced subject clauses, an analysis which is dismissed by Enger (2004), who also shows that any last-resort default analysis runs into serious troubles. Corbett (2006: 150) speaks of extension in use of the default, but last resort defaults cannot be extended, if there is some other choice. Enger (2004) shows that Norwegian and Swedish pancake sentences are largely semantically conditioned (low individuation) and are subject to Corbett's Agreement Hierarchy. Following Widmark (1966), he also points out that the syntax of the subject NP plays a certain role. In (41) the common gender form (M/F) of the predicative adjective is possible if the subject has an adjective attribute, but is ungrammatical if the subject is a bare noun.

(41)   Norwegian (Indo-European, Germanic; Enger 2004: 24)
       Russisk   vodka   er   sunn   / sunt.
       Russian.M.SG vodka(M).SG be.PRS healthy.M/F.SG / healthy.N.SG
       'Russian vodka is healthy.'

If neutral gender and in particular its extensions in Scandinavian languages are semantic, this means that non-noun controllers can be as meaningful in classification as noun classes and should not necessarily be considered to be assigned by default.

In a diachronic perspective, this means that if noun classes have become obligatory for nouns in the sense that every noun must trigger a gender under certain circumstances, there will usually also be obligatory gender agreement with some non-noun controllers. A neutral gender may originate as a default, but the existence of unique neutral genders, as in Spanish, and of expansive neutral gender, as in Scandinavian, shows that neutral genders can become phenomena of their own. Put differently, default genders can acquire semantic content.

6.6 From classes of single items to classes of larger sets

Many classifiers and genders have originally a very restricted range of application which can be gradually extended. According to Erbaugh (1986: 428), Chinese classifiers start out as specific for single items both in diachrony and in child acquisition, and several of the commonly used Mandarin classifiers, such as *běn* for 'books' and *duǒ* for 'flowers' (also 'clouds'), still tend to be restricted to single or few concepts in spoken Mandarin of adults. The Chinese general classifiers Mandarin *ge* and in earlier periods *méi* have developed from words for 'bamboo' and 'trunk of bamboo tree' and can be shown to have gradually extended their range of application (Erbaugh 1986: 429).

The Ngan'gityemerri 'thing'-class *yerr-* has developed from *yawurr/yewirr* 'tree', "a natural extension of the allocation to this class of such traditional artefacts as woomeras, spears, shields, coolamons etc, which are all made from the timber of trees" (Reid 1990: 309). Similar developments are found in other Australian languages. According to Allan (1977: 300), a classifier for trees and objects is perhaps the most common inanimate classifier.

The Ateker [=Teso-Turkana] group of East Nilotic has developed a third gender (in addition to the East Nilotic two gender masculine-feminine opposition, as in Bari; see §3) from an anaphoric noun **(né)ní* 'that place (just referred to)' (Dimmendaal 1983: 219; Heine & Reh 1984: 228). In Turkana, an Ateker language, "[t]he new gender has lost virtually all traces of its locative origin" (Heine & Reh 1984: 229) and has mostly a diminutive function. In another East Nilotic language, Maasai [Masai], only one noun *wwéjì* 'place' belongs to the third gender, which indicates place (Tucker & Mpaayei 1955: 15; Payne 1998: 160).

Not only individual nouns, but also, for instance, person names, nominalizations and diminutives (or particular types of them) can serve as starting points for the development of larger sets of classes. Similar to extensions from the use with particular nouns are extensions from other very specific functions. In Iroquoian languages, a feminine(-indefinite) gender in Five Nations Iroquois has developed from a generic and indefinite human index on verbs (still represented in Cherokee, Southern Iroquoian; Mithun 2014: 141). This development is an extension of referent-based gender rather than of lexical gender. In Mohawk (Iroquoian, Northern Iroquoian), the feminine-indefinite gender is mostly used for older women and for expressing respect, but individual speakers use it for specific sets of referents. "Often mothers are initially shocked to realize that they use different gender prefixes for different daughters" (Mithun 2014: 138).

Many languages have some sort of respect or honorific distinction especially for women. Respect can originally be associated with specific nouns, as in the case of Lak (Nakh-Daghestanian). In Lak female nouns originally were gender II with the exception of *duš* 'girl, daughter' gender III. *Duš* 'girl, daughter' served as a so-called *Trojan horse* (Corbett 1991: 100) to transfer all female nouns to gender III except older family members, because this gender is associated with politeness. In two different Polish dialect areas transitional to Czech and Slovak (Indo-European, Slavic), specific morphological formations for diminutives and patronyms for unmarried women, which happen to be neuter and masculine respectively, are the origins for neuter and masculine gender use for unmarried women (Corbett 1991: 101). As in Mohawk, it may play a role that the communities are small and everybody knows each other for keeping track of the sets of referents.

In some varieties of Swiss German, nicknames for women are either neuter or feminine depending on their morphological pattern. Accordingly, the anaphoric pronouns referring to specific women whom one knows well are either neuter or feminine, and the neuter pronoun *ääs* 'it' can be used contrastively. Bosch (1988: 218) argues for Standard German that the neuter pronoun *es* 'it' never can be accented, since the marked (emphatic) pronoun reflects a classification of referents. If Bosch's descriptive-content hypothesis is true, this means that the set of referents is part of the descriptive content of Bernese German neuter and feminine genders. In (42), there are two different women or girls with the name *Susanne* with different diminutive-based nicknames, one of which is feminine (*Suslə*) and one of which is neuter (*Susi*). The referents can be tracked by using the corresponding emphatic forms of personal pronouns in contrastive focus.

(42) Bernese Swiss German (Indo-European, Germanic; constructed example)
    D   Suslə   ʊ   ds   Susi   sötə   beedi   choo.
    DEF.SG.F Susle(F) and DEF.SG.N Susi(N) should.COND.3PL both.PL come.INF
    Sıı   ısch   scho   daa, abər ƐƐS no   nıd.
    SHE be.PRS.3SG already here, but   IT   not yet.

    'Susle(DIM.F) and Susi(DIM.N) are both supposed to come. SHE is here already, but "IT" is not yet here.'

The Mohawk, Polish and Swiss German examples show that extensions to general sets is not only relevant for lexical, but also for referent-based gender.

Since every noun class has its own history, it will usually be the case that different classes in the same languages are at entirely different levels of generalization. Mandarin, for instance, has a special classifier for 'books', *běn*, as opposed to the general classifier *ge*. The Ngan'gityemerri *kurum/kurim* 'canegrass spear' class is opposed to the much more general 'thing' class *yerr-*. It is hence astonishing that there are languages with a roughly equal distribution of nouns across genders. This is the more likely the lower the number of genders is, since the general tendency for Zipfian distributions is hard to do away with in larger sets of items. According to Zipf's Law (1935), the frequency of a form is inversely proportional to its frequency rank. This entails that different forms will greatly differ in frequency.

Noun classes with very limited scope are not restricted to early stages of development. It is common that a gender disappears by steadily losing its members until nearly no members are left. Standard Swedish has largely lost the opposition between masculine and feminine in nouns, but retains the distinction for anaphoric gender in personal pronouns, and, to a certain extent, masculine in weak adjectives (see Dahl 2000b, as well as Di Garbo & Miestamo 2019 [this volume]). Traces of the earlier ability of nouns to trigger feminine are the anaphoric use of the personal pronoun *hon* 'she' with the antecedent *människa* 'human being', and with *klocka* 'clock' (Teleman et al. 1999: 61). However, as will be discussed in §7.7, such a development has typically a component of idiomatization, which is characteristic for relics.

7 The complexity of agreement

7.1 Toward a definition of agreement

In this section we will define agreement as an asymmetric specific relation involving displaced information between a syntactically potentially complex controller and a syntactically potentially complex target. The rest of §7.1 has the aim of motivating this definition. §7.2 deals with specific relationships in agreement, §7.3 with complex controllers and §7.4 with complex targets. In §7.5 we argue that features are a mature form of displaced information. Viewed in the dynamic perspective adopted in this chapter, agreement can gradually develop when nouns decategorialize to gender targets (§7.6). But targets can also have properties of controllers and agreement can be idiomatic, which contributes to the fuzzy character of agreement (§7.7).

Throughout §7 we will use the term *complex* in three rather different, but still connected, senses. As elsewhere in the chapter, we conceive of complexity as absolute descriptive complexity (see §2). Thus, *complex* means 'non-trivial in structure, so that an exhaustive description cannot be short'. The sheer length of this section will suggest that gender agreement is complex. However, this has much to do with *complex* in the sense of 'consisting of different, but related phenomena'. The phenomena commonly subsumed under agreement in the typological literature are of many different, but yet related kinds. We will argue here that this can be accounted for by the dynamic approach. Different kinds of agreement or agreement-like phenomena have different kinds of origin and represent different stages of maturity of agreement. Throughout the section, we will emphasize the importance of identifying some kind of unequivocal specific relationship between the elements involved in agreement. As we will show, this requirement can only be maintained if the units linked by agreement can be viewed as elements that can consist of several words (complex targets and complex controllers). *Complex* therefore also has the sense 'consisting of several elements'. Agreement is also complex in the sense of number of items involved, which, however, limits its complexity in the sense of transparency. We claim that agreement relations can always be seen as one-to-one relations. This comes at the cost of rejecting the idea that agreement is simply a direct relationship between two words. In gender, the word(s) or context(s) triggering the choice of a grammatical value of a marker do not originate in the word on which the category is marked, which is what we call displacement of information, the very essence of agreement. If information is displaced, this happens in the form of a chain (from one chain link to another) and this chain can have more than two links. As we will show, it is not uncommon that there can be many links in the information transfer chain.

Agreement is one of the most traditional notions in linguistics. However, modern linguists very much disagree about its nature and whether it is a useful concept. While Corbett (2006) understands agreement in terms of the highly abstract notion of morphosyntactic feature triggered by a controller and expressed on a target (a conception compatible with many formal approaches), Croft (2013) questions the usefulness of the concept of agreement and Haspelmath (2018) holds that agreement is poorly defined. Haspelmath suggests to replace the notion of (potential) agreement target in the definition of gender by "noun-associated form", which he defines as "an adnominal modifier (article, demonstrative, adjective, or numeral), or a verbal argument index (subject or object index), or an anaphoric pronoun". One of Haspelmath's arguments is that noun-associated forms are often used in situations when the corresponding noun is not overtly present. This argument has been well-known at least since Barlow's (1999: 190) discourse-oriented approach to agreement. Barlow conceives of agreement as a process of feature unification, a view shared by Corbett (2006) and approaches within Lexical-Functional Grammar (e.g., Kuhn & Sadler 2007). This implies that gender marked forms need not actually be controlled and can occur on their own, such as the isolated utterance in Spanish *Bella!* [beautiful.F.SG] '(You are/she is) beautiful!' While the unification approach accounts for syntactically non-controlled targets, it has the disadvantage that it models agreement as a symmetric relation.

In our view the concept of feature shared by a controller and a target captures the idea that agreement is a form of displaced information. The form where gender is realized is not where gender originates. The information necessary to determine the gender value comes from another part of the utterance, be it from a word or sequence of words elsewhere in the sentence or discourse or be it from the context.

We think that our definition of agreement has the potential of building a bridge between the extreme positions of either viewing agreement in highly abstract terms or doing away with the notion of agreement altogether. In our view, morphosyntactic features are highly mature forms of displaced information. This understanding of morphosyntactic features allows us to put agreement into a dynamic perspective, where abstract features can be seen as emergent.

Gender marking is the forced choice from a set of redundant marking options on an element that is typically not a noun (the target). The choice is externally determined by an overt, typically nominal, element (the controller) or by the context. In the latter case we will speak of a latent controller, as in Tasmowski-De Ryck & Verluyten's (1982: 328) famous French example (43), where there is no syntactic antecedent for the anaphoric pronoun.

(43) French (Indo-European, Romance; Tasmowski-De Ryck & Verluyten 1982: 328)
      (John is trying to stuff a large table (*la table*, feminine) in the trunk of his car; Mary says:)
      *Tu n'arriveras jamais à **la** [F]/*le [M] faire entrer dans la voiture.*
      'You will never manage to get it into the car.'

In (43), the latent controller is lexical. The displaced feature originates in a specific lexical item in a specific word form (singular) which must be activated in the speaker's mind when she utters the target. The controller is not overtly present in syntax, but there is still displaced information from a latent lexical item to a target and there is an asymmetric relation between the latent controller and the target.

A consequence of externally forced choice (the use of *la* or *le* in (43) is not random) is that the target bears some typically nominal information, which can be some referent-based property, such as animacy, sex, size or shape, or some lexical feature of a noun, as in (43). In gender agreement, this is always displaced information. Displaced information is hence a defining criterion of gender agreement. However, there may be intermediate cases where it is unclear whether the choice of a marker is externally determined (by syntax or discourse), especially if the target is a noun or a noun phrase. As we will see, this is highly important from a diachronic perspective since gender agreement, at least in some cases, can be shown to evolve from the decategorialization of nouns (see §7.6). Agreement, as we conceive of it, is partly fuzzy. On the one hand, there are clear cases of agreement; on the other hand, there are phenomena which only have some properties of agreement, and the latter are important for understanding how agreement evolves diachronically.

Much of the disagreement about the notion of agreement comes from attempts to define agreement uniformly syntactically (e.g. Hengeveld 2012 and Passer

2016b)[17] or uniformly in terms of discourse (e.g., Barlow 1999). This has to do with the fuzzy nature of coreferentiality. Many agreement phenomena can be subsumed under Moravcsik's (1978: 363) Coreferentiality Principle, according to which all agreement targets include reference to the controller nominal. The Coreferentiality Principle is too narrow, as shown by Corbett (2006), since targets sometimes agree with non-coreferential controllers, for instance, if the gender of the possessee is marked on the possessor (see §7.6). However, coreferentiality is neither strictly opposed to lack of reference nor to completely independent reference, and, as a consequence, lack of reference is not strictly opposed to completely independent reference. Attributive adjectives in an NP are arguably coreferential with the head noun of the NP, but since it is the NP as a whole that refers, it is unclear whether reference need be invoked at all in this context. Croft (2013) argues that there is no principled difference between independent reference and dependent reference, which leads him to an independent reference analysis of "agreement" as indexation.

The information displaced through agreement marking can consist of features, such as gender and number, with very limited sets of possible values. Features are a mature form of displaced information, but displaced information is not restricted to features: it can be just a condition (a context where a certain choice of marker is made, whereby that context is information relevant for the choice). Corbett (2006, chap. 6) keeps features and conditions apart. We think that the two are just two different forms of displaced information in agreement and features are often mature conditions (which also explains why features often cumulate, see §9).

Agreement is syntactic to the extent that it involves words or groups of words as targets and controllers, but the relation between controller and target can be semantic and it can be inter-sentential. Our definition differs from Corbett's (2006: 4) in seeing the domain as part of the syntactic target. For instance, a target is not an adjective qua part of speech, but an adjective in a specific syntactic environment, such as attributive or predicative.

The visualization in Figure 3 captures some core ideas of our definition of agreement. Controller and target can consist of several words (small boxes within a larger box). They are linked by a specific relation, which can be syntactic or se-

---

[17]Hengeveld (2012), van Rijn (2016) and Passer (2016b) only distinguish between independent reference and agreement as the result of a syntactic feature copying-mechanism not involving reference. In their view, attributive adjectives exhibiting gender are an instance of agreement exactly because they do not refer. This entails a narrow definition of agreement, especially manifest in Passer (2016b: 86), who argues that concordial class systems must have a range of language specific modifiers, i.e. agreement within the NP.

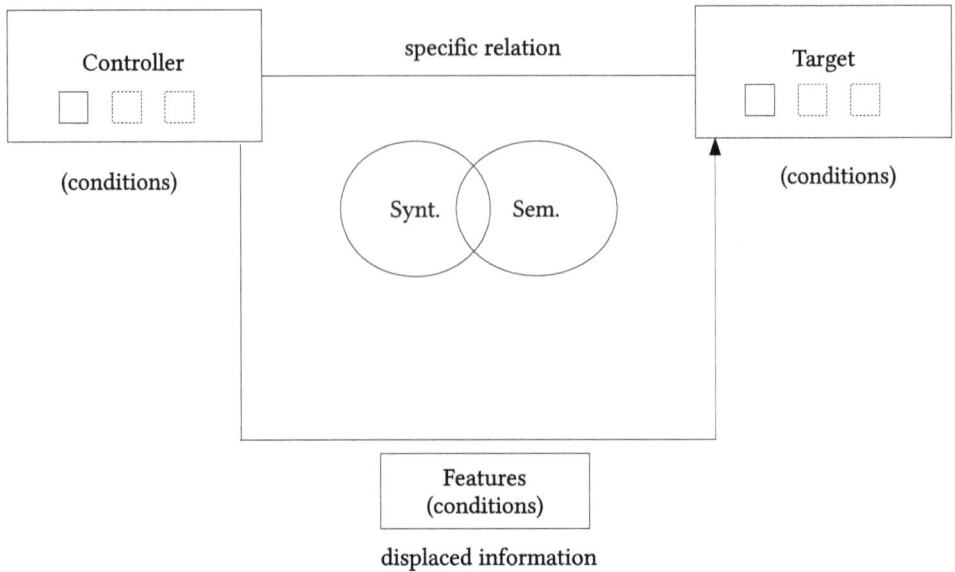

Figure 3: A model of agreement

mantic, and the information expressed by agreement and realized on the target is displaced information, in the sense that it does not originate in the target. It can consist of features or a feature or a condition on a feature.

Unlike Corbett, we think that the notion of relation is an indispensable defining term of agreement. Our definition is consistent in this respect with Lehmann, who requests "a grammatical or semantic syntagmatic relation" between controller and target (Lehmann 1982: 203). However, we think it need not be syntagmatic, since the controller can be contextual. Coreferentiality is an example of a specific relationship that can hold between a controller and a target. Our claim is that there is always some specific relationship between target and controller in agreement. The relationship must be specific, because it must be unequivocal. This does not exclude occasional instances of ambiguity, but agreement is basically a one-to-one relationship or association, not a one-to-many or many-to-many relationship between controller and target. This entails that targets are sometimes complex in the sense that they consist of FORMAL GROUPS, a term that we take from Croft's (2001: 190) critique of the notion of constituent. A formal group can be a phrase or constituent, but it can also be another kind of syntactic grouping (which need not be a continuous string of words). Agreement is a means of indicating syntactic grouping (groups of controller and target or target groups or controller groups) parallel to, but not necessarily congruent with, constituency.

Sometimes a word displaying an agreement marker does not entertain any specific or exclusive relation with the controller if considered in isolation, but only when considered in terms of a formal group it is part of. This is evidence for syntactically complex targets. Consider (44) from Italian with object agreement in the participle of *dovere* 'must' in the verbal formal group *ho dovuti chiudere* 'had to close' preceded by the object clitic which triggers the agreement. The object is semantically an object of the verb *chiudere* 'to close', but the whole sequence consisting of three verbs is a unit when it comes to argument structure. In terms of Rizzi (1982), the modal auxiliary and the lexical verb form a verbal complex. As further elaborated in §7.4, the verbal complex in (44) is an instance of a complex target or target group. The clitic, which is coreferential with 'pralines and biscuits' in (44), is an object of the whole verbal complex, not just of 'must', and as an object of the whole verbal expression it triggers object agreement, which happens to be realized on the modal verb, because the participle is the only form in the verbal complex where object agreement can be realized. Furthermore, *[q]ueste praline e questi biscotti* 'these pralines and biscuits' is an instance of a complex controller with gender resolution (in Italian feminine and masculine is masculine); see §7.3 for complex controllers.

(44) Italian (Indo-European; Romance; constructed, with inspiration of text examples)

Queste	praline	e	questi	biscotti	li	ho
this.F.PL	praline(F).PL	and	this.M.PL	biscuits(M).PL	3M.PL.ACC	have.PRS.1SG

dovuti	letteralmente	chiudere	sotto	chiave.
must.PTCP.PST.M.PL	literal.ADV	close.INF	under	key(M).SG

'Those pralines and biscuits I had to keep literally under lock and key.'

The agreement patterns in (44) can be described as an INFORMATION TRANSFER CHAIN (see Wälchli 2018) consisting of at least ten steps: The masculine plural marker -*i* (i) on the target word *dovuti* (ii) is part of the target group *dovuti chiudere* (iii), which receives masculine plural agreement from the pronoun *li* (iv), serving as controller under the condition that it precedes the verb (cf. *ho dovuto chiuder-li*, when the object clitic follows the verbal complex) (v), and is itself a target controlled by the controller group *queste praline e questi biscotti* (vi), whose gender results from gender resolution between the word-forms *praline* and *biscotti* (vii), whose word-form values feminine plural and masculine plural (viii) result from number inflection of the feminine lexeme *pralina* and the masculine noun *biscotto* (xi), which receive their lexical gender by formal gender assignment (x).

Above we have said that the specific relationship can be of different kinds. This is the topic of the next subsection.

7.2 Specific relationships in agreement

It is not the purpose of this section to give an exhaustive treatment of all possible specific relationships that can hold in agreement. What we want to point out here is that coreference is not the only kind of specific relationship that can hold in agreement and that a specific relationship can be semantic (in that case agreement can be inter-sentential) or formal (in that case agreement is usually intra-sentential). The latter part of this section will be devoted to adjacency, which is an under-researched phenomenon often encountered in agreement. We will argue that adjacency may qualify as a specific relationship in agreement.

The clearest case of agreement blatantly violating Moravcsik's (1978: 363) Coreferentiality Principle is gender in Archi (Nakh-Daghestanian, Lezgic). Archi has excessive agreement in the clause with the absolutive argument as controller. In (45) not only the verb 'make' agrees with the absolutive argument of the clause, but the pronominal arguments in the ergative and dative cases and the adverb 'quickly' do so too.

(45) Archi (Nakh-Daghestanian, Lezgic; Bond et al. 2016: 3)
   Nena<b>u   *do:ˤzu-b*   *χˤon*
   1PL.INCL.ERG<III.SG> be.big.ATTR-III.SG cow(III)[SG.ABS]
   b-ela<b>u   *dit:a<b>u*   *χir*   *a<b>u*
   III.SG-1PL.INCL-DAT<III.SG> quickly<III.SG> behind <III.SG>make.PFV
   'We quickly drove the big cow to us (home).'

In our view, agreement here marks the whole clause as a formal group; put differently, the agreement target is the whole clause (see §7.4 for complex targets). Agreement with the same noun class is realized wherever it can be morphologically marked in the clause. This is actually less excessive in Archi than (45) suggests, because agreement can be spelled out only occasionally in the Archi clause. Agreement appears only in about one third of the verbs, in the ergative only in the inclusive plural, in the dative only in first person pronouns, and only in 13 of 392 adverbs (Bond et al. 2016: 70). In clauses with two verbs with different absolutives, so-called biabsolutive constructions, there are two formal groups for agreement (Chumakina & Bond 2016: 90–111).

The agreement relation in Archi is a specific relationship in the sense that it is a unique relationship between the head of the absolutive NP (controller) and its clause (target). Since this is a syntactic dependency relationship, Archi agreement is intra-sentential, as opposed to coreference, which is semantic and can be inter-sentential. However, coreference is not the only possible kind of specific semantic relationship in agreement.

CO-CONCEPTUALITY – where controller and target express identity of concept, but not identity of reference – is another important specific relationship in gender agreement. Unlike co-referentiality, there is usually no agreement in number, since number is a property of the referent, not of the lexical noun expressing the concept (except for pluralia tantum, see Wälchli 2017 for Latvian). If we consider examples from the literature on anaphoric pronouns without explicit antecedents, such as *Either no letter was sent, or **it** got lost* and *Watch out for that snake. **They** are poisonous* (Bosch 1988: 211), there is no relationship of co-reference between noun and pronoun. The anaphoric pronoun simply stands for something that is of the same kind as the noun (the same concept); *it* is a letter and *they* are snakes, irrespective of their reference and whether they are referential at all. The so-called "donkey sentences" also sort here. This term was first introduced by the medieval philosopher Walter Burleigh around 1328 based on the Latin *Omnis homo habens **asinum*** [donkey.ACC.SG.M] *videt illum* [DEM.ACC.SG.M] 'Every man having a donkey sees it' (Seuren 2009: 269). In languages with lexical gender, such as Latin, there is usually agreement in gender in such cases of co-conceptuality.

Co-conceptuality is particularly important for independent adjectives and numerals and other independent elements as was discussed in §4. Like anaphoric pronouns, independent adjectives typically express some sort of anaphoric relationship, which, however, does not imply identity of reference, but identity of concept. This is illustrated in (46) from German.

(46)   German (Indo-European, Germanic): independent adjective expressing
       co-conceptuality
       Das mit dem <u>Hemd</u> [shirt(N)] *leuchtet mir so langsam auch ein... ja, **ein***
       weißes [INDF.NOM.SG.N white.NOM.SG.N] *wäre in der Tat besser gewesen.*
       [After a non-successful job application:] 'The thing with the shirt starts
       becoming clear to me, too...yes, a white one would indeed have been
       better.'
       http://www.bewerbung-forum.de [2018-11-06]

It might be objected that (46) is a case of ellipsis of the head noun. However, the form of attributive adjectives or numerals with head nouns and of independent adjectives or numerals without head nouns is not always the same in all languages, which is an argument that independent adjectives and numerals are not attributive adjectives and numerals with ellipsis. In German, the independent numeral 'one' follows a different declension pattern (originally pronominal endings): (speaking of shirts) *ein-es ist hellgrau* [one-NOM.SG.N.PRON be.PRS.3SG light.gray] 'one is light gray' as opposed to *ein Hemd ist hellgrau* [one.NOM.SG.N shirt be.PRS.3SG light.gray] 'one shirt is light gray'. Wälchli (2017) discusses the case of Dundaga Latvian, where there is gender agreement only in NPs with head nouns, but not in independent adjectives (which only have number agreement; see example (31) in §4.4). As far as the Animacy Hierarchy is concerned, independent adjectives behave like pronouns. In (47) from German there is semantic (referent-based) agreement with independent adjectives rather than lexical agreement. With attributive adjectives, semantic agreement is ungrammatical (*das*[N] *ältere Mädchen*(N), **die*[F] *ältere Mädchen*(N) 'the older girl').

(47) German (Indo-European, Germanic): co-conceptuality linked to coreference by means of part-whole relationship
      <u>*Zwei Mädchen*</u> [girl(N).PL] *im Alter von sieben und acht Jahren sind am Samstag in Schwarzenberg am Böhmerwald (Bezirk Rohrbach) von der Holzleiter eines Hochstandes gestürzt. **Die** [DEF.NOM.SG.F] **ältere** der beiden war ausgerutscht und hatte **die** [DEF.ACC.SG.F] **jüngere** mitgerissen.*
      'Two girls aged seven and eight years fell from the wooden ladder of a tree stand in Schwarzenberg am Böhmerwald (district of Rohrbach) on Saturday. **The elder one** of the two had slipped and had dragged **the younger one** with her.'
      http://www.salzburg.com/nachrichten/oesterreich/chronik/sn/artikel/
      zwei-maedchen-in-ooe-von-hochstand-gestuerzt-und-verletzt-209318
      [accessed 2017-06-05]

In the rest of this section we will focus on adjacency as a further potential specific relationship in agreement.

ADJACENCY in agreement means that controller and target or target and controller immediately follow each other. Target and/or controller can consist of several words. Adjacency between controller and target is frequent in most languages with gender, which is natural, since agreement is often local. According to Corbett (2006), local agreement is more canonical than distal agreement. But most treatments of gender do not pay any particular attention to adjacency. We think that adjacency is an important issue in agreement that deserves particular attention because there are several languages where gender agreement is pre-dominantly or exclusively adjacent.

Since adjacency is unequivocal, it has the potential of qualifying as a specific relationship between controller and target. Thus, it is a candidate for a type of specific relationship between controller and target on a par with coreference and other specific relationships.

It is well-known that linearity plays an important role in phonology, notably in sandhi phenomena, sound changes that take place at word- or morpheme-boundaries. As already mentioned in §6.4, some instances of gender agreement originate in sandhi. This adds a developmental perspective to the study of adja-cency in gender agreement. In cases where sandhi is involved in the origin of gender agreement, adjacency may reflect preservation of an earlier phonological motivation.

The importance of sandhi phenomena in agreement is well-known from Celtic languages. In all Celtic languages, feminine nouns have "mutated" onsets fol-lowing an article: Irish *bean* 'woman(F)', *an bhean* 'the woman'; Welsh *pont* 'bridge(F)', *y bont* 'the bridge' (Fife & King 1986: 480). Here it looks as if the controller noun is at the same time the target. However, morpho-syntactically it is rather the article which is the target with the gender marker being realized phonologically on the following word. In the case of postposed adjectives, it is just the other way round. In Breton *ur verc'h vras* 'a big girl' (*merc'h* 'girl', *bras* 'big'), *vras* 'big' looks as if it displays agreement with its initial mutation, but the mutation is in fact diachronically caused by the feminine noun preceding it (Fife & King 1986: 480). (For the possessive pronoun in Welsh see Wälchli 2019 [this volume].)

Let us now turn to the discussion of languages in which target and controller in gender agreement almost always are adjacent. In Uduk, a language with two noun classes termed class 1 and class 2, gender targets immediately precede gen-der controllers (see Killian 2019 [in Volume I]). At the same time, coreference does not seem to play any major role. If there are two or more words in a noun phrase, the head noun and the modifier have genders of their own.[18] Gender in Uduk does not usually have the function of signaling that two words belong to the same constituent or are coreferential. The gender marker is simply triggered by the gender of the following word. In (48) the preposition *kí* is followed by a class 1 noun (*yil* 'year'). With a following class 2 noun it would be *ká*. The mod-ifier 'small', however, is class 2, as are all modifiers derived from stative verbs

---

[18]For one single exception involving prenominal modifiers, see Killian (2015: 128).

with the suffix -*gàʔ*. This is why the associative marker, which links words in the NP, takes a class 2 marker. Since the gender markers are clitics in some case forms (see Killian 2019 [in Volume I]), the words on which the gender marker may appear make sometimes rather unexpected targets, such as the adverbial subordinator *gòm* in (48).

(48) Uduk (Koman; Killian 2015: 382)
    gòm=à   '*cí*   *yǐsà 'bór-ó'd*   *á'dī kí*   *màsh* *kī-Ø*
    for=CL2 'child(CL2) NEG good:IPFV-3SG 3SG NARR marry with-CL1
    yìl=à   *gwǎ'd-gàʔ*
    year(CL1)=ASS.CL2 small-NMLZ(CL2)
    'Because it's not good for the child to marry early.'

It is not entirely obvious what the target is in this case. In one possible analysis, *gòm* is the gender target, because this word bears the gender marker. In another possible analysis, which we prefer, the gender target is the clitic =*à* which happens to require a host for phonological rather than morphosyntactic reasons.

While almost all gender agreement in Uduk is adjacent, the Taa languages West !Xõo [=West Xoon] and East !Xõo [=East Taa] (Tuu [=Southern Khoisan], Taa) have several different kinds of agreement, only one of which exhibits adjacency. Agreement preceding the controller is necessarily adjacent, agreement within the NP with the NP head noun as controller is not. Adjacency agreement is illustrated in (49) with a compound. Its first part, which is not the head of the compound, triggers agreement on the preceding word. In Taa languages, the gender of the whole compound often differs from the gender of the parts of the compound. In (49), *ǁkx'oe nǁaen* [rain house.PL] 'clouds' has gender CL2A[SG]/CL2A[PL], but *ǁkx'oe* 'rain' (only singular) has gender 3 and *nǁahe* SG (*nǁaen* PL) 'house' has gender CL3[SG]/CL1[PL]. Adjacent gender in Taa languages is always controlled by the immediately following noun, which is the first part of the compound, *ǁkx'oe* 'rain(CL3)' in (49), rather than the whole compound 'cloud(CL2A)'. In (50), there is an associative plural formed from a person name. The associative plural has gender 4. However, the adjacency agreement is triggered by the gender of the person name, which is gender 1.

(49) West !Xõo (Tuu, Taa; Güldemann 2004): adjacency and compound gender
    n *si* *nǀa=e* *ǁkx'oe*   *nǁaen*   *ka*   *ǁari*
    1SG IPFV see=CL3 [rain(CL3) house.PL(CL1)](CL2A) REL.CL2A many
    ka
    REL.CL2A
    'I see many clouds.'

(50)   West !Xõo (Tuu, Taa; Güldemann 2006): adjacency and associative plural
    nna   *n/a=i*   *Tom-tu*   *ku*   *lai* *k=i*
    1SG:PRF see=CL1 [Tom(CL1)-ASS.PL](CL4) REL.CL4 stay OBLIQUE=CL1
    dertien   *ku*
    TOPONYM(CL1) REL.CL4
    'I have seen Tom and them who were at post 13.'

Some clitic hosts, such as the question particle /V in (51) (*V* means that the vowel must come from agreement), never occur without a following gender clitic. There is thus no gender marking, if there is no clitic host. If (51) were not a question, there would not be any gender marker.

(51)   East !Xõo (Tuu, Taa; Traill 1994: 18)
    /=ú   *tûu*   *à*   *sîl*
    Q=CL4 people(CL4) TENSE come
    'Did the people come?'

A third language where adjacency plays an important role is Nalca. Gender is triggered by the immediately preceding constituent. In (52) the noun *heik* 'hamlet' is followed by two case markers, dative plus comitative, which together express the notion of source. Case markers and gender markers are mutually dependent on each other and hence almost always co-occur in the case-number word following the noun. In (52), *heik* 'hamlet' is default noun *e*-gender, which is why the first case-number word in (52) is default noun *e*-gender. However, since the controller cannot control anything but the gender of the immediately following target, the second case-gender word is default phrase *a*-gender (which is never triggered by a lexical noun). There is no adjacency condition on the demonstrative suffix, which is repeated in both case-number words.

(52)   Nalca (Nuclear Trans-New Guinea, Mek; New Testament 40021001;
    Wälchli 2018)
    heik   *e-nye-k*   *a-nye-b*   *dara*
    hamlet DN-DEM-DAT DP-DEM-COM/ABL TOP
    'from this hamlet'

As argued by Wälchli (2018), gender in Nalca partly derives from sandhi phenomena, which motivates adjacency diachronically.

In both Nalca and Uduk, person names are important gender controllers (see Killian 2019 [in Volume I] for Uduk). In the Oceanic languages spoken on the island of Makira, gender classes have developed from an extension of person name markers, and, as discussed in §6.4, one of five classes in Owa originates from sandhi phenomena. Person names rarely have attributes. Thus it is natural that person name markers and person names are typically adjacent.

Adjacency-based gender developing from person name markers is not particularly complex when it first develops. There is only one agreement target, person name markers, and gender need not be specified in the noun lexicon, since it is organized by the animacy hierarchy (see §3). Person name markers can then travel down the animacy hierarchy, first expanding to older kinship terms and to other words typically expressing unique reference, in Makira languages also to the pronoun 'who'. Both Mek languages and Makira languages illustrate complexification in terms of number of classes (in Mek from two in Una and Eipo to four to six in Nalca, depending on whether only classes with lexical controllers or all classes are counted, and in Makira from two in Arosi to four in Kahua and five in Owa). Uduk gender is considerably more complex in terms of gender assignment (see Killian 2019 [in Volume I]) and it is not known how the system has developed. Gender in Taa languages is the most complex among the languages discussed here and nothing is known about the origin of the system.

7.3 Complex controllers

Complex controllers, where the controller consists of more than one word, are well-known from gender resolution in coordination, but also inalienable possession, names consisting of several words, and nominalizations. They provide evidence for gender being assigned to a group of words rather than to a single word. In this section we will consider evidence from inalienable possession in Paumari, from German restaurant names and Taa nominalizations. The section also discusses Nalca, where complex controllers are pervasive.

The assumption of complex controllers is uncontroversial for gender resolution in coordination, as illustrated in (44) in §7.1. However, gender resolution is not restricted to coordination. Consider (53) from Paumari, a language with two different gender systems: masculine/feminine and *ka*- vs. non-*ka*-noun classes. In Paumari, there is gender resolution in inalienable possession in the *ka*- vs. non-*ka* gender system. "If either the possessor, or the possessed noun (or both) belong to the *ka*- class, a modifier takes the *ka*- class marking, no matter which one of the two it modifies" (Aikhenvald 2010: 240). Put differently, *ka*-/non-*ka* gender in Paumari inalienable possession is computed with formal criteria in the same way as in gender resolution in coordination. In (53) the possessor is *ka* and the possessed noun is non-*ka*. The adjective displays *ka*-agreement whether it modifies the possessor or the possessed noun.[19] The possessor *bodi* 'mouth(N.*KA*;F)' also takes *ka-* because it agrees with *ojoro* 'turtle(*KA*;F)'.

(53) Paumari (Arawan, Aikhenvald 2010: 240): gender resolution in
      inalienable possession
      ojoro   *ka-bodi-ni*   *ka-karaho*
      turtle(*KA*;F) *KA*-mouth(N.*KA*;F)-3SG.F.DERIV *KA*-big
      'big mouth of a turtle' or 'mouth of a big turtle'

Further evidence for complex controllers comes from cases where gender is assigned on the level of group of words rather than on the level of words, which can hold for names consisting of several words. Plank (2015) discusses German restaurant names, which often can be neuter irrespective of the gender of the head noun.[20] The German lexeme *Orkan* 'hurricane' is masculine. However, in (54), *Orkan* is used as name for a restaurant and is neuter. (55) illustrates the same phenomenon with a name consisting of more than one word. *Oma* 'grandma' is feminine, but it is the whole expression *Oma Plüsch* 'grandma Plush' that is the restaurant name and as a restaurant name consisting of two words it is neuter.

(54) German (Indo-European, Germanic; Angerer 2009: 132)
      Hinter der   *wohl*   *schmalsten*   *Eingangstüre*
      behind DEF.GEN.SG.F probably narrow.SUPERL.GEN.SG.F entrance.door(F)
      Regensburgs   *verbirgt*   *sich* **das**   *Orkan.*
      Regensburg.GEN hide.PRS.3SG RFL DEF.NOM.SG.N hurricane(M)
      'The Orkan is hidden behind the probably narrowest door in Regensburg.'

(55) German (Indo-European, Germanic; tripadvisor.de [2018])
      Das   *Oma*   *Plüsch liegt*   *direkt* *an der*
      DEF.NOM.SG.N grandma(F) Plüsch lie.PRS.3SG directly at DEF.DAT.SG.F
      Donau.
      Danube(F)
      'Oma Plüsch is located directly at the River Danube.'

---

[19] For similar phenomena in the related language Jarawara, where the *ka*/non-*ka*-gender was lost, see Dixon (2000) and §3.4.

[20] According to Plank (2015), recategorization with default-neuter for German restaurants pragmatically indicates the distance of the name to gastronomy. Traditional names for restaurants, such as *Die Sonne* [the.F sun(F)] and *der Ratskeller* [the.M council.cellar(M)] are not neuter. Neuter gender for German restaurants is not obligatory.

Adjectives as parts of names commit restaurant names to the gender of their lexical head: *der Bayerische Bahnhof* [the.M.SG Bavarian.M/F/N.SG railway_station(M)], even if the adjective cannot inflect: *die Schweizer Grenze* [the.F.SG Swiss.ADJ border(F)]. This only holds if the adjective is part of the name. With non-restrictive adjectives neuter is possible: *das spießige Vier Jahreszeiten* [the.N.SG petty-bourgeois.M/F/N.SG four seasons.PL] (Plank 2015). To state this in more general terms, if the lexical head is already combined with a potential target before the name is completed, the noun phrase has already committed itself to a gender, thus gender assigned to the name as a whole is no longer available. The same rule holds, for instance, for names of roses, which can be default-feminine unless they contain an adjective (*die Helmut Schmidt, die Gruß an Helgoland* [the.F.SG greeting(M.SG) to Helgoland], but *der Gelbe Engel* [the.M.SG yellow angel(M)]).[21]

While complex controllers in German are limited to names, Nalca has them all over. In Nalca there is a general alternation between one of four lexical genders – masculine *be-*, feminine *ge-*, phonologically assigned CV-gender *ne-* (the controller has the structure CV or V), and default noun *e*-gender – and default phrasal gender *a-*, which is never controlled by a lexical noun. The switch is syntactically determined. Having certain modifiers ("allies") helps the noun impose its lexical gender, having certain other modifiers ("obstacles") conditions the phrasal default. Most nouns cannot impose their lexical gender unless they have an attribute ally that helps them impose their gender, as in (56) about boys' initiation rites, where *me* 'boy, child' with lexical CV-gender *ne-* triggers *ne-* only if there is an adjective in the NP, but has default phrase *a-* if it is bare in the NP.

(56) Nalca (Nuclear Trans-New Guinea, Mek; Binzell n.d.; Wälchli 2018: 71)
      me   *a-ra*   *gɛlɛlinga* *sɔob-vka*
      child(CV) DP-TOP unnoticed enclose.in.netbag-CVB
      bɔ-ba-lam-ek.   *Nauba me*   *ne-ra* *al-biyok*
      carry-go-HAB/IPFV-PST.3PL big   child(CV) CV-TOP 3SG-alone
      ba-lam-ok.   *Mek me*   *ne-ra* *sɔob-oka*
      go-IPFV-PST.3SG small child(CV) CV-TOP enclose.in.netbag-CVB

---

[21]Sometimes the gender of names is paradigmatically inherited – names of roses (F), apples (M), pears (F), beers (N), and wines (M) have the gender of their general noun as default. However, in case of restaurants (N), ships (F), motorcycles (F), and cars (M), the default-gender is not inherited from a general noun.

bɔ-ba-lam-ek.

carry-go-HAB/IPFV-PST.3PL

'They carried the boy away secretly in a netbag. A big boy went by himself. A small boy they carried in a netbag.'

There is a parallel in Mopán Maya, where gender also has developed from an extension of person name markers. Gender in Mopán Maya is marked only on one target, the "gender marker" proposed to the noun or adjective+noun, which distinguishes masculine *aj* and feminine *ix* (Contini-Morava & Danziger 2018). Only a minority of nouns have gender, most nouns take the article *a* instead (which, unlike gender markers, is not compatible with possessive pronouns). Nouns that are not gendered when used in isolation may sometimes option-ally have a gender marker if there is an attributive adjective. Contini-Morava & Danziger (2018: 138) give an example from a story where *a ch'o'oj=o* [ART rat=ECHO] 'rat' is first introduced without gender and then occurs with adjec-tives and gender markers as *aj noxi' ch'o'oj=o* [GM.M big rat=ECHO] and *aj tz'i' ch'o'oj=o* [GM.M small rat=ECHO] with a gender switch very similar to that in the Nalca example (56). The difference is that Nalca *a-* default phrase gender is for-mally integrated in the gender system and the alternation is more systematic in Nalca.

In some languages, sentential nominalizations can be gender controllers. Nalca sentential nominalizations, if not followed by a noun, can take one of three phrasal suffixes and each of the three resulting constructions without a nominal head takes another gender. Two of the three suffixes are homonymous and are distinguished only by the gender they control (Wälchli 2018): male nominaliza-tions with suffix *-nya* (57) take masculine gender *be-* and thing-nominalizations with suffix *-nya* (58) take neuter gender *ne-* (which happens to have the same form as CV-gender in (56)).

(57)   Nalca (Nuclear Trans-New Guinea, Mek; New Testament, 44010021; Wälchli 2018: 80)

    *... [ugun-da na   e-le-nu-lum]-**nya**   **be-ra, na-ra***

    2PL-TOP   1SG[22] search-IPFV-OBJ.1SG-PRS.2PL-**NMLZ.M** **M-TOP** 1SG-TOP

    al-an   ...

    3SG-DEM

    '... I am he whom you are looking for!', lit. 'I am he, the one [you are looking for me]'

---

[22]In Nalca nominalizations, O is often zero marked, but 'thing' nominalizations tend to have a dative-marked O as in (58).

(58) Nalca (Nuclear Trans-New Guinea, Mek; New Testament, 43006026; Wälchli 2018: 80)

... *[ugun-da na-k   e-le-nu-lum]-**nya***   ***ne**-ne-ra* ...
   2PL-TOP 1SG-DAT search-IPFV-OBJ.1SG-PRS.2PL-**NMLZ.N** N-DEM-TOP

'...you seek me not [because you saw signs]...', lit. 'this fact that [you are looking for me]'

Nalca nominalizations are morphologically marked, but there is also a semantic component, which is strengthened by the homonymy of two different morphological markers. There is no competition with lexical gender as there are no lexical heads in the construction. The sentential nominalization with its morphological marker must immediately precede the gender target (adjacency agreement, see §7.2).

A similar construction is found in East !Xõo, where, however, nominalizations can only take one gender. The nominalization suffix -*sà* can attach to the verb stem (*!qāhe-sà* [hunt-NMLZ(CL2)] 'hunting') or to a verb phrase, the subject of the nominalization being expressed by a possessor in a POSSESSOR /V+GENDER.MARKER POSSESSED construction. The preposition /V takes the gender of the immediately adjacent following controller. The only available controller is the nominalized verb phrase, which is a constituent without any lexical head from which the gender of the nominalization derives.

(59) East !Xõo (Tuu, Taa; Traill 1994: 30; Güldemann 2004: 7)

   ùh ń́   bà   /ɡ̄-n   là   /ùã̄   /àũ̄ /nàa
   CL4 TENSE ASPECT refuse-1SG POSS.CL2 hold/give.CL2 tobacco(CL2)
   /nēe-sà
   to.3-NMLZ(CL2)

'They disapprove of my giving him tobacco.'

To summarize, there is a diverse set of formal syntactic groups that can all function as complex controllers. These include NP-coordination (gender resolution), possessed and possessor in inalienable possession, names consisting of several words, nominalizations, and – in Nalca – any kind of noun phrase. Since compounds are also groups of words, we can also add compounds taking compound gender, as in Khasi (see §6.3), as a further type of formal groups serving as complex controllers.

7.4 Complex targets

Target groups or complex targets must be invoked whenever the agreement rela-tion applies between the controller and a formal group of words. This is the case, for instance, if the target is a complex predicate consisting of several verbs (lex-ical verb and auxiliary) which share the same argument structure. This is most clearly visible if there is agreement with the object and the agreement is realized on an auxiliary as in (44) from Italian discussed in §7.1.

Haspelmath (1999) discusses the Italian data together with two languages where agreement goes with the absolutive to which we turn now: Godoberi (Nakh-Daghestanian, Andic) and Hindi and Urdu (Indo-European, Indo-Aryan). In (60) from Hindi/Urdu, the feminine noun 'bread' is the object of 'eat', but all three verbs in the verb complex display agreement. This means that the three verbs together make up one complex target. (61) from Godoberi shows so-called "long distance agreement", which Haspelmath (1999) analyzes as an instance of clause-union. In our terms, the four verbs in (61) together constitute a formal group sharing the object argument and are a single complex target, with the neuter plural of the absolutive realized on three of them ('want' never takes agreement).

(60)   Hindi/Urdu (Indo-European, Indo-Aryan; Wunderlich 1994: 23;
       Haspelmath 1999: 147)
       Raam ne   roṭii   khaa-nii   caah-ii   thii.
       Ram   ERG bread(F)[SG] eat-INF.F.SG want.PST-F.SG be.PST.F.SG
       'Ram had wanted to eat bread.'

(61)   Godoberi (Nakh-Daghestanian, Andic; Haspelmath 1999: 143)
       ilu-ɬi   quči-be   r-al-u   r-uL-i
       mother-DAT book(N)-PL[ABS] PL.N-read-CVB.PST PL.N-finish-INF
       q'ʷaraʕ-anta   ru-k'-a.
       want-CVB.PRS PL.N-be-AOR
       'Mother wanted to finish reading the books.'

Nakh-Daghestanian languages are known for their extensive clausal agree-ment, which takes different forms in different languages. In Godoberi all verbs of a unified clause together constitute an agreement target (see also the similar case of Archi in §7.2).

Complex gender targets involving complex predicates also occur in Coastal Marind. In (62) the patient *ebta* 'sago thatch' is an argument of the transitive verb *takun* 'make roof', but agreement is shown on the auxiliary *balen* 'finish (intr./tr.)'.[23]

(62) Coastal Marind (Anim, Marindic; Bruno Olsson, p.c.)
      ebta   *takun*   *mbya nak-ap-ba<h>in*
      sago.thatch(IV) make.roof NEG   1.A-CONTESSIVE-finish<IV.U>
      'I didn't finish making the sago thatch roofing.'

In discussing agreement in case, Lehmann (1982: 222) points out that viewing the head noun as controller of agreement is problematic notably when an NP lacks a head noun. This also holds for gender in independent headless NPs, such as Italian *Tu sei la più bella* 'you are the most beautiful one (F)' (see §4). Here it is obviously not the article controlling feminine gender on the adjective or vice versa, but the whole headless noun phrase in the predicate is a target group assigned feminine singular by a latent contextual controller.

If attributes in headless NPs form target groups, the question arises as to whether a series of target words within the same NP could generally be considered to constitute a target group. In many languages gender agreement with multiple targets in an NP is a way to signal that these elements all belong together in one formal group (which can be contiguous or non-contiguous). This would then mean that in NP agreement the head noun is the controller and the whole NP is the target. A potential problem is then that the head noun controlling the NP is also part of the NP. Lehmann (1982: 223) suggests that this could be solved with the following condition "If B is the head of an NP A, B is not said to agree." This may seem entirely ad hoc at first glance. However, if we take into account that agreement is displaced information, it is a priori excluded that the controller can be part of the target. Target groups are formal groups, but not all formal groups are syntactic constituents. The easiest solution is to say that in NP agreement, the target group is the NP minus the head noun. What we have said for NPs here also applies to clauses in the Daghestanian languages Archi and Godoberi where the whole clause can be the agreement target (see §7.2).

A further case of complex targets are gendered clauses in Ngan'gityemerri serving as relative clauses, discussed in §4.3.

Table 16 summarizes the kinds of formal groups involved in complex controllers and complex targets mentioned in §7.3 and §7.4.

---

[23]For similar phenomena involving person in another language in South New Guinea, Nen (Morehead-Wasur), see Evans (2015).

Table 16: Formal groups serving as complex controllers and complex targets in gender agreement

	Formal groups manifest in gender agreement
Complex controllers	NP coordination
	Inalienable possession
	Names consisting of several words
	Nominalizations
	Compounds
	Complex noun phrases
Complex targets	Complex predicates
	Clauses
	Noun phrases
	Gendered clauses (relative clauses)

7.5 Features as mature conditions

Morphosyntactic features are a highly mature form of information transfer. In non-mature gender systems it is often difficult to identify a [NUMBER] feature. For instance, Ngan'gityemerri has a noun class *awa-* glossed 'mob' for a group of people (Reid 1990: 296), but number does not otherwise interact with gender. If we consider what makes gender a good feature, it is pretty much the same characteristics that are traditionally invoked for delimiting genders from classifiers: there is a closed set of values with up to twenty members (Dixon 1982: 215), the same system of values applies to different targets, all nouns are controllers, and gender markers are bound elements on target words. All these properties are indications of maturity (see also §6). In our view, features are emergent and develop through grammaticalization, thus there is no reason to assume a universal set of morphosyntactic features. The existence of languages with two parallel concurrent gender systems, such as Paumari (Aikhenvald 2010) and Burmeso (isolate; Donohue 2001), is an argument against a universal set of features (see also Dahl 2000b, Corbett et al. 2017: 252 and Svärd 2019 [in Volume I], Liljegren 2019 [in Volume I], and Sinnemäki 2019 [this volume], for other languages with two parallel gender systems).

Further evidence that features are not all there is to displaced information in agreement comes from what Corbett 2006 calls conditions. Conditions are "factors which are not themselves realized directly in agreement" (Corbett 2006: 176).

As a rule of thumb, features, but not conditions, are usually glossed. Many examples of conditions pertain to the realm of animacy and related notions such as individuation. In Miya (Afro-Asiatic, West Chadic), attributive demonstratives take plural agreement only if the controller is animate. Since the masculine-feminine gender opposition is neutralized in the plural in Miya, this entails the peculiar pattern that in the plural masculine and feminine are realized only with inanimate controllers: *nákən víyayúw-awàw* [this.M.SG fireplace(M)-PL] 'these fireplaces' (Schuh 1998: 193; Corbett 2006: 178). Recall from §7.4 that groups of verbs in some Nakh-Daghestanian languages can form target groups, a phenomenon often referred to as "long distance agreement". In Tsez (Nakh-Daghestanian, Tsezic) "long distance agreement" is conditioned by topicality. A target group of several verbs agrees with the absolutive of the subordinate verb only if the S or O of the subordinate clause is a topic (Polinsky & Comrie 1999; Corbett 2006: 197).

Conditions are conditions on agreement. As a consequence, if a condition turns into a feature, the result is usually a combination of two features in cumulative exponence. If features develop from conditions it is no coincidence that features often cumulate with each other. Since animacy is a very frequent type of condition, it is no coincidence that animate gender or other gender values reflecting animacy frequently cumulate with other agreement features, such as number (this is the topic of §8).

Corbett (2006, chap. 6) distinguishes absolute conditions, factors that always determine a certain choice of agreement value (the two examples given so far in the previous paragraph), and relative conditions, factors that favor a certain optional choice of agreement value. We change the terms to *obligatory* and *optional*, which we think are more easily understandable. In Russian, controllers consisting of two conjuncts are more likely to trigger plural agreement when animate than when inanimate, which is an instance of an optional (relative) condition on agreement (Corbett 2006: 179).

When conditions develop into features, it is reasonable to assume that they are first optional. This suggests the following grammaticalization path (63):

(63) Grammaticalization path from condition to feature
      optional condition on agreement > obligatory condition on agreement >
      gender (= cumulative feature)

Consider the example of (in)animate subgenders in Russian and other Slavic languages (Corbett 1991: 42, 2006: 118; see also §3.5). In Russian, only the major declension class for feminine nouns has dedicated accusative forms, and only in the singular. Masculine singular nouns and all plural nouns take the genitive form if animate and the nominative form if inanimate. In Serbian-Croatian-Bosnian, only the masculine singular is affected, so there are only two subgenders in the masculine. Slavic (in)animate subgenders originate as a condition on case, but in Russian animacy has gone quite a long way to become lexical gender, as the subgender of most nouns is fixed irrespective of their referent-based animacy (see §3.5). For instance, *konkurent* 'competitor' is always animate; however, *duši* 'souls(F)' (in feminines, the animacy distinction is visible only in the plural), The Pentagon and The White House are never animate. Russian has undergone the development in (63). Huntley (1980) surveys evidence from several Slavic languages demonstrating how the category was extended from object function to use with other functions of the accusative with prepositions, and from definite human to human and animate. In Polish the genitive singular form is further extended to individualized inanimates (Björn Wiemer, p.c.).

In Slavic there was already gender (masculine, feminine and neuter) before the development in (63). The path in (63) is possible also when there is no gender originally. However, there must be some form of agreement already. An interesting example in this respect is Lakhota (Siouan) with plural actor and undergoer agreement on the verb with animate nouns, which Sinnemäki (2019 [this volume]), following Van Valin (1977: 36–37), classifies as an instance of gender. Another possible interpretation is that the "enclitic =*pi* indicates plurality of all human subjects" (Mithun 1999: 508) and that there is no verbal agreement at all in Lakhota verbs. The question as to whether animacy in Lakhota can be interpreted as a feature is very much dependent on how number, which it conditions, is interpreted. A condition cannot turn into agreement if the category which it conditions is not agreement.

Pnar attributive adjectives, discussed in §4.3, illustrate that an animacy distinction can emerge in a language with gender without connection to that gender system. Recall from §4.3 (example (29)) that one type of attributive adjectives in Pnar optionally takes the preposed nominalizer *wa*. However, with human head nouns, the nominalizer *wa* is obligatory with this adjective type. This is an optional condition as far as non-human nouns are concerned, and an obligatory condition as far as human nouns are concerned.

We may conclude that features can evolve from conditions on agreement and that if there is a feature in agreement already, another one, especially if animacy-based, can more easily join it in cumulative expression (realized by the same marker).

7.6 Nominal gender targets and the decategorialization of nouns

Agreement usually has nominal controllers and non-nominal targets. Nominal is used here in the sense of a cover term for nouns, noun phrases and formal groups of nouns. However, nouns outside their prototypical discourse function of referring (Croft 2001: 87) in modification or predication use tend to lose some of their nominal properties. Hopper & Thompson (1984: 711) call this decategorialization. Decategorialization of nouns is highly relevant for gender, since the possibility to serve as a target for gender may be a property of nouns undergoing decategorialization.

An important kind of nominal target is adnominal possessors. The double nature of possessors is most obvious in independent possessors which can either agree with the possessed or with the possessor (the latter is person indexing) and in some languages, such as German (see, e.g., Wälchli 2019 [this volume]) and Biak, they agree with both.[24] Adjectivized possessors are more inclined to agree with the head noun than nominal possessors. However, adjectivization does not always preclude possessors from being controllers for modifiers themselves, as in (64) from Upper Sorbian. It is unexpected that the Sorbian adjective can trigger agreement in (64), but given that this is the case, it is not unexpected that gender here is referent-based (since there is no lexical noun that could trigger the agreement).

(64)   Upper Sorbian (Indo-European, Slavic; Schuster-Šewc 1976: 27; Corbett 2006: 62)

    w [naš-eho   nan]-ow-ej   chěž-i
    in our-GEN.SG.M father-POSS.ADJ-LOC.SG.F house(F)-LOC.SG

    'in our father's house'

NOMINAL GENDER TARGETS (nouns or noun phrases that are gender targets) are a heterogeneous group of phenomena where a noun or noun phrase looks as if it was an agreement target of another noun or NP. (65) from German is an example of a nominal gender target. Most German nouns for professions have to mark gender derivationally (derivational gender). The predicate noun carries a redundant marking whose choice is determined externally, in (65) by the referent of the subject.

---

[24]Biak (Austronesian, Cenderawasih Bay) distinguishes animates and inanimates only in the plural. Body parts that occur in pairs are often animate, as in *tanduk v<y>e=s-ya* [horn <3SG>POSS=3PL.ANIM-SPEC] 'its horns (of one animal)' (van den Heuvel 2006: 106). Excrements, such as 'spit', are plural and inanimate: *an inf se=na* [NMLZ spit 3PL.ANIM.POSS=3PL.INAN.SPEC] 'their spit (of those people)' (van den Heuvel 2006: 273).

(65) German (Indo-European, Germanic): predicate professional noun marked
for gender

Angela Merkel ist   die   beste
Angela Merkel be.PRS.3SG DEF.NOM.SG.F best.NOM.SG.WEAK

Kanzlerin,   die   wir   je   hatten.
chancellor.DERIV.FEM REL.ACC.SG.F we.NOM ever have.PST.3PL

'Angela Merkel is the best chancellor we ever had.'
www.plattentests.de/mobile/forum.php?action=showThread&id=89713
[2018-10-10]

Despite its female derivational suffix *-in*, *Kanzlerin* in (65) denotes the whole
set of male and female Chancellors of Germany (otherwise the set could not
be restricted by 'best'), among which there only was a single female one so far.
The same holds when Margaret Thatcher in 2013 was called *Großbritanniens um-
strittenste Premierministerin* 'Great Britain's most controversial prime minister'
(www.spiegel.de › Politik › Ausland › Tories Apr 11, 2013).

While adjectives do not agree in predicative position in German, superlative
predicates mark gender agreement in the singular on the article. The superlative predicate necessitates a forced choice of gender, which is determined externally. In (66) there are two competing NPs with different lexical gender, differ-
ing also in their level of taxonomy. In German there is usually agreement by
co-conceptualization with the hyperonym in the construction type instantiated
in (66), in Latvian with the hyponym (67), and Italian is mixed, as illustrated in
(68–69).

(66) German (Indo-European, Germanic): agreement by co-conceptualization
with hyperonym

Von   allen   Tieren   ist   der   Löwe
from all.DAT.PL animal(N).DAT.PL be.PRS.3SG DEF.NOM.SG.M lion(M)

das   majestätischste.
DEF.NOM.SG.N majestic.SUPERL

'Among all animals the lion is the most majestic one.'

(67) Latvian (Indo-European, Baltic): agreement by co-conceptualization with
hyponym

No   visiem   zvēriem   lapsa   ir
from all.DAT.PL.M animal(M).DAT.PL fox(F).NOM.SG be.PRS.3

visgudrākā.
all.smart.COMP.NOM.SG.F.DEF

'Among all animals, the fox is the smartest one.'

(68) Italian (Indo-European, Romance): agreement by co-conceptualization
with hyponym

Tra   tutti   i   fiori   la   rosa   è
among all.PL.M DEF.PL.M flower(M).PL DEF.SG.F rose(F).SG be.PRS.3SG

la   più   bella.
DEF.SG.F more beautiful.SG.F

'Among all flowers, the rose is the most beautiful one.'

(69) Italian (Indo-European, Romance): agreement by co-conceptualization
with hyperonym

Tra   tutti   i   paesi   la   Svizzera
among all.PL.M DEF.PL.M country(M).PL DEF.SG.F Switzerland(F).SG

è   il   più   neutrale.
be.PRS.3SG DEF.SG.M more neutral.SG

'Among all countries, Switzerland is the most neutral one.'

Nominal targets are highly relevant for gender from a diachronic point of view since it is well-known that gender markers can grammaticalize from nouns (Heine & Reh 1984: 225). Since grammaticalization from nouns to gender markers is gradual, there must be intermediate cases between noun targets and agreement proper with non-noun targets.

Yagua (Peba-Yagua) and other Amazonian languages demonstrate how agreement with noun targets can gradually give rise to agreement by decategorialization of nouns. Yagua has a large set of classificatory formatives, many of which can be shown to originate from nouns (Payne 1986: 120), such as *jạ́ạ́* 'water' which is also the classifier for liquid. In attributive constructions as in (70), the classifier can be repeated, which looks like agreement.

(70) Yagua (Peba-Yagua; Payne 1986: 126)
jityạạ-jạ́ạ́   vánuqui-jạ́ạ́
breast-CLF:LIQUID hot-CLF:LIQUID
'hot milk'

Based on evidence from another Amazonian language, Miraña, which is not genealogically related to Yagua, Grinevald & Seifart (2004: 278–279) argue that noun classes may grammaticalize from such constructions as (70) in Yagua where classifiers are used as repeaters.

It is particularly interesting in Yagua that different kinds of elements display different degrees of decategorialization. Attributes expressing qualities in Yagua are nouns and not adjectives and can also carry a non-classifying nominalizer, as in *mucata-y-sara* [boil-INTR-NMLZ] 'boiled'. The major function of the classifier in modifiers is to nominalize the modifier and marking is actually rare, since many adjective-like concepts are inherently nominal and need not be nominalized (Payne 1986: 127). However, with demonstratives and numerals, decategorialization is more advanced. Demonstrative and numeral roots cannot stand without suffixation of a classifier, but classifiers do not cause a change in word class (Payne 1986: 127). Agreement is not obligatory, since the general inanimate classifier *-ra* can be used on a demonstrative with any head noun.

When nominal targets develop into agreement proper, the agreement marker may originate from a noun, as in Yagua, but it can also originate from a nominal derivation marker. Dressler & Doleschal (1990) show that Italian agent nouns in appositive use, such as *una risposta rivelatrice* [one.SG.F answer(F).SG reveal.AGN.F.SG] 'a revealing answer', *uno sguardo rivelatore* [one.SG.M glance(M).SG reveal.AGN.M.SG] 'a revealing look' agree in gender, which testifies to their adjectivization (see also Luraghi 2015: 75–76 for examples from other Indo-European languages).

A development from nominal targets to agreement proper also occurs in cases of gendered clauses turning into relative clauses, as in Ngan'gityemerri (Reid 1997) discussed in §4.3.

Decategorialization of nouns also occurs in the development of person name markers as in Iraya (Austronesian, North Mangyan; data from the New Testament) *laki Howan* 'John' (from *lalaki* 'man') and *bayi Mariya* 'Mary' (from *babayi* 'woman'), *laki Satanas* 'the devil'. For the development of nouns and NPs to anaphoric gender markers see Wälchli (2019 [this volume]). As shown by Mithun (1986), object noun incorporation may develop into a marker of verb classification. In the Northern Iroquoian languages, the incorporated elements are nominal, as in (71):

(71) Cayuga (Iroquoian, Northern Iroquoian; Mithun 1986): noun
    incorporation in classificatory use
    So:wá:s akh-náhskw-aę'.
    dog   I-**domestic.animal**-have
    'I have a (pet) dog.'

In the Southern Iroquoian language Cherokee, only relics of noun incorporation are left in the form of distinctions of a closed set of choices for a few verbs ('to give a living thing/liquid/a long, rigid object/a flexible object/else') (Mithun 1986: 392). According to Mithun (1986), verb classifiers may express noun classification. Passer (2016a), however, emphasizes the differences between (supposed) verb classifiers and nominal classification based on a diverse sample of thirteen languages. Even though it is a matter of debate how far verb classifiers can reach in becoming classifiers, they certainly belong to the complex of phenomena where decategorialization of nouns is involved in the development of some sort of asymmetric coreference relationship, even though it is not the core function of verb classifiers to classify nouns.

7.7 Target-controlled gender and idiomatization of gender agreement

The basic idea of the notion of agreement is that the feature value is selected by the controller. However, in some cases, the target contributes to the choice or selects the value entirely, which, similarly to nominal targets treated in §7.6, contributes to make agreement fuzzy.

Mohawk (Iroquoian) has four genders: masculine, feminine-indefinite, feminine-zoic, and neuter. Neuter differs from feminine-zoic only by not allowing for dual and plural number. Gender is expressed cumulatively with number and person in verbal prefixes. According to Mithun (2014: 155), relatively few verb stems can be used with either animate or inanimate arguments. "[V]erbs for growing, catching, burying, and having a proper name require grammatically animate patients, that is, they routinely occur with Zoic Patient prefixes" (Mithun 2014: 155). The verb for getting ripe, however, requires neuter gender. The gender for corn, for instance, is zoic when it is described as growing or short and neuter when it is ripe or dry (72):

(72) Mohawk (Iroquoian, Northern Iroquoian; Mithun 2014: 154)
    o-nenhst-E'   *ken'=ok*
    N-corn-NOUN.SUFFIX small=just
    *ni-**konti**-hneni-es-on's*
    PARTITIVE-3ZOIC.PL.AGT.**length**-be.long-DISTR
    'The corn (i.e., corn stalks) are (ZOIC) very short.'

In Mawng, there are five genders, masculine, feminine, land, vegetation, and edible, which, among other things, are distinguished for S and O arguments in verbal prefixes (A arguments distinguish only masculine vs. non-masculine)

(Singer 2012: 984). However, many verbs tend to have different meanings with different gender prefixes. At the same time there are few overt nouns (Singer 2018: 117). Each gender has several semantic domains associated with it. For instance, liquids are land gender, plant food is edible gender, most animals are masculine, and crabs are feminine. Hence, the Mawng verb *wa* 'consume' usually means 'drink' with land gender, 'eat plant food' with edible gender, 'eat animal food' with masculine gender, and 'eat crab' with feminine gender. In other instances, gender marking on verbs is even more idiomatic. For instance, the Mawng verb *-apti* 'have, hold' tends to have land gender when used in the meaning 'understand'. Explicit objects are often missing and most nouns for knowledge are land gender, but *mayali* 'knowledge' in (73) is vegetation gender. With this noun, *-apti* 'understand' can either take controller-induced vegetation gender or target-induced land gender:

(73) Mawng (Iwajdian Proper; Singer 2012: 972)
      *K-**ang**-apti-Ø*   *ma-lijap*
      PRS-3N_M>3LAND-understand-N_PST VEGETATION-little
      mayali.
      knowledge(VEGETATION)
      'She understands a little bit of knowledge.'

When asked to express 'drink blood' with the noun *maningul* 'blood (vegetation gender)', a native speaker prefers target-induced land gender (Singer 2012: 970), since liquids are usually land-gender.

Controller-induced gender is nothing else but lexical gender (see §3). Target-induced gender is the verbal equivalent of referent-based gender. Target-induced gender and referent-based gender are both opposed to lexical gender. If the term verbal gender were not already taken (*genus verbi* = voice), we might use this label here for the classification of events rather than referents. Singer (2012: 978) draws the parallel to classificatory noun incorporation in Mawng's neighbor Bininj Kun-Wok (Gunwinyguan) (see §7.6 for noun incorporation in Iroquoian).

Mawng also has many cases of so-called lexicalized agreement (agreement with an argument that does not exist; Singer 2011). For instance, the verb *-marranyi* 'wave (at OBL)' always has third person land gender in the prefix where direct object is marked, but never has an identifiable direct object. According to Singer (2011: 640) lexicalized agreement is also found in a number of other Northern Australian languages spoken near to Mawng, such as Tiwi (isolate) and Gaagudju (isolate). It also occurs in Southern Tiwa (Kiowa-Tanoan; Frantz 1995: 84, "empty arguments") and in Ket (Yeniseian). However, Ket pseudo-actant markers (Vajda 2003: 79) in, among other things, involuntary causatives and stative resultatives, differ from Mawng in that they always can be interpreted as (default) neuter gender. Despite the complexity of the Ket verb morphology, this is actually not that much different from dummy subjects in Germanic languages such as English *it rains*.

If we extend the notion of lexicalized agreement to free pronouns, idioms with pronouns such as English *to make it* 'to succeed' or *to rough it* 'to live without usual conveniences' (famous through Mark Twain's travel book *Roughing It*) can also be considered idiomatized agreement. An example with a masculine idiomatized pronoun from a Germanic language variety is Bernese Swiss German *er git ihm!* [he give.PRS.3SG him] 'he makes an effort, hurries up' (Greyerz & Bietenhard 1997: 125) with a semantic shift 'hit a male person in a fight' > 'make an effort'. An example of a gender relic in an idiom in Germanic is the specification of time in more conservative varieties of Standard Swedish with the feminine personal pronoun *hon* 'she':

(74) Swedish (Indo-European, Germanic; Teleman et al. 1999: 276): feminine
      gender relic with time idiom
      *Hur mycket är   klockan/**hon**?   – **Hon** är   väl bortåt tre.*
      how much be.PRS clock.DEF.SG.CM/she   she be.PRS well towards three

      'How much is the time/"she"? –"She" is around three, I guess.'

Idiomatization involving gender agreement may take many different shapes. In the Torricelli language Walman (Dryer 2019 [in Volume I]), masculine is mainly restricted to human males, some larger animals and a few quasi-animate natural phenomena. In a few idioms, however, nouns that are usually feminine or pluralia tantum are masculine, notably *olokol* 'mountain(PLT)' and *anako* 'sky(F)' in idioms for 'to thunder' and *won* 'chest(F)' in idioms expressing emotions.

If gender is only retained in idioms, it disappears as a grammatical category. In this, gender is not different from any other grammatical category. In Iwaidja (Iwaidjan Proper), which is related to Mawng, gender is lost entirely and in Garig-Ilgar (Iwaidjan Proper), it is reduced to a two-value system (masculine vs. non-masculine) (Evans 2000: 115). Relics of object gender agreement can only be found in idioms (Evans 2000 calls them "pseudo-argument affixes"). Neuter gender (=Mawng land gender) and vegetable gender in Garig-Ilgar and Iwaidja still appear with a few verb roots, such as 'consume' and 'know' in idiomatic expressions in contexts where it is productive in Mawng (Evans 2000: 116; Singer 2011: 643). This can be compared to the many idioms in Swedish that retain case endings, as *till handa* 'at hand' and many other examples with an old genitive plural ending *-a*.

7.8 Summary

Agreement is prototypically a relationship between nouns and noun-associated forms. The prototypical discourse function of nouns is to express referents and nouns have a tendency to decategorialize if they are used in other functions, such as predication and modification. Decategorializing nouns and noun phrases gradually lose their ability to refer by themselves and some of their marking can then be reanalyzed as displaced information of referring expressions elsewhere in discourse. This displacement of information need not be syntactic, but can also be paradigmatic. There is not always an overt controller, which makes it impossible to view agreement as a purely syntactic process.

In this section we have seen that agreement is much more complex than just a syntactic relationship between two words. The relationship can be semantic and agreement can be inter-sentential. Both controllers and targets may be complex and consist of several words. To the extent that agreement is syntactic, its function is to indicate formal groups, and these formal groups can be of three different kinds: controller groups, target groups and the grouping of controller and target. Even though agreement has the potential of indicating discontinuous groups with considerable distance between the elements, agreement is often local and it is not uncommon for controller and target to be adjacent. In several cases from widely different languages, gender agreement requires adjacency, which is an underresearched phenomenon. Much of the fuzziness of agreement derives from the fuzziness of coreference, the most important specific relationship that can hold between controller and target. However, as we have seen in §7.2, coreference is by far not the only kind of relationship between controller and target.

8 Cumulation of gender with number, case and person

Gender marking systems are more often than not conflated with the encoding of other morphosyntactic features such as number, case, and person. In §8.1, we consider cumulation with number, in §8.2 cumulation with case and/or person. §8.3 puts cumulation into the wider context of the formalization of gender.

8.1 Gender and number

Patterns of interaction between gender and number seem to be particularly prominent in the functioning of gender systems, and, in fact, number is claimed to be "the category most often realized together with gender" (Corbett 1991: 189). Creissels et al. (2008) formulate an Africa-specific generalization on the nature of this relation. They claim that African languages devoid of gender tend to have less grammaticalized strategies for the marking of nominal plurality, whereas in languages with gender, number distinctions tend to be obligatory and expressed both through nominal and non-nominal marking, often in cumulation with gender. Di Garbo (2014) and Di Garbo & Agbetsoamedo (2018) bring empirical support to this claim by investigating patterns of exponence of gender and number values in two partially overlapping samples.[25] Di Garbo (2014) is based on a sample of 100 African languages (84 with gender, 36 without). The sample used by Di Garbo & Verkerk (2018) is based on the gendered subset of the dataset in Di Garbo (2014), and thus consists of 84 languages, all of which have gender. In line with Creissels et al. (2008), the study by Di Garbo (2014: 134) reveals that, in the languages of Africa, pervasive patterns of encoding on noun-associated forms almost always involve both gender and number, and that, in the absence of gender, number marking tends to remain optional and to operate at the phrasal level (one marker per noun phrase). The study also concludes that cumulative exponence of gender and number is by and large the most pervasive pattern of encoding in both nominal and non-nominal (noun-associated forms) domains of gender marking. Out of a sample of 84 languages, only the North-Central Atlantic language Wamey is found to display non-cumulative encodings of gender and number, both on nouns and on all relevant noun-associated forms. In this language, however, non-cumulative exponence of gender and number is the result of a recent innovation whereby the plural prefix of gender 1/2 (to which human nouns are typically assigned) became the default plural marker, generalized to all nouns and gender- and number-inflecting forms, independently of the animacy of the noun referent (Di Garbo & Agbetsoamedo 2018: 187). A similar development is attested in the Kinshasa variety of Lingala (Atlantic-Congo, Central-Western Bantu), but only in the nominal domain. In Kinshasa Lingala, nouns can receive double plural marking: by means of a cumulative gender/number marker and the plural prefix *ba-*, which, as in the case of Wamey, originally was the plural prefix for nouns of gender 1/2, most typically human, but which is now used as a generalized plural marker, with human and non-human nouns alike (Di Garbo & Agbetsoamedo 2018: 188). In addition to investigating the distribution of cumulative exponence of gender and number, Di Garbo & Agbetsoamedo (2018) also survey the occurrence of gender syncretism in the context of non-singular number values. The results show that syncretism of gender in the context of number is also very widespread in the languages of the sample (attested in 67 out of 84

---

[25]See also Güldemann & Fiedler (2019 [in Volume I]) for a thorough discussion of co-exponence of gender and number in Niger-Congo gender systems.

languages), and that its occurrence always presupposes cumulative exponence of gender and number values.

These findings offer an interesting parallel to earlier results by Carstairs (1987), who finds a similar relationship between syncretism and cumulative exponence in the domain of case and number marking: case distinctions are more likely to be syncretized in the context of plural number than any number value in the context of any case distinction. In addition, these patterns of syncretism always presuppose cumulative exponence between the two features. Carstairs (1987) interprets these findings as pointing to the existence of functional asymmetries between case and number. Di Garbo & Agbetsoamedo (2018: 205–206) suggest that the same reading could be applied to the results on gender and number. When non-cumulative exponence of gender and number emerges from the reanalysis of earlier cumulative systems of encodings (as in the case of Wamey and Kinshasa Lingala), this is likely to be linked to the development of new (and initially semantically motivated) strategies for the marking of nominal plurality. Similarly, the distribution of patterns of syncretism involving gender and number is strongly asymmetrical, with gender – and not number – being the morphosyntactic feature that is most likely to be syncretized.

There are various ways in which an asymmetric relationship between gender and number makes sense from a functional point of view. On the one hand, number has a more obviously semantic core function than gender. On the other hand, if gender preferably tends to develop in markers that already express another grammatical category, then the functional asymmetry between gender and number must also be interpreted in a developmental perspective. This is well in line with Nichols' (1992: 142) hypothesis that "agreement triggers noun classification (rather than vice versa)". Here are some examples where it has been argued that gender markers have developed in close connection to number markers.

In various Berber and Semitic languages, the feminine *t* also has singulative and diminutive functions. Mettouchi (2000: 221) argues that the diminutive and singulative (partitive) function of the *t-* marker in Berber is diachronically prior to the feminine function (see also §5.2). Similarly, it has been suggested that the Arabic gender system was not sex-based originally. Moscati (1964: 86) speaks of "a more complex system of classes within which the category of number has to be included as well".

The Khasian languages have innovated feminine pronouns for second and third person singular (Daladier 2011: 184), which at least partly seem to derive from the second and third plural forms not distinguishing gender with different vocalism for singular and plural forms (Khasi 2PL *phi*, 2SG.F *pha*, [vs. 2SG.M *me*], 3PL *ki*, 3SG.F *ka*, [vs. 3SG.M *'u*]).

Interesting is also the case of Yagua mentioned by Wälchli (2019 [this volume]), where a woman who has given birth to a child or children is referred to with dual number. Payne (1985: 42) does not consider Yagua to have gender, but Yagua is obviously an example of a language where sex can condition the use of number.

8.2 Gender and case and person

Given the pervasiveness of number as the the category type most obviously connected with gender, any other category type will look meager in comparison. Moreover, case cannot be expected to be equally prominent because case is more restricted cross-linguistically than number. However, we think that case is also very relevant for the cumulative character of gender and this mainly for two reasons.

First, gender in anaphoric function in free and bound pronouns tends to exhibit some form of suppletion or neutralization according to grammatical relation (that is, grammatical case, if case is not restricted to dependent marking, but also includes indexical head marking on verbs), as shown by Wälchli (2019 [this volume]) specifically for feminine gender (but there is no reason to believe that feminine is exceptional in this respect). In this function, case occurs together with gender most typically in personal pronouns and pronominal affixes. Hence, here we deal with cumulation of gender with person and case rather than with case only. In addition, one person, the third, is clearly more dominant than others, and, within third person, the third person singular is more dominant than the plural, which in turn brings us back to the dominance of number as the feature with which gender interacts the most.

Second, there are several instances where gender displays systematic syncretism patterns with case, which can sometimes be shown to go back to the very origin of gender. In other instances, the origins of the patterns remain unexplained.

A well-known source of animacy in gender is differential case marking. In §3 and §7.5 we have discussed the example of Slavic, where animacy in gender has developed from differential object marking. Luraghi (2011: 456) argues that the neuter vs. non-neuter distinction in Indo-European has developed from differential subject case marking. In both Slavic and Proto-Indo-European, the origin of gender from case entails a cumulation of gender and case marking, with case in actor and undergoer roles neutralized in the less animate gender. In both Slavic and Proto-Indo-European, there is already case agreement within the NP when gender develops. In Indo-European, forms from two different demonstrative stems, animate (*so) and inanimate (*to), were integrated into an already existing case agreement system (Luraghi 2011: 456).

Two instances where the origin of pervasive syncretism patterns between case and gender are not known are Algonquian and Uduk. Algonquian languages have systematic syncretism between singular obviative and inanimate plural (where proximate and obviative are not distinguished; see Table 15 in §6.4). In Uduk, there is a syncretism of class 1 ergative case and class 2 accusative and associative cases (see §5.2 and Killian 2019 [in Volume I]).

In some languages of New Guinea, notably in Nalca (Mek) and in Abau (Sepik), gender and case are expressed in the same word adjacent to the head noun. Svärd (2019 [in Volume I]) speaks of "case marker hosts". In Mek, it can be shown that gender was originally restricted to a few postpositions distinguishing case functions and was secondarily extended to other postpositions in Nalca by analogy (Wälchli 2018).

What links gender together with case in several of the instances discussed so far is animacy (see also §3 and §3.2). While connections between gender and case due to animacy effects can be expected to be related predominantly to grammatical case, there are also interesting connections between gender and local cases. In some languages, locatives are well-connected with gender systems, in others they are completely outside of it. In many Bantu languages, locatives are integrated in gender systems (see, e.g., Bresnan & Kanerva 1989 for Nyanja [=Chicheŵa]). In Meskwaki, however, the locative case lacks gender or number distinctions (Thomason 2003: 12). In several of the Oceanic languages spoken on the Island of Makira, a place gender is developing from the local preposition *i* (see §6.4). These languages thus can help us understand how locative and gender can be intertwined. In Owa, *i* can still be interpreted as a preposition when used in isolation, but in the "sentence medial" form, used among other things before objects and following prepositional verbs, nouns of the location class (mainly place names) must take *ki* (<*k+i*), which is *k-* plus class marker: *tanga-a k-i Jerusalem* [to-3sg MEDIAL-LOC J.] 'to Jerusalem' as opposed to *tanga-a k-o Herod* [to-3sg MEDIAL-M H.] 'to Herod'. Therefore, Mellow (2013: 26) lists zero for "sentence initial" and *ki* for "sentence medial" article forms of the location-noun class.

8.3 Cumulation and the degree of formalization of gender

In this section we will argue that there is a correlation between cumulation of gender with other grammatical categories and the degree of formalization of gender, as represented by obligatoriness of gender agreement and noun classification, as well as by number of agreement targets. The degree of formalization in gender and classifier languages has been investigated by Passer (2016b). Passer compiles two indexes consisting of seven features each, measuring the "Dimension of Form" and the "Dimension of Transparency" of gender and classifier systems. These indexes are used to investigate the degree of grammaticalization of systems of nominal classification (classifiers and gender; for gender, which he defines very narrowly, he uses the term "concord"). Passer argues that conventionalization (reducing transparency) and formalization can be conceived of as independent pathways of systems of nominal classification. With its 37 systems from 36 languages, Passer's sample is not particularly large, but it has the advantage that it has world-wide scope, is stratified and also comprises both gender and classifier systems. Passer takes for granted that the Form features and the Transparency features form two dimensions, but the extent to which the features cluster can actually be tested on the basis of Passer's database. Figure 4 shows a hierarchical clustering of a comparison of the ranking of the 14 features and the two indexes with squared Spearman's Rho (which is equally sensitive to positive and negative correlations; varclus() in the R Hmisc library described in Harrell 2001).

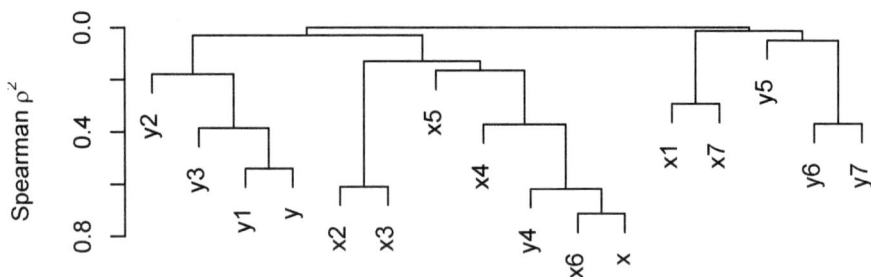

Legend: x total formalization value, x1 inventory size, x2 host number (targets within NP), x3 locus operandi (targets outside of the NP), x4 obligatoriness, x5 boundedness, x6 multiple marking on various types of targets in the NP, x7 exhaustivity of classification, y total transparency value, y1 degree of semantic assignment, y2 number of different assignment rule types, y3 number of assignment rules, y4 INDEPENDENCE FROM OTHER GRAMMATICAL CATEGORIES, y5 discreteness of markers, y6 redundancy, y7 flexibility

Figure 4: Clustering of Passer's (2016b) Form (x) and Transparency (y) features

Figure 4 suggests that there are actually more than two dimensions and that the total indexes do not reflect all of their components equally well. The three first transparency features (y1–3), and apparently also the whole y-index, measure similar things, viz. how transparent assignment is, ranging from semantic to opaque. Degree of formalization (x) seems indeed to be an important issue, but, as it turns out, y4 (in)dependence of other grammatical categories – even though arguably indicating transparency – actually correlates with multiple marking on various types of targets in the NP (x6), obligatoriness (x4), and boundedness (x5), which seems to indicate that it is a characteristic property of a grammaticalized category of gender to exhibit interdependence with other grammatical categories.

We do not want to suggest here that gender does not exist if it does not cumulate with number, case, or person. However, where there is gender and no cumulation, gender tends to have a low degree of formalization. Notably, gender has a tendency not to be obligatory and not to be marked on multiple agreement targets, if it does not cumulate with other categories. Let us consider a few cases in point.

Within Sino-Tibetan, Limbu (van Driem 1987: 21) and other Kiranti languages (Ebert 2003b: 508) have a very limited masculine-feminine gender opposition on attributive adjectives (one target type). The suffixes, masculine *-pa/ba* and feminine *-ma*, although they can be shown to be of nominal origin (*ma* and *pa* also mean 'mother' and 'father', for instance, in Camling; Ebert 2003a: 535), are common derivational suffixes in adjectives throughout Tibeto-Burman languages. In Classical Tibetan (Sino-Tibetan, Bodish), adjectives have nominal suffixes (*-pa/-ma/-po/-mo* or *-ka*): *chen-po* 'large', *legs-pa* 'good', *gsha-ma* 'worthy'; "a few adjectives may express the natural gender of their referent by alternating the masculine *pa/po* and feminine *ma/mo* suffixes, but most adjective forms are fixed" (DeLancey 2003: 373). Not all adjectives, where the markers occur, do agree and agreement is not obligatory even in those adjectives where it occurs.

The Hindu Kush Indo-Aryan languages Khowar, Kalasha, and Dameli (Liljegren 2019 [in Volume I]) distinguish animacy in the root of the copula. Number and person are marked through suffixes attached to the animate/inanimate roots, and thus do not cumulate with the morpheme where animacy is marked.

Mopán Maya masculine and feminine gender (originating from person name markers) have only a single marking target. Only a minority of nouns are gendered and the gender marker can sometimes be omitted (Contini-Morava & Danziger 2018: 133).

In Ngan'gityemerri (discussed in §4.3, included in Passer's sample), gender does not cumulate and not all nouns are classified in noun classes.

In languages where gender has been borrowed, gender is often not in cumulation with another grammatical category and not obligatory. For instance,

Chamorro has borrowed the Spanish masculine and feminine gender markers as -*o*/*u* and -*a* along with Spanish words which results in a semi-productive sex-based type of gender system without cumulative exponence (Stolz 2012; Di Garbo & Miestamo 2019 [this volume]).

However, before hasting to conclusions, it is important to note that degree of formalization has played an important role in delimiting gender from classifiers. Notably, obligatoriness is a traditional feature used for distinguishing between classifiers and gender (e.g., Dixon 1982: 160: "a grouping of all the nouns of a language [...] so that there is some overt indication of the class of a noun within any sentence in which it occurs"). According to these criteria, most of the languages discussed in this section would count as lacking gender. By applying these criteria, there is thus a danger of excluding by definition languages where gender has limited degree of formalization (see also Wälchli 2019 [this volume]). Yet, we have chosen to make the connection between gender and cumulation explicit in our definition of gender, which contains the statement that gender typically exhibits cumulative exponence with number, case, and/or person (see §1). However, this does not mean that categories lacking cumulation with other categories should be excluded from the study of grammatical gender.

8.4 Summary

To sum up, cumulation of gender with number, case and/or person is pervasive across the languages of the world. In addition, in a few cases we are able to establish through diachronic comparison that cumulative exponence with other morphosyntactic features can be reconstructed, and thus exists from the very origin of the history of a language- and/or family-specific gender system. This can most likely be explained with the fact that gender tends to develop from pre-existing grammatical systems. For instance, gender may arise as a condition on the distribution of a specific number value (as in animacy-constrained plural marking) or case distinction (as in differential argument marking). More research is needed to explore the diachronic relationship between gender and number, case, and/or person, but it is fair to say that interdependence of gender with these other grammatical category types is the rule rather than the exception. This typological finding is in need of diachronic explanation in each individual instance.

Cumulative exponence is a violation of the Principle of One-Meaning–One-Form (one and the same affix is associated with two or more grammatical meanings) and the Principle of Independence (the encoding of gender distinctions is dependent on number, case, and/or person values) and thus qualifies as a phenomenon that fosters complexity (see §2). The fact that gender typically has cumulation with other nominal morphosyntactic features naturally means that gender is usually complex.

9 Lexical plurality and grammatical gender

9.1 Introduction

In many languages, certain nouns tend to be inherently specified for number, that is, to display lexicalized number values. This fact has been claimed to blur the boundaries between the gender and number domain. The gender systems of the Papuan languages Coastal Marind and Walman, described by Olsson (2019 [in Volume I]) and Dryer (2019 [in Volume I]) are a case in point, which we discuss in this section in the light of the larger typological context.

The label pluralia tantum is typically used in the literature to refer to nouns that only exist in the plural-marked form, as in English *scissors, trousers, leftovers,* and *supplies.*[26] Broadly speaking, pluralia tantum nouns fall within the wider domain of LEXICAL PLURALITY. The term encompasses a variety of semantic and formal phenomena, both morphological and syntactic, which stem from the fact that plurality is a lexicalized property of a given noun, or, simply put, part of what there is to know about it (Acquaviva 2008: 2). In this section we use the labels LEXICAL PLURALS and LEXICAL PLURAL NOUNS as general terms to refer both to pluralia tantum nouns, that is, nouns with fixed plural number, as well as to nouns that are inherently plural, but that are not necessarily marked as plural.

Previous studies both on the spoken and signed modality (Koptjevskaja-Tamm & Wälchli 2001; van der Meer 2015; Börstell et al. 2017) show that some broader semantic domains may be identified as recurrent attractors of lexical plurality across languages, while languages differ considerably with respect to the specific concepts that tend to be associated with lexical plurality. In Table 17 we list some major semantic domains – they need not necessarily exclude each other – that have been shown to be most typically associated with lexical plurality. We illustrate each semantic domain with one exemplar concept with an English label. Notice that the concept chosen to exemplify a particular semantic domain need not to be a lexical plural of English, which is indicated by small caps.

Concepts typically expressed by lexical plurals differ in whether they are countable or non-countable, a distinction that not necessarily neatly aligns with

---

[26]For a recent, typologically informed, classification of types of pluralia tantum nouns, see Corbett (2018).

Table 17: Semantic domains associated with nominal lexical plurality across languages

Semantic domain	Exemplar concept
Abstract[a]	ANGER
Collectives	CATTLE
Dual entities/Internally complex concept	GLASSES
Disease	MEASLES
Festivities and time intervals	SEASON
Liquids and masses	SALIVA
Locations	WOODS
Situations/activities involving more than one participant	FIGHT

[a]Abstract nouns can be either count or non-count and it is reasonable to suspect that it is the latter type that is especially likely to be attracted by the lexical plurality domain. We are grateful to Östen Dahl for this suggestion.

the domains in Table 17. Countable units may refer to what we may think of as singular entities. The English nouns *leftovers* and *supplies* have a mass noun reading and it is not possible to talk about one item of them. Liquids and masses are usually non-countable, but also abstract concepts often belong to this category. Conversely, we can talk about *a pair of scissors/trousers*, which, in this respect, behave as count nouns. Languages differ as to whether they use special constructions to count multiple instances of a particular entity denoted by countable lexical plural nouns (as in English *one pair of scissors/trousers*), a topic which is not further addressed here.

As mentioned above, in spoken languages, nouns that are lexically plural typically only occur in the plural form. A parallel situation is found in the signed modality where lexical plurality is associated with double-handed signs, what Börstell et al. (2017) refer to as ARTICULATORY PLURALITY. Similarly to the spoken modality, where pluralia tantum nouns are typically marked by regular, productive number morphology, double-handed articulation is used in sign languages to mark non-lexical, compositional plurality with various types of signs (Carl Börstell, p.c.).

9.2 Lexical plurality and grammatical gender: a crosslinguistic overview

If a language has number agreement, lexical plural nouns typically trigger plural agreement, and the formal marking patterns are typically indistinguishable from those triggered by morphological plurals. While this would seem to be a rather unproblematic fact, it turns out that in languages with grammatical gender and large classes of lexical plural nouns, lexical plurality may come to interact so closely with the morphosyntactic encoding of gender that the two domains (gender and number) may appear to be merged into one. This is the situation that we encounter in two of the Papuan languages investigated in the first volume of this work, Coastal Marind (Olsson 2019) and Walman (Dryer 2019). Let us briefly summarize the Coastal Marind and Walman situations (for more extensive analyses, we refer to the individual chapters).

There are four genders in Coastal Marind: masculine, feminine, and two inanimate genders, which Olsson refers to as gender I, II, III, and IV. While gender I and II vary according to number (singular and plural), the two inanimate genders are number-invariant. In addition, the plural marker used for the two animate genders (I and II) and the marker of gender IV are the same, and this syncretism is systematic across all agreement targets, even through the patterns of suppletion that regulate argument indexing on verbs. While male humans are gender I and female humans gender II, there are no strong tendencies that help predict which inanimate nouns should be assigned to gender III and which other ones to gender IV. Nevertheless, some regularities can be detected. For instance, some of the semantic domains that are typically associated with lexical plurality tend to cluster in gender IV (e.g., internally complex objects, diseases, heterogeneous objects). This, together with the fact that the plural marker of the animate genders is systematically syncretic with the marker of gender IV, suggests that there might be an even tighter relationship between gender IV and nominal plurality. According to Olsson, this relationship can be understood in diachronic terms. He speculates that at least some of the gender IV nouns are the diachronic descendants of a large class of pluralia tantum nouns which, as such, used to trigger semantically motivated plural agreement, the same plural agreement pattern triggered by animate masculine and feminine nouns. Such an originally coherent class of pluralia tantum nouns later expanded "resulting in a large, semantically heterogeneous residue gender, with a small core that still reflects the 'plural semantics' of the original pluralia tantum grouping" (Olsson 2019 [in Volume I], p. 219).

Walman has two clear-cut gender values, masculine and feminine. In addition, together with the diminutive, Dryer (2019 [in Volume I]) describes lexical plural nouns as a gender-like phenomenon. Lexical plurals in Walman are not marked as plural, but can be described as syntactically pluralia tantum nouns because, independently of whether their denotational meaning is singular or plural, they always trigger plural agreement. Semantically, the range of meanings expressed by lexical plural nouns in Walman strongly overlaps with the semantic groupings identified in the typological literature on the topic: objects consisting of multiple parts, dual entities (especially body parts coming in pairs), mass nouns. While there can be mismatches (not all mass nouns are, for instance, pluralia tantum), the semantic makeup of this class of nouns is highly consistent. According to Dryer, what could justify describing the Walman pluralia tantum nouns as an independent gender value, alongside masculine and feminine, is the sheer number of lexemes in this class: 81 instances of lexical plurals are attested in Dryer's corpus, as opposed to 40 instances of masculine nouns.

Interactions between lexical plurality and grammatical gender similar to those attested in Coastal Marind and Walman are also found in other New Guinean languages. An interesting parallel to Coastal Marind is, for instance, the Ok language Mian. In Mian, along with the masculine and feminine genders there are two inanimate genders: neuter 1, which is sensitive to number distinctions, and neuter 2, which is number-invariant and whose marker is the same as the plural of neuter 1 (for a detailed description of the gender system of Mian, see Fedden (2011). Olsson (2019 [in Volume I]) notes that in Mian the overlap between neuter 2 nouns and the semantic domains typically associated with lexical plurality is even stronger than in Coastal Marind.[27] In his survey of gender systems in the languages of New Guinea, Svärd (2019 [in Volume I]) mentions the case of another New Guinean language, Ama (Left May), where lexical plurals systematically align with one gender value in a way that is at least partially reminiscent of the Coastal Marind system. There are three genders in Ama – masculine, feminine, compound – and nouns that are semantically connected with lexical plurality (in particular, nouns denoting objects having many parts and mass nouns) are always assigned to the compound gender (Årsjö 1999: 68). In sum, the language-specific and cross-linguistic data presented in separate contributions to the two volumes of this work show that a number of genealogically unrelated New-Guinean languages have classes of nouns, which fall in between

---

[27]Depending on the genealogical classification adopted, Anim and Ok, the language families to which Coastal Marind and Mian, respectively, belong, may be also seen as distantly related members of the Trans New Guinea phylum (see §11.1).

representing a proper gender value and an unusually large class of nouns with fixed plural number/lexicalized plurality. The spread of this pattern within New Guinea and its role as a possible characteristic feature of the gender systems of this area would deserve to be further investigated.

There are a few typological parallels to the New Guinean languages discussed above, where, other things being equal, lexical plurality has an impact on patterns of encoding in the domain of gender and number agreement. One such parallel is Cushitic languages, or at least a subset of them. Cushitic languages are a branch of the Afro-Asiatic family, spreading from Eritrea all the way down to Tanzania and consisting of approximately 40 languages, further divided into four subgroups: Agaw, Beja, East Cushitic, and South Cushitic. Nominal number marking in Cushitic is typically not obligatory. Speakers can leave nouns unmarked for number or use a variety of derivational suffixes and/or morphophonological strategies to mark a noun as singular or plural. In the literature on Cushitic languages, number-unmarked nouns are referred to as nouns with general number or as transnumeral nouns, whereas the derivational singular and plural morphemes are labeled as singulative and plurative. Cushitic languages typically have sex-based gender systems with a masculine-feminine distinction. Yet, some languages of the family are described as having three genders, with the third gender class beyond masculine and feminine being traditionally referred to as "the plural". There are two main scenarios under which some Cushitic languages have been analyzed as displaying a tripartite gender system with a distinction between masculine, feminine and plural gender.

Under the first scenario, languages have agreement patterns that are used to signal that the controller is plural, but that are not used with all plural controllers. This is, for instance, the case of the East Cushitic language Baiso. The gender and number agreement system of Baiso has been described in detail by Corbett & Hayward (1987) and Corbett (2000). In the following, we provide a brief overview of its most relevant properties.

Baiso has two gender distinctions in the singular, masculine and feminine. Verbs agree in gender and number with the subject. With the majority of plural-marked nouns, the agreement pattern triggered by the verb is the same as the one triggered by masculine singular nouns, irrespective of whether the noun is masculine or feminine. This is illustrated in examples (75) and (76), which show gender and number agreement with masculine singular and plural nouns, and feminine singular and plural nouns, respectively.

(75) Baiso (Afro-Asiatic, East Cushitic; Corbett 2000: 181): gender and number agreement with masculine nouns

    a. *lúban*   *hudure*
       lion(M).GENERAL slept.M

       'The lion slept.'

    b. *luban-jool hudure*
       lion-PL   slept.M

       'The lions slept.'

(76) Baiso (Afro-Asiatic, East Cushitic; Corbett 2000: 182): gender and number agreement with feminine nouns

    a. *kimbír*   *hudurte*
       bird(F).GENERAL slept.F

       'The bird slept.'

    b. *kimbir-jool hudure*
       bird-PL   slept.M

       'The birds slept.'

In addition to the two verb forms exemplified in (75) and (76), Baiso has a third verb form, which is only used when the subject (i.e., the controller noun) is the third person plural pronoun, a noun marked by the paucal suffix or one of the underived nouns listed in Table 18. Because it is used with third person plural pronouns, this third verb form is traditionally glossed as PL, "plural". The use of the plural verb form with two paucal-marked nouns (one masculine and one feminine) is illustrated in (77).

(77) Baiso (Afro-Asiatic, East Cushitic; Corbett 2000: 181–182): plural agreement

    a. *luban-jaa hudureene*
       lion-PAUC slept.PL

       'A few lions slept.'

    b. *kimbir-jaa hudureene*
       bird-PAUC slept.PL

       'A few birds slept.'

Table 18: Underived nouns selecting plural agreement in Baiso, adapted from Corbett & Hayward (1987: 9)

Semantic groupings	Nouns
Body parts	*ilkoo* 'tooth, teeth'; *kalaljaa* 'kidneys'; *luḳḳaa* 'foot, feet, leg(s)'; *iḷọ o* 'eye(s)'; *ogorroo* 'hair'; *moo* 'hips, lumber region'
Collectives	*saé* 'cattle'
Mass nouns	*eenoo* 'milk'; *soo* 'meat'; *udú* 'faeces'
Objects coming in pairs	*keferoo* 'sandals'

The eleven nouns in Table 18 always select the plural verb form. The noun for 'kidneys', *kalaljaa*, can be described as a "paucal tantum" noun as it is only attested in the paucal-marked form (Corbett & Hayward 1987: 9). The suffix *-oo*, in which many of the nouns listed in the table end, is a productive plural suffix in several Omo-Tana languages, a subgroup within East Cushitic to which Baiso also belongs. However, *-oo* is not a productive plural suffix in Baiso (Corbett & Hayward 1987: 19). Within Cushitic studies, the agreement pattern illustrated in (77) has been analyzed as the morphosyntactic realization of a third gender, the plural gender (Mous 2008: 146). The analysis is motivated by the fact that the nouns listed in Table 18 select plural agreement even though they are morphologically underived for number. For these nouns, plurality is a lexically specified feature as masculine and feminine are for other nouns. Corbett & Hayward (1987) and Corbett (2012) describe the peculiar agreement preferences of the nouns listed in Table 18 as lexical exceptions and reject the analysis of plural as a gender value. Semantically these nouns tend to denote collectives ('cattle'), entities that are prone to occur as pairs ('kidneys'), or masses ('meat'). They always select plural agreement because they are semantically and lexically plural. Di Garbo (2014: 121–127) develops this line of reasoning one step further and describes Baiso as a language with a split system of number agreement. While the majority of nouns that undergo regular morphological plural marking do not trigger dedicated plural agreement but an agreement pattern that is syncretic with the one triggered by masculine singular nouns, as in examples (75) and (76), dedicated plural agreement is used only with a closed set of controllers: plural pronouns, paucal-marked nouns, the lexical plurals and a handful of plural-marked nouns that tend to denote small groups. Di Garbo (2014) speculates that the split number agreement system attested in Baiso is semantically motivated and that the controllers of dedicated plural agreement rank higher on a scale of semantic plurality than derived plural nouns.

There is yet another profile of languages within Cushitic that has been analyzed as displaying a tripartite gender system with plural as a gender value along with masculine and feminine. These are languages that have dedicated patterns of plural agreement that are used with all plural controllers: third person plural pronouns, derived plurals (that is, nouns that are morphologically marked as plural), and nouns that are unmarked for number but nevertheless control plural agreement. In these languages, gender distinctions are always neutralized in the plural. In addition, in these languages nouns that are number-unmarked but that always trigger plural agreement constitute a rather large lexical class. This large class of inherently plural nouns encompasses both typically lexical plural concepts and concepts that are not associated with lexical plurality, somewhat similarly to nouns of gender IV in Coastal Marind. An example of such a language is Konso, an East Cushitic language spoken in Ethiopia. Konso displays subject agreement on the verb, which has three different inflectional forms depending on whether the subject argument is masculine (78a), feminine (78b) or plural (78c and d). The masculine and feminine forms are used if the subject is singular, the plural form is used if the subject is a plural-marked noun (78c) or a noun that is lexically specified as plural (78d). Definite markers, which are suffixed to nouns, only distinguish between singular and plural. The plural form of the definite marker is used both with overtly plural-marked nouns and with nouns that are lexically specified as plural.

(78) Konso (Afro-Asiatic, East Cushitic; adapted from Tsegaye 2017: 36–37): gender and number agreement

a. *ćmayta-siʔ*   *i=kutiʔ-ay*
   old.man-DEF.SG 3=sit.down-PFV.3M

   'The old man sat down.'

b. *aleeta-siʔ*   *i=piʔ-t-i*
   hut-DEF.SG 3=fall-3F-PFV

   'The hut fell.'

c. *laha-dd́-siniʔ*   *i=muk-i-n*
   ram-PL-DEF.PL 3=sell-pass-IPFV.FUT-3PL

   'The rams will be sold.'

d. *filaa-sini?*   *i=pat-i-n*
comb-**DEF.PL** 3=be.broken-**PFV-PL**
'The comb disappeared.'

Orkaydo (2013) and Tsegaye (2017) analyze the plural agreement pattern, as realized on verbs and definite markers, as the morphosyntactic manifestation of a gender value. According to this analysis, plural-marked nouns are also considered to be plural in gender. The main arguments that Orkaydo (2013) and Tsegaye (2017) present in support of the plural as a gender-value analysis in Konso are: (i) the large number of nouns that are underived for number and only trigger plural agreement[28] and (ii) the fact that not all of these nouns are semantically analyzable as instances of lexical plurals.[29]

The possibility of positing an independent gender value for lexical plural/pluralia tantum nouns has also been defended for Russian by Zaliznjak (1977). Russian has a tripartite gender system with a masculine-feminine-neuter distinction that is further subject to a number of animacy-based conditions. Gender distinctions are neutralized in the plural. Pluralia tantum nouns always trigger plural agreement, irrespectively of whether they refer to singular or plural entities. This is illustrated in (79).

(79)   Russian (Indo-European, Slavic; Corbett 2012: 237)
odn-i   *san-i*
one-**PL.NOM** sledge-**PL.NOM**
'one sledge'

In virtue of the properties illustrated in (79), according to Zaliznjak, pluralia tantum nouns in Russian are better analyzed as representing one independent agreement class, and thus one independent gender value.

Corbett (2012: 237–238) notices that *plural-as-a-gender-value* analyses have only been proposed for languages where gender distinctions are systematically neutralized in the plural. This is the case for Russian and indeed this is also the case for Coastal Marind, Walman, Baiso and Konso. In languages where gender distinctions are maintained in the plural, lexical plurals are usually distributed

---

[28] Orkaydo (2013: 318–330) lists 471 Konso nouns. Out of these, 92 are classified as being inherently plural (or, following his analysis, plural in gender), 134 as feminine, and 245 as masculine.
[29] By inspecting the meanings of the 92 nouns classified by Orkaydo (2013: 318–330) as inherently plural we found that more than half of them (about 50) have denotational meanings that align with the most typical semantic domains of lexical plurality (e.g., mass nouns, body parts coming in pairs, names of activities requiring multiple participants).

across different gender values, but still share the properties of carrying only plural morphology and/or of only triggering plural agreement. This is for instance the case of Italian, where the plurale tantum noun *pantaloni* 'trousers' is masculine and selects only masculine plural agreement while the plurale tantum *forbici* 'scissors' is feminine and selects only feminine plural agreement as in *i pantaloni* 'the.F.PL trousers' and *le forbici* 'the.M.PL scissors'. Analyzing Italian pluralia tantum nouns as belonging to separate gender values would then mean positing at least two different lexical plural genders in the language, one formally overlapping with the masculine plural and one with the feminine plural. Corbett (2012: 237–238) uses this argument to reject the cross-linguistic validity of *plural-as-a-gender-value* analyses. Conversely, he stresses that in languages where gender distinctions are neutralized in the plural, lexical plural nouns are de facto outside the system of gender distinctions because this system is only active in the context of singular number, which they are devoid of. The exceptional agreement preferences of these nouns are thus to be analyzed as a consequence of them being irregular from the point of view of number and not of gender.

While we agree that having or not having gender distinctions in the plural is a relevant typological parameter to take into account when assessing the type of encodings that lexical plurality may trigger in the domain of gender and number agreement, we believe that language-specific analyses where lexically plural nouns are described as making up a gender value of their own *should not* be a priori considered to be fallacious. The descriptive adequacy of language-specific categories should always be distinguished from what is generalizable across languages with the support of typologically adequate comparative concepts (Haspelmath 2010). Arguing, and demonstrating, that lexical plural nouns in some gendered languages exhibit gender-like properties does not amount to say that the lexical plural nouns of all languages with gender should be analyzed as instances of an independent gender value. In languages like Coastal Marind and Konso, the lexicalization of the plural number value and the presence of large classes of nouns with fixed plural number, which only trigger plural agreement, clearly blurs the distinction between the gender and number domain.

9.3 Extreme lexicalization of number values in Kiowa-Tanoan

In addition to the cases mentioned in §9.2, the gender system of yet other languages may be described as being entirely based on the lexicalization of number values.[30]

---

[30]This subsection was written by Bruno Olsson. We are very thankful to Bruno for his general contribution to our discussion of gender and lexical plurality.

The most extreme cases of lexicalization of number values are arguably found in the languages of the Kiowa-Tanoan family of North America, illustrated here with Kiowa data from Sutton (2014: 310) and Watkins & McKenzie (1984: 78). Kiowa distinguishes singular, dual and plural numbers through a combination of suffixation on nouns and indexing prefixes on verbs. Nouns occur in two forms: the unmarked basic form and the inverse form, derived by suffixation. For every noun in the language it must be specified whether the noun occurs in the basic or the inverse form when reference is made to one, two or three or more entities (the labels basic and inverse are specific to the Kiowa-Tanoan descriptive tradition and should not be confused with similar labels in other grammatical traditions). For example, *tógúl* 'young man' is used in the basic form for reference to one or two young men, whereas the inverse form *tógú·dɔ́* must be used for reference to three or more young men. This contrasts with the noun *'ɔnsó·* 'feet', which occurs in its basic form when reference is made to two or more feet, but in the inverse form *'ɔnsôy* when reference is made to a single foot. For other nouns the basic form refers to two instances of the referent, as with *'álɔ·* '(pair of) apples', whose inverse form *'álɔ·bɔ* is used to refer to one apple or three or more apples. A fourth type of nouns lacks the inverse form and occurs in the basic form regardless of the cardinality of the referents.

Each noun in the language exhibits the basic-inverse alternation according to one of these four patterns. In the Kiowa-Tanoan literature the four patterns are referred to as noun classes and numbered I-IV (following Wonderly et al. 1954). Nouns in the four superclasses are further divided into subclasses according to their combinatorics with verb prefixes indexing person/number of core arguments. The intransitive third person paradigm consists of four prefixes: singular Ø-, dual *ę̀-*, plural *gyà-* and inverse *è-*. The inverse verb prefix occurs whenever the inverse form of the noun is used, and the singular and dual disambiguate the number reference of nouns in their basic form. It is the behavior of the plural prefix that reveals the need for subclasses. For example, some class II nouns ('bucket', 'saw', 'arrow') trigger the plural prefix when reference is made to three or more entities, while other class II nouns ('bed sheet', 'peg, stake', 'peyote, cactus') trigger the singular prefix when reference is made to three or more entities; these two patterns form subclasses IIa and IIb. When the full range of indexing patterns is taken into account, the total number of subclasses is between 7 (e.g. Watkins & McKenzie 1984) and 9 (Harbour 2008; the difference in granularity depends on whether some marginal patterns are counted as their own subclasses or not).

It is clear from Wonderly et al.'s (1954) use of the term *noun classes* that researchers realized early on that the Kiowa-Tanoan system of number marking amounts to a form of noun classification. Nichols' (1992: 141) conclusion that "noun classification appears to have arisen out of number agreement in the Kiowa-Tanoan family" explicitly couches this in diachronic terms (an interpretation repeated by Aikhenvald 2000: 377 and Luraghi 2011: 451).

The parallel with languages such as Coastal Marind, Walman, Konso and Baiso is most evident in the class of Kiowa nouns that trigger invariant plural prefixation on the verb regardless of the cardinality of the referent (class IVc in Watkins & McKenzie 1984). According to Harbour (2008: 46) this class consists of objects composed of several parts ('trousers', 'book', 'necklace', 'tepee', 'headdress'; the multi-part semantics are also noted by Merrifield 1959: 270, "a single item is looked upon as having several constituent parts"), granular mass nouns ('flour', 'salt', 'sand') and abstracts ('problem', 'dance', 'word, language'), which echoes the pluralia tantum-like semantics of the nouns discussed for Coastal Marind, Walman, Konso and Baiso. The important difference is that Kiowa takes the lexicalization much further, and requires that every noun in the language be specified for its "inherent number". For some of the Kiowa noun classes this can be expressed straightforwardly as an inherent number value, so that Kiowa $k^h\acute{ɔ}\cdot d\acute{e}$ 'trousers' (class IVc) is inherently plural, and $\hat{ʔ}\acute{a}lɔ\cdot$ '(pair of) apples' (class III) is inherently dual. For other classes the pattern is more complicated, as with *tól* 'peg, stake' (class IIb) which triggers singular verb prefix when the cardinality of the referent is 1, the dual prefix with cardinality 2, but the singular also when cardinality is 3 and higher.

We think that the Kiowa-Tanoan systems of "inherent number" must be considered gender according to the Hockettian conception of gender as "classes of nouns reflected in the behavior of associated words". This also seems to be the contention of Harbour, who – working in the Chomskyan tradition – equates the Kiowa noun classes with Indo-European gender, with the main difference residing in their semantic basis: the former is based on number and the latter on sex. For our purposes, the important point is that Kiowa-Tanoan languages represent the extreme end of a spectrum in which the organization of nominal number in a language can be more or less gender-like. Further towards the other end of the spectrum we find languages such as Coastal Marind, Walman, Konso and Baiso, in which lexicalized number (in this case, plurality) appears to have blurred the line between gender and number to a much lesser degree.

9.4 Summary

We believe that a particularly promising direction of research on the interaction between gender and lexical plurality lies in diachrony and, in particular, in examining how the encoding of lexical plurality affects the evolution of gender and number agreement systems. Olsson (2019 [in Volume I]) suggests that a plausible explanation for the peculiar configuration of gender IV in Coastal Marind is that this agreement class evolved from a smaller nucleus of pluralia tantum nouns (which selected plural agreement because semantically plural) and only gradually came to include non-plural types of nouns. A similar hypothesis could be tested on Konso and other Cushitic languages exhibiting large classes of lexical plural nouns. Another promising area of investigation in this domain would be taking a closer look at languages like Baiso, where only certain types of agreement controllers, among which the lexical plurals, trigger the use of dedicated plural agreement, whereas the majority of morphologically plural nouns trigger agreement patterns that are syncretic with either masculine or feminine singular agreement. These languages, where, synchronically, there seems to be a split in the agreement patterns associated with nominal plurality, offer an interesting test case for hypotheses about the evolution and grammaticalization of number agreement, a topic that goes beyond the scope of the present volume.

10 System evolution

10.1 Introduction

System is probably the most commonly unexplained term in the literature on grammatical gender and thus arguably rather void of meaning. However, in this section, we will argue that the notion of system is highly important from a developmental point of view. Furthermore, the relationship between complexity and system needs to be sorted out. The Latin adjective *complex* 'weaved together' and the Ancient Greek noun *sústēma* '(what is) standing together' are very close in their original meanings. It is thus not surprising that complexity is often understood in linguistics as system complexity, which somehow wrongly takes for granted that complexity is necessarily connected to systems, especially if complexity is understood in terms of description length.

A very simple way of defining system in linguistics is to say that it is an opposition of at least two markers, and in this sense gender is always organized in terms of systems. However, this simple definition does not capture many of the systematic properties of mature gender. Gender connects different parts of language structure (one might say that it is always a multiple-interface phenomenon): syntax, semantics, and morphology are always involved. Lexicon is fundamentally involved to the extent that gender is lexical. Even phonology is sometimes involved, notably if there is phonological gender assignment. Mature gender systems imply a high degree of internal organization and, from a developmental perspective, it is interesting to consider how such complex systems can emerge.

In §10.2 we introduce the notion of co-evolution (a set of more than one diachronic change, which are at least partly dependent on each other), which is crucial for processes of system emergence. In §10.3 we discuss various approaches dealing with contextualization of variability where variation that is not accounted for is remotivated. In §10.4 we will argue that co-evolution in both rise and reduction of gender can take the form of cascades of anomalies.

10.2 Co-evolution

Diachronic processes, such as sound change, analogy, reanalysis, grammaticalization, and semantic shift, are often viewed as individual changes. One sound, morpheme, construction or meaning turns into another sound, morpheme, construction or meaning. However, changes can also co-occur in a sequence of connected events. The probably best-known example are push and drag chains of several sound changes that co-determine each other, such as the great vowel shift in English. Since gender consists of systems of at least two markers, individual diachronic processes are usually not sufficient for the modelling of the emergence and evolution of gender. Of course, it cannot be excluded that several changes that may result in a gender system co-occur accidentally, but more often than not there will be some sort of co-evolution of several changes in the evolution of gender.

Even a maximally simple gender system, such as the Japanese (Japonic) grammatical anaphors, *kanojo* 'she' (from the attributive form of the obsolete distal demonstrative in its attributive form *kano* plus the Sino-Japanese form *jo* for 'woman') and *kare* 'he' (from the independent form of the obsolete distal demonstrative; see Ishiyama 2008 and Wälchli 2019 [this volume]), is difficult to imagine without some sort of co-evolution. It is true that the loss of the distal demonstrative series *kano/kare* is a shared development that is important for rendering both forms opaque, but the forms are still heterogeneous. One is a complex NP, the other one is just a simplex demonstrative form. The development of *kare* to masculine 'he' presupposes a semantic shift of narrowing to masculine, and this process is hard to imagine without co-evolution of a parallel feminine form that makes that narrowing possible.

It is thus not surprising that the general literature on grammaticalization, which focuses on individual cases of grammaticalization, says very little about the origin of gender. Heine & Kuteva (2002) only list a few cases such as MAN ('man', 'male', 'person') > THIRD PERSON PRONOUN in ‖Ani (Khoe-Kwadi, Khoe), Lendu (Central Sudanic, Lenduic), and Zande.

10.3 Contextualization of variability

In a system, there are markers and a division of labor among them. It is a reasonable assumption that the markers (often of rather heterogeneous origin) are there first and that the division of labor is put into place in a second step. Here we will discuss two approaches that can help us understand how this can happen: Lass' (1990) concept of exaptation and the experimental research on iterated artificial language learning by Kirby and Smith and collaborators (Kirby et al. 2008; Smith & Wonnacott 2010).

Lass (1990) borrows the term EXAPTATION from biology where it means the "opportunistic co-optation of a feature whose origin is unrelated or only marginally related to its later use" (Lass 1990: 80), such as when the dinosaur ancestors of birds happen to have feathers which later turn out to be useful for flying. Linguistic exaptation is the development by which junk that is kept (instead of being relegated) is later used for some other purpose. Lass (1990) discusses the following two examples. (i) Indo-European distinguished perfect and aorist in the past, a distinction which was lost in Germanic, where the perfect and aorist stem forms were redeployed as singular and plural past stems in strong verbs. (ii) The Dutch alternation between suffix -e and Zero in attributive adjectives expressing gender and number agreement was redeployed in Afrikaans as an expression of various classes of adjectives (among other things, simple versus complex/compound adjectives).

Smith & Wonnacott (2010) use iterated learning modelled in an experiment as a tool for investigating the cultural evolution of language. One group of participants is presented with some stimuli they have to learn and the next group of participants has to learn the language reproduced by the first group and so on in several "generations". The equivalent of Lass' "junk" is free variation in the input. In Smith & Wonnacott's (2010) experiment, learners were presented with nouns denoting animals with the two artificial plural words *fip* and *tay* distributed entirely randomly in the input for the first "generation". This junk, or pattern of free variation between two plural marking strategies, was redeployed in iterative learning. Smith & Wonnacott's (2010) call this PROBABILITY-MATCHING BEHAVIOR: the learners reproduce markers more or less with the same proportion of frequency that the markers have in the input. However, as a consequence of transmission over several generations, the distribution of markers is made predictable by linking it to particular conditions, in this case the use of markers is made predictable by lexical conditioning. "A typical fifth-participant language exhibits [...] predictable variability [...] for instance, *fip* used to mark plurality on *cow* and *pig*, *tay* used to mark plurality on *rabbit* and *giraffe*" (Smith & Wonnacott 2010: 447). The learners thus developed some sort of lexical gender. While the token frequency of markers changes very little, there is a change from zero predictability to full or almost full predictability. As a consequence, conditional entropy drops, and if entropy is considered a measure of complexity, complexity drops. (Even though system complexity increases as we go from one grammatical distinction, number, to two, number and gender).

Lass' and Smith & Wonnacott's examples have in common that there is a co-evolution of many changes. Parallel changes take place in all Germanic strong verbs, all Afrikaans attributive adjectives and all nouns denoting animals in the experiment. Unmotivated alternations are conditioned, which makes the alternation predictable (lower complexity as meaning and form are better aligned) at the cost of a lower independence (higher complexity according to the Principle of Independence), while the number of markers remains constant.

In §7.5 and §8 we have seen that gender may emerge as a condition on an already existing grammatical category. This may seem strange if viewed as a complexification in terms of the Principle of Indepencence without any obvious benefit since grammatical gender does not seem to provide any communicative benefit. However, rise of gender is better understandable if we assume that the stage before there was gender contained some markers whose use was largely unpredictable. In more general terms, we can assume that the stages that precede the development of gender contain anomalies where some formal distinctions are poorly motivated. This can, for instance, be due to sound change, to decategorialization of nouns, or to anaphoric NPs having become opaque (as in Japanese).

10.4 Reduction and rise of gender as cascades of anomalies

Gender system evolution often involves a sequence of changes where the first change introduces increasing complexity in the form of unpredictable variability and subsequent changes restore order. Such an initial change introducing idiosyncratic patterning can be regular sound change. A well-studied example is the loss of gender agreement in the predicative adjective (but not in the attributive adjective) in German (Fleischer 2007a, Fleischer 2007b and the literature surveyed there). Old High German and Old Saxon had two competing inflectional paradigms of adjectives, one with endings originating from the pronominal paradigm and one with nominal endings. The nominal endings happened to be reduced to zero by regular sound change in all three genders in the nominative singular and in the nominative neuter plural. The idiosyncratic distribution created by phonological erosion is reflected quite accurately in Old Saxon in predicative use (SG 0%, M.PL 99%, F.PL 95%, N.PL 29%; Fleischer 2007a: Table 9). In Early Old High German, two opposite tendencies can be observed in predicative use. On the one hand, inflection tends to be lost in the forms where it was preserved. On the other hand, inflection is also partly reintroduced by analogy to the forms where it was not lost by sound law. Inflected forms spread most easily to the neuter plural and to a lesser extent also to the feminine singular, which happened to have the same pronominal ending as the neuter plural (N.SG 0%, M.SG 1%, F.SG 8%, N.PL 64%, F.PL 79%, M.PL 80%; Fleischer 2007a: Table 11). While the uninflected forms were generalized in predicative use in Middle High German and Modern German, the inflected forms were generalized in Highest Alemannic dialects with support of language contacts with Romance languages (Fleischer 2007b). In attributive use, the inflected pronominal forms with gender and number agreement were generalized in all varieties of German.

In the development simulated by Polinsky & Van Everbroeck (2003) for the transition from Latin to Old French, "the major push for the restructuring of the gender system came from phonological changes (loss of vowel length, loss of word-final segments)" (Polinsky & Van Everbroeck 2003: 385). Neuter merged with masculine in the singular and with feminine in the plural (as preserved in Romanian). In early Old French text, Romanian-like neuter nouns had been reduced to about 4.6% as compared to 21.1% neuter in Classical Latin.

There are also cascades of changes where an anomaly is remedied by restructuring which entails another anomaly which again calls for restructuring which in its turn is an anomaly and so on. Such a cascade of changes is responsible for a strange pattern in some Tamian Latvian dialects in northern Kurzeme where demonstratives do not agree in gender anymore (only in number and case) and always take the masculine form (80).

(80) Kandava Latvian (Indo-European, Baltic; Graudiņa 1958; Rudzīte 1964: 65; Wälchli 2018: 144)

un tas   cūkgans   a   visàm   tiẽm
and that.NOM.SG.M swineherd(M).NOM.SG with all.DAT.PL.F that.DAT.PL.M

cūkam   tur i   palic:s.
swine(F).DAT.PL there be.PRS.3 stay.PST.PTCP.ACT.NOM.SG.M

'and this swineherd had remained there with all those pigs'

The starting point is a regular sound change (triggered by language contact with the Finnic contact language Livonian) where short vowels in final syllables of words longer than one syllable are lost. This causes gender neutralization (of masculine and feminine) in the accusative plural in nouns. Demonstratives are monosyllables and monosyllables are not affected by the sound change entailing neutralization. However, the neutralization is extended to them by analogy. The masculine accusative plural form in demonstratives is generalized also with feminine controllers. Since there is a syncretism of feminine plural accusative and nominative, the use of masculine forms instead of feminine is extended also to the nominative plural, which causes the gender opposition in the demonstrative plural forms to be maintained only in the dative (attested in the dialect of Zlēkas). This is a new anomaly, the dative is less frequent than the nominative; thus masculine is further expanded to all plural forms in the demonstrative (attested in Puze and Pope). Demonstratives are the only target in these varieties that inflects for gender only in the singular and not in the plural. This is still an anomaly. In the dialect of Dundaga, the generalized use of masculine forms in demonstratives is further extended to all case-number forms of the demonstrative (see Wälchli 2017).

Wälchli (2018) considers the rise of gender in Nalca from the point of view of system emergence. The development in Nalca implies a large number of minor changes of different kinds (grammaticalization, analogy, and reanalysis) that all must have taken place within a short period of time. There are instances of grammaticalization (female person name marker *ge* from *gel* 'woman'), instances of reanalysis (*nimi ara* [men TOP] > *nim e-ra* [men DN-TOP]), and instances of analogical extension such as when gender is extended to the comitative postposition (*be-b/ge-b/ne-b/e-b/a-b* instead of just *ab* as in other Mek languages). Most of these developments are highly language-specific and are triggered by local anomalies that give to rise to new anomalies which again trigger further changes. As a whole, the development in Nalca is a highly specific development, which gives rise to a gender system with highly specific properties. However, since gender systems often exhibit highly specific properties, it can be assumed that complex system emergence of the kind that it can be reconstructed for Nalca may have taken place in other gender systems as well.

11 Areal and genealogical patterns and external factors

In this section, we will discuss patterns in gender that go beyond language-internal implications. §11.1 deals with genealogical and areal patterns. §11.2 addresses external factors in the ecology of languages.

11.1 Areal and genealogical patterns

If we take the nine language families in the world with more than a hundred languages (according to Hammarström et al. 2018), gender can arguably be reconstructed for the proto-language in three of them (Atlantic-Congo, Afro-Asiatic and Indo-European), which testifies to the diachronic stability of gender. However, in all three families there are also a considerable number of languages that have lost gender. And, at least if we adopt a broad definition of gender, the remaining six large language families (Austronesian, Sino-Tibetan, Nuclear Trans-New Guinea, Pama-Nyungan, Otomanguean, Austroasiatic) all have some languages with gender, and in all six families, gender must have emerged more than once. What contributes to the impression that gender is genealogically stable is its entrenchment in specific morphological marking patterns, which makes gender an interesting feature to look at for traditional historical linguistics. As Nichols (2003: 303) puts it, "[f]or genders, with their clear formal exponents, it is very obviously not the abstract typological feature but particular form-function pairings that are transmitted from ancestor to daughter language".

However, old morphological material does not necessarily guarantee wide distribution across a large language family. A case in point is gender in Classical Tibetan and Kiranti languages discussed in §8.3, where masculine -pa/po and feminine -ma/mo are common derivational suffixes in adjectives throughout Tibeto-Burman languages, so it cannot be excluded that gender in Sino-Tibetan might be old.

There is probably a bias toward discussing stable gender in historical linguistics more often than instable gender. This is understandable since only morphologically entrenched stable gender is useful for establishing genealogical groupings of languages. There are so far no general surveys of the development of gender across Austronesian, Sino-Tibetan, Nuclear Trans-New Guinea, Otomanguean or Austroasiatic (for Australian languages, however, see Dixon 2002: 449–514), and no general surveys for the loss of gender across Atlantic-Congo, Afro-Asiatic or Indo-European.

Classifiers are more prone to areal diffusion than grammatical gender (see Seifart 2010: 730–731 and the references given there). However, this does not mean that language contact is irrelevant for gender. Nichols (2003: 300) argues that gender is a cluster phenomenon in the sense that it is most easily preserved where languages with gender are neighbors of (usually) related languages with gender. Put differently, gender is "of high stability only when reinforced by gender systems in neighboring languages" (Nichols 2003: 303) and languages that lose gender are typically neighbors of each other. This does not only hold for gender in general, but also for particular gender agreement targets, as the preservation of gender in predicative adjectives in Highest Alemannic German dialects due to contacts with Romance languages discussed in §10.4 (Fleischer 2007b).

The findings of Liljegren (2019 [in Volume I]) on the distribution of gender in Hindu Kush Indo-Aryan are well in line with Nichols' (2003) suggestion. Liljegren identifies areal patterns both in the loss of gender, but also in the emergence of a new gender opposition based on animacy. Liljegren also highlights the diachronic dimension. The two Chitral group languages, Khowar and Kalasha, which have lost the Indo-Aryan masculine-feminine opposition and developed a new gender system based on animacy are likely to reflect a first wave of Indo-Aryan settlers in the Hindu Kush area. Languages with concurrent sex- and animacy-based systems are spoken in the vicinity of Chitral languages.

Areal patterns in the development of gender within clusters of languages of the same family can also be identified in other areas. Within the Austroasiatic Khasian branch, War-Jaintia is clearly more distantly related to Khasi than Lyngngam based on evidence from lexical data (Nagaraja et al. 2013: 6). However, the similarities of gender systems rather follow areal patterns where the westernmost language Lyngngam (Nagaraja 1996) has the most rudimentary system among the Khasian languages (see also Di Garbo & Miestamo 2019 [this volume]). In Northern Australia, the Ngan'gityemerri Nangikurrunggurr (Southern Daly) nominal classification system is more similar to that of Marithiel (Western Daly) than to that of Murriny Patha, even though Murriny Patha (Southern Daly) is a closer genealogical relative. Marrithiyel and Ngan'gityemerri "share the larger, central classes, have a number of formally cognate classifiers, and display the same range of agreement patterns" (Green 1997: 233). In central New Guinea, Anim and Ok have very similar gender systems (see Olsson 2019 [in Volume I]). They are so similar in form and function that they are likely cognates (Usher & Suter 2015: 118). However, lexical comparison does not suggest any close genealogical relationship of Anim and Ok (E. Suter, p.c.). According to Seifart (2007), the systems of nominal classsification in Huitotoan and Boran are so strikingly similar, that entirely independent development is unlikely, but no common proto-system can be reconstructed.

11.2 External factors

As argued by Dahl (2019 [in Volume I]) it is not easily possible to establish any correlations between grammatical gender and ecological parameters, such as population size or degree of contact and there is no positive correlation with morphological complexity (Nichols 2019 [in Volume I]). This contrasts with evidence from other typological features where extralinguistic ecological factors are clearly reflected in typological distributions (Lupyan & Dale 2010; Sinnemäki 2014a). Sinnemäki & Di Garbo (2018) do not find any significant relationship between the number of gender distinctions (including whether or not a language has gender) and sociolinguistic variables, whereas degree of inflectional synthesis in the verb is clearly sensitive to population dynamics. It is, of course, possible that number of genders does not accurately represent the complexity of gender and that other properties of gender systems must be used (for which large scale data sets are not availabe) to establish a relationship with factors of population dynamics. However, Blasi et al. (2017) do not find any evidence for adaptive patterns in gender marking even when looking at adjectival modifiers and personal pronouns in creole languages. The results from the large-scale quantitative studies conducted so far thus suggest that, if there are correlations between gender typology and sociolinguistic factors, they are rather subtle, so that they are unlikely to be covered in large typological databases.

A problem with large typological databases is that they often do not take into account dialects. The number of genders in Bininj Kun-Wok ranges from four in the central Kunwinjku dialect to zero in Kune, with Gun-djeihmi having three genders. According to Evans (1997), considerable differences in grammatical gender across dialects of Bininj Kun-Wok reflect social relationships with speakers of neighboring languages. In the *WALS* database, the number of genders listed for Bininj Kun-Wok is simply "four". As Evans (1997: 105) puts it, deep regularities cannot always be seen in the shallow perspective of one dialect. Karatsareas (2014) shows that not all varieties of Koineic Greek are equally conservative, especially not the different varieties of Greek in Asia Minor. In Greek in Asia Minor the number of genders ranges from three (like in Modern Greek in Greece) in Pontic Greek (but with major restructuring of the system) to zero in Cappadocian Greek. Karatsareas (2009) argues that the loss of gender in Pontic Greek results from an interplay of heavy language contact with Turkish and language-internal analogical levellings. Interestingly, dialects of Ancient Greek in Asia Minor not surviving to the present were already undergoing restructuring of their gender systems due to substrate from Anatolian languages, which had only two genders (common and neuter) (Brixhe 1994: 176). As in Greek, in Latvian gender restructuring of very different kinds occur in peripheral dialects with intensive language contact, in this case with Finnic (Livonian and Estonian) (see Wälchli 2017). Like Greek varieties in Asia Minor, the Tamian Latvian dialects are highly endangered.

There is thus evidence from a fair number of particular cases that a large proportion of non-native speakers and/or intensive language contacts with languages lacking grammatical gender can entail massive restructuring in gender systems which can, but need not, entail a reduction of the number of genders (see also Trudgill 2011: 24). In a study of 36 languages distributed among 15 sets of closely related languages, Di Garbo (forthcoming) finds that in Eurasia radical reduction, loss and emergence of gender agreement tend to cluster around language family edges, which is consistent with the findings of Nichols (2003). "Loss of gender agreement tends to prevail under circumstances in which the demographically dominant and/or more prestigious language lacks grammatical gender. On the other hand, borrowing of gender agreement patterns may be favored when the demographically dominant and/or more prestigious language has grammatical gender" (Di Garbo forthcoming, see also Di Garbo & Miestamo 2019 [this volume]). Prestige of languages with gender also plays a role in cases of language planning as reflected in the gender system of the Makanza variety of Lingala that was designed by missionaries (Meeuwis 2013; see also Di Garbo forthcoming and Di Garbo & Miestamo 2019 [this volume]). Di Garbo (forthcoming) launches the hypothesis that gender marking may actually have important ties to the way in which speakers and speech communities construe their linguistic identity in opposition to that of their neighbors. A case in point is the mixed language Michif which preserves both the gender system of French and the gender system of Cree (Bakker 1997; Di Garbo forthcoming).

12 Conclusions

In this chapter we have addressed grammatical gender and its complexity (as defined in §2) from a dynamic perspective. We found that dynamic comparative concepts of the form *From X to Y*, as summarized in Table 19, are highly useful to describe the typology of gender. Often it is the case that less mature gender is a source for more mature complex gender, which contributes to the view that complexity in gender is something that can grow over time.

Our starting point was a dynamic definition of gender in §1, repeated here for convenience.

> Definition of gender adopted in this chapter:
> Gender is a grammatical category type with a semantic core of animacy and/or sex reflecting classes of referents, which have a propensity to turn into classes of noun lexemes. It is overtly marked on noun-associated forms. It typically exhibits cumulative exponence with number, case, and/or person. Gender is organized in the form of systems.

Table 19: Less mature gender as source for more mature gender

Simpler earlier stage can develop into a...	...more mature stage	
Referent-based gender >	Lexical gender	§3
Marker in independent use >	Gender in adnominal use	§4
One-to-one assignment >	Many-to-one assignment	§6.2
Semantic gender assignment >	Opaque gender assignment	§6.3
Semantic assignment ("covert" gender) >	Formal assignment ("overt" gender)	§6.4
Morphological assignment or sandhi >	Phonological assignment	§6.4
Classes of single items >	Classes of larger sets	§6.6
Condition on another feature >	Gender feature	§7.5
Apposition and nominal gender targets >	Non-nominal gender targets	§7.5
Non-idiomatic gender >	Idiomatic use of gender	§7.7

This definition goes beyond the traditional Hockettian definition, which is based on two critieria: noun classes and agreement. Our definition is dynamic in the sense that it expresses the fact that gender is an evolving category type, where gender has a semantic core of animacy and/or sex and exhibits hierarchical patterning according to the animacy hierarchy above some cutoff point in the animate segment of the hierarchy (§3). The semantic core and the hierarchical patterning reflect referent-based gender. Gender becomes lexical only as a secondary development. Put differently, the organization of gender in terms of noun classes is a mature phenomenon. Incipient gender need not have noun classes and in the process of gender loss, lexical gender can be lost before referent-based gender is lost. In several language groups, gender can be shown to originate from top segments of the animacy/individuation hierarchy and then move further down the hierarchy as it further develops. Gender thrives in symbiosis with nouns, but does not usually originate as noun classes. When associated with nouns, gender tends to lexicalize. Gender assignment can be semantic, formal, and/or opaque (§5 and §6). Gender has mechanisms to restore semantic assignment for animate referents if gender assignment for animate referents has become opaque (§6.3). In some languages, gender assignment can be flexible. Through flexible gender assignment speakers modify the construal of noun referents, targeting properties such as size and/or countability (§5).

Gender is a special case of nominal marking on noun-associated words where the number of values is larger than one. But there are also many cases of nominal marking with value one without opposition of gender values. Omission of head nouns in NPs and subsequent explicit nominal marking of non-headed NPs seems to be an important driving force for the accumulation of nominal morphology as the marking of independent modifiers can be transferred to modifiers in headed NPs (§4).

Agreement is complex in the sense that it can involve syntactically complex controllers and syntactically complex targets and in the sense that the relationship between controller and target can be of various kinds: syntactic and strictly intra-sentential, semantic and inter-sentential, or purely contextual in the case of latent controllers. There is always a specific relationship between controller and target in agreement, but this specific relationship need not necessarily be coreference. Features are a highly mature form of agreement and features may develop from conditions. Gender requires displacement (realization on another element than the one triggering it) in order to be considered a grammatical category. Overt marking of gender on nouns is distinct from gender as a grammatical category, and relates to derivation rather than agreement (§7).

Gender systems almost always imply cumulation with number, case and/or person. This is so pervasive that we have decided to include this peculiarity in the definition of gender. Number and case also play an important role for the emergence of gender systems. In general, it seems to be the very essence of gender that it interacts with other grammatical domains, such as number, person, case, and evaluation. To the extent that interaction with other grammatical categories is counted as complexity according to the Principle of Independence, gender is almost always complex. Gender is thus arguably complex by definition. Cumulation with number, case and/or person has not been taken into account sufficiently in the literature pointing out the similarities between gender and classifiers. Classifiers are similar to gender in that they are classes of referents or classes of noun lexemes. However, classifiers do not tend to interact with number and case in the way gender does (§8).

As gender, number can be entrenched in the lexicon in the form of classes of pluralia tantum, and pluralia tantum can further develop into gender values. It is, of course, possible to exclude pluralia tantum from gender by definition, but it is not clear whether this is useful since it is the very essence of gender to be connected to other grammatical categories, and among them number is the most important one (§9).

Gender is organized in terms of systems that connect different parts of language structure (lexicon, syntax, morphology, semantics, phonology) in order to efficiently and orderly assign values to markers. Although the origin of many gender systems is unknown, different kinds of diachronic approaches are indispensable for understanding how gender emerges and evolves as systems (§10).

Gender is stable diachronically in the sense that it is highly entrenched in specific morphosyntactic marking. Gender displays areal patterns especially in groups of closely related languages. Especially in non-mature stages, gender seems to spread across closely related languages or languages with similar typological profiles. Gender is often lost or restructured in languages with intensive contacts with languages lacking gender or displaying different gender systems. There is no obvious general relationship between the typology of gender and language ecology, but larger proportions of non-native speakers and higher population size seem to go together with restructuring in gender marking (§11).

Gender, noun classes and agreement are among the most discussed topics in the linguistic literature, but there are still many open questions which could only be touched upon in this chapter or are not addressed at all. As the literature is growing, there is also a need of integrative surveys, even if only partial ones, like this chapter. We hope that this chapter, and the two volumes as a whole, will stimulate further descriptions of gender in particular languages and dialects, new large-scale typological studies, and more comprehensive surveys of the research than this chapter provides.

Acknowledgments

We would like to thank Östen Dahl, Pernilla Hallonsten Halling, Martin Haspelmath, Don Killian, Bruno Olsson, and three anonymous reviewers for numerous highly useful and thought-provoking comments, which helped us improve this chapter in multiple ways. We are also grateful to Maria Koptjevskaja-Tamm and Björn Wiemer for answering our questions about Slavic languages, and to Sebastian Nordhoff, Felix Kopecky and Martin Haspelmath for their advice and assistance when preparing the final version of the text. Most of all we would like to thank Bruno Olsson, the editor of this chapter, who has done much more for this chapter than you ever might expect from an editor.

Symbols and special abbreviations

The abbreviations and symbols listed below are not found in the Leipzig Glossing Rules:

{}	gender with which the morphological form is more commonly associated
[]	non-overt element
()	inherent category
I, II, III, …	Genders I, II, III, etc.

A	actor	INT	interrogative (Coastal Marind)
ACT	active		
ACT	actualis (Coastal Marind)	ITER	iterative mood (Meskwaki)
AGN	agentive noun		
AGT	grammatical agent	*KA*	*ka*-class (Paumari)
ANIM	animate gender	LNK	linker
AOR	aorist	MAKE	light verb 'make' (Oksapmin)
ASS	associative case (Uduk)		
ATTR	attributive (Archi)	N_	non-
CL	class	N1	neuter 1 (Mian)
CL1 etc.	class 1 etc.	N2	neuter 2 (Mian)
CM	common gender; common noun marker (not person name marker: Tagalog)	NARR	narrative
		Neg.indef	negative indefinite pronoun
		NEUT	neutral orientation (Coastal Marind)
Cmpl	complement clause		
COMP	comparative	NF	non-finite (Pnar §4.3)
CV	CV gender (Nalca)	N_M	non-masculine
DERIV	derivation	NOMIN	nominal marker
DETR	detransitivizing "emphatic" form of verb (Bari)	Num	numeral
		N.UNI	non-uniqueness
		OBV	obviative
ECHO	prosodic echo vowel	PAUC	paucal
EMPH	emphatic clitic or particle	PLT	plurale tantum
DIM	diminutive	PN	proper name marker
DN	default noun gender (Nalca)	Poss	possessive pronoun
		POSS	possessive (affix)
DP	default phrase gender (Nalca)	PRED	predicator (Mian)
		PRON	pronominal inflection
GEN	genitive; possession (Pnar)	REAL	realis
		REFL.POSS	reflexive possessive
Gen	noun possessor	Rel	relative clause
GM	gender marker (Mopán Maya)	SPEC	specific
		SUPERL	superlative
HAB	habitual	U	undergoer
HUM	human	UNI	uniqueness
INAN	inanimate gender	WEAK	weak declension
Int	interrogative		

Translations of New Testaments used

Iraya N. T. 1991. The New Testament in Iraya. http://listen.bible.is/IRYOMF/Matt/1.

Kahua Bible. 2011. Buka Apuna (I Lotu Katolika). The Bible in Kahua. http://bibles.org/agw-KCB/Gen/int. Bible Society of the South Pacific.

Nalca N.T. n.d. Translated by Samuel and Jeremy Souga and Roger Doriot.

Una N. T. 2007. Translated by Wilem Balyo, Titus Bitibalyo, Melkias Kipka and Gipson Malyo, with consultant input from Dick and Margreet Kroneman (SIL) and Lourens de Vries (UBS). The permission to use the Una N.T. by the Indonesian Bible Society is gratefully acknowledged.

References

Acquaviva, Paolo. 2008. *Lexical plurals: A morphosyntactic approach.* Oxford: Oxford University Press.

Aikhenvald, Alexandra Y. 2000. *Classifiers: A typology of noun categorization devices.* Oxford: Oxford University Press.

Aikhenvald, Alexandra Y. 2010. Gender, noun class and language obsolescence: The case of Paumarí. In Eithne B. Carlin & Simon van de Kerke (eds.), *Linguistics and archaeology in the Americas: The historization of language and society,* 235–252. Leiden: Brill.

Aikhenvald, Alexandra Y. 2012. Round women and long men: Shape, size, and the meanings of gender in New Guinea and beyond. *Anthropological Linguistics* 54. 33–86.

Aikhenvald, Alexandra Y. 2016. *How gender shapes the world.* Oxford: Oxford University Press.

Aksenov, A. T. 1984. K probleme èkstralingvističeskoj motivacii grammatičeskoj kategorii roda [About the problem of the extralinguistic motivation of the category of gender]. *Voprosy jazykoznanija* 1. 14–25.

Allan, Keith. 1977. Classifiers. *Language* 53(2). 285–311.

Anderson, Judi Lynn. 1989. *Comaltepec Chinantec syntax* (Studies in Chinantec Languages 3). Arlington: Summer Institute of Linguistics.

Angerer, Martin. 2009. *Regensburg: Für Anfänger und Fortgeschrittene.* Regensburg: Donau Live.

Årsjö, Britten. 1999. *Words in Ama.* Uppsala: Uppsala University. (MA thesis).

Audring, Jenny. 2009. Gender assignment and gender agreement: Evidence from pronominal gender languages. *Morphology* 18(2). 93–116.

Audring, Jenny. 2014. Gender as a complex feature. *Language Sciences* 43. 5–17.

Audring, Jenny. 2017. Calibrating complexity: How complex is a gender system? *Language Sciences* 60. 53–68.

Audring, Jenny. 2019. Canonical, complex, complicated? In Francesca Di Garbo, Bruno Olsson & Bernhard Wälchli (eds.), *Grammatical gender and linguistic complexity: Volume I: General issues and specific studies*, 15–52. Berlin: Language Science Press. DOI:10.5281/zenodo.3462756

Audring, Jenny & Sebastian Fedden. 2018. Introduction. In Sebastian Fedden, Jenny Audring & G. Greville Corbett (eds.), *Non-canonical gender systems*, 3–22. Oxford: Oxford University Press.

Baker, Mark. 2003. *Lexical categories: Verbs, nouns, and adjectives*. Cambridge University Press: Cambridge.

Bakker, Peter. 1997. *A language of our own: The genesis of Michif, the mixed Cree-French language of the Canadian Métis*. Oxford: Oxford University Press.

Barlow, Michael. 1999. Agreement as a discourse phenomenon. *Folia Linguistica* 33(2). 187–210.

Becher, Jutta. 2001. *Untersuchungen zum Sprachwandel in Wolof aus diachroner und synchroner Perspektive*. Universität Hamburg. (Doctoral dissertation).

Beguinot, Francesco. 1942. *Il berbero nefûsi di Fassâṭo*. Roma: Istituto per l'Oriente.

Binzell, John. n.d. Nalca original texts. 8 texts collected by John Binzell around 1975. 16 pages, manuscript.

Blasi, Damian E., Susanne M. Michaelis & Martin Haspelmath. 2017. Grammars are robustly transmitted even during the emergence of creole languages. *Nature Human Behaviour* 1(10). 723–729. DOI:10.1038/s41562-017-0192-4

Bond, Oliver, Greville G. Corbett, Marina Chumakina & Dunstan Brown (eds.). 2016. *Archi: Complexities of agreement in cross-theoretical perspective*. Oxford: Oxford University Press.

Börstell, Carl, Ryan Lepic & Gal Belsitzman. 2017. Articulatory plurality is a property of lexical plurals across sign languages. *Linguisticæ Investigationes* 39. 392–408. Special issssue on "Lexical plurals and beyond" edited by Peter Lauwers and Marie Lammert.

Bosch, Peter. 1988. Representing and accessing focussed referents. *Language and Cognitive Processes* 3(3). 207–232.

Bresnan, Joan & Jonni Kanerva. 1989. Locative inversion in Chicheŵa: A case study in factorization in grammar. *Linguistic Inquiry* 20(1). 1–50.

Brixhe, Claude. 1994. Le phrygien. In Françoise Bader (ed.), *Langues indo-européennes*, 165–178. Paris: CNRS Éditions.

Bybee, Joan. 1985. *Morphology: The study of the relation between meaning and form.* Amsterdam: John Benjamins.

Capell, Arthur. 1982. *Arosi grammar* (Pacific Linguistics B 20). Canberra: Australian National University.

Capell, Arthur & Heather H. Hinch. 1970. *Maung grammar: Texts and vocabulary.* The Hague: Mouton.

Caro Reina, Javier. 2018. The grammaticalization of the terms of address *en* and *na* as onymic markers in Catalan. In Friedhelm Debus, Rita Heuser & Damaris Nübling (eds.), *Linguistik der Familiennamen*, 175–204. Hildesheim: Olms.

Carstairs, Andrew. 1987. *Allomorphy in inflection.* London: Croom Helm.

Carter, Hazel. 2002. *An outline of Chitonga grammar.* Lousaka: Bookwords Publishers.

Chumakina, Marina & Oliver Bond. 2016. Competing controllers and agreement potential. In Oliver Bond, Greville Corbett, Marina Chumakina & Dunstan Brown (eds.), *Archi: Complexities of agreement in cross-theoretical perspective*, 77–117. Oxford: Oxford University Press.

Comrie, Bernard & Tania Kuteva. 2013. Relativization on subjects. In Matthew S. Dryer & Martin Haspelmath (eds.), *The world atlas of language structures online*. Leipzig: Max Planck Institute for Evolutionary Anthropology. https://wals.info/chapter/122.

Contini-Morava, Ellen & Eve Danziger. 2018. Non-canonical gender in Mopan Maya. In Sebastian Fedden, Jenny Audring & Greville Corbett (eds.), *Non-canonical gender systems*, 129–146. Oxford: Oxford University Press.

Contini-Morava, Ellen & Marcin Kilarski. 2013. Functions of nominal classification. *Language Sciences* 40. 263–299.

Corbett, Greville G. 1991. *Gender.* Cambridge: Cambridge University Press.

Corbett, Greville G. 2000. *Number.* Cambridge: Cambridge University Press.

Corbett, Greville G. 2006. *Agreement.* Cambridge: Cambridge University Press.

Corbett, Greville G. 2012. *Features.* Cambridge: Cambridge University Press.

Corbett, Greville G. 2013. Systems of gender assignment. In Matthew S. Dryer & Martin Haspelmath (eds.), *The world atlas of language structures online*. Leipzig: Max Planck Institute for Evolutionary Anthropology. http://wals.info/chapter/32.

Corbett, Greville G. 2014. Gender typology. In Greville G. Corbett (ed.), *The expression of gender*, 87–130. Berlin: Mouton De Gruyter.

Corbett, Greville G. 2018. Pluralia tantum nouns and the theory of features: A typology of nouns with non-canonical number properties. *Morphology* 29(1). 51–108. DOI:10.1007/s11525-018-9336-0

Corbett, Greville G. & Sebastian Fedden. 2016. Canonical gender. *Journal of Linguistics* 52(3). 495–531.

Corbett, Greville G., Sebastian Fedden & Raphael Finkel. 2017. Single versus concurrent feature systems: Nominal classification in Mian. *Linguistic Typology* 21(2). 209–260.

Corbett, Greville G. & Norman Fraser. 1999. Default genders. In Barbara Unterbeck & Matti Rissanen (eds.), *Gender in grammar and cognition*, 55–97. Berlin: Mouton de Gruyter.

Corbett, Greville G. & Richard J. Hayward. 1987. Gender and number in Bayso. *Lingua* 73(1–2). 195–222.

Cornish, Frances. 1987. Anaphoric pronouns: Under linguistic control, or signalling particular discourse representations? *Journal of Semantics* 5(3). 233–260.

Crazzolara, Joseph Pasquale. 1955. *A study of the Acooli language: Grammar and vocabulary*. 2nd edn. London: Oxford University Press.

Creissels, Denis. 1999. Origine et évolution des diminutifs et augmentatifs dans quelques langues africaines. *Silexicales* 2. 29–35.

Creissels, Denis, Gerrit J. Dimmendaal, Zygmunt Frajzyngier & Christa König. 2008. Africa as a morphosyntactic area. In Bernd Heine & Derek Nurse (eds.), *A linguistic geography of Africa*, 86–150. Cambridge: Cambridge University Press.

Croft, William. 1994. Semantic universals in classifier systems. *Word* 45(2). 145–171.

Croft, William. 2001. *Radical construction grammar: Syntactic theory in typological perspective*. Oxford: Oxford University Press.

Croft, William. 2003. *Typology and universals*. 2nd edn. Cambridge: Cambridge University Press.

Croft, William. 2005. Word classes, parts of speech, and syntactic argumentation. *Linguistic Typology* 9(3). 431–441.

Croft, William. 2013. Agreement as anaphora, anaphora as coreference. In Dik Bakker & Martin Haspelmath (eds.), *Languages across boundaries: Studies in memory of Anna Siewierska*, 95–118. Berlin: De Gruyter.

Dahl, Östen. 2000a. Animacy and the notion of semantic gender. In Barbara Unterbeck (ed.), *Gender in grammar and cognition*. Vol. 1: *Animacy and the notion of semantic gender: Approaches to gender*, 99–115. Berlin: Mouton de Gruyter.

Dahl, Östen. 2000b. Elementary gender distinctions. In Matti Rissanen, Terttu Nevalainen & Mirja Saari (eds.), *Gender in grammar and cognition*. Vol. 2: *Elementary gender distinctions: Manifestations of gender* (Trends in Linguistics. Studies and Monographs 124), 577–593. Berlin: de Gruyter.

Dahl, Östen. 2004. *The growth and maintenance of linguistic complexity*. Amsterdam: John Benjamins.

Dahl, Östen. 2019. Gender: esoteric or exoteric? In Francesca Di Garbo, Bruno Olsson & Bernhard Wälchli (eds.), *Grammatical gender and linguistic complexity: Volume I: General issues and specific studies*, 53–61. Berlin: Language Science Press. DOI:10.5281/zenodo.3462758

Daladier, Anne. 2011. The group Pnaric-War-Lyngngam and Khasi as a branch of Pnaric. *Journal of the Southeast Asian Linguistics Society* 4(2). 169–206.

de Hollenbach, Elena E. 1995. Cuatro morfemas funcionales en las lenguas mixtecanas. In *Vitalidad e influencia de las lenguas indígenas en Latinoamérica: II coloquio Mauricio Swadesh*, 284–293. Universidad Nacional Autónoma de México.

DeLancey, Scott. 2003. Classical Tibetan. In Graham Thurgood & Randy J. LaPolla (eds.), *The Sino-Tibetan languages* (Routledge Language Family Series), 253–269. London & New York: Routledge.

Delbrück, Berthold. 1883. *Vergleichende Syntax der indogermanischen Sprachen*. Erster Theil. Strassburg: Trübner.

Di Garbo, Francesca. 2014. *Gender and its interaction with number and evaluative morphology: An intra- and intergenealogical typological survey of Africa*. Stockholm University. (Doctoral dissertation).

Di Garbo, Francesca. 2016. Exploring grammatical complexity crosslinguistically: The case of gender. *Linguistic Discovery* 14(1). 46–85.

Di Garbo, Francesca. forthcoming. The complexity of grammatical gender and language ecology. In Peter Arkadiev & Francesco Gardani (eds.), *The complexities of morphology*. Oxford: Oxford University Press.

Di Garbo, Francesca & Yvonne Agbetsoamedo. 2018. Non-canonical gender in African languages: A typological survey of interactions between gender and number, and gender and evaluative morphology. In Sebastian Fedden, Jenny Audring & Greville Corbett (eds.), *Non-canonical gender systems*, 176–210. Oxford: Oxford University Press.

Di Garbo, Francesca & Matti Miestamo. 2019. The evolving complexity of gender agreement systems. In Francesca Di Garbo, Bruno Olsson & Bernhard Wälchli (eds.), *Grammatical gender and linguistic complexity: Volume II: World-wide comparative studies*, 15–60. Berlin: Language Science Press. DOI:10.5281/zenodo.3462778

Di Garbo, Francesca & Annemarie Verkerk. 2018. The evolution of Bantu gender marking systems: Typology, phylogeny and social history. Plenary lecture at the 51th Meeting of the Societas Linguistica Europaea. Tallinn (Estonia).

Dietze, Joachim. 1973. Die Entwicklung der altrussischen Kategorie der Beseeltheit im 13. Und 14. Jahrhundert. *Zeitschrift für Slawistik* 18(1). 261–272.

Dimmendaal, Gerrit. 1983. *The Turkana language.* Dordrecht: Foris Publications.

Dixon, Robert M. W. 1972. *The Dyirbal language of North Queensland.* Cambridge: Cambridge University Press.

Dixon, Robert M. W. 1977. *A grammar of Yidiɲ.* Cambridge: Cambridge University Press.

Dixon, Robert M. W. 1979. Ergativity. *Language* 55. 59–138.

Dixon, Robert M. W. 1982. *'Where Have all the adjectives gone?' and other essays in semantics and syntax.* Berlin: Mouton de Gruyter.

Dixon, Robert M. W. 2000. Categories of the noun phrase in Jarawara. *Journal of Linguistics* 36(3). 487–510.

Dixon, Robert M. W. 2002. *Australian languages: Their nature and development* (Cambridge Language Surveys). Cambridge: Cambridge University Press.

Donoghue, Emma. 2010. *Room.* New York: Little, Brown & Company.

Donohue, Mark. 2001. Animacy, class and gender in Burmeso. In Andrew Pawley, Malcolm Ross & Darrell Tryon (eds.), *The boy from Bundaberg: Studies in Melanesian linguistics in honour of Tom Dutton* (Pacific Linguistics 514), 97–115. Canberra: Australian National University.

Donohue, Mark. 2004. A grammar of the Skou language of New Guinea. http://pubman.mpdl.mpg.de/pubman/item/escidoc:402710/component/escidoc:402709/skou%5C_donohue2004%5C_s.pdf, accessed 2015-2-6. Unpublished manuscript.

Dost, Ascander & Vera Gribanova. 2006. Definiteness marking in the Bulgarian. In Donald Baumer, David Montero & Michael Scanlon (eds.), *Proceedings of the 25th West Coast Conference on Formal Linguistics*, 132–140. Somerville, MA: Cascadilla Proceedings Project.

Dravniece, Sofija. 2008. *Dundagas izloksnes teksti.* Brigita Bušmane (ed.). Rīga: LU Latviešu valodas institūts.

Dressler, Wolfgang & Ursula Doleschal. 1990. Gender agreement via derivational morphology. *Acta Linguistica Hungarica* 40. 115–137.

Dryer, Matthew S. 2019. Gender in Walman. In Francesca Di Garbo, Bruno Olsson & Bernhard Wälchli (eds.), *Grammatical gender and linguistic complexity: Volume I: General issues and specific studies*, 171–196. Berlin: Language Science Press. DOI:10.5281/zenodo.3462766

Ebert, Karen. 2003a. Camling. In Graham Thurgood & Randy J. LaPolla (eds.), *The Sino-Tibetan languages*, 533–545. London: Routledge.

Ebert, Karen. 2003b. Kiranti languages: An overview. In Graham Thurgood & Randy J. LaPolla (eds.), *The Sino-Tibetan languages*, 505–517. London: Routledge.

Enger, Hans-Olav. 2004. Scandinavian pancake sentences as semantic agreement. *Nordic Journal of Linguistics* 27(1). 5–34.

Enger, Hans-Olav & Greville G. Corbett. 2012. Definiteness, gender, and hybrids: Evidence from Norwegian dialects. *Journal of Germanic Linguistics* 24(4). 287–324.

Epps, Patience. 2008. *A grammar of Hup*. Berlin: Mouton de Gruyter.

Epps, Patience. 2012. Between headed and headless relative clauses. In Bernard Comrie & Zarina Estrada-Fernández (eds.), *Relative clauses in languages of the Americas: A typological overview*, 191–211. Amsterdam: John Benjamins.

Erbaugh, Mary. 1986. Taking stock: The development of Chinese noun classifiers historically and in young children. In Colette Grinevald Craig (ed.), *Noun classes and categorization*, 399–436. Amsterdam: John Benjamins.

Evans, Nicholas. 1994. The problem of body parts and noun class membership in Australian languages. *University of Melbourne Working Papers in Linguistics* 14. 1–8.

Evans, Nicholas. 1997. Head classes and agreement classes in the Mayali dialect chain. In Mark Harvey & Nicholas Reid (eds.), *Nominal classification in Aboriginal Australia*, 105–146. Amsterdam: John Benjamins.

Evans, Nicholas. 2000. Iwaidjan: A very un-Australian language family. *Linguistic Typology* 4. 91–142.

Evans, Nicholas. 2003. *Bininj Gun-Wok: A pan-dialectal grammar of Mayali, Kunwinjku and Kune*. Canberra: Pacific Linguistics.

Evans, Nicholas. 2015. Valency in Nen. In Andrej Malchukov & Bernard Comrie (eds.), *Valency classes in the world's languages*. Vol. 2: *Valency in Nen: Case studies from Austronesia and the Pacific, the Americas, and theoretical outlook*, 1069–1116. Berlin: Mouton de Gruyter.

Faarlund, Jan Terie. 1977. Embedded clause reduction in Scandinavian gender agreement. *Journal of Linguistics* 13. 153–168.

Fedden, Sebastian. 2010. Ditransitives in Mian. In Andrej Malchukov, Martin Haspelmath & Bernard Comrie (eds.), *Studies in ditransitive constructions: A comparative handbook*, 456–485. Berlin: Mouton de Gruyter.

Fedden, Sebastian. 2011. *A grammar of Mian*. Berlin: Mouton de Gruyter.

Fedden, Sebastian & Greville G. Corbett. 2017. Gender and classifiers in concurrent systems: Refining the typology of nominal classification. *Glossa: A journal of general linguistics* 2(1). 1–47. DOI:10.5334/gjgl.177

Fife, James & Gareth King. 1986. Celtic (Indo-European). In Andrew Spencer & Arnold Zwicky (eds.), *Handbook of morphology*, 477–499. Oxford: Blackwell.

Fischer, Olga, Ans van Kemenade, Willem Koopman & Wim van der Wurff (eds.). 2000. *The syntax of Early English*. Cambridge: Cambridge University Press.

Fleischer, Jürg. 2007a. Das prädikative Adjektiv und Partizip im Althochdeutschen und Altniederdeutschen. *Sprachwissenschaft* 32. 279–348.

Fleischer, Jürg. 2007b. Zur Herkunft des flektierten prädikativen Adjektivs im Höchstalemannischen. *Zeitschrift für Dialektologie und Linguistik* 74(2–3). 196–240.

Foley, William A. & Robert D. Van Valin. 1984. *Functional syntax and universal grammar*. Cambridge: Cambridge University Press.

Frantz, Donald. 1995. Southern Tiwa argument structure. In Clifford S. Burgess, Katarzyna Dziwirek & Donna Gerdts (eds.), *Grammatical relations: Theoretical approaches to empirical questions*, 75–98. Stanford: CSLI.

Gabelentz, Georg von der. 1891. *Die Sprachwissenschaft, ihre Aufgaben, Methoden und bisherige Ergebnisse*. Leipzig: Tauchnitz.

Gerdts, Donna B. 2013. The purview effect: Feminine gender on inanimates in Halkomelem Salish. In Chundra Cathcart, I-Hsuan Chen, Greg Finley, Shinae Kang, Clare S. Sandy & Elise Stickles (eds.), *Proceedings of the 37th annual meeting of the Berkeley Linguistics Society*, 417–426. Berkeley: Berkeley Linguistics Society.

Gore, Edward Cline. 1926. *A Zande grammar*. London: Sheldon Press.

Graudiņa, Milda. 1958. Laidzes un Kandavas izloksne [The dialects of Laizde and Kandava]. Rīga. University of Latvia Kandidata disertācija [=PhD dissertation].

Green, Ian. 1997. Nominal classification in Marrithiyel. In Mark Harvey & Nicholas Reid (eds.), *Nominal classification in Aboriginal Australia*, 229–253. Amsterdam: John Benjamins.

Greenberg, Joseph H. 1978. How does a language acquire gender markers? In Joseph H. Greenberg, Charles Ferguson & Edith Moravcsik (eds.), *Universals of human language*. Vol. 3: *How does a language acquire gender markers?: Word structure*, 47–82. Stanford: Stanford University Press.

Greyerz, Otto von & Ruth Bietenhard. 1997. *Berndeutsches Wörterbuch*. 6th edn. Muri bei Bern: Cosmos.

Grinevald Craig, Colette. 1977. *The structure of Jacaltec*. Austin: University of Texas Press.

Grinevald, Colette & Frank Seifart. 2004. Noun classes in African and Amazonian languages: Towards a comparison. *Linguistic Typology* 8(2). 243–285.

Güldemann, Tom. 1999. Head-initial meets head-final: Nominal suffixes in eastern and southern Bantu from a historical perspective. *Studies in African Linguistics* 29. 49–91.

Güldemann, Tom. 2004. Linear order as a basic morphosyntactic factor in Non-Khoe Khoisan. Paper presented at the the Syntax of the World's Languages conference in Leipzig, 8 August 2004.

Güldemann, Tom. 2006. "Janus-headed" nominals: The morphosyntax of agreement in Taa. Paper presented at the International Conference "Rara & Rarissima – collecting and interpreting unusual characteristics of human languages", Leipzig, 29 March–1 April 2006.

Güldemann, Tom & Ines Fiedler. 2019. Niger-Congo "noun classes" conflate gender with deriflection. In Francesca Di Garbo, Bruno Olsson & Bernhard Wälchli (eds.), *Grammatical gender and linguistic complexity: Volume I: General issues and specific studies*, 95–145. Berlin: Language Science Press. DOI:10.5281/zenodo.3462762

Haas, Mary R. 1940. Tunica. In *Handbook of American Indian Languages*, vol. 4, 1–143. New York: Augustin.

Hammarström, Harald, Robert Forkel & Martin Haspelmath (eds.). 2018. *Glottolog 3.2*. Jena: Max Planck Institute for the Science of Human History. http://glottolog.org/.

Handschuh, Corinna. 2018. Distinct marking of common and proper nouns in Oceanic (and beyond): Synchronic variation in from and function and historical implications. International Conference of Austronesian Linguistics, 17–20 July, 2018, Abstract book, 130–131. University of Antananarivo, Ambohitsaina.

Harbour, Daniel. 2008. *Morphosemantic number: From Kiowa noun classes to UG number features* (Studies in Natural Language and Linguistic Theory 69). Dordrecht: Springer.

Harrell, Frank E. 2001. *Regression modeling strategies: With applications to linear models, logistic regression, and survival analysis*. New York: Springer.

Haspelmath, Martin. 1999. Long distance agreement in Godoberi (Daghestanian) complement clauses. *Folia Linguistica* 33(2). 131–151.

Haspelmath, Martin. 2010. Comparative concepts and descriptive categories in crosslinguistic studies. *Language* 86(3). 663–687.

Haspelmath, Martin. 2013. Occurrence of nominal plurality. In Matthew S. Dryer & Martin Haspelmath (eds.), *The world atlas of language structures online*.

Leipzig: Max Planck Institute for Evolutionary Anthropology. https://wals. info/chapter/34.

Haspelmath, Martin. 2018. Toward a new conceptual framework for comparing gender systems and some so-called classifier systems. Talk presented at Stockholm University, Department of Linguistics on April 13, 2018.

Haugen, Einar. 1972. The ecology of language. In Answar Dil (ed.), *The ecology of language: Essays by Einar Haugen*, 325–339. Stanford: Stanford University Press.

Heath, Jeffrey. 1975. Some functional relationships in grammar. *Language* 51(1). 89–104.

Heine, Bernd. 1982. African noun class systems. In Hansjakob Seiler & Christian Lehmann (eds.), *Apprehension: Das sprachliche Erfassen von Gegenständen, Teil I: Bereich und Ordnung der Phänomene*, 189–216. Tübingen: Narr.

Heine, Bernd & Tania Kuteva. 2002. *World lexicon of grammaticalization*. Cambridge: Cambridge University Press.

Heine, Bernd & Mechthild Reh. 1984. *Grammaticalization and reanalysis in African languages* (Kölner Beiträge zur Afrikanistik 1). Hamburg: Buske.

Heine, Bernd & Rainer Vossen. 1983. On the origin of gender in Eastern Nilotic. In Rainer Vossen & Marianne Bechhaus-Gerst (eds.), *Nilotic studies: Proceedings of the international symposium on languages and history of the Nilotic peoples, Cologne, January 4-6, 1982*, 245–268. Cologne: Reimer.

Hengeveld, Kees. 2012. Referential markers and agreement markers in Functional Discourse Grammar. *Language Sciences* 34(4). 468–479.

Herrmann, Tania. 2005. Relative clauses in English dialects of the British Isles. In Bernd Kortmann, Tanja Herrmann, Lukas Pietsch & Susanne Wagner (eds.), *A comparative grammar of British English dialects: Agreement, gender, relative clauses*, 1–123. Berlin: Mouton de Gruyter.

Himmelmann, Nikolaus. 2001. Articles. In Martin Haspelmath, Ekkehard König, Wulf Oesterreicher & Wolfgang Raible (eds.), *Language typology and language universals: An international handbook*, 831–841. Berlin: Mouton de Gruyter.

Hockett, Charles F. 1958. *A course in modern linguistics*. New York: Macmillan.

Hopper, Paul J. & Sandra A. Thompson. 1984. The discourse basis for lexical categories in universal grammar. *Language* 60(4). 703–752.

Hudson, Joyce. 1985. *Grammatical and semantic aspects of Fitzroy Valley Kriol* (Work Papers of SIL-AAB, Series A, Vol. 8). Darwin: Summer Institute of Linguistics.

Huntley, David. 1980. The evolution of genitive-accusative animate and personal nouns in Slavic dialects. In Jacek Fisiak (ed.), *Historical morphology* (Trends in Linguistics: Studies and Monographs 17), 189–212. The Hague: Mouton.

Ishiyama, Osamu. 2008. *Diachronic perspectives on personal pronouns in Japanese.* State University of New York at Buffalo. (Doctoral dissertation).

Jespersen, Otto. 1949. *A modern English grammar on historical principles, part II.* London: George Allen & Unwin Ltd.

Johnston, Raymond Leslie. 1980. *Nakanai of New Britain. The grammar of an Oceanic language* (Pacific linguistics B70). Canberra: Australian National University.

Jurafsky, Daniel. 1996. Universal tendencies in the semantics of the diminutive. *Language* 72. 533–578.

Karatsareas, Petros. 2009. The loss of grammatical gender in Cappadocian Greek. *Transactions of the Philological Society* 107. 196–230.

Karatsareas, Petros. 2014. On the diachrony of gender in Asia Minor Greek: The development of semantic agreement in Pontic. *Language Sciences* 43. 77–101.

Kayser, MSC., Alois. 1993. *Nauru grammar.* Edited by Karl H. Rensch. Yarralumla (Australia): Embassy of the Federal Republic of Germany.

Kibrik, Andrej A. 2011. *Reference in discourse.* Oxford: Oxford University Press.

Kilarski, Marcin. 2013. *Nominal classification: A history of its study from the classical period to the present.* Amsterdam: John Benjamins.

Killian, Don. 2015. *Topics in Uduk phonology and morphosyntax.* University of Helsinki. (Doctoral dissertation).

Killian, Don. 2019. Gender in Uduk. In Francesca Di Garbo, Bruno Olsson & Bernhard Wälchli (eds.), *Grammatical gender and linguistic complexity: Volume I: General issues and specific studies*, 147–168. Berlin: Language Science Press. DOI:10.5281/zenodo.3462764

Kirby, Simon, Hannah Cornish & Kenny Smith. 2008. Cumulative cultural evolution in the laboratory: An experimental approach to the origins of structure in human language. *Proceedings of the National Academy of Sciences* 105(31). 10681–10686. DOI:10.1073/pnas.0707835105

Kohnen, Fr. Bernardo. 1933. *Shilluk grammar, with a little Shilluk-English dictionary.* Verona: Missioni Africane.

Koptjevskaja-Tamm, Maria. 2005. Maria's ring of gold: Adnominal possession and non-anchoring relations in the European languages. In Ji-yung Kim, Yu Lander & Barbara H. Partee (eds.), *Possessives and beyond: Semantics and syntax*, 155–181. Amherst, MA: GLSA Publications.

Koptjevskaja-Tamm, Maria & Bernhard Wälchli. 2001. The Circum-Baltic languages: An areal-typological approach. In Östen Dahl & Maria Koptjevskaja-Tamm (eds.), *Circum-Baltic languages: Typology and contact*, vol. 2, 615–750. Amsterdam: John Benjamins.

Kuhn, Jonas & Louisa Sadler. 2007. Single conjunct agreement and the formal treatment of coordination in LFG. In Miriam Butt & Tracy Holloway King (eds.), *On-line Proceedings of the LFG2007 Conference*. http://journals.linguisticsociety.org/proceedings/index.php/BLS/issue/view/120.

Kusters, Wouter. 2003. *Linguistic complexity: The influence of social change on verbal inflections*. University of Leiden. (Doctoral dissertation). Utrecht: LOT.

Kusters, Wouter. 2008. Complexity in linguistic theory, language learning and language change. In Matti Miestamo, Kaius Sinnemäki & Fred Karlsson (eds.), *Language complexity: Typology, contact, change*, 3–22. Amsterdam: John Benjamins.

Lass, Roger. 1990. How to do things with junk: Exaptation in language evolution. *Journal of Linguistics* 26. 79–102.

Leeding, Velma J. 1989. *Anindilyakwa phonology and morphology*. University of Sydney. (Doctoral dissertation).

Lehmann, Christian. 1982. Universal and typological aspects of agreement. In Hansjakob Seiler & Franz Josef Stachowiak (eds.), *Apprehension: Das sprachliche Erfassen von Gegenständen*. Vol. 2: *Universal and typological aspects of agreement: Die Techniken und ihre Zusammenhänge in Einzelsprachen*, 201–267. Tübingen: Narr.

Lehmann, Christian. 1984. *Der Relativsatz. Typologie seiner Strukturen, Theorie seiner Funktionen, Kompendium seiner Grammatik* (Language Universals Series 3). Tübingen: Gunter Narr.

Liljegren, Henrik. 2019. Gender typology and gender (in)stability in Hindu Kush Indo-Aryan languages. In Francesca Di Garbo, Bruno Olsson & Bernhard Wälchli (eds.), *Grammatical gender and linguistic complexity: Volume I: General issues and specific studies*, 279–328. Berlin: Language Science Press. DOI:10.5281/zenodo.3462772

Lindström, Eva. 1995. Animacy in interrogative pronouns. In Inger Moen, Hanne Gram Simonsen & Helge Lødrup (eds.), *Papers from the 16th Scandinavian Conference of Linguistics*, 307–315. Oslo: University of Oslo.

Loughnane, Robyn. 2009. *A grammar of Oksapmin*. University of Melbourne. (Doctoral dissertation).

Lupyan, Gary & Rick Dale. 2010. Language structure is partly determined by social structure. *PLOS one* 5(1). e8559.

Luraghi, Silvia. 2011. The origin of the Proto-Indo-European gender system: Typological considerations. *Folia Linguistica* 45(2). 435–464.

Luraghi, Silvia. 2015. From non-canonical to canonical agreement. In Hans Amstutz, Andreas Dorn, Matthias Müller, Miriam Ronsdorf & Sami Uljas (eds.), *Fuzzy boundaries*, 71–88. Hamburg: Widmaier.

Lyons, Christopher. 1999. *Definiteness*. Cambridge: Cambridge University Press.

Malkiel, Yakov. 1957–1958. Diachronic hypercharacterization in Romance. *Archivum Linguisticum* 9–10. 79–113, 1–36.

Mathiot, Madeleine & Marjorie Roberts. 1978. Sex roles as revealed through referential gender in American English. In Madeleine Mathiot (ed.), *Boas, Sapir and Whorf revisited*, 1–47. The Hague: Mouton.

McWhorter, John. 2001. The world's simplest grammars are creole grammars. *Linguistic Typology* 5(2-3). 125–166.

Meeuwis, Michael. 2013. Lingala. In Susanne Michaelis, Philippe Maurer, Martin Haspelmath & Magnus Huber (eds.), *The survey of pidgin and creole languages*. Vol. 3: *Lingala: Contact languages based on languages from Africa, Asia, Australia and the Americas*, 25–33. Oxford: Oxford University Press.

Meillet, Antoine. 1897. *Recherches sur l'emploi du génitif-accusatif en vieux-slave* (Bulletin de l'Ecole des hautes études 115). Paris: Bouillon.

Mellow, Greg. 2013. *A dictionary of Owa: A language of the Solomon Islands*. Berlin: De Gruyter Mouton.

Merrifield, William R. 1959. Classification of Kiowa nouns. *International Journal of American Linguistics* 25(4). 269–271.

Mettouchi, Amina. 2000. La "t" n'est-il qu'une marque de féminin en berbère (kabyle)? *Faits de Langue* 14. 217–225.

Miestamo, Matti. 2008. Grammatical complexity in a cross-linguistic perspective. In Matti Miestamo, Kaius Sinnemäki & Fred Karlsson (eds.), *Language complexity: Typology, contact, change*, 23–41. Amsterdam: John Benjamins.

Miestamo, Matti, Kaius Sinnemäki & Fred Karlsson (eds.). 2008. *Language complexity: Typology, contact, change*. Amsterdam: John Benjamins.

Mithun, Marianne. 1986. The convergence of noun classification systems. In Colette Craig (ed.), *Noun classes and categorization. Proceedings of a symposium on categorization and noun classification, Eugene, Oregon, October 1983*, 379–397. Amsterdam: John Benjamins.

Mithun, Marianne. 1999. *The languages of native North America*. Cambridge: Cambridge University Press.

Mithun, Marianne. 2014. Gender and culture. In Greville Corbett (ed.), *The expression of gender*, 132–160. Berlin: Mouton de Gruyter.

Moravcsik, Edith. 1978. Agreement. In Joseph Greenberg (ed.), *Universals of human language*. Vol. 4: *Agreement: Syntax*, 331–374. Standord: Stanford University Press.

Moravcsik, Edith. 1994. Parts and wholes in definite article constructions. Paper presented at the Pre-inaugural meeting of ALT, Konstanz, November 30.

Moscati, Sabatino. 1964. *An introduction to the comparative grammar of the Semitic languages*. Wiesbaden: Otto Harrasowitz.

Mous, Maarten. 2008. Number as an exponent of gender in Cushitic. In Zygmunt Frajzyngier & Erin Shay (eds.), *Interaction of morphology and syntax: Case studies in Afroasiatic*, 137–160. Amsterdam: John Benjamins.

Nagaraja, Keralapura Shreenivasaiah. 1996. The status of Lyngngam. *Mon-Khmer Studies: A Journal of Southeast Asian Linguistics and Languages* 26. 37–50.

Nagaraja, Keralapura Shreenivasaiah, Paul Sidwell & Simon J. Greenhill. 2013. A lexicostatistical study of the Khasian languages: Khasi, Pnar, Lyngngam, and War. *Mon-Khmer Studies* 42. 1–11.

Nau, Nicole. 1999. Was schlägt der Kasus? Zu Paradigmen und Formengebrauch von Interrogativpronomina. *Sprachtypologie und Universalienforschung* 52. 130–150.

Nau, Nicole. 2011. Declension classes in Latvian and Latgalian: Morphomics vs. morphophonology. *Baltic Linguistics* 2. 141–177.

Newman, Paul. 1979. Explaining Hausa feminines. *Studies in African Linguistics* 10(2). 197–226.

Nichols, Johanna. 1992. *Linguistic diversity in space and time*. Chicago: University of Chicago Press.

Nichols, Johanna. 2003. Diversity and stability in language. In Brian D. Joseph & Richard D. Janda (eds.), *The handbook of historical linguistics*, 283–310. Oxford: Blackwell.

Nichols, Johanna. 2009. Linguistic complexity: A comprehensive definition and survey. In Geoffrey Sampson, David Gil & Peter Trudgill (eds.), *Language complexity as an evolving variable*, 110–125. Oxford: Oxford University Press.

Nichols, Johanna. 2019. Why is gender so complex? Some typological considerations. In Francesca Di Garbo, Bruno Olsson & Bernhard Wälchli (eds.), *Grammatical gender and linguistic complexity: Volume I: General issues and specific studies*, 63–92. Berlin: Language Science Press. DOI:10.5281/zenodo.3462760

Olsson, Bruno. 2017. *The Coastal Marind language*. Singapore: Nanyang Technological University. (Doctoral dissertation).

Olsson, Bruno. 2019. The gender system of Coastal Marind. In Francesca Di Garbo, Bruno Olsson & Bernhard Wälchli (eds.), *Grammatical gender and linguistic complexity: Volume I: General issues and specific studies*, 197–223. Berlin: Language Science Press. DOI:10.5281/zenodo.3462768

Oomen, Antoinette. 1981. Gender and plurality in Rendille. *Afroasiatic linguistics* 8(1). 35–75.

Orkaydo, Ongaye Oda. 2013. *A grammar of Konso*. Utrecht: LOT: Netherlands Graduate School of Linguistics. (Doctoral dissertation).

Parker, Enid M. & Richard J. Hayward. 1985. *An Afar-English-French dictionary (with grammatical notes in English)*. London: School of Oriental & African Studies (SOAS). 308.

Passer, Matthias Benjamin. 2016a. (What) do verb classifiers classify? *Lingua* 174(1). 16–44.

Passer, Matthias Benjamin. 2016b. *The typology and diachrony of nominal classification*. Utrecht: University of Amsterdam. (Doctoral dissertation).

Pawley, Andrew. 2004. Using *he* and *she* for inanimate referents in English: Questions of grammar and world view. In Nick J. Enfield (ed.), *Ethnosyntax, explorations in grammar and culture*, 110–137. Oxford: Oxford University Press.

Payne, Doris L. 1985. *Aspects of the grammar of Yagua: A typological perspective*. University of California, Los Angeles. (Doctoral dissertation).

Payne, Doris L. 1986. Noun classification in Yagua. In Colette G. Craig (ed.), *Noun classes and categorization. Proceedings of a symposium on categorization and noun classification, Eugene, Oregon, October 1983*, 113–131. Amsterdam: John Benjamins.

Payne, Doris L. 1998. Maasai gender in typological perspective. *Studies in African Linguistics* 27(2). 159–175.

Penchoen, Thomas. 1973. *Etude syntaxique d'un parler berbère (Ait-Frah de l'Aurès)*. Napoli: Centro di studi magrebini.

Petrollino, Sara. 2016. *A grammar of Hamar: A South Omotic language of Ethiopia*. Cologne: Köppe.

Plank, Frans. 2015. Genus im Gastgewerbe. Mit einem Nachtrag: Der/das Zwiebelfisch und die Tiefe der Jahre. Manuscript.

Plaster, Keith & Maria Polinsky. 2007. Women are not dangerous things: Gender and categorization. *Harvard Working Papers in Linguistics* 12. 1–44.

Polinsky, Maria & Bernard Comrie. 1999. Agreement in Tsez. *Folia Linguistica* 33(2). 109–130.

Polinsky, Maria & Ezra Van Everbroeck. 2003. Development of gender classifications: Modeling the historical change from Latin to French. *Language* 79. 356–390.

Rabel-Heymann, Lili. 1977. Gender in Khasi nouns. *Mon-Khmer Studies* 6. 247–272.

Reid, Nicholas. 1990. *Ngan'gityemerri: A language of the Daly River region, Northern Territory of Australia.* Canberra: Australian National University. (Doctoral dissertation).

Reid, Nicholas. 1997. Class and classifier in Ngan'gityemerri. In Mark Harvey & Nicholas Reid (eds.), *Nominal classification in Aboriginal Australia*, 165–225. Amsterdam: John Benjamins.

Ring, Hiram. 2015. *A grammar of Pnar.* Singapore: Nanyang Technological University. (Doctoral dissertation).

Rissanen, Matti. 1997. The pronominalization of *one*. In Matti Rissanen, Merja Kytö & Kirsi Heikkonen (eds.), *Grammaticalization at work. Studies of long-term developments in English*, 87–143. Berlin: Mouton de Gruyter.

Rizzi, Luigi. 1982. A restructuring rule. In Luigi Rizzi (ed.), *Issues on Italian syntax*, 1–48. Dordrecht: Foris.

Rudzīte, Marta. 1964. *Latviešu izlokšņu teksti [Texts in Latvian dialects].* Rīgā: Latvijas Valsts universitāte. Reprinted in Rudzīte, Marta 2005. *Darbi latviešu dialektoloģijā*, 173–251. Rīga: LU Akadēmiskais apgāds.

Russell, Bertrand. 1905. On denoting. *Mind, New Series* 14. 479–493.

Sagna, Serge. 2011. Semantic categorizations in the Gújjolaay Eegimaa collectives and distributives. In Oliver Bond, Peter K. Austin, David Nathan & Marten Lutz (eds.), *Proceedings of Conference on Language Documentation and Linguistic Theory 3*, 237–246. London: Department of Linguistics, SOAS.

Sampson, Geoffrey, David Gil & Peter Trudgill (eds.). 2009. *Language complexity as an evolving variable.* Oxford: Oxford University Press.

Santos Sachot, Rosine. 1996. *Le mey.* Paris: Université de la Sorbonne Nouvelle. (Doctoral dissertation).

Sasse, Hans-Jürgen. 1993. Syntactic categories and subcategories. In Joachim Jakobs, Arnim von Stechow, Wolfgang Sternefeld & Theo Vennemann (eds.), *Syntax: Ein internationales Handbuch zeitgenössicher Forschung / An international handbook of contemporary research*, 646–686. Berlin: Walter de Gruter.

Schachter, Paul & Fe T. Otanes. 1972. *Tagalog reference grammar.* Berkeley: University of California Press. Reprinted in 1983.

Schuh, Russell G. 1998. *A grammar of Miya* (University of California Publications in Linguistics 130). Berkeley & Los Angeles: University of California Press. 414.

Schuster-Šewc, Heinz. 1976. *Gramatika hornjoserbskeje rěče [Grammar of Upper Sorbian].* Vol. 2: Syntaksa. Bautzen: Domowina.

Seifart, Frank. 2005. *The structure and use of shape-based noun classes in Miraña.* Nijmegen: Radboud Universiteit Nijmegen. (Doctoral dissertation).

Seifart, Frank. 2007. The prehistory of nominal classification in Witotoan languages. *International Journal of American Linguistics* 73(4). 411–445.

Seifart, Frank. 2010. Nominal classification. *Language and Linguistics Compass* 4(8). 719–736.

Seifart, Frank. 2018. The semantic reduction of the noun universe and the diachrony of nominal classification. In William B. McGregor & Søren Wichmann (eds.), *The diachrony of classification systems*, 9–32. Amsterdam: John Benjamins.

Senft, Gunter. 1985. Klassifikationspartikel im Kilivila: Glossen zu ihrer morphologischen Rolle, ihrem Inventar und ihrer Funktion in Satz und Diskurs. *Linguistische Berichte* 99. 373–393.

Senft, Gunter. 1986. *Kilivila: The language of the Trobriand islanders.* Berlin: Mouton de Gruyter.

Senft, Gunter. 1993. A grammaticalization hypothesis on the origin of Kilivila classificatory particles. *Sprachtypologie und Universalieforschung* 46(2). 100–112.

Seuren, Pieter A. M. 2009. Donkey sentences. In Keith Allan (ed.), *Concise encyclopedia of semantics*, 269–271. Oxford: Elsevier.

Siemund, Peter. 2008. *Pronominal gender in English: A study of English varieties from a cross-linguistic perspective.* New York: Routledge.

Siemund, Peter & Florian Dolberg. 2011. From lexical to referential gender: An analysis of gender change in medieval English based on two historical documents. *Folia Linguistica* 45(2). 489–534. DOI 10.1515/flin.2011.018.

Silverstein, Michael. 1976. Hierarchy of features and ergativity. In Robert M. W. Dixon (ed.), *Grammatical categories in Australian languages*, 112–190. New Jersey: Humanities Press.

Singer, Ruth. 2011. Typologising idiomaticity: Noun-verb idioms and their relations. *Linguistic Typology* 15. 625–569.

Singer, Ruth. 2012. Do nominal classifiers mediate selectional restrictions? An investigation of the function of semantically-based nominal classifiers in Mawng (Iwaidjan, Australian). *Linguistics* 50. 995–990.

Singer, Ruth. 2018. Beyond the classifier/gender dichotomy: The role of flexibility in a more integrated typology of nominal classification. In Sebastian Fedden, Jenny Audring & Greville G. Corbett (eds.), *Non-canonical gender systems*, 100–128. Oxford: Oxford University Press.

Sinnemäki, Kaius. 2014a. Cognitive processing, language typology, and variation. *WIREs Cognitive Science* 5(4). 477–487.

Sinnemäki, Kaius. 2014b. Complexity trade-offs: A case study. In Frederick J. Newmeyer & Laurel B. Preston (eds.), *Measuring grammatical complexity*, 179–201. Oxford: Oxford University Press.

Sinnemäki, Kaius. 2019. On the distribution and complexity of gender and numeral classifiers. In Francesca Di Garbo, Bruno Olsson & Bernhard Wälchli (eds.), *Grammatical gender and linguistic complexity: Volume II: World-wide comparative studies*, 133–200. Berlin: Language Science Press. DOI:10.5281/zenodo.3462782

Sinnemäki, Kaius & Francesca Di Garbo. 2018. Language structures may adapt to the sociolinguistic environment, but it matters what and how you count: A typological study of verbal and nominal complexity. *Frontiers in Psychology* 9. DOI:10.3389/fpsyg.2018.01141

Small, Priscilla C. 1990. A syntactic sketch of Coatzospan Mixtec. In C. Henry Bradley & Barbara E. Hollenbach (eds.), *Studies in the syntax of Mixtecan languages 2* (Summer Institute of Linguistics and the University of Texas at Arlington Publications in Linguistics 90), 261–479. Dallas: Summer Institute of Linguistics & the University of Texas at Arlington.

Smith-Stark, Thomas Cedric. 1974. The plurality split. In Michael W. La Galy, Robert A. Fox & Anthony Bruck (eds.), *Papers from the 10th regional meeting of the Chicago Linguistic Society*, 657–661. Chicago: Chicago Linguistics Society.

Smith, Kenny & Elizabeth Wonnacott. 2010. Eliminating unpredictable variation through iterated learning. *Cognition* 116. 444–449.

Spagnolo, Lorenzo M. 1933. *Bari grammar*. Verona: Missioni Africane.

Stolz, Thomas. 2012. Survival in a niche. On gender-copy in Chamorro (and sundry languages). In Martine Vanhove, Thomas Stolz, Aina Urdze & Hitomi Otsuka (eds.), *Morphologies in contact*, 93–140. Munich: Akademie-Verlag.

Straus, Anne Terry & Robert Brightman. 1982. The implacable raspberry. *Papers in Linguistics* 15. 97–137. DOI:10.1080/08351818209370564

Sutton, Logan. 2014. *Kiowa-Tanoan: A synchronic and diachronic study*. Albuquerque: University of New Mexico. (Doctoral dissertation).

Svärd, Erik. 2019. Gender in New Guinea. In Francesca Di Garbo, Bruno Olsson & Bernhard Wälchli (eds.), *Grammatical gender and linguistic complexity: Volume I: General issues and specific studies*, 225–276. Berlin: Language Science Press. DOI:10.5281/zenodo.3462770

Swanton, John R. 1921. The Tunica language. *International Journal of American Linguistics* 2(1/2). 1–39.

Tasmowski-De Ryck, Liliane & Paul Verluyten. 1982. Linguistic control of pronouns. *Journal of Semantics* 1. 323–346.

Teleman, Ulf, Staffan Hellberg & Erik Andersson. 1999. *Svenska Akademiens grammatik [Grammar of the Swedish Academy]*. Vol. 2: Ord. Stockholm: Nordstedts.

Thiesen, Wesley & David Weber. 2012. *A grammar of Bora with special attention to tone* (SIL International Publications in Linguistics 148). Dallas: SIL International.

Thomason, Lucy Grey. 2003. *The proximate and obviative contrast in Meskwaki.* University of Texas at Austin. (Doctoral dissertation).

Traill, Anthony. 1994. *A !Xóõ dictionary.* Cologne: Rüdiger Köppe Verlag.

Trudgill, Peter. 2011. *Sociolinguistic typology: Social determinants of linguistic complexity.* New York: Oxford University Press.

Tsegaye, Mulugeta. 2017. *Plural gender: Behavior evidence for plural as a value of Cushitic gender with reference to Konso.* Leiden: Leiden University. (Doctoral dissertation).

Tucker, A. N. & J. Tompo Ole Mpaayei. 1955. *A Maasai grammar with vocabulary* (Publications of the African Institute, Leyden 2). London: Longmans, Green & Co.

Universals Archive. n.d. *Konstanz universals archive.* https://typo.uni-konstanz.de/archive/. Compiled by Frans Plank and collaborators.

Usher, Timothy & Edgar Suter. 2015. The Anim languages of Southern New Guinea. *Oceanic Linguistics* 54(1). 110–142.

Vajda, Edward J. 2003. Ket verb structure in typological perspective. *STUF - Language Typology and Universals* 56(1-2). 55–92. DOI:10.1524/stuf.2003.56.12.55

van den Heuvel, Wilco. 2006. *Biak: Description of an Austronesian language of Papua.* Vrije Universiteit Amsterdam. (Doctoral dissertation).

van der Meer, Suzanne. 2015. *The distribution of P-nouns in Cushitic.* Leiden University. (MA thesis).

Van Valin, Robert D. 1977. *Aspects of Lakhota syntax: A study of Lakhota (Teton Dakota) syntax and its implications for universal grammar.* University of California, Berkeley. (Doctoral dissertation).

van Driem, Georg. 1987. *A grammar of Limbu.* Berlin: Mouton de Gruyter.

van Rijn, Marlou. 2016. The grammaticalization of possessive person marking: A typological approach. *Transaction of the Philological Society* 114(2). 233–276.

Verhaar, John W. M. 1995. *Toward a reference grammar of Tok Pisin: An experiment in corpus linguistics* (Oceanic Linguistics Special Publication 26). Honolulu: University of Hawai'i Press.

Verkerk, Annemarie. 2014. Change in Bantu noun class systems. Poster presented at the Nijmegen Lectures 2014 (Nijmegen, 27–29 January 2014).

Wälchli, Bernhard. 2017. The incomplete story of feminine gender loss in Northwestern Latvian dialects. *Baltic Linguistics* 8. 143–214.

Wälchli, Bernhard. 2018. The rise of gender in Nalca (Mek, Tanah Papua): The drift towards the canonical gender attractor. In Sebastian Fedden, Jenny Audring & Greville G. Corbett (eds.), *Non-canonical gender systems*, 68–99. Oxford: Oxford University Press.

Wälchli, Bernhard. 2019. The feminine anaphoric gender gram, incipient gender marking, maturity, and extracting anaphoric gender markers from parallel texts. In Francesca Di Garbo, Bruno Olsson & Bernhard Wälchli (eds.), *Grammatical gender and linguistic complexity: Volume II: World-wide comparative studies*, 61–131. Berlin: Language Science Press. DOI:10.5281/zenodo.3462780

Watkins, Laurel J. & Parker McKenzie. 1984. *A grammar of Kiowa*. Lincoln: University of Nebraska Press.

Weidert, Alfons. 1975. *I Tkong Amwi: Deskriptive Analyse eines Wardialekts des Khasi* (Neuindidische Studien). Wiesbaden: Otto Harrassowitz.

Widmark, Gun. 1966. Den inkongruenta neutrala predikatsfyllnaden och dess plats i svenskans genussystem [The non-agreeing neuter complement and its place in the current Swedish gender system]. *Nysvenska studier* 46. 91–135.

Wolfart, H. Christoph. 1973. *Plains Cree: A grammatical study* (Transactions of the American Philosophical Society, New Series 63.5). Philadelphia: American Philosophical Society.

Wonderly, William L., Paul L. Kirk & Lorna F. Gibson. 1954. Number in Kiowa: Nouns, demonstratives, and adjectives. *International Journal of American Linguistics* 20. 1–7.

Wunderlich, Dieter. 1994. Towards a lexicon-based theory of agreement. *Theoretical Linguistics* 20. 1–35.

Zaliznjak, Andrey A. 1977. *Grammatičeskij slovar' russkogo jazyka: Slovoizmenenie [Grammatical dictionary of Russian: Inflection]*. Moskva: Russkij Jazyk.

Zipf, George Kingsley. 1935. *The psycho-biology of language. An introduction to dynamic philology*. Boston: Houghton Mifflin.

Appendix: List of topics with short definitions and where these are treated in the chapter

Absolute complexity: complexity as an objective property of grammatical domains (§2.1).

Absolute condition: also obligatory condition: condition that always determines a certain choice of agreement value (§7.5).

Adjacency: controller and target or target and controller follow each other immediately. A possible specific relationship in agreement (§7.2).

Adnominal use (of nominal morphology): marker on an adnominal modifier or dependent in an NP with a noun head or NP marker in a NP with a noun head (§4.1).

Adnominal modifier: modifier in an NP with a head noun, such as attributive adjective, relative clause with a head noun, attributive demonstrative and attributive numeral (§4.1).

Agentivity: semantic connection between animacy and inanimate objects, responsible for the fact that agentive nouns are more likely to take an animate gender (§3.3 (i)).

Agreement: an asymmetric specific relation between a controller and a target involving displaced information. Agreement is syntactic to the extent that it involves words or groups of words as targets and controllers, but the relation between controller and target can be semantic (as in inter-sentential agreement). Controllers can be latent (contextual, semantic) (§7.1).

Agreement Hierarchy: more distal controllers are more likely to trigger semantic agreement along a hierarchy attributive < predicate < relative pronoun < personal pronoun (Corbett 1991: 226) (§3.6).

Anaphor, pl. anaphora: linguistic element that is lacking clear independent reference and picks up reference through connection with another element.

Animacy distinctions: the linguistic encoding of the ontological difference between living and non-living beings.

Animacy hierarchy: certain patterns of language structure (e.g., plural marking, differential object marking) are more likely to emerge/be synchronically restricted to humans and or highly animate entities only. Based on these effects, types of entities can be arranged on a hierarchy of degree of animacy: speaker > addressee > 3rd person > kinship terms > other humans > "higher" animals > "lower" animals > discrete inanimates > nondiscrete inanimates (Smith-Stark 1974; Corbett 2000; Haspelmath 2013).

Apposition: two nominal constituents in the same case role and not in a predicative relationship and not in a relationship of subordination (none of the two is the head of the other one) (§4.3).

Areal pattern: distribution of linguistic properties across languages in a geographical area that cannot be explained by obvious genealogical relation of languages (§11.1).

Articulatory plurality: lexical plurality expressed with double-hand signs in sign languages (§9.1).

Associated gender: noun receiving its gender through a link with another noun (§3.4).

Augmentative: grammatical construction that, in its basic meaning, expresses that a given entity is bigger than its standard size (§5.2).

Canonical Approach: theoretical and methodological approach to the typological study of morphosyntactic features developed by Greville Corbett. The approach is based on the idea that, for every morphosyntactic phenomenon, there exists a space of crosslinguistic variation and that attested language-specific systems are situated in this space in ways that more or less correspond to a certain identified base of comparison (Audring & Fedden 2018: 2) (§1).

Case: marker of grammatical relation or oblique semantic role, often cumulating with gender (§8.2).

Classifiers: cover term for numeral classifiers, noun classifiers, and possessive classifiers, and some further minor types of classifiers (§1).

Co-conceptuality: a specific relationship in agreement where controller and target express identity of concept (but not identity of reference) (§7.2).

Co-evolution: a set of more than one diachronic change that are at least partly dependent on each other (§10.2).

Complex controller: the agreement controller consists of several words (§7.3).

Complex: (i) non-trivial in structure, so that an exhaustive description cannot be short. But also (ii) consisting of several elements and (iii) heterogeneous, consisting of various, but related phenomena (§1).

Complex target: the agreement target consists of several words. These constitute a formal group (§7.4).

Compound gender: the gender of a compound is different from the gender of its head (§6.2).

Concurrent gender systems: two or more than two gender systems that are largely independent of each other within the same language (§1).

Condition: factor provoking the choice of an agreement value, can be absolute or relative (§7.5).

Contrastive focus: emphasis of a choice of argument as opposed to another or other possible choices, induces transparency in gender-marked anaphoric pronouns by activating the descriptive content of gender (§3.6).

Controller: formal or contextual element triggering the choice of a marker of a grammatical category (such as gender or number) (§7.1).

Coreferentiality: a specific relationship in agreement where controller and target have identity of reference (§7.2).

Covert marking of gender: extent to which nouns lack formal gender assignment (§6.4).

Cumulation: expression of two or more grammatical categories in the same morpheme (§8).

Decategorialization of nouns: nouns losing some of their prototypical properties, notably when used in non-referential contexts (e.g., predicatively) (§7.6).

Declension class: morphological paradigm (according to number, case, and/or any other nominal grammatical category) characterizing a subset of nouns (§1, §6.4).

Default: rest category for gender assignment, usually thought of as last resort (§6.5).

Derivational gender: gender in nominal targets expressed on nouns by derivational morphology (§3.4, §7.6).

Description length: from an information theory perspective, one of the ways of measuring system complexity. The longer its description, the more complex the system (§2.1).

Descriptive complexity: (or Kolmogorov complexity), the information required to describe a system (the longer the description the more complex the system) (§2.1).

Differential case marking: a grammatical relation is indicated by different case forms or appositions, often depending on animacy and/or definiteness (§8.2).

Differential object marking: the grammatical relation object is indicated by different case forms or appositions, often depending on animacy and/or definiteness (§3.5).

Diminutive: grammatical construction that, in its basic meaning, expresses that a given entity is smaller than its standard size. Additional meanings associated with diminutive constructions are: affection, partitive, female (see Jurafsky 1996 for a full list) (§5.2).

Displacement (of information): the word or context triggering the choice of a grammatical value of a marker does not originate in the word on which the category is marked (§6.4).

Dynamic approach: viewing a set of related phenomena as something that can emerge, evolve and disappear in accordance with certain diachronic pathways of development and assuming that these developments are crucial for the understanding of the phenomena (§1).

Ecology of languages: the interaction between any given language and its natural and/or social environment (Haugen 1972) (§11.2).

Feature: a fully paradigmaticized grammatical category type expressed by systematic morphological marking. Typical examples of features are: gender, number, case, person, and tense (Corbett 2012) (§7.5).

Formal assignment: morphological and/or phonological gender assignment and opposed to semantic gender assignment (§5.1, §6.4).

Formal group: several words together constituting a syntactic unit (can but need not be a constituent; Croft 2001: 190) (§7.1).

Gender: gender is a grammatical category type with a semantic core of animacy and/or sex reflecting classes of referents, which have a propensity to turn into classes of noun lexemes. It is overtly marked on noun-associated forms. It typically exhibits cumulative expression with number, case, and/or person. Gender is organized in the form of systems (§1).

Gender assignment: rationale determining the gender of a noun (can be semantic or formal) (§5).

Gender recategorization: the phenomenon whereby gender assignment is not fixed but subject to variation based on reference construal. Synonymous with: *flexible/manipulable gender assignment*. But also used for reconceptualization of same referent in discourse (§3.7).

Gender resolution: the gender of a complex controller is determined by means of interaction between the genders of at least two of its parts (§7.3).

Gendered clause: subordinate clause (often an independent relative clause) bearing a gender marker (§4.3).

Gender value: one gender from the set of genders in a gender system (§1).

Grammatical anaphor: anaphor intermediate between pronoun (third person pronoun) and noun (noun in anaphoric function like *that man*) (§4.3).

Headedness reversal: a semantic modifier or dependent of a phrase is its formal head (§4.3).

Hierarchical patterning: organization of the structure of a grammatical category according to a hierarchy (§3).

Hybrid noun: noun that can trigger two or more different gender values (but often only one of them is lexical gender) (§3.6).

Hypercharacterization: diachronic process whereby a marker is added that overtly indicates a category that the element already had before (§6.4).

Idiomatization of gender: a particular use of gender is restricted to idioms or an idiom (§7.7).

Independent modifier: modifier in an NP without a head noun, such as free relative clause, pronominal demonstratives and pronominal numerals (§4.1).

Independent nominal morphology: grammatical marking in an NP without a head noun (§4.1).

Indexation: an index is a bound or free grammatical marker – prototypically a marker of person – that denotes the argument itself. One argument can be marked several times by different indexes, which are then in a relationship of coreference (§7.1).

Individuation hierarchy: version of the animacy hierarchy subdividing inanimates into tangible objects, abstracts and mass nouns (Sasse 1993) (§3.2).

Information transfer chain: displacement of information in agreement in several steps, e.g., from gender assignment to noun lexeme to word-form to complex controller to complex target to word within target to gender marker realized on that word (§7.1).

Inherited gender: the possessor determines the gender of a noun or NP (§3.4).

Inter-sentential agreement: controller and target in agreement are or can be in different sentences (§7.1).

Intra-sentential agreement: controller and target in agreement occur within the same sentence (§7.1).

Inventory complexity: the number of distinctions in a grammatical system (§2.1).

Latent controller: a contextual controller that is not realized in syntax (§7.1).

Lexical gender: classes of noun lexemes distinguished on noun-associated forms (§3.1).

Local agreement: agreement within the noun phrase (§4.1).

Mature phenomenon: a phenomenon with a non-trivial prehistory (Dahl 2004: 2) (§1).

Many-to-one gender assignment: the same gender value is the outcome of several assignment rules (§6.2).

Morphological gender assignment: the gender value of a controller is determined by some of its inherent morphological properties (e.g., its declension class) (§5.1, §6.4).

Neutral gender: agreement form used for agreement with non-noun controllers, such as infinitive phrases, clauses, interjections and quoted phrases (§6.5).

Nomifier: cover term for gender and classifiers (§1).

Nominal gender targets: nouns or noun phrases that are gender targets (typically decategorialized nouns) (§7.6).

Nominal morphology: cover term for non-lexical markers within the noun phrase (§4.1).

Non-noun controllers: a controller in agreement that is not a noun, see neutral gender (§6.5).

Noun-associated form: an adnominal modifier (article, demonstrative, adjective, or numeral), or a verbal argument index, or an anaphoric pronoun (§1).

Noun class: same as gender, but emphasizing classes of noun lexemes (§1).

Noun incorporation: compound of a noun (usually in object function) and its verbal head. Has classifying potential to the extent the incorporated nouns are hyperonymic (§7.6).

Nominal target: agreement is imposed on a noun or noun phrase (§7.6).

Number: grammatical category marking number of referents (singular, plural, dual, non-singular etc.), frequently cumulating with gender (§8.1).

One-to-one gender assignment: every gender assignment rule applies to another gender value (§6.2).

Opaque gender assignment: non-formal gender assignment that is not general but characterized by numerous exceptions (§5.1, §6.3).

Overt marking of gender: extent to which nouns exhibit formal gender assignment (§5.1, §6.4).

Person: grammatical category indicating whether or not a referent is a speech act participant and which one (speaker or addressee), marked in free or bound personal pronouns (also called indexes). It may be sensitive to honorific distinctions. Person frequently cumulates with gender (§8.2).

Person name marker: marker indicating that an element is a name of a person, can be a general person name marker or distinguish male and female names; also called proprial article, but not all person name markers are articles and "proprial" and "proper name" does not specify that the markers tend to be dedicated to person names rather than place names (§3.5).

Phonological gender assignment: the gender value of a controller is determined by some of its inherent phonological properties (§5.1, §6.4).

Plurale tantum, pl. Pluralia tantum: literally, noun that only exists in the plural, but more broadly noun exhibiting lexical plurality (plural is a lexicalized property of a noun) (§9).

Principle of Contrast: captures the observation that in systems with opaque gender assignment nouns in a semantic field preferably have a dominant gender, but some salient nouns in the field tend to contrast with them and take an opposite gender (§6.3).

Principle of Fewer Distinctions (also Principle of Economy): measure of inventory complexity stating that the fewer distinctions made the less complex the domain (§2.1).

Principle of One-Meaning–One-Form (also Principle of Transparency): measure of transparency whereby the less complex grammatical phenomenon is one where there is a one-to-one correspondence between meaning and form (§2.1).

Principle of Independence: measure of complexity whereby the less complex grammatical domain/pattern of encoding is the one that is NOT dependent on another grammatical domain/pattern of encoding (§2.1).

Power: semantic connection between animacy and inanimate objects concerning objects endowed with some inherent potential of agency (§3.3 (iv)).

Pronominal articles: use of personal pronouns (third person and occasionally others) with noun phrases often with some restriction to referential, specific or animate (§3.5).

Pronominal gender systems: gender systems with pronouns as the only agreement target (§3.2).

Purview: semantic connection between animacy and inanimate objects concerning objects that belong to or relate to a human or animate referent, are perceived as human or animate in size, shape, or function, or are spoken about by humans (Gerdts 2013) (§3.3 (iii)).

Reconceptualization of referents (also called recategorization): switch of gender in a sequence of coreferential expressions due to association with different gender controllers with different gender (§3.7).

Referent-based gender: Dahl's (2000a) "referential gender". Classes of referents distinguished on noun-associated forms (§3.1).

Relative condition, also optional condition: factor that favors a certain optional choice of agreement value (§7.5).

Relevance: the meaning of an element is relevant to another to the extent its semantic content interferes with the meaning of the other element (Bybee 1985) (§6.4).

Repeater: classifier with the same form as the noun classified (§4.3).

Sandhi: phonological processes across word boundaries (§6.4).

Salience: semantic connection between animacy and inanimate objects based on the fact that discourse prominence of referents can be viewed as an aspect of animacy (§3.3 (ii)).

Semantic agreement: agreement with a referent-based controller (i.e., referent-based gender), often not local, can be inter-sentential. Follows the Agreement Hierarchy (§3.6).

Semantic gender assignment: the gender value of a controller is determined by some of its semantic properties, can be lexical gender or referent-based gender (§5.1).

Specific relationship in agreement: property rendering the relation between controller and target unequivocal, e.g. coreference, co-conceptualization, certain kind of syntactic dependency, adjacency (§7.2).

System: minimally an opposition of at least two markers; however, often much more organized. If the notion is restricted to the more complex cases: highly organized language-specific complexes with both paradigmatic and syntagmatic components that play an important role in the architecture of grammar (however that architecture is modeled). Systems must constantly and actively be dealt with in production and comprehension, which presupposes a high degree of adaptability to previously non-encountered discourse contexts (§1).

System evolution: cover term for all kinds of changes in the structure of systems and in particular including changes that entail the emergence of a system (§10).

Target: element or group of elements on which an agreement marker is realized (§7.1).

Target-controlled gender: the target restricts the choice of the gender value or contributes to the choice of gender value in another way (at the same time as there is displacement) (§7.7).

Unification: assumption that features of elements in an agreement relation are combined, which results in a symmetric interpretation of agreement. With unification, certain kinds of feature mismatches are tolerated and can be accounted for. Our approach does not provide feature mismatches, but accounts for the relevant phenomena with information transfer chains with several chain links (§7.1).

Uniqueness: a set of referents with a single member. Since animates are often unique (especially when referred to by person names), uniqueness is a semantic connection between animacy and inanimate objects (§3.3 (iv)).

Name index

Abbott, Miriam, 177
Acquaviva, Paolo, 309
Adelaar, Willem F. H., 177
Agbetsoamedo, Yvonne, 35, 59, 302, 303
Ahland, Colleen Anne, 170
Aikhenvald, Alexandra Y., 18, 97, 107, 133, 134, 138, 140, 142, 143, 146, 150, 153, 159–161, 170, 176, 177, 202, 253, 254, 260–262, 284, 285, 291, 320
Åkerberg, Bengt, 29, 60
Aksenov, A. T., 213
Allan, Keith, 270
Alungum, John, 139, 176
Anderson, Judi Lynn., 217
Anderson, Neil, 81
Andrason, Alexander, 136
Andronov, Michail S., 93, 99
Angerer, Martin, 285
Applegate, Richard B., 173
Appleyard, David L., 170
Arensen, Jonathan E., 170
Arppe, Antti, 147
Årsjö, Britten, 81, 92, 175, 312
Artawa, Ketut, 174
Atkinson, Quentin D., 167
Audring, Jenny, 1, 15, 18, 20, 26, 30, 49–51, 63, 64, 133, 208–212, 226, 230, 356

Baayen, R. Harald, 148, 166, 167

Baird, Louise, 174, 176
Baker, Mark, 203
Bakker, Peter, 47, 48, 60, 330
Balode, Laimute, 59
Barlow, Michael, 275
Barr, Dale J., 148, 156, 166, 167
Bates, Douglas, 146, 166, 167
Beam de Azcona, Rosemary Grace, 173
Becher, Jutta, 263
Beguinot, Francesco, 253
Benton, Joseph. B., 83
Bentz, Christian, 134, 144, 145, 147
Berry, Christine, 176
Berry, Keith, 176
Betts, La Vera, 93
Bhattacharya, Sudhibhushan, 172
Bickel, Balthasar, 136, 141, 144, 145, 148, 153, 160, 164, 167, 168
Bietenhard, Ruth, 300
Binzell, John, 286
Birk, David B. W., 171
Bisang, Walter, 137
Blasi, Damian E., 329
Bliese, Loren F., 170
Boas, Franz, 173
Bokamba, Eyamba, 48, 59
Bond, Oliver, 278
Borgman, Donald M., 178
Bornkessel-Schlesewsky, Ina, 160
Börstell, Carl, 309, 310

Bosch, Peter, 67, 226, 271, 279
Bowles, Joshua Wayne, 178
Bradley, David P., 104
Braine, Jean Critchfield, 172
Brandao, Ana, 177
Breslow, Norman E., 145
Bresnan, Joan, 160, 305
Brightman, Robert, 218, 226
Brixhe, Claude, 329
Brody, Michal, 173
Bromley, H. Myron, 176
Brown, Jessica, 175
Bruce, Leslie P., 175
Bunn, Gordon, 99
Burling, Robbins, 172
Burton, Michael L., 168
Bybee, Joan, 63, 265, 363

Campbell, Barbara, 176
Campbell, Carl, 176
Campbell, Judy, 176
Campbell, Lyle, 144, 146
Canonici, Noverino N., 170
Capell, Arthur, 171, 220, 261, 264
Capen, Carole Jamieson, 104
Carlin, Eithne, 170
Carlson, Robert, 171
Carlson, Terry, 176
Caro Reina, Javier, 222
Carstairs, Andrew, 303
Carter, Hazel, 251
Caughley, Ross Charles, 173
Chafe, Wallace, 173
Chandralai, Dileep, 172
Charachidzé, Georges, 172
Chumakina, Marina, 278
Church, Kenneth Ward, 77
Clayton, David G., 145
Clendon, Mark, 171

Comrie, Bernard, 234, 292
Contini-Morava, Ellen, 84, 158, 161, 216, 251, 266, 287, 307
Corbett, Greville G., 1, 23, 24, 38, 62, 66, 68, 133, 134, 138, 141, 142, 146, 149, 150, 154, 161, 164, 170–178, 202, 203, 206, 213, 220, 226, 230, 247–250, 263, 265–270, 273, 275, 280, 291, 292, 294, 301, 309, 313–315, 317, 318, 355, 356, 358
Corris, Miriam, 175
Craig, Colette, 107, 173
Crazzolara, Joseph Pasquale, 242
Creissels, Denis, 256, 301, 302
Croft, William, 68, 203, 205, 213, 214, 228, 232, 273, 275, 294, 359
Crouch, Sophie Elizabeth, 174
Curnow, Timothy J., 177
Curzan, Anne, 26
Cysouw, Michael, 74, 144, 145, 162, 164

da Silva Facundes, Sidney, 177
Dahl, Östen, 1, 17, 18, 24, 38, 62, 63, 65, 74, 110, 135, 136, 153, 161, 162, 164, 202, 203, 213, 232, 246, 248–250, 259, 267, 272, 291, 328, 360
Daladier, Anne, 303
Dale, Rick, 329
Danziger, Eve, 84, 216, 287, 307
Davies, William D., 173
Day, Christopher, 107, 173
de Boeck, Egide, 59
de Earl, Catalina, 105
de Hollenbach, Elena E., 236
de Kondo, Riena W., 101
de Suárez, Yolanda Lastra, 173

de Vries, Lourens, 176
Dediu, Dan, 162, 164
DeLancey, Scott, 307
Delbrück, Berthold, 263
Dench, Alan, 171
Derbyshire, Desmond C., 142, 149, 176–178
Di Garbo, Francesca, 1, 15, 16, 18–20, 24, 48, 94, 133, 208–211, 227, 244, 250, 252–254, 256, 272, 302, 303, 308, 315, 328–330
Dickens, Patrick, 170
Dietze, Joachim, 221, 222
Dimmendaal, Gerrit, 270
Dingemanse, Mark, 35
Dixon, Robert M. W., 18, 133, 138, 171, 176, 177, 205, 214, 219, 220, 237, 258, 285, 291, 308, 327
Doble, Marion, 176
Dobson, Rose M., 93
Dol, Philomena, 176
Dolberg, Florian, 24, 215
Doleschal, Ursula, 297
Donohue, Mark, 168, 291
Dost, Ascander, 265
Dougherty, Janet W. D., 175
Dravniece, Sofija, 245
Dressler, Wolfgang, 297
Dryer, Matthew S., 143, 144, 150, 206, 213, 215, 253, 300, 309, 311, 312
Duke, Janet, 29, 60
Dunn, Michael, 145, 167
Durie, Mark, 172
Dutton, Tom E., 176

Earl, Roberto, 105
Eaton, Helen, 171
Ebert, Karen, 307

Edenmyr, Niklas, 170
Elias, David Lyndon, 170
Elliott, Eric Bryant, 174
Emeneau, Murray B., 141, 159
Enger, Hans-Olav, 265, 266, 268, 269
England, Nora C., 106
Epps, Patience, 177, 236, 237
Erbaugh, Mary, 269
Evans, Nicholas, 59, 100, 218, 220, 264, 290, 300, 329
Everett, Daniel L., 177

Faarlund, Jan Terie, 268
Farr, Cynthia, 176
Fedden, Sebastian, 66, 87, 138, 176, 206, 219, 227, 240, 250, 312, 356
Feldman, Harry, 175
Fiedler, Ines, 35, 204, 264, 265, 302
Fife, James, 281
Fischer, Olga, 231, 232
Fleischer, Jürg, 324, 325, 328
Foley, William A., 175, 227
Foreman, Velma, 175
Forstmeier, Wolfang, 156
Fortune, George, 170
Frantz, Donald, 299
Fraser, Norman, 268
Frenda, Alessio, 34, 60
Fung, Pascale, 77

Gabelentz, Georg von der, 247
Gandour, Jack, 137
Garland, Roger, 81
Garland, Susan, 81
Gblem-Poidi, Massanvi Honorine, 35, 36
Gelman, Andrew, 145, 147
Georgopoulos, Carol Perkins, 175

Gerdts, Donna B., 174, 217, 219, 363
Ghosh, Arun, 159, 172
Gil, David, 134, 140–143, 149, 150, 161,
    170–178
Givón, Talmy, 66
Glinert, Lewis, 171
Good, Jeff, 137
Gore, Edward Cline, 171, 215
Goswami, G. C., 172
Goudswaard, Nelleke Elisabeth, 174
Granberry, Julian, 173
Graudiņa, Milda, 325
Green, Diana, 134
Green, Ian, 328
Greenberg, Joseph H., 16, 38, 52, 146,
    202, 227, 263
Greyerz, Otto von, 300
Gribanova, Vera, 265
Gries, Stefan Th., 166
Grimm, Scott, 171
Grinevald Craig, Colette, 107, 227
Grinevald, Colette, 38, 138, 140, 263,
    296
Guirardello, Raquel, 177
Güldemann, Tom, 35, 204, 256, 264,
    265, 282, 283, 288, 302

Haan, Johnson Welem, 175
Haas, Mary R., 174, 261
Hagman, Roy Stephen, 170
Haiman, John, 176
Halekoh, Ulrich, 146, 156
Hammarström, Harald, 21, 168, 214,
    327
Handschuh, Corinna, 223
Hanna, H. Morcos, 170
Harbour, Daniel, 319, 320
Hardin, James W., 166
Harrell, Frank E., 306

Harrell, Richard S., 170
Harris, Alice C., 146
Hart, Helen, 177
Harvey, Mark, 171
Haspelmath, Martin, 94, 98, 143, 205,
    273, 289, 318, 356
Haude, Katharina, 177
Haugen, Einar, 358
Hawkins, John A., 158
Hayward, Dick, 170
Hayward, Richard J., 248, 313, 315
Heath, G. R., 173
Heath, Jeffrey, 171, 227
Heeschen, Volker, 96
Heine, Bernd, 38, 202, 224, 232, 242,
    270, 296, 323
Hemmilä, Ritva, 176
Henadeerage, Deepthi Kumara, 172
Hengeveld, Kees, 274, 275
Her, One-Soon, 140
Herrmann, Tania, 231
Hess, H. Harwood, 173
Hesse, Ronald, 176
Hilbe, Joseph W., 166
Hill, Jennifer, 145, 147
Himmelmann, Nikolaus, 224
Hinch, Heather H., 171, 220, 261
Hinkson, Mercedes O., 174
Hintikka, Jaakko, 69
Hockett, Charles F., 62
Hoffman, Carl, 170
Højsgaard, Søren, 146, 156
Holvoet, Axel, 59
Hopper, Paul J., 294
Horton, A. E., 170
Hualde, José Ignacio, 42, 43, 59
Huber, Christian, 44
Huber, Juliette, 176

Hudson, Joyce, 234
Huldén, Lars, 29, 36, 60
Hultman, Oskar Fredrik, 36, 60
Hundius, Harald, 137
Hunn, Eugene S., 105
Hunt, Katharine Dorothy, 174
Huntley, David, 221, 293
Hurd, Conrad, 175
Hurd, Phyllis W., 175
Hymes, Dell Hathaway, 173

Ingkaphirom, Preeya, 137
Inglis, Douglas, 137
Ishiyama, Osamu, 98, 99, 322
Iwasaki, Shoichi, 137

Jaeger, T. Florian, 134, 145
Jakobi, Angelika, 170
Janhunen, Juha, 149
Jendraschek, Gerd, 175
Jensen, John Thayer, 175
Jespersen, Otto, 231
Johnston, Raymond Leslie, 223
Jones, Paula, 177
Jones, Wendell, 177
Jukes, Anthony, 175
Jun, Akamine, 175
Jung, Ingrid, 84
Jurafsky, Daniel, 358

Kaiser, Stefan, 172
Kalnača, Anna, 172
Kamwangamalu, Nkonko Mudi-
    panu, 170
Kanerva, Jonni, 305
Karatsareas, Petros, 30–33, 59, 214,
    227, 329
Kaufman, Terrence S., 40, 173
Kayser Alois, MSC., 237

Keels, Jack, 101
Kennard, Edward, 174
Kern, Barbara, 177
Kibrik, Andrej A., 67, 87, 94, 99, 227,
    229
Kiessling, Roland, 170
Kilarski, Marcin, 133, 158, 161, 202,
    251, 266
Killian, Don, 96, 170, 219, 229, 248–
    250, 259, 262, 281–284, 305
Kimball, Amelia E., 166, 167
King, Gareth, 281
Kirby, Simon, 323
Klaiman, M. H., 172
Klamer, Marian, 176
Kliegl, Reinhold, 166, 167
Kohnen, Fr. Bernardo, 242
Kölver, Ulrike, 137
Koptjevskaja-Tamm, Maria, 59, 242,
    309
Kosaka, Ryuichi, 173
Kramer, Ruth, 161
Kretzschmar Jr., William A., 136
Kroeker, Menno H., 100
Krute, Laurence Dana, 177
Kuhn, Jonas, 273
Kulas, Jack, 69
Kusters, Wouter, 17, 135, 160, 208
Kuteva, Tania, 234, 323

Lass, Roger, 323
Laycock, Donald C., 175
Lee, Alan, 100
Leeding, Velma J., 218
Lehmann, Christian, 204, 232, 239,
    276, 290
Leslau, Wolf, 170
Leufkens, Sterre, 16
Levinson, Stephen C., 69, 145

Li, Charles N., 140, 141
Lichtenberk, Frantisek, 175
Liljegren, Henrik, 206, 211, 291, 307, 328
Lindström, Eva, 175, 244
Lock, Arjen, 82, 141, 175
Lomas, G. C. J., 176
Loos, Eugene, 177
Loughnane, Robyn, 225
Louwerse, John, 176
Lowe, Ivan, 100
Lowing, Aretta, 81
Lowing, Richard, 81
Luoma, Pirkko, 176
Lupyan, Gary, 329
Luraghi, Silvia, 38, 62, 146, 161, 162, 203, 297, 304, 320
Lynch, John, 175
Lyons, Christopher, 222

Macaulay, Monica, 104, 173
Machal, Marcelo, 101
Macri, Martha J., 104
Maddieson, Ian, 165
Maechler, Martin, 146, 167
Maho, Jouni, 27
Malkiel, Yakov, 263
Matasović, Ranko, 16, 38, 172
Mathiot, Madeleine, 217
Matras, Yaron, 161
McGregor, Ronald S., 172
McGregor, William B., 171
McKenzie, Parker, 319, 320
McWhorter, John, 1, 160, 210
Meeuwis, Michael, 27, 48, 59, 170, 330
Meillet, Antoine, 221
Mellow, Greg, 108, 229, 264, 305

Merchán, Hernanda Ana Joaquina, 101
Merlan, Francesca C., 171
Merrifield, William R., 320
Mettouchi, Amina, 256, 303
Meyer, David, 146
Miestamo, Matti, 17, 25, 52, 134, 135, 137, 158, 165, 208–211, 227, 244, 272, 308, 328, 330
Mihas, Elena, 177
Milles, Karin, 95
Minor, Eugene E., 101
Mithun, Marianne, 149, 173, 270, 293, 297, 298
Moore, Denny, 178
Moran, Dorothy, 176
Moran, Paul, 176
Moravcsik, Edith, 204, 232
Morris, Cliff, 174
Moscati, Sabatino, 303
Mosel, Ulrike, 175
Mous, Maarten, 83, 84, 170, 315
Mpaayei, J. Tompo Ole, 270
Müller, Adam, 176
Munshi, Sadaf, 172
Murane, Elizabeth, 175
Mushin, Ilona, 171
Muysken, Pieter C., 177

Nagaraja, Keralapura Shreenivasaiah, 328
Nau, Nicole, 244, 266
Newman, Paul, 263
Nichols, Johanna, 1, 16, 38, 60, 65, 134, 138, 141–143, 153, 154, 161, 162, 164, 167, 170–176, 203, 205, 208–212, 229, 230, 327, 328, 330
Nicolova, Ruselina, 172

Nordlinger, Rachel, 171

Oakes, Michael P., 174
Olsson, Bruno, 206, 218, 219, 251, 309, 311, 312, 321, 328
Oomen, Antoinette, 263
Orkaydo, Ongaye Oda, 317
Ortiz de Urbina, Jon, 59
Osborne, C. R., 171
Otanes, Fe T., 174, 223
Otsuka, Yuko, 175
Owens, Jonathan, 170

Pandharipande, Rajeshwari, 172
Paradis, Carole, 96, 120
Parker, Enid M., 248
Passer, Matthias Benjamin, 2, 16, 138, 142, 161, 163, 164, 178, 205, 238, 249, 274, 275, 298, 305
Pawley, Andrew, 50, 216, 217
Payne, David L., 177
Payne, Doris L., 93, 142, 143, 149, 170, 176–178, 270, 296, 297, 304
Peeke, M. Catherine, 178
Penchoen, Thomas, 170, 252
Pensalfini, Robert, 171
Pet, Willen Jan Agricola, 177
Peterson, David A., 153
Petrollino, Sara, 255
Phillips, Colin, 175
Plank, Frans, 68, 285, 286
Plaster, Keith, 146, 153, 220, 258, 259
Polinsky, Maria, 146, 153, 220, 258, 259, 263, 292, 325
Poppe, Nicholas, 171
Premsrirat, Suwilai, 172
Priestly, Tom M. S., 26, 30

Quesada, J. Diego, 173

Quigley, Susan R., 176

Rabel-Heymann, Lili, 258, 259, 266
Ramirez, Henri, 178
Rau, Der-Hwa Victoria, 174
Reed, Irene, 173
Reesink, Ger P., 176
Reh, Mechthild, 170, 224, 232, 270, 296
Rehg, Kenneth L., 175
Reid, Nicholas, 38, 240, 241, 263, 270, 291, 297
Rennison, John R., 171
Rich, Rolland G., 178
Riddle, Elizabeth M., 160, 161
Ring, Hiram, 136, 137, 141, 172, 230, 243, 244, 267
Rissanen, Matti, 233
Rizzi, Luigi, 277
Roberts, Marjorie, 217
Roberts, Sarah J., 160
Robinson, Stuart Payton, 176
Ross, Malcolm, 175
Rudzīte, Marta, 37, 325
Russell, Bertrand, 222

Saad, George, 177
Sadler, Louisa, 273
Sagna, Serge, 253
Sakel, Jeanette, 177
Samarin, William J., 171
Sampson, Geoffrey, 209
Sándalo, Filomena, 82
Sanders, Arden G., 87
Sanders, Joy, 87
Sands, Bonny, 170
Santos Sachot, Rosine, 251
Sapir, J. David, 171
Sarvasy, Hannah Sacha, 79

Sasse, Hans-Jürgen, 33, 214, 360
Schachter, Paul, 174, 223
Schellinger, Wolfgang, 68
Schielzeth, Holger, 156
Schiffman, Harold F., 172
Schlesewsky, Matthias, 160
Schuh, Russell G., 170, 292
Schultze-Berndt, Eva, 171
Schuster-Šewc, Heinz, 294
Scorza, David, 176
Scott, Graham, 81
Seifart, Frank, 25, 38, 67, 111, 138, 146,
        161, 202, 205, 227, 238, 249,
        258, 262, 263, 296, 327, 328
Senft, Gunter, 237, 238
Serzisko, Fritz, 138
Seuren, Pieter A. M., 279
Sharpe, Margaret C., 171
Shklovsky, Kirill, 140
Shosted, Ryan K., 134, 165
Siemund, Peter, 24, 214, 215
Siewierska, Anna, 165
Silverstein, Michael, 214
Singer, Ruth, 253, 299, 300
Sinnemäki, Kaius, 134, 135, 137, 138,
        143, 144, 158, 160, 165, 208,
        210, 211, 243, 247, 291, 293,
        329
Skopeteas, Stavros, 173
Skribnik, Elena, 171
Small, Priscilla C., 104, 235, 236
Smith, Kenny, 323, 324
Smith-Stark, Thomas Cedric, 356
Sohl, Damian G., 175
Soubrier, Aude, 35, 59
Spagnolo, Lorenzo M., 231
Speck, Charles H., 104, 105
Spriggs, Ruth, 175

Spruit, Arie, 172
Sridhar, Shikaripur N., 172
Staley, William E., 176
Stark, Sharon L., 103
Stebbins, Tonya, 175
Steever, Sanford B., 159
Stilo, Donald, 30, 46, 60
Stolz, Thomas, 41, 42, 60, 308
Straus, Anne Terry, 218, 226
Suter, Edgar, 328
Sutton, Logan, 173, 319
Svärd, Erik, 24, 175, 176, 206, 223, 248,
        249, 253, 259, 261, 291, 305,
        312
Swanton, John R., 173, 219

Tamuli, Jyotiprakash, 172
Tang, Chih-Chen Jane, 175
Tasmowski-De Ryck, Liliane, 274
Tayul, Julius, 175
Teleman, Ulf, 272, 300
Terrill, Angela, 175
Tharp, Doug, 175
Thiesen, Wesley, 177, 239
Thomason, Lucy Grey, 228, 267, 305
Thomason, Sarah G., 40, 59
Thompson, Sandra A., 140, 141, 294
Thurgood, Graham, 172
Thurman, Robert C., 100
Tomasello, Michael, 71, 86
Topping, Donald M., 174
Traill, Anthony., 283, 288
Tripp, Robert, 177
Trudgill, Peter, 1, 40, 65, 160, 161, 330
Trussel, Stephen, 65
Tsegaye, Mulugeta, 316, 317
Tucker, A. N., 270

Usher, Timothy, 328

Vafaeian, Ghazaleh, 89
Vajda, Edward J., 300
van den Berg, Helma, 172
van den Heuvel, Wilco, 294
van der Meer, Suzanne, 309
van der Voort, Hein, 177
van Driem, Georg, 84, 307
van Engelenhoven, Aone, 174
Van Everbroeck, Ezra, 263, 325
van Rijn, Marlou, 275
van Staden, Miriam, 176
Van Valin, Robert D., 174, 227, 293
Velie, Daniel, 177
Verhaar, John W. M., 230, 234
Verkerk, Annemarie, 256, 302
Verluyten, Paul, 274
Vincent, Lois E., 81
Vossen, Rainer, 38, 242

Wade, Terence, 172
Wälchli, Bernhard, 25, 36–40, 59, 60,
        63, 65, 74, 82, 94, 110, 223,
        224, 226, 236, 244, 245, 264,
        266, 268, 277, 279–281, 283,
        286–288, 294, 297, 304, 305,
        308, 309, 322, 325, 326, 329
Wash, Suzanne, 173
Waterhouse, Viola, 174
Watkins, Laurel J., 319, 320
Watters, John Robert, 170
Weber, David, 239
Weber, David John, 177
Weidert, Alfons, 220
Westrum, Peter N., 176
Wheeler, Alva Lee, 177
Wickham, H., 146
Widmark, Gun, 269
Willett, Thomas Leslie, 174

Williams-van Klinken, Catharina,
        174
Williamson, Kay, 38
Wilson, Particia R., 175
Winter, Bodo, 134, 144, 145, 147
Wolfart, H. Christoph, 173, 226
Wonderly, William L., 319
Wonnacott, Elizabeth, 323, 324
Wu, Jing-Ian Joy, 174
Wunderlich, Dieter, 289

Yarshater, Ehsan, 60

Z'graggen, John, 175
Zaicz, Gábor, 173
Zaliznjak, Andrey A., 317
Zavala, Roberto, 107
Zeileis, Achim, 146

Language index

Abau, 82, 83, 124, 141, 175, 224, 261, 305

Abkhaz, 172

Abun, 176

Acehnese, 172

Acoli, 242, 243

Acoma, 173

Adang, 175

Afar, 248

Afrikaans, 86, 123, 323, 324

Afro-Asiatic, 64, 84, 128, 170, 171, 252, 253, 262, 263, 292, 313, 314, 316, 327

Agaw, 313

Aghul, 21, 28, 37, 60

Ainu, 171

Akan, 5

Akateko, 77, 97, 106, 107, 120

Alagwa, 170

Alamblak, 175

Alawa, 171

Albanian, 172

Albanian, Gheg, 123

Alemannic, 123, 325, 328

Algic, 130, 173, 218, 226, 228

Algonquian, 173, 218, 221, 226, 228, 267, 305

Altaic, 128, 171

Alto-Orinoco, 177

Ama, 64, 65, 77, 81, 83, 87, 89, 92, 124, 175, 262, 312

Amarakaeri, 177

Amazonian, 38, 296

Ambulas, 124, 175

Amele, 176

Amharic, 124, 170

Amis, 174

Amwi, 220

Anatolian, 329

Ancient Greek, 321, 329

Angami Naga, 77, 120

Angan, 176

Anim, 7, 218, 219, 290, 312, 328

Animere, 35

Anindilyakwa, 218

Ankave, 120

Apurinã, 125, 177

Arabela, 178

Arabic, 303

Arabic (Egyptian), 170

Arabic (Moroccan), 170

Arai, 64, 129

Arapesh, 176

Arapesh (Mountain), 176

Arapesh, Bumbita, 124

Arauan, 130, 176

Araucanian, 130, 177

Arawak, 177

Arawakan, 64, 73, 84, 130, 134, 158, 160, 177

Arawan, 219, 220, 260, 285

Arbore, 170

Archi, 21, 60, 67, 89, 278, 279, 289, 290, 334
Argyroúpolis Pontic, 31
Arhuacic, 177
Armenian, 73, 172
Arosi, 264, 284
Asháninka, 84, 85, 125
Ashéninka Pajonal, 84, 85, 125
Ashéninka Perené, 177
Ashéninka, Pichis, 84, 125
Aslian, 171
Assamese, 172
Atakapa, 173
Atayal, 174
Atayalic, 174
Ateker, 270
Athapaskan, 173
Atlantic, 171, 251, 253, 255, 263, 302
Atlantic-Congo, 35, 38, 59, 215, 251, 253, 255, 263, 302, 327
Au, 89–91, 124, 176
Auhelawa, 81
Australian, 129
Australian Kriol, 234
Austroasiatic, 46, 59, 107, 129, 136, 159, 171, 172, 220, 224, 230, 243, 327, 328
Austronesian, 7, 19, 40, 41, 60, 65, 73, 98, 106, 108, 129, 154, 170, 172, 174, 175, 222, 223, 229, 237, 238, 250, 264, 294, 297, 327
Avar, 84, 85, 123, 172
Avar-Andic-Tsezic, 172
Awa, 81, 126
Awa Pit, 177
Awara, 176
Awju-Dumut, 176

Awtuw, 175
Axó Cappadocian, 33
Aymaran, 130, 177
Aztecan, 174

Bagvalal, 172
Baining, 175
Baiso, 313–315, 317, 320, 321
Bajau (Sama), 175
Balinese, 174
Baltic, 30, 172, 244, 245, 263, 266, 268, 295, 325
Balto-Slavic, 21, 27, 59
Bana, 124
Bangala, 48
Baniwa, 177
Bantoid, 142, 170
Bantu, 5, 22, 27, 48, 59, 251, 255, 256, 302, 305
Baré, 177
Barasana Eduria, 125
Barasano, 177
Barbacoan, 130, 177
Barbareño, 173
Bari, 230, 231, 242, 243, 246, 261, 270, 334
Barito, 170
Barupu, 175
Baruya, 84
Basque, 21, 40, 42, 43, 59, 84, 128, 172
Basque, Lekeitio, 21, 40, 42, 43, 45, 59
Batak (Karo), 174
Begak-Ida'an, 174
Beja, 313
Belize Kriol, 89
Belize Kriol English, 90, 113, 124
Bengali, 146, 159, 172
Berber, 170, 252, 253, 256, 303
Berik, 176

Biak, 294
Biangai, 84
Bimin, 124
Binanderean, 176
Bine, 87, 125
Bininj Kun-Wok, 241, 248, 264, 299,
    329
Bird's Head, 176
Biu-Mandara, 170
Bodic, 43, 44, 60, 172
Bodo-Garo, 172
Bora, 98, 102, 122, 177, 227, 238–240,
    245, 246, 262
Boran, 38, 138, 177, 227, 238, 239, 258,
    263, 328
Border, 175
Bougainville, East, 175
Brahui, 172
Breton, 123, 281
British English dialects, 231
Buglere, 127
Bukiyip, 124
Bulgarian, 123, 172, 265
Bunuban, 171
Burarra, 124
Buriat, 171
Burmese, 173
Burmese-Lolo, 173
Burmeso, 291
Burushaski, 8, 172

Cacua, 125
Cahuapanan, 130, 177
Camling, 307
Camsa, 130
Candoshi-Shapra, 130
Canela-Krahô, 177
Cantonese, 173
Capanahua, 177

Caquinte, 84, 85, 125
Carapana, 77, 125
Carib, 130
Caribbean, 177
Catalan, 123, 222
Cayuga, 297
Cayuvava, 177
Celebic, 174
Celtic, 21, 60, 281
Chadic, 170, 263, 292
Cham, 172
Chamorro, 19, 21, 40–43, 45, 50, 60,
    174, 308
Chapacura-Wanham, 177
Chayahuita, 177
Chechen, 84, 85, 123, 172
Chepang, 173
Cherokee, 270, 298
Cheyenne, 218, 226
Chibcha-Duit, 177
Chibchan, 130, 173, 177
Chicheŵa, 305
Chichimec, 173
Chichimeca-Jonaz, 173
Chimakuan, 173
Chimariko, 173
Chinantec, Comaltepec, 217
Chinese, 90, 173, 269
Chinook (Upper), 173
Chipaya, 125, 131
Chiquihuitlan, 103
Chiquitano, 125
Chitimacha, 173
Chitral, 8, 211, 328
Choco, 130, 177
Choctaw, 173
Chontal (Huamelultec Oaxaca), 174
Chuave, 98, 100, 120

Chuj, 106, 107, 120

Chukchi, 172

Chukotko-Kamchatkan, 172

Chumash, 173

Chuvash, 171

Classical Tibetan, 307, 327

Coastal Marind, 7, 218, 219, 251, 289, 290, 309, 311, 312, 316–318, 320, 321, 334

Coos (Hanis), 173

Coosan, 173

Cornish, 228

Cree, 47, 48, 226, 330

Cree (Plains), 173

Croatian, 123, 293

Cross River, 170

Cubeo, 125

Cuiba, 98, 101, 122

Cuicatec, 85, 104

Cuicatec, Tepeuxila, 103, 121

Cuicatec, Teutila, 84, 85, 120

Culina, 176

Cushitic, 84, 87, 170, 248, 262, 263, 313–316, 321

Czech, 123, 270

Daga, 175

Dagaare, 171

Daghestanian, 290

Dameli, 307

Dangaléat, 124

Dani, 176

Dani (Lower Grand Valley), 176

Danish, 29, 123, 226

Dargwa, 172

Datooga, 170

Dawro, 124

Defoid, 170

Dení, 176

Desano, 125

Diegueño (Mesa Grande), 173

Diola-Fogny, 171

Dizi, 170

Djambarrpuyngu, 126

Djingili, 171

Dravidian, 93, 98, 99, 128, 159, 172, 248

Drehu, 174

Dumo, 175

Dutch, 123, 323

Dyirbal, 171, 220, 221, 257–261

East Bird's Head, 129

East Papuan, 129

East Taa, 282

East !Xõo, 282, 283, 288

Eegimaa, 253

Eipo, 21, 40, 60, 223, 284

Ejagham, 170

Ekari, 176

Elfdalian, 21, 29, 60

Endo, 81, 126

Engan, 176

English, 9, 24, 26, 42, 50, 63–65, 68, 70, 74, 75, 77–80, 85, 89, 90, 98, 100, 111, 113, 123, 140, 149, 172, 204, 214–217, 219, 227, 230–234, 246, 300, 309, 310, 322

Epena Pedee, 177

Erromangan, 174

Eshtehardi, 21, 46, 60

Eskimo-Aleut, 130, 173

Esperanto, 83, 93, 120

Estonian, 75, 233, 234, 244, 329

Evenki, 171

Faiwal, 124

Faroese, 123
Fasu, 126
Fijian, 175
Finisterre-Huon, 176
Finnic, 173, 233, 244, 326, 329
Finnish, 29, 173, 233
Folopa, 81, 127
Fore, 81, 127
Formosan, 174
French, 30, 47, 48, 87, 123, 139, 172,
    228, 263, 274, 325, 330
Fula, 171
Fur, 170
Futuna-Aniwa, 175

Gaagudju, 171, 299
Galela, 124
Gamo, 124
Garifuna, 64, 75, 77, 125
Garig-Ilgar, 300
Garo, 172
Garrwa, 171
Gavião, 178
Gbaya-Manza-Ngbaka, 171
Gbeya Bossangoa, 171
Ge-Kaingang, 177
Geelvink Bay, 129
Georgian, 172
German, 24, 72, 87, 89, 90, 123, 172,
    212, 215, 225, 234, 246, 271,
    279, 280, 284–286, 294, 295,
    324, 325, 328
Germanic, 21, 26, 30, 60, 172, 212, 226,
    232, 268, 269, 271, 279, 280,
    285, 295, 300, 323, 324
Ghana-Togo-Mountain, 5, 22, 35, 59
Gitksan, 174
Gitonga, 251, 252, 254, 255
Godoberi, 289, 290

Gofa, 124
Golin, 98–100, 120
Gooniyandi, 171
Greek, 21, 30–34, 49, 59, 75, 123, 227,
    329
Greek, Cappadocian, 21, 28, 32–34,
    59, 329
Greek, Pharasiot, 32, 33
Greek, Pontic, 21, 28, 31, 33, 34, 49,
    59, 329
Greek, Rumeic, 21, 28, 31–34, 50, 59
Greek, Silliot, 31
Guahiban, 98, 101, 102, 130
Guahibo, 101, 122
Guaicuruan, 82
Guang, 5
Guaraní, 178
Guayabero, 98, 101, 122
Gude, 124
Gujarati, 84, 85, 123
Gumuz, 170
Gunin, 171
Gunwinyguan, 37, 59, 171, 218, 241,
    299
Gur, 171
Gurung, 172

Hadza, 170
Haida, 173
Halkomelem, 174, 217, 219, 220
Halmaheran, 176
Hamar, 255
Harakmbet, 130, 177
Hatam, 176
Hausa, 64, 77, 124, 170, 263
Hawaiian, 175
Hawaiian Pidgin, 124
Hebrew, 171

Hindi, 43, 84, 85, 89, 92, 123, 141, 172, 289
Hindu Kush Indo-Aryan, 8, 307, 328
Hixkaryana, 177
Hmong Daw, 172
Hmong-Mien, 129, 172
Hokan, 130, 173
Hua, 176
Huave, 82, 126
Huavean, 130
Huitoto, 102, 122, 177
Huitoto, Minica, 98, 101, 102, 122
Huitoto, Murui, 98, 102
Huitotoan, 177, 328
Huli, 176
Hungarian, 173
Hunzib, 172
Hup, 177, 236–240, 245

Iaai, 175
Iatmul, 124, 175
Icelandic, 123
Igbo, 171
Ignaciano, 125
Igo, 22, 28, 35, 36, 59
Ika, 177
Ikposo, 22, 35, 59
Imonda, 175
Indic, 141, 159, 172
Indo-Aryan, 8, 43–45, 85, 87, 159, 214, 289, 328
Indo-European, 16, 18, 24, 26, 27, 30–33, 38, 59, 60, 63, 68, 73, 77, 78, 90, 92, 93, 128, 141, 144, 159, 172, 212, 214, 221, 222, 226, 232, 244, 245, 250, 263, 265, 266, 268–271, 274, 277, 279, 280, 285, 289, 294–297, 300, 304, 317, 320, 323, 325, 327
Indonesian, 75, 174
Ineseño, 173
Ingush, 172
Iranian, 8, 21, 30, 46, 60, 73, 159, 172
Iraqw, 83–85, 124, 170
Iraya, 82, 126, 297
Irish, 21, 28, 34, 60, 217, 281
Iroquoian, 130, 173, 270, 297–299
Iroquois, Five Nations, 270
Italian, 30, 123, 250, 251, 277, 289, 290, 295–297, 318
Iwaidja, 300
Iwaidjan, 171
Iwam, 124, 175
Ixil, 106, 107, 120

Jacaltec, 94, 97, 106, 107, 120, 173, 227
Jamamadi, 176
Jaminjung, 171
Jangshung, 21, 44, 45, 60
Japanese, 81, 94, 95, 97–99, 109, 120, 128, 172, 322, 324
Jaqaru, 177
Jarawara, 176, 219, 220, 285
Javanese, 174
Jivaro, 177
Jivaroan, 131, 177
Ju Kung, 170
Jur Modo, 124
Jul'hoan, 170

Kâte, 176
Kabyle, 77, 85, 124
Kadai, 173
Kadiweu, 82–84, 127
Kadu, 170
Kadugli, 170

Kafa, 124
Kafteji, 21, 30, 46, 60
Kahua, 223, 264, 284
Kaingang, 77, 122
Kalasha, 8, 211, 307, 328
Kam-Tai, 173
Kamasau, 87, 124
Kambera, 174
Kana, 159, 170
Kanjobalan, 97
Kannada, 98, 99, 123, 172, 248
Kanuri, 171
Karkar-Yuri, 129
Karok, 173
Kartvelian, 172
Kashmiri, 8
Kayabi, 83, 93, 122, 224
Ke'o, 174
Kebar, 176
Kegboid, 159
Kelasi, 21, 28, 30, 46, 60
Kemant, 170
Keresan, 173
Ket, 261, 299, 300
Kewa, 176
Khalkha, 171
Khasi, 21, 46, 59, 224, 257, 258, 260,
        261, 266, 267, 288, 303, 328
Khasian, 21, 46, 47, 59, 136, 141, 172,
        220, 224, 230, 243, 303, 328
Khmer, 95, 106, 120, 172
Khmu', 172
Khoe, 224, 323
Khoe-Kwadi, 170
Khoekhoe, 170, 224
Khoisan, 282
Khowar, 8, 211, 307, 328
Kilivila, 175, 237, 238, 246, 247

Kinshasa Lingala, 27, 28, 48, 59, 302,
        303
Kiowa, 173, 319, 320
Kiowa-Tanoan, 173, 299, 319, 320
Kiranti, 307, 327
Kiribati, 65, 66, 70, 82, 97, 98, 102, 111,
        120
Kiwai, 175
Klamath, 173
Klamath-Modoc, 173
Klon, 176
Kobon, 176
Koiari, 176
Koman, 6, 170, 219, 229, 250, 282
Kombai, 176
Kombio-Arapesh, 176
Komi-Zyrian, 173
Konso, 262, 316–318, 320, 321
Konua, 176
Korafe, 176
Kordofanian, 170
Korean, 128, 172
Koreguaje, 125
Korku, 172
Koromfe, 171
Koyra Chiini, 171
Kriol, Australian, 234
Krongo, 170
Kuliak, 170
Kundjeyhmi, 22, 28, 37, 59
Kune, 22, 28, 59, 329
Kunwinjku, 22, 59, 329
Kuot, 78, 124, 175
Kurdish, 89, 92, 123
Kutenai, 173
Kwa, 35, 36
Kwanga, 124
Kwazá, 177

Kwoma, 124
Kx'a, 170
Kxoe, 224, 232

Lachi, 173
Lahu, 173
Lak, 270
Lak-Dargwa, 172
Lakhota, 174, 293
Lango, 170
Latin, 87, 89, 92, 123, 222, 263, 268, 279, 321, 325
Latvian, 21, 27, 28, 36, 59, 77, 86, 87, 89, 92, 123, 172, 244, 245, 266, 279, 295, 325, 329
Latvian, Dundaga, 244–246, 280, 326
Latvian, Kandava, 325
Lavukaleve, 175
Left May, 64, 129, 175, 312
Lendu, 323
Leti, 174
Lezgian, 28, 172
Lezgic, 21, 37, 60, 172, 278
Limbu, 84, 307
Lingala, 22, 46, 48, 59, 170, 302, 330
Lithuanian, 30, 123, 244, 268
Livonian, 244, 326, 329
Low Saxon, 123
Lower Sepik, 175
Lower Sepik-Ramu, 175
Luganda, 142, 170
Lugbara, 170
Luiseño, 174
Luvale, 170
Lyngngam, 21, 46, 59, 328

Máku, 177
Maasai, 170, 270
Machiguenga, 85, 125

Macro-Ge, 131, 177
Macuna, 125
Macushi, 177
Madang, 176
Magahi, 159
Mahakiranti, 173
Maidu, 173
Makasae, 176
Makassar, 175
Makira languages, 284
Maku, 131
Malagasy, 170
Malakmalak, 171
Malayalam, 93, 120
Malayo-Polynesian, 174
Malayo-Sumbawan, 172, 174
Mali, 175
Maltese, 85, 124
Malto, 159
Mam, 106
Mam, Todos Santos, 106, 120
Manambu, 254, 261
Mandan, 174
Mandarin, 90, 140–142, 146, 173, 269, 271
Mande, 170
Mandinka, 170
Mangarrayi, 171
Mangarrayi-Maran, 171
Mapudungun, 177
Marathi, 123, 141, 172
Margi, 170
Maricopa, 173
Marithiel, 328
Martuthunira, 171
Mataco-Guaicuru, 131
Mawng, 171, 220, 253, 298–300
Maya, Mopán, 84, 216, 229, 287, 307,

334

Mayan, 87, 97, 106, 107, 130, 139, 140, 173, 216

Maybrat, 176

Mazatec, 103, 104

Mazatec, Ayautla, 81, 126

Mazatec, Chiquihuitlan, 104, 121

Mek, 21, 39, 40, 60, 82, 96, 110, 176, 223, 224, 283, 284, 286–288, 305, 326

Mende, 124

Menominee, 218

Meskwaki, 228, 267, 305, 334

Mian, 87, 124, 176, 224, 227, 239, 240, 246, 261, 312, 334

Michif, 19, 22, 46–48, 60, 330

Micronesian, 65

Minangkabau, 174

Miraña, 138, 227, 238, 262, 296

Mirndi, 171

Miskito, 173

Misumalpan, 173

Miwok, 174

Mixe-Zoque, 130

Mixtec, 84, 104, 236, 239, 246, 247

Mixtec, Atatlahuca, 121

Mixtec, Ayutla, 236

Mixtec, Chalcatongo, 95, 104, 173

Mixtec, Coatzospan, 84, 104, 121, 235, 236, 239, 240, 246

Mixtec, Diuxi-Tilantongo, 121

Mixtec, Jamiltepec, 121

Mixtec, Ocotepec, 121

Mixtec, Peñoles, 121

Mixtec, Pinotepa Nacional, 121

Mixtec, San Juan Colorado, 121

Mixtec, San Miguel, 103, 104, 121

Mixtec, Silacayoapan, 121

Mixtec, Southern Puebla, 121

Mixtec, Tezoatlan, 121

Mixtec, Yosondúa, 121

Mixtecan, 173

Mixtepec Zapotec, 105

Miya, 170, 292

Mocoví, 82–84, 127

Mohawk, 270, 271, 298

Mokilese, 175

Monde, 178

Mongolic, 171

Mordvin, 173

Moru-Ma'di, 170

Mosetén, 177

Motuna, 175, 254

Mountain Koiali, 81, 127

Movima, 177

Mpur, 176

Mufian, 124, 139, 176

Muinane, 102, 122

Muisca, 177

Munda, 172

Mundurukú, 142, 143, 178

Mura, 177

Murle, 170

Murriny Patha, 328

Murui, 122

Muskogean, 173

Mwaghavul, 83, 84, 124

Na-Dene, 67, 130, 173

Naasioi, 120

Nadahup, 177

Nafusi, 253

Nagatman, 176

Nahuatl (Tetelcingo), 174

Nakanai, 223

Nakh, 172

Nakh-Daghestanian, 60, 67, 87, 89, 172, 270, 278, 289, 292
Nalca, 21, 39, 40, 45, 50, 60, 79, 82–84, 126, 176, 223, 224, 229, 264, 268, 283, 284, 286–288, 305, 326, 334
Nama, 224
Nambikuara, 98, 100, 122
Nambiquaran, 100, 131
Nanai, 171
Nangikurrunggurr, 240, 241, 328
Nasioi, 175
Nauru, 237
Navajo, 67, 173
Ndu, 254
Ndyuka, 177
Nebaj, 106, 107
Nen, 290
Nenets, 173
Nepali, 141
Ngalum, 124
Ngan'gityemerri, 38, 240–242, 246, 247, 263, 270, 271, 290, 291, 297, 307, 328
Ngiyambaa, 171
Nicobarese, 172
Niger-Congo, 5, 36, 73, 96, 128, 138, 142, 159, 170, 171, 302
Nilo-Saharan, 128
Nilotic, 38, 170, 230, 231, 242, 247, 270
Nivkh, 172
No, 28, 232, 250
Nomatsiguenga, 84, 125, 177
North Bougainville, 261
North Caucasian, 128
North Halmaheran, 82
Northern Daly, 171
Northern Khmer, 107

Norwegian, 123, 226, 266, 268, 269
Nubian, 170
Nubian (Dongolese), 170
Numic, 174
Nunggubuyu, 171
Nuristani, 8
Nyanja, 305

O'odham, 174
Ocaina, 177
Oceanic, 174, 175, 223, 229, 232, 237, 238, 250, 264, 283, 305
Ojibwa, 218
Ok, 7, 73, 176, 224, 225, 240, 312, 328
Oksapmin, 120, 224, 225, 240, 334
Old High German, 325
Old Russian, 221
Old Saxon, 324, 325
Old Spanish, 263
Olo, 124, 176
Omo-Tana, 315
Omotic, 255
Oregon Coast, 173
Orejón, 177
Orig, 170
Oromo (Harar), 170
Otomí (Mezquital), 173
Otomanguean, 87, 102, 106, 111, 130, 158, 173, 217, 235, 236, 327
Otomian, 173
Owa, 77, 106, 108, 109, 120, 223, 229, 264, 284, 305

Paez, 84, 131
Paiute, 174
Paiwan, 175
Palai, 213
Palauan, 175
Palaung-Khmuic, 172

Palikur, 134, 158, 177
Pama-Nyungan, 171, 257, 327
Panare, 177
Panjabi, Eastern, 84, 85, 123, 214
Panoan, 131, 177
Parecis, 83, 177
Pashai, 8
Paumari, 78, 125, 176, 260–262, 284, 285, 291, 334
Peba-Yaguan, 131, 177
Penutian, 173, 174
Permic, 173
Persian, 172
Pharasiot, 32
Piapoco, 125
Piaroa, 177
Pileni, 175
Pipil, 174
Pirahã, 177
Piratapuyo, 125
Piro, 177
Pnar, 21, 46, 59, 136, 137, 141, 172, 230, 242–244, 246, 267, 293, 334
Pohnpeian, 175
Polish, 123, 270, 271, 293
Popoloca, 103, 104, 109, 111
Popoloca, San Marcos Tlalcoyalco, 84, 121
Popoloca, Tlalcoyalco, 103, 111
Portuguese, 123
Punjabi, 214
Purus, 177

Qafar, 170
Qaqet, 124
Quechua (Huallaga), 177
Quechua (Imbabura), 177
Quechuan, 73, 131, 158, 177
Quileute, 173

Ram, 175
Rapanui, 175
Rashad, 170
Rawa, 81, 126
Rendille, 263
Retuara, 160
Rikbaktsa, 122
Romance, 30, 139, 172, 224, 250, 263, 274, 277, 296, 325, 328
Romani, Sinte, 123
Romani, Vlax, 123
Romanian, 123, 325
Ros Much, 60
Rotokas, 124, 176, 261
Russian, 18, 123, 172, 221, 222, 239, 248, 269, 292, 293, 317

Sáliban, 177
Sabaot, 81, 126
Safeyoka, 81, 126
Sahaptin (Umatilla), 174
Saharan, 171
Salinan, 174
Salish, 174, 217, 219
Sama-Bajaw, 175
Samoyedic, 173
Sandawe, 171
Sanskrit, 99
Santali, 159, 172
Sanuma, 178
Satere-Mawe, 82, 126
Sawu, 174
Scandinavian, 29, 74, 268, 269
Selee, 22, 35, 59
Semelai, 171
Semitic, 170, 171, 303
Seneca, 173
Sentani, 175
Sepik, 124, 129, 141, 175, 224, 305

Sepik Hill, 175
Serbian, 293
Shilluk, 242
Shipibo-Konibo, 177
Shona, 170
Shumashti, 8
Shumcho, 21, 40, 43–45, 60
sign languages, 310, 356
Sinhala, 172
Sino-Tibetan, 40, 43, 73, 98, 99, 129,
        140, 172, 173, 307, 327
Siona, 125, 177
Siouan, 174, 293
Siriano, 125
Siwai, 254
Sko, 260
Skou, 175, 260, 261
Slavic, 18, 172, 221, 222, 263, 265, 270,
        292–294, 304, 317, 333
Slavonic, Old Church, 123
Slovak, 270
So, 170
Somali, 124
Songhay, 171
Sorbian, 294
Sorbian, Upper, 294
South Tairora, 81, 99
Southern Daly, 38, 240, 241, 328
Southern Puebla, 84
Southern Rincón Zapotec, 105
Southern Tiwa, 299
Spanish, 41–43, 45, 50, 104, 123, 263,
        268, 269, 273, 308
Standard Greek, 31–33
Sudanic, 170, 323
Suena, 176
Sulka, 175
Supyire, 171

Surmic, 170
Swahili, 170
Swedish, 21, 28, 29, 36, 49, 60, 74, 75,
        95, 113, 123, 226, 268, 269,
        271, 300
Swedish, Karleby, 28, 29, 36, 60
Swedish, Ostrobothnian, 29
Swiss German, 271, 300

Taa, 282–284, 288
Taba, 175
Tabaru, 124
Tacanan, 131
Tachelhit, 85, 124, 252
Tagalog, 174, 222, 226, 229, 334
Tai-Kadai, 173
Tainae, 176
Tairora, 81, 99, 126
Takelma, 174
Talamanca, 173
Tama Sepik, 175
Tamasheq, 85, 124
Tamil, 123, 172
Tanah, 39
Tarahumara, Low, 81
Tat, 279
Tatar, 171
Tatic, 30
Tatuyo, 125
Taulil, 175
Tawala, 175
Tehit, 176
Teiwa, 176
Telefol, 125, 176
Telugu, 99
Tenharim, 93, 122, 224
Teop, 175, 223, 250
Tepehua (Tlachichilco), 174
Tepehuan, 174

Tepiman, 174
Tequistlatecan, 174
Teribe, 173
Terêna, 177
Tetun, 174
Thai, 136, 137, 173
Thebor, 21, 43, 44, 60
Thompson, 174
Tibeto-Burman, 8, 60, 307, 327
Ticuna, 125, 131
Tidore, 176
Tigré, 170
Timor-Alor-Pantar, 175
Tiwi, 171, 220, 299
Tlingit, 173
Tobelo, 124
Tok Pisin, 75, 79, 80, 230, 231, 234
Tol, 131, 174
Tongan, 175
Toqabaqita, 175
Tor-Orya, 176
Torricelli, 6, 129, 139, 176, 300
Totonacan, 130, 174
Trans-New Guinea, 7, 39, 73, 81, 96,
    98, 129, 158, 176, 223–225,
    240, 283, 286–288, 327
Trinitario, 125
Trique, 236
Triqui, 103, 104
Triqui, Copala, 121
Triqui, San Martin Itunyoso, 121
Trumai, 177
Tsez, 292
Tsimane, 125, 131
Tsimshian, 174
Tucano, 125, 178
Tucanoan, 73, 87, 131, 158, 160, 177,
    178

Tukang Besi, 174
Tungusic, 171
Tunica, 174, 219, 261
Tupi, 131
Tupi-Guaraní, 178
Tupian, 83, 93, 142, 178, 224
Turkana, 270
Turkic, 8, 73, 171
Turkish, 31, 34, 69, 70, 75, 78, 90, 171,
    329
Tuu, 282, 283, 288
Tuvaluan, 175
Tuvan, 171
Tuyuca, 125, 178
Tzeltal, 173
Tzeltal, Petalcingo, 139, 140
Tzutujil, 173

Uab Meto, 82, 126
Ubangi, 171, 215
Udi, 21, 28, 37, 60
Uduk, 6, 72, 96, 112, 120, 170, 219, 229,
    248–250, 259, 262, 281–284,
    305, 334
Ugric, 173
Ukrainian, 123
Ulithian, 175
Umbu-Ungu, 81, 126
Una, 40, 176, 223, 224, 227, 284
Ungarinjin, 171
Upper Pokomo, 79
Uradhi, 171
Uralic, 128, 173, 233
Urarina, 131
Urdu, 289
Urim, 176
Uru, 131
Usan, 176
Uto-Aztecan, 73, 130, 158, 174

Viet-Muong, 172
Vietnamese, 108, 172

Wè Northern, 96, 120
Waigali, 172
Waimaha, 125
Walman, 6, 213, 215, 254, 300, 309, 311, 312, 317, 320
Wambaya, 171
Wamey, 251, 252, 302, 303
Waorani, 131, 178
Wapei-Palei, 176
Wappo, 174
Wappo-Yukian, 174
War-Jaintia, 220, 328
War-Jaintia, Amwi variety, 220
Warapu, 175
Wardaman, 171
Warekena, 177
Wari', 177
Warndarang, 171
Waurá, 177
Wayuu, 125
Welsh, 87, 89, 91, 92, 123, 281
West Himalayish, 44
West Papuan, 129, 158
West Xoon, 282
West !Xõo, 282, 283
Western Daly, 328
Wissel Lakes-Kemandoga, 176
Witotoan, 98, 101, 102, 131
Wojokeso, 81, 126
Wolaytta, 124
Wolof, 263
Worora, 171
Worrorran, 171

Xaasongaxango, 79

Yagua, 85, 93, 94, 125, 143, 177, 296, 297, 304
Yale, 96, 110, 176
Yangmanic, 171
Yanomam, 131, 178
Yapese, 175
Yau, 79
Yawa, 124
Yawelmani, 174
Yessan-Mayo, 124, 175
Yidiñ, 97, 171, 258
Yimas, 175
Yine, 125
Yingkarta, 171
Yokuts, 174
Yonggom, 124
Yoruba, 170
Yucatec, 173
Yuchi, 174
Yucuna, 125, 160
Yukaghir, 173
Yukaghir, Kolyma, 173
Yuman, 173
Yup'ik, 173
Yuracare, 131
Yurok, 173

Zande, 171, 215, 323
Zaparoan, 131, 178
Zapotec, 104, 105
Zapotec (Coatlán), 173
Zapotec, Amatlan, 103, 122
Zapotec, Chichicapan, 83, 127
Zapotec, Lachixio, 122
Zapotec, Miahuatlan, 77, 83, 127
Zapotec, Ozoltepec, 121
Zapotec, Quioquitani Quieri, 121
Zapotec, Rincon, 121

Zapotec, Santo Domingo Albar-
    radas, 122
Zapotec, Southern Rincon, 122
Zapotec, Texmelucan, 84, 104, 105,
    122
Zapotecan, 83, 173
Zome, 98, 99, 108, 109, 120
Zulu, 170
Zuni, 174

‖Ani, 323

Lightning Source UK Ltd.
Milton Keynes UK
UKHW032141270223
417761UK00010B/563

9 783961 101818